From
GIFTEDNESS
to
GIFTED

Reflecting Theory
in Practice

EDUCATION

From GIFTEDNESS *to* GIFTED EDUCATION

Reflecting Theory in Practice

Edited by
**Jonathan A. Plucker, Ph.D., Anne N. Rinn, Ph.D.,
and Matthew C. Makel, Ph.D.**

PRUFROCK PRESS INC.
WACO, TEXAS

DEDICATION

For Peni and Steve Plucker and Kay and Tom Whitman, who have
supported me, my work, and my family unconditionally.—JAP

For my parents, Randy and Carol Rinn, who were my first teachers and the
hardest working people I've ever known. Dad, enjoy your retirement!—ANR

For Mrs. Sandy Strobel Johnson and Mrs. Pat Gabriel, who
taught me when I was young and whose passion and dedication
inspire me to help those who are young now.—MCM

Prufrock Press Inc.
P.O. Box 8813
Waco, TX 76714-8813
Phone: (800) 998-2208
Fax: (800) 240-0333
http://www.prufrock.com

Table of Contents

Introduction

*Jonathan A. Plucker, Anne N. Rinn,
and Matthew C. Makel*

Meeting the needs of advanced students has a long history in the United States (Robinson & Jolly, 2013). In 1868, the superintendent of St. Louis schools began a program specifically dedicated to serving students who were able to accelerate through the elementary grades more quickly than their peers. Indeed, acceleration was the most common approach to serving bright children in the late 1800s and the early 1900s in the United States. But, over the past 150 years or so, how best to identify and serve gifted students has remained a constant, controversial question for researchers, practitioners, families, and policymakers. And, in that 150 years, numerous perspectives have been offered.

More recently, the field of gifted education and talent development has experienced a range of conceptual and instructional advances, moving the field to a point of conceptual richness and diversity that would have been hard to imagine even 15 years ago. However, despite a large number of books on the topics of gifted education and talent development, we could not find a single resource collecting each of the various approaches to serving gifted and talented students. Although there are high-quality books focusing on conceptual perspectives or systems and models perspectives, the combination of both perspectives is generally found only in introductory textbooks, which by necessity also include a range of other topics. This limits the space for discussion of how our theories and conceptions connect to practical application. And, in a field like gifted education, practical application is paramount.

Broadly speaking, the importance of evidence-based practices in gifted education cannot be overstated, but the actual practices being used in schools are often not evidence-based (e.g., 30 minutes a week in a pull-out program is likely not the most effective educational intervention available, despite being quite common). This implementation gap is closing, but we are in the midst of a long journey in this regard. In an effort to contribute to closing the implementation gap, we wanted to create a single volume that provided readers with the information needed to explicitly connect the conceptual and practical perspectives. Various views of giftedness and talent may be separated by common language, relying on different terms, combined different ways, but converge on a fairly unified vision of how to identify and serve gifted and talented students. With this shared destination envisioned, it is largely up to us to make *reflecting theory in practice* a reality so that we can best serve gifted and talented individuals.

SELECTION OF AUTHORS AND TOPICS

We sought to provide a comprehensive summary of major models and conceptual directions in the field of gifted education and talent development with ample descriptions of their potential application. We started by identifying the conceptual work that appears to be most widely discussed in the field, then attempted to identify new and emerging perspectives that could soon grow to hold an important place in the field. Finally, and with a bit of a twist, we included major intervention strategies, with the intent of having authors work backward, in a way, to discuss the conceptual and empirical foundations of popular interventions, such as acceleration and grouping.

Although we strove to be comprehensive, we readily acknowledge that other important perspectives exist—the book could only be so long! In addition, a few major thinkers were not able to write chapters, and a couple of chapters were not submitted in time to be included. Regardless, we believe the coverage in this book offers readers a strong foundation for examining how theory can, should, and often does become reflected in our practices.

Selecting authors for each topic was straightforward. For example, George Betts was asked to write about his Autonomous Learner Model, Joe Renzulli and Sally Reis were asked to write about their work, and Françoys Gagné was invited to describe his model and its application. The work of such authors introducing their own ideas once again constitute the majority of the book, and we are grateful for their quick, enthusiastic responses. For other, broader chapters, we invited people we consider to be authoritative thinkers on important topics related to gifted education and talent development (i.e., our colleagues from the Belin-Blank Center wrote about acceleration). We should note that the turnaround time for authors was almost unreasonably short. Authors had roughly 4 months from invitation to the revision deadline to submit their chapters in highly polished form.

Our enthusiasm for this book is based in large part on the quality content that our colleagues provided, for which we are appreciative.

ORGANIZATION OF EACH CHAPTER

We invited authors to write chapters that address three questions from their perspective, with the responses to the second and third questions getting the lion's share of attention in each chapter. First, we asked authors to define from their (theoretical/conceptual) perspective, what does it mean to be gifted/talented? We also asked them to include a brief description of their definition of giftedness/talent/exceptional performance. Second, we asked the authors to describe how individuals develop gifts and talents according to their conception. Third, we asked authors to outline how they would ideally advise educators to develop their students' gifts and talents. Further, if practitioners have implemented their approach, what research support regarding the efficacy of those efforts exists? Essentially, we wanted authors to introduce their definition upfront, discuss their conceptual/theoretical approach, and then examine how each approach can be put into practice.

Each chapter concludes with take-home summary points. Additionally, to provide interested readers with an avenue to delve deeper, each set of authors provides explicit suggestions for further, recommended readings. These suggestions guide readers to related work and/or foundational work related to the theory, conception, or intervention discussed in each chapter.

ORGANIZATION OF THE BOOK

We have organized the chapters based roughly on when the ideas discussed by the authors were first published. The intent is to tell a story about how ideas in the field have evolved over time. Of course, given space limitations, not every potentially valuable perspective could be included. But many authors addressed how they stand "on the shoulders of giants," providing a historical bedrock to their work specifically and the entire volume generally, even if it lies below the surface. Because some of the ideas discussed in the book were developed long ago, they have had greater opportunity to develop their specific story than some of the more recently developed conceptions. But, just as age need not be equated with decrepitude, as we discuss below, youth need not be equated with callowness. If anything, we believe the chapters provide a unique and fresh perspective on the field: We are moving in such exciting directions!

In the first chapter on academic acceleration, Assouline, Lupkowski-Shoplik, and Colangelo discuss one of the oldest interventions for gifted students. The chapter reports on the long history of acceleration, its varied means of implementation, and research evidence for acceleration. The authors then describe three types of acceleration intervention models to illustrate the variety of ways acceleration can effectively be implemented for gifted students.

In Chapter 2, Renzulli and Reis discuss the Three-Ring Conception of Giftedness/Triad Model, which focuses on "gifted behaviors" that appear when a student has sufficient talent in three interlocking clusters of abilities: above-average cognitive ability, task commitment, and creativity. They show how the Three-Ring model can serve as the foundation for the Schoolwide Enrichment Model to develop student talents.

In Chapter 3, Brody writes about the Talent Search model that was originally developed by Julian Stanley in the 1970s. Although this model is often associated with national talent searches affiliated with universities, Brody's chapter shows readers how the same core principles can be applied in school settings through acceleration, flexible placement, curricular modification, and extracurricular activities. These practices will help facilitate more individualization of student learning experiences that focuses on individual growth and goals.

Gentry and Tay discuss another of the oldest interventions in our field, ability grouping, in Chapter 4. They provide an overview of the empirical research to support grouping high-ability students, including both benefits to students and myths associated with grouping. Gentry and Tay then present the Total School Cluster Grouping Model, which was designed to serve all students in a school.

In Chapter 5, Betts, Carey, and Kapushion discuss Betts's Autonomous Learner Model, which is designed to help practitioners meet the needs of the whole gifted child by focusing on an individual's cognitive, emotional, social, and physical development. Betts and colleagues show how the model can be used to facilitate the growth of students as autonomous learners. Specific strategies for practitioners are outlined to illustrate how a gifted child can move from *student* to *learner*.

Portenga provides an overview of the development of athletic talent in Chapter 6. By outlining the Self-Regulated Model of Athletic Talent Development, Portenga provides a perspective that has important implications for advanced learning and performance. The chapter's focus on athletics has valuable perspectives for those working both with athletic talent development and advanced learning in academic domains.

In his chapter on the Integrative Model of Talent Development, Gagné introduces a large set of terms that are often thrown about without clear articulation and sometimes treated synonymously. Gagné has continually modified and refined his model to reflect his deepening understanding of how giftedness differs from talent, the origin of an individual's giftedness, how talent development occurs, and the ways in which we can best foster the development of academic talent.

In Chapter 8, Ford, Wright, Grantham, and Moore describe various models for addressing giftedness through a cultural lens, which requires educators to acknowledge the cultural context of each and every student. The authors describe a number of useful models and tools for addressing equity in gifted education, including the Ford Venn Diagram and Bloom-Banks Matrix.

In Chapter 9, Ziegler and Vialle describe the influential actiotope model, with an emphasis on how it can be applied to influence all aspects of gifted education programming and, more to the point, the lives of gifted students. The authors provide clear direction on how to apply the model to a range of educational contexts.

Although sociocultural theories have been widely applied in education and other fields for decades, they are infrequently applied to gifted education. Plucker, McWilliams, and Guo describe in Chapter 10 how sociocultural approaches to gifted education and talent development offer a unique perspective on identification of talent and interventions for helping students develop their abilities.

In Chapter 11, Subotnik, Worrell, and Olszewski-Kubilius take a domain-specific and developmental perspective of giftedness and talent development and focus on what opportunities are needed to develop talent and what cognitive and psychosocial factors are required for its cultivation. In their model, they highlight two types of individuals, performers and producers, and the similarities and differences each needs to develop talent.

In their explanation of the Advanced Academics perspective in Chapter 12, Peters, Erstad, and Matthews use multiple hypothetical students to illustrate the importance of educational context when determining how best to identify and serve students. Their attention to the rationale behind identification and (more importantly) services is used to draw readers away from traditional age-based grouping into a schoolwide Response to Intervention model that shifts education more toward age-irrelevant contexts that match instruction with students' current readiness to learn.

Csermely describes in Chapter 13 the concept of talent development networks, which are being implemented on a large scale within and across several European countries. He describes the nature of these networks, the conceptual reasoning behind them, and how students participating in these networks can and should be supported.

In Chapter 14, Siegle, McCoach, and Bloomfield present their Achievement Orientation Model, which focuses largely on individuals' self-perceptions and how those affect the development of giftedness and talent. By outlining both personal characteristics and environmental situations that affect when and how students can be successful, Siegle and McCoach present the optimal conditions necessary for student achievement.

In the next chapter, Plucker, Peters, and Schmalensee provide an overview of the excellence gap intervention model, which is intended to provide guidance to educators seeking to reduce and eventually eliminate excellence gaps. Their model differs from some of the other conceptions in that its primary purpose, rather than describe how people develop gifts and talents, is to guide interventions the help ensure equity *and* excellence.

Coming from a psychological perspective, Simonton introduces his genetics and talent typology in Chapter 16. In this final chapter, Simonton tackles an issue that is often considered hazardous: genetic influences on talent. Simonton shows the intellectual history of both genetic and environmental influences on talent development and performance. Namely, he states that talent development must consider three continua: simple versus complex, additive versus multiplicative, and static versus dynamic. This taxonomy is then used to introduce different ways genetic and environmental influences play a role in talent development.

SUGGESTIONS FOR HOW TO READ THIS BOOK

As a guide for readers as they compare and contrast components of the conceptions described in this volume, we pose a number of questions for the reader to consider. It may make sense to read through a chapter (or the entire volume) before going back and considering each of these questions. Individual chapters may not directly address all of the following topics. However, as is often the case, what is left unsaid can be just as important as what is said.

How Have Our Conceptions Changed Over Time?

One of our motivations for arranging the chapters in rough chronological order was to provide you with a sense of development over time. Certain goals, desired outcomes, terms, and recommended interventions, among other factors, have changed over time. What are the major developmental trends in the field's conceptual approaches, and where do you see these trends leading in the future?

How Does Time-Since-Publication Impact the Available Evidence and Sophistication of a Model or Intervention?

An idea that has been around for nearly a century has far longer to be assessed, evaluated, and refined than one developed in the last few years. Thus, lack of empirical support should not necessarily be held against relatively new models and ideas—an absence of evidence is not evidence of an absence of benefit. Nevertheless, one can reasonably expect ideas generated decades earlier to have a body of evidence associated with them. To what extent do the varying degrees of empirical support influence your evaluation of each theory or model? Are some models just easier to evaluate via research than others?

Does It Matter That the Theories do Not Have the Same Goals?

Every theory, model, or intervention in this book is clearly related to gifted education and talent development. But you do not have to read more than two or three chapters to see that they do not all have the same general goals. How do the goals of each model impact your analysis of its strengths and weaknesses?

To What Degree Does the Field of Gifted Education and Talent Development Struggle With the Jangle Fallacy?

George Bernard Shaw and Oscar Wilde are often credited with saying that England and America are two countries separated by the same language. Common examples are the use of sweaters versus jumpers or chips versus crisps. Different words are used to describe the same thing in different contexts, which in the social sciences is often referred to as the jangle fallacy. To what extent are various conceptions of giftedness separated by the same language? If Springfield schools identify and serve "gifted students" using essentially the same practices as Sunnydale schools to identify and serve "talented students," do the label differences really matter if the substantive experiences are similar? Perhaps more importantly, does the diversity of language used in these chapters inhibit the field, or is that a red herring?

Are the Data Best Described by the Theory?

The purpose of a theory or conception is not to tell a good story. It is to explain and predict subsequent outcomes. A theory may predict a particular outcome accurately, but is that theory the best predictor of those data? Although no one would confuse gifted education with physics, we are reminded of classic Newtownian mechanics and Einstein's theory of relativity. Einstein did not prove Newton incorrect, but improved upon his work, particularly in the special instance of extreme speeds. In the case of gifted education and talent development, we remain far from the classic mechanics level of theory sophistication, which makes it all the more important that we carefully consider our theories and whether alternative explanations would better explain and predict performance. As you consider each conceptual approach, are there better ways to reach the goals of interest?

Is the Ultimate Value of a Theory or Model Determined by its Practical Usefulness, or Is That Often Beside the Point?

Some models may not have practical value, in that they end up influencing actual practice with students in limited ways (if at all). The theories that do readily appear to have practical value are often embraced, but it is possible to argue that theory is often intended to influence how a broader field thinks about itself, and that an ongoing evolution of theory is necessary for any field to thrive, even if some of the theories and supporting research during this long-term development have little impact on practice (Flexner, 1939/2017). For example, many facets of Einstein's theory of relativity are only just being supported by data, with practical applications appearing only decades later (and with some still quite distant). To what extent does practical utility (i.e., being able to impact student lives positively) factor into your analysis of each conception?

In a Related (But Opposite) Vein, Does the Soundness of the Conceptual Foundations of Our Evidence-Based Practices Matter?

Some strategies that are widely endorsed by and used within the field (e.g., acceleration, ability grouping) have conceptual bases that are somewhat beside the point—they work well, we have extensive research evidence to support them, and educators have become skilled at using them. But it is also widely accepted that fields can only move forward when research is used to examine the theoretical foundations, in the hope that we can evaluate those conceptual models and revise them based on data. In this way, we can build on our theories, gradually improving them, which then leads to better interventions, which leads to better theories, etc. To what degree should you consider a well-supported intervention's conceptual base when examining the usefulness of the intervention?

How do We Spot and Stop a Zombie?

In a wonderfully titled paper, "A Vast Graveyard of Undead Theories," Ferguson and Heene (2012) argued that some systemic problems in academic publishing reduced psychology's ability to assess when theories were false, thus creating undead zombie theories that were not alive, per se, but also could not be considered dead and gone. In the case of gifted education, zombies may be theories, conceptions, or educational practices. They are zombies because they remain in practice or influential despite data disconfirming them. If a theory cannot be falsified (shown to be wrong), then it is not a theory. When reading, look for the specific claims and predictions made in each chapter. Could such claims be proven false? Is evidence provided to support such claims?

How Can We Move the Field of Gifted Education and Talent Development Forward From Here?

Vartanian (2014) noted that one goal of theory is for it to become more complex over time, building on previous theories, often by subsuming them, and pushing others to the sidelines. In our field, we also have an expectation that at least some practical benefit will eventually emerge from our theoretical work. We also noted that the practical implications for some of the perspectives are similar. How do these diverse expectations and trends influence your sense of how to move the field forward?

CONCLUSION

This book has selfish origins: We wanted to produce a resource that we could use in our classes and share with our colleagues that addressed a need in the field. As a result, this book is in many ways an experiment. We wondered if it were possible for the best thinkers in our field to present their conceptual work within a context of practical application, we played around with classic versus more contemporary approaches, and we gambled a bit on where the exciting new directions for the field would be. In addition, we encouraged the authors to be "intellectually playful" (i.e., have fun with these chapters!). We like to think that all of these risks paid off, but we are obviously biased. We would love to hear from readers about what worked and did not work in this volume. Did we miss a theory or model that should have been included? Should we extend beyond gifted education and talent development and touch on related constructs, such as intelligence, creativity, motivation, etc.? Did the format, with authors encouraged to spend half their chapter on theory and half on practice, work for most chapters? Is there a better way to organize the chapters than our chronological approach? What features could be added to increase the book's readability and usefulness? Your feedback will be very helpful to us, both as we use the book ourselves and as we plan for future editions.

But for now, we will end this introduction by once again thanking the authors for producing such high-quality work, on deadline, and according to the specifications we provided to them (a very rare occurrence for edited volumes!). And we thank readers for picking up this book and working through the often provocative material. It is our sincere hope that we have provided a volume whose pages will soon be reflected in practice.

REFERENCES

Ferguson, C. J., & Heene, M. (2012). A vast graveyard of undead theories: Publication bias and psychological science's aversion to the null. *Perspectives on Psychological Science, 7,* 555–561. doi:10.1177/1745691612459059

Flexner, A. (1939/2017). *The usefulness of useless knowledge.* Princeton, NJ: Princeton University Press.

Robinson, A., & Jolly, J. (Eds.). (2013). *A century of contributions to gifted education: Illuminating lives.* New York, NY: Routledge.

Vartanian, O. (2014). Toward a cumulative psychological science of aesthetics, creativity, and the arts. *Psychology of Aesthetics, Creativity, and the Arts, 8,* 15–17.

CHAPTER 1

Academic Acceleration

THE THEORY APPLIED

Susan G. Assouline, Ann Lupkowski-Shoplik, and Nicholas Colangelo

INTRODUCTION

Educators, educational researchers, educational policy makers, parents, and students can agree that schools implement educational interventions to have a positive impact on student learning. Some interventions have little research evidence whereas others (e.g., one or more of the 20 forms of academic acceleration; Southern & Jones, 2015) represent interventions with a robust research record. Since the mid-20th century, when Pressey (1949) defined academic acceleration as an educational intervention that moves high-ability students through an educational program at a rate faster or an age younger than typical, the research supporting acceleration has been consistently positive (Steenbergen-Hu, Makel, & Olszewski-Kubilius, 2016). However, despite unequivocal research findings that support academic acceleration, implementation remains sporadic or inconsistent at best and ignored or renounced at worst. A watershed national report, *A Nation Deceived: How Schools Hold Back America's Brightest Students* (Colangelo, Assouline, & Gross, 2004) identified multiple myths and excuses impeding the implementation of academic acceleration over the last half of the 20th century, such as detriment to an individual's social-emotional development or concern that accelerating a student is not fair to other students (Borland, 1989;

Gold, 1965). Assouline, Colangelo, VanTassel-Baska, and Lupkowski-Shoplik (2015) updated the 2004 Colangelo et al. report and offered fresh evidence of the unambiguous effectiveness of the intervention known as academic acceleration within the context of 21st-century educational issues. Given the strong research support for the intervention, it is logical to ask if the research findings have translated into everyday practice or policy.

Relative to everyday practice with gifted students, the National Association for Gifted Children (NAGC) promotes academic acceleration as a research-based intervention. Paragraph one from the NAGC position paper on acceleration stated that acceleration is "one of the cornerstones of exemplary gifted education practices" (NAGC, n.d.). Paragraph four of the position paper (NAGC, n.d.) continued with,

> Talent search programs at selected universities provide early assessment of advanced mathematical and verbal abilities in students such that decisions on appropriate accelerative options can be constructed inside and outside of schools . . . several acceleration opportunities can be accessed through online coursework in specific content areas.

Despite this positive endorsement by NAGC, the country's leading gifted education advocacy organization, the school-based intervention of gifted education and the research-supported intervention of acceleration remain disconnected. Every 2 years, NAGC collaborates with the Council of State Directors of Programs for the Gifted (CSDPG) to create a report on the state of gifted education. The 2014–2015 report revealed that 80% of the 42 states completing the survey reported a mandate related to gifted and talented education; however, only 13 of the reporting states had policy specifically permitting acceleration strategies. The others have policies that allow the local educational agencies to determine acceleration policies or do not specify a state policy on acceleration. Currently, no state explicitly denies acceleration.

Acceleration can be accomplished in at least 20 different ways (Southern & Jones, 2015; see Table 1.1), including early entrance to kindergarten, curriculum compacting, grade-skipping, dual enrollment, mentoring, extracurricular programs, college-level classes in high school (e.g., Advanced Placement), and credit by examination. Acceleration is both a delivery system and curriculum intervention. The various forms (Rogers, 2015) typically fall into one of two broad categories: (a) whole-grade acceleration, including grade-skipping, early access to kindergarten or first grade, or early entrance to college; and (b) content or subject acceleration when students are moved up for only one subject, such as reading or math, but remain with their age-peers for other subjects.

TABLE 1.1

Forms of Acceleration (Southern & Jones, 2015) Indicated in the Pyramid of Accelerative Opportunities

Forms of Grade-Skipping:
a.   Early admission to kindergarten
b.   Early admission to first grade
c.   Grade-skipping
d.   Acceleration in college
e.   Early graduation from high school or college
f.   Early entrance into middle school, high school, or college
g.   Accelerated/honors high school or residential high school on a college campus
Forms of Subject Acceleration:
h.   Subject-matter acceleration/partial acceleration
i.   Advanced Placement
j.   Continuous progress
k.   Self-paced instruction
l.   Combined classes
m.   Telescoping curriculum
n.   Distance learning courses
o.   Concurrent/dual enrollment
p.   Credit by examination
Less Accelerative Opportunities:
q.   International Baccalaureate program
r.   Extracurricular programs
s.   Mentoring
t.   Curriculum compacting (the time saved by compacting the curriculum is typically used to provide enrichment)

The purpose of this chapter is to highlight three acceleration interventions, (a) above-level testing, (b) content acceleration in math, and, (c) Advanced Placement. Each intervention is practical in its approach and grounded in university-based partnerships. The identification process for each of the three interventions varies. However, the goal of each intervention is to address the needs of academically talented students through one or more forms of acceleration. Although we do not adhere to a single definition of gifted and talented, we regard a gifted student as an individual who is ready to learn advanced material, in more depth, at a faster rate, and earlier age than their grade cohort or their age-peers. These are students who are typically considered very high achievers, a concept that is operationalized through their performance on grade-level standardized tests. Typically, these high achievers earn scores that are near or have hit the ceiling of the grade-level test. Therefore, one major process for determining which students are ready for advanced material is above-level testing. This is a practical approach that focuses on readiness to move ahead in specific subjects, rather than labeling a student as "gifted" or "not gifted."

Above-level testing, presented first, is offered on a large-scale basis through university-based talent search programs grounded in Stanley's (1996) Talent Search model. The second intervention, an accelerated math program, includes early above-level assessment information that comprises many characteristics of the Talent Search model (Brody, 2009; Stanley, 2005). Finally, Advanced Placement is described as an intervention that can level the playing field by equalizing opportunities for students who may be at risk for access to advanced learning opportunities (Plucker & Harris, 2015). The Advanced Placement program described here occurs in small and/or rural schools throughout a predominately rural state and addresses the importance of accessibility to advanced programming for academically able students who are at risk due to economic vulnerability or geographic isolation.

All three interventions share the common feature of a school-university partnership. They are also pragmatic in their approach because the programs focus on students' talents and abilities in specific content areas and adjust the level and pace of the content to match what students are ready to learn.

ABOVE-LEVEL TESTING THROUGH UNIVERSITY TALENT SEARCH PROGRAMS: THE MODEL

Above-level testing is the core of the Study of Mathematically Precocious Youth (SMPY), founded by Julian Stanley in 1971. Julian Stanley's purpose in establishing SMPY was to help students "who reason extremely well mathematically to find the educational resources they need to achieve their full potential" (Brody & Stanley, 2005). Through SMPY, Stanley offered bright seventh and eighth graders the opportunity to take the College Board's SAT as an above-grade-level test. Rather than matching students to a pre-established "gifted program" (Assouline & Lupkowski-Shoplik, 2012) in a school setting or devoting time and energy to conceptualizing "giftedness," he had a very simple goal: to discover students at varying levels of mathematical reasoning ability and help them to develop their mathematical aptitude by moving through the math curriculum at a pace matching their abilities. The testing paradigm Stanley initiated was called a "talent search"; the first large-scale implementation of the Talent Search Model took place at Johns Hopkins University in the early 1980s (Stanley, 2005). That testing program evolved into a comprehensive center (the Center for Talented Youth, or CTY) that includes above-level testing as well as various other associated programs, for example, the Study of Exceptional Talent, focused on talent development (Subotnik, Olszewski-Kubilius, & Worrell, 2011) of very bright students (see Linda Brody's chapter, this volume, for more information about other resources provided by university-based talent searches).

SMPY relocated to Vanderbilt University in 1998 and SMPY codirectors, Camilla Benbow and David Lubinski, and their team of researchers (Lubinski, 2004; Lubinski & Benbow, 2006; Lubinski, Webb, Morelock, & Benbow, 2001; Wai, 2015) have contributed enormously to the acceleration literature. CTY and other talent search organizations, including those at Duke and Northwestern University or university-based gifted education centers, such as the Belin-Blank Center at the University of Iowa, expanded this simple, yet elegant model of above-level testing to (a) include an array of above-level assessments and (b) broaden the talent pool sample to include a more diverse population relative to age, grade, ethnicity, and socioeconomic status (Assouline, Ihrig, & Mahatmya, 2017; Assouline, Lupkowski-Shoplik, & Colangelo, 2018). The suite of assessments used as above-level tests includes the SAT or ACT for seventh and eighth graders (Lupkowski-Shoplik, Benbow, Assouline, & Brody, 2003), and the Secondary School Admission Test, School and College Abilities Test, and Explore[1] tests for younger students (Lupkowski-Shoplik & Assouline, 1993; Lupkowski-Shoplik & Swiatek, 1999; Mills & Barnett, 1992).

The Talent Search model uses a two-step process, beginning with grade-level achievement tests. Students in the top range of the grade-level test (usually scoring at the 90th or 95th percentile or higher) are invited to participate; these students' scores are represented in Bell Curve A in Figure 1.1. When bright students take a grade-level standardized test, the test does not have enough difficult items to measure high-achieving students' achievements. Psychologists say the students have "hit the ceiling" of the test; therefore, they require a more challenging test (i.e., an above-level test) to determine aptitude or readiness for advanced curriculum. In the second step of the process, above-level testing, the students are invited to take a test developed for older students. Above-level test scores earned by talent search participants revealed a new bell curve (see Bell Curve B in Figure 1.1).

What is important here is not simply the fact that the bright students' performances on the above-level tests result in a score distribution similar to that of a normal curve, but that the above-level testing differentiates among various levels of aptitude (e.g., *talented* from *exceptionally talented* students). This information offers a better idea of students' capabilities so that educators can tailor educational opportunities to students' abilities and needs. To help educators and parents understand the implications of above-level test scores and how they can

---

1   Explore, developed by ACT (ACT, 2013), was retired in 2016. The Belin-Blank Center licensed content developed by ACT that was designed to measure academic progress of junior high students and provided an above-level test on an online platform, I-Excel, which is available as an above-level test for high-achieving fourth through sixth graders.

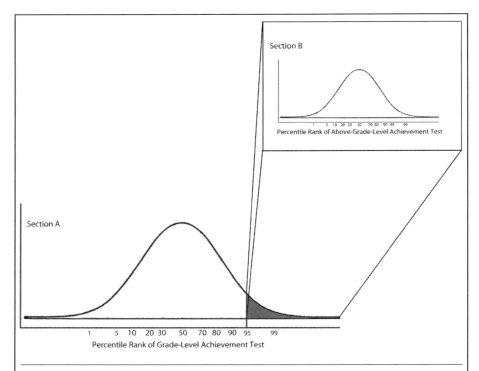

Section B

Percentile Rank of Above-Grade-Level Achievement Test

Section A

1   5   10   20 30   50   70 80   90   95   99
Percentile Rank of Grade-Level Achievement Test

Figure 1.1. From *Developing Math Talent: A Comprehensive Guide to Math Education for Gifted Students in Elementary and Middle School* (2nd ed., p. 145), by S. Assouline and A. Lupkowski-Shoplik, 2011, Waco, TX: Prufrock Press. Copyright 2011 by Prufrock Press. Reprinted with permission.

help guide educational decisions, Assouline and Lupkowski-Shoplik (2011) linked scores earned on above-level tests to specific educational opportunities in the Pyramid of Educational Options. As an extension of this same thought process, in this chapter, we show how the scores on above-level tests can be related to the 20 forms of acceleration described by Southern and Jones (2015) and created a new pyramid, the Pyramid of Accelerative Opportunities (see Figure 1.2). This pyramid helps educators and families to understand the extent of a student's readiness for acceleration and helps them to consider specific educational opportunities that might be appropriate for the student. This type of information is used routinely by the university-based talent searches to match students to their summer, weekend, and online programs. Although above-level testing is still an under-used option for high-achieving students (Assouline & Lupkowski-Shoplik, 2012), it increasingly is used by elementary and middle schools when they conduct their own above-level testing activities to discover students in need of accelerative opportunities (Assouline et al., 2017).

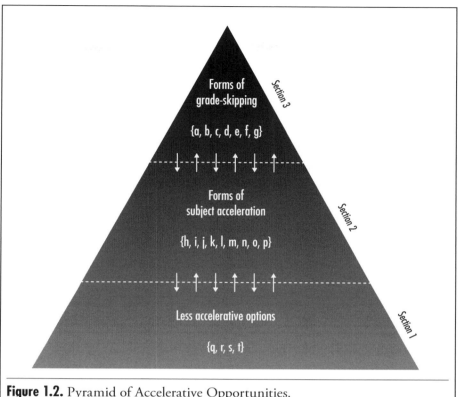

Figure 1.2. Pyramid of Accelerative Opportunities.

All students taking the above-level test can be considered high achievers or academically talented, because they have already scored in the top 5% to 10% of their age group on grade-level tests. It is appropriate for all of these students to take advantage of opportunities shown in the bottom section (Section 1) of the pyramid, including challenging educational opportunities that may be routinely provided by the school, such as enrichment-oriented activities. However, students who earn progressively higher scores on the above-level test demonstrate greater aptitude in the content areas measured by the above-level test and likely would benefit from and should participate in more accelerative options. These include the opportunities listed in the middle section (Section 2) of the pyramid, characterized by subject-matter acceleration. Students who perform at this level on an above-level test are often ready to move up one or more grades in their particular strength area because they have performed at or above the 50th percentile when compared to the older group of students on the above-level test. See Table 1.2 for an explanation of the above-level test percentile rankings corresponding to each section of the pyramid. The score ranges and percentile rankings are meant to be guidelines about readiness for acceleration, not stringent rules used to match accelerative opportunities to students' achievements and needs.

TABLE 1.2

Explanation of Forms of Acceleration Within the Pyramid of Acceleration Opportunities

Section 1, Less Accelerative Opportunities	Students earning scores below the 50th percentile when compared to the older group	Example: Seventh-grade students earning scores below 500 on the College Board's SAT
Section 2, Forms of Subject Acceleration	Students earning scores from the 50th percentile through the 74th percentile	Example: Seventh-grade students earning scores between 500 and 600 on the College Board's SAT
Section 3, Forms of Grade-Skipping	Students earning scores above the 75th percentile	Example: Seventh-grade students earning scores above 600 on the College Board's SAT

Students who earn very high scores (in the top section, Section 3, of the Pyramid of Accelerative Opportunities) should consider the most accelerative options. These students score in the top quartile (at the 75th percentile or above) when compared to older students taking the above-level test; therefore, by definition, they demonstrate extreme aptitude in their strength area. They have an aptitude for the material that is typically presented to older students, which suggests they are ready for more extraordinary challenges. Above-level tests are very useful in gathering information to inform these decisions. Additional tools (i.e., the *Iowa Acceleration Scale*, Assouline et al., 2009) include above-level testing in domain-specific areas as an important component of the process designed to ensure well-thought-out decisions about readiness for grade-skipping.

CONTENT ACCELERATION THROUGH THE UNIVERSITY OF MINNESOTA'S TALENTED YOUTH MATHEMATICS PROGRAM

Starting in the mid-1970s as an outgrowth of Stanley's above-level testing model and SMPY research (Keynes & Rogness, 2011), the University of Minnesota's Talented Youth Mathematics Program (UMTYMP) illustrates an effective acceleration program developed by schools and universities working together on behalf of talented youth. UMTYMP, administered by the University of Minnesota's School of Mathematics Center for Educational Programs, focuses on mathematically talented sixth to 12th graders.

As described on the program's website, http://www.mathcep.umn.edu/umtymp, UMTYMP identifies mathematically talented students and provides them with a rigorous curriculum that will result in significant acceleration in math. The purpose of UMTYMP is to discover exceptionally talented students who will benefit from a challenging, stimulating program where students work at a fast pace with other exceptionally mathematically talented students of similar ages. UMTYMP is available to students attending public or nonpublic schools, as well as those who are homeschooled, and approximately 400 students per year take their math courses through UMTYMP rather than in their own schools.

Eligible students have scored at the 95th percentile or above on a standardized mathematics achievement test or have been recommended by a teacher or school counselor to take the UMTYMP exam. Students then are invited to take the UMTYMP Algebra Qualifying Exam. This exam is a specialized aptitude examination using prealgebra mathematics knowledge. Students who are successful on this exam demonstrate mastery of elementary and junior high school mathematics as well as excellent problem-solving skills and strategies. The exam stresses accuracy, understanding, and speed. Students may participate in UMTYMP practice sessions to learn about the testing process and work with University of Minnesota faculty members to develop their reasoning skills and test-taking strategies.

In addition to taking the entrance exam, students are required to complete an application and submit essays. The admissions team uses a holistic admissions process, including information from the entrance exam, student applications, and student-written essays. The committee is looking for more subjective indicators of readiness, such as maturity demonstrated by students who are not only ready for advanced mathematics courses, but who are also mature enough to sit in a 2-hour class, stay focused, and take notes.

Once accepted into the program, students complete 4 years' worth of high school math in a 2-year period. Successful students later move on to the 3-year calculus component, which includes concepts in linear algebra, differential equations, multivariable calculus, and vector analysis.

Minnesota Statute 120B.14, passed in 1984, requires schools to grant high school credit on their transcripts for students who have completed courses through UMTYMP. Therefore, there is no need for students to take math courses in their home schools. Nonpublic schools are not required to follow this state law, but most of them take a similar approach. The goal is for UMTYMP students not to have to retake calculus or any other math course taken through the program. Students receive University of Minnesota credit for completing the calculus component; students are able to complete nearly half of the requirements for a math degree by the time they graduate from high school. Also, some funding for the program is provided by the state of Minnesota.

UMTYMP is impressive because Minnesota state policy requires that schools recognize exceptionally talented students' need for acceleration and additional challenge in mathematics. The implications of this state policy are that even Minnesota students from small or underresourced schools can participate in challenging courses with intellectual peers. Schools outside of Minnesota can replicate this program by (1) recognizing that students with a variety of levels of academic abilities exist, (2) utilizing the research-supported method of above-level testing to discover academically talented students, and (3) making efforts to systematically accelerate students in content areas, recognizing that some students are ready to move ahead long before many of their age-peers.

Advanced Placement and the Equalization of Opportunity

The role of postsecondary education in ensuring that individuals have the best opportunity for finding a meaningful career, which contributes to lifelong satisfaction and well-being, cannot be overstated (Ma, Pender, & Welch, 2016). This notion was recognized well before current practice. Just before World War II, the Ford Foundation offered scholarships to high-school-aged students (younger than 16) so that they could enroll in one of a few selected postsecondary institutions prior to joining the military (see Colangelo et al., 2004 for a brief history of acceleration during the 20th century). Although this specific program was eventually phased out, the Ford Foundation continued to demonstrate prescience regarding the importance of college-level opportunities for high school students through its establishment of the College Board Advanced Placement (AP) program in the mid-1950s. Over the past seven decades, the AP program has grown exponentially (College Board, 2016) from the original (1955–1956) 104 schools with 1,229 students taking 2,199 exams to the 2015–2016 demographics of 21,953 schools with 2,611,127 students taking 4,704,980 exams in one or more of 37 subjects.

The Advanced Placement program has several components, with the primary being first-year college-level coursework delivered to high school students. Upon completion of a course, students take the national AP exam and the scores, which are on a scale of 1–5, offer a consistent indicator of accomplishment. An AP exam score of 5 corresponds to excellent work in a commensurate college course. An AP exam score of 3 is recognized by many colleges and universities as a qualifying score for college credit. The AP exam provides an objective standard of achievement irrelevant of school size, location, ethnicity, or economic status. College credit notwithstanding, the most important component of the AP course is the advanced content delivered in a setting with similar-aged students who are interested in the topic, followed by taking the AP exam (Warne, 2017). Bleske-Rechek, Lubinski, and Benbow (2004) presented the College Board's Advanced Placement (AP) program as a gold standard of advanced, rigorous curriculum for all participants. The benefits occur during the students' high school years and well into college; students who benefitted from AP coursework in high school are more likely to graduate college in 4 years or fewer (Hargrove, Godin, & Dodd, 2008; Mattern, Marini, & Shaw, 2013) and earn an advanced degree (Bleske-Rechek et al., 2004). Warne (2017) has noted, however, that some recent research studies on the effectiveness of AP courses show findings that are less clear-cut; when studies control for confounding variables, the effect of participating in AP courses is smaller, although still positive. Students who earn scores of 3, 4, or 5 on an AP test experience the greatest benefits, as measured by increased ACT scores (Warne, Larsen, Anderson, & Odasso, 2015).

The benefits associated with the AP program suggest that as many college-bound students as possible should have access to AP. Yet, as reported in the College Board's (2014) *10th Annual AP Report to the Nation*, nearly 300,000 students who demonstrate readiness for AP coursework are not accessing the coursework, and many of those students attend schools where AP is not an option. In 2013, the participation rate for taking an AP exam for the entire United States was 33.2% (nearly doubled from the previous 10 years, or 18.9% in 2003). However, many rural states report significantly lower percentages of participation. Although the 2013 AP exam participation rate of 17.9% in rural states was double the 2003 AP exam participation rate, it is still only half the rate of the U.S. overall. Not experiencing the same benefits with respect to academic rigor as their urban or suburban counterparts may have unintended consequences—especially for college-ready students. For example, fewer individuals from rural communities attend 4-year colleges. In December 2016, the United States Census Bureau reported that nearly one out of three adults in urban areas have a bachelor's degree; however, only one in five adults in rural areas do (U.S. Department of Agriculture, 2018).

There are multiple reasons why rural schools have difficulty offering AP, including logistics, finances, and limited resources (Azano, Callahan, Missett, & Brunner, 2014; Colangelo, Assouline, Baldus, & New, 2003). However, technology can make AP accessible in places where it was once only read about, not experienced. For example, since 2000, the State of Iowa has supported a partnership among schools and the University of Iowa's Belin-Blank Center to create an online AP Academy.

The Iowa Online Advanced Placement Academy: University/K–12 Partnership at Its Best

Funded by a state legislative initiative in partnership with the University of Iowa's Belin-Blank Center, the Iowa Online Advanced Placement Academy (IOAPA) was formed to offer greater accessibility to the AP program for high schools with limited access to AP. Although there is a special focus on rural and/ or small districts because the primary goal is reducing the impact of geographical barriers, IOAPA is available to any accredited high school in Iowa. The administration of the program by the Belin-Blank Center for Gifted Education and Talent Development is a critical component of the success of the program because of the expertise in gifted education provided by the staff. IOAPA includes five main components: (a) online AP coursework; (b) an in-school mentor (usually a gifted and talented teacher), who serves as a liaison between the school and the university level administration of the program; (c) online, instructor-led AP exam reviews; (d) an Advanced Placement Teacher Training Institute, with instructors provided by College Board consultants; and (e) above-level assessment to middle school students that provides specific data indicating readiness for accelerated programming, which is intended to prepare them for the AP coursework in high school.

The online nature of the course offers flexibility that traditional brick-and-mortar courses cannot provide; progress is self-paced and coursework can be completed virtually anywhere with Internet access. This is ideal for gifted students in rural schools who may prefer a faster pace and/or have complicated schedules due to participation in several extracurricular activities (a hallmark of small, rural schools).

THEORETICAL BASIS AND RESEARCH SUPPORT

Above-level testing, which is also an accelerative intervention with a modest effect size (Rogers, 2015), is a hallmark of SMPY's work and considered the genesis for several other acceleration strategies. Above-level testing was very much research-based and grounded in Hollingworth's (1942) pioneering work using above-level testing and Terman's (1925) longitudinal research studies on gifted students (Brody & Stanley, 2005). The researchers at SMPY carefully documented their findings from the very beginning of the study (e.g., Keating, 1976; Stanley, Keating, & Fox, 1974). SMPY was based on sound theory and research (Brody & Stanley, 2005), including three principles from developmental psychology:

1. learning is sequential and developmental;
2. there are individual differences among students, including the rate at which children learn; and
3. effective teaching involves matching the child's readiness to learn with the level of curriculum, including consideration of pace and complexity of the material.

Highly able students need a faster pace and access to higher level content compared to average learners (Assouline et al., 2018), and the most efficacious way to provide the appropriate level of curriculum for highly able learners is through academic acceleration. Accelerated students are more likely to be challenged and engaged while they are in school, and they often perform better academically than their peers in the same grade (Wells, Lohman, & Marron, 2009).

Above-level testing information can help us understand which students are ready for specific academic challenges, especially one or more of the 20 forms of acceleration, thus informing educational practice. This information helps us to match the level and pace of curriculum and other educational opportunities to the needs of the students (Olszewski-Kubilius, 2015). Additionally, differences measured at a relatively young age are meaningful in terms of what these students produce years later (Wai, 2015). They tend to continue pursuing these challenges throughout their schooling (Olszewski-Kubilius, 2015).

Longitudinal studies have revealed that accelerated students pursue more challenging majors, attend more prestigious colleges, and demonstrate outstanding achievements (Wai, 2015). Accelerated students have higher productivity rates, earn more money in their careers, and advance in their careers more rapidly than older, similar-ability, nonaccelerated peers. Even years after these students are out of school, they are just as satisfied with their lives and careers as nonaccelerated students, putting to rest the fear of potential negative social effects of acceleration (McClarty, 2015). Many students identified before the age of 13 as profoundly mathematically or verbally talented developed into truly outstanding producers in their respective fields (Kell, Lubinski, & Benbow, 2013).

Despite these unequivocally positive findings about the academic benefits, some educators and parents remain skeptical about the impact of acceleration on students' psychological adjustment. Cross, Andersen, and Mammadov (2015) found positive, although small effects. The research on the social-emotional development of accelerated students is not as robust and clear as the research on the academic effects of acceleration; however, as an intervention, acceleration has positive effects on the psychological and social-emotional development of students (Rogers, 2015).

CONCLUSION

Academic acceleration has an extensive and robust research base and a history of effectiveness with gifted students. Research indicates positive outcomes on both academic and social dimensions. However, myths about negative effects of acceleration have minimized the widespread use of this intervention as part of gifted programming in schools. Recently, there has been greater acknowledgement and acceptance of acceleration due to continued research by a number of scholars.

Two publications by the Belin-Blank Center, *A Nation Deceived: How Schools Hold Back America's Brightest Students* (Colangelo et al., 2004) and *A Nation Empowered: How Evidence Trumps the Excuses Holding Back America's Brightest Students* (Assouline et al., 2015), as well as the explicit statement of support for acceleration by NAGC, positively impacted the field of gifted and talented education. Therefore, although we recognize there is still work to do, there is reason for optimism that acceleration will play a stronger role in schools.

Assessing a student's readiness for acceleration is critical. Above-level testing, based on the work of Julian Stanley, is the essence of the Talent Search model and the predominant method of identification for out-of-school talent development opportunities through acceleration. The University of Minnesota's Talented Youth Mathematics Program uses a combination of testing, teacher/counselor recommendations, and interviews to serve mathematically talented students throughout Minnesota. The Iowa Online Advanced Placement Academy uses teacher recommendations, past course performance, and student interest/motivation to assess readiness for AP.

Whereas there may be some variations in identification or delivery of the three acceleration interventions presented, each focuses on identifying students who are ready for fast-paced and advanced content. Acceleration is the essence of programming for gifted students. The greater the talent in an area, the greater the need for more highly accelerative interventions as defined by the Pyramid of Accelerative Opportunities in this chapter.

Lastly, acceleration minimizes the social and political issues that confront some general enrichment programming for gifted students, which may be considered as unnecessarily exclusive or elitist. The elegance of acceleration is that it demands a high level of readiness to succeed at a fast pace and with advanced content. If a student is not ready for acceleration in a particular content area, then that student will not benefit from (and likely will not want) such an intervention. The converse is true, thus our definition of giftedness connects student readiness and willingness to learn advanced material. This is a sound rationale for programming for gifted students.

Major Takeaways

1. Acceleration works because it effectively matches the curriculum to the abilities and achievements of gifted students (Assouline et al., 2015); the intervention also has positive effects on students' psychological and social-emotional development.

2. Acceleration yields positive short-term academic, psychological, and social-emotional effects (Rogers, 2015), which accumulate into long-term benefits (McClarty, 2015).

3. The Talent Search Model of above-level testing differs from the school-based general gifted education model (Assouline & Lupkowski-Shoplik, 2012); however, the variety of levels of ability and individual differences measured through above-level testing (Assouline et al., 2018) provides meaningful information that can help educators understand which students are ready for accelerated academic challenges, thus informing educational practices.

4. Longitudinal studies demonstrate that accelerated students pursue more challenging majors, attend more prestigious colleges, and demonstrate outstanding achievements (Wai, 2015).

5. Despite the multiple advantages of acceleration as an intervention, acceleration strategies are not frequently taught in colleges of education; therefore, teachers and administrators simply have not had the opportunity to learn about them and are therefore hesitant to use them (Assouline et al., 2015; Siegle, Wilson, & Little, 2013).

RECOMMENDED READINGS AND RESOURCES

Assouline, S., Colangelo, N., VanTassel-Baska, J., & Lupkowski-Shoplik, A. (Eds.). (2015). *A nation empowered: Evidence trumps the excuses that hold back America's brightest students* (Vol. 1). Iowa City: University of Iowa, The Connie Belin & Jacqueline N. Blank International Center for Gifted Education and Talent Development.

Assouline, S., Colangelo, N., & VanTassel-Baska, J. (Eds.). (2015). *A nation empowered: Evidence trumps the excuses that hold back America's brightest students* (Vol. 2). Iowa City: University of Iowa, The Connie Belin & Jacqueline N. Blank International Center for Gifted Education and Talent Development.

Assouline, S. G., & Lupkowski-Shoplik, A. (2011). *Developing math talent: A comprehensive guide to math education for gifted students in elementary and middle school* (2nd ed.). Waco, TX: Prufrock Press.

Assouline, S. G., & Lupkowski-Shoplik, A. (2012). The Talent Search model of gifted identification. *Journal of Psychoeducational Assessment, 30*(1), 45–59.

Belin-Blank Exceptional Student Talent Search (in-school testing program)—http://www.belinblank.org/talent-search

REFERENCES

ACT, Inc. (2013). *ACT Explore technical manual.* Iowa City, IA: Author. Retrieved from https://www.act.org/content/dam/act/unsecured/documents/Explore-TechManual.pdf

Assouline, S. G., Colangelo, N., Lupkowski-Shoplik, A. E., Lipscomb, J., & Forstadt, L. (2009). *Iowa Acceleration Scale Manual* (3rd ed.). Scottsdale, AZ: Great Potential Press.

Assouline, S., Colangelo, N., VanTassel-Baska, J., & Lupkowski-Shoplik, A. (Eds.). (2015). *A nation empowered: Evidence trumps the excuses that hold back America's brightest students* (Vol. 2). Iowa City: University of Iowa, The Connie Belin & Jacqueline N. Blank International Center for Gifted Education and Talent Development.

Assouline, S. G., Ihrig, L. M., & Mahatmya, D. (2017). Closing the excellence gap: Investigation of an expanded talent search model for student selection into an extracurricular STEM program in rural middle schools. *Gifted Child Quarterly.* Advance online publication. doi:10.1177/0016986217701833

Assouline, S. G., & Lupkowski-Shoplik, A. (2011). *Developing math talent: A comprehensive guide to math education for gifted students in elementary and middle school* (2nd eds.). Waco, TX: Prufrock Press.

Assouline, S. G., & Lupkowski-Shoplik, A. (2012). The Talent Search model of gifted identification. *Journal of Psychoeducational Assessment, 30*(1), 45–59.

Assouline, S. G., Lupkowski-Shoplik, A., & Colangelo, N. (2018). Acceleration and the talent search model: Transforming the school culture. In S. I. Pfeiffer, E. Shaunessy-Dedrick, & M. Foley-Nicpon (Ed.), *APA handbook of giftedness and talent* (pp. 333–346). Washington, DC: American Psychological Association.

Azano, A. P., Callahan, C. M., Missett, T. C., & Brunner, M. (2014). Understanding the experiences of gifted education teachers and fidelity of implementation in rural schools. *Journal of Advanced Academics, 25,* 88–100. doi:10.1177/1932202X14524405

Bleske-Rechek, A., Lubinski, D., & Benbow, C. P. (2004). Meeting the educational needs of special populations: Advanced Placement's role in developing exceptional human capital. *Psychological Science, 15,* 217–224. doi:10.1111/j.0956-7976.2004.00655.x

Borland, J. H. (1989). *Planning and implementing programs for the gifted.* New York, NY: Teachers College Press.

Brody, L. E. (2009). The Johns Hopkins talent search model for identifying and developing exceptional mathematical and verbal abilities. In. L V. Shavinina (Ed.), *International handbook on giftedness* (pp. 999–1016). New York, NY: Springer Science + Business Media.

Brody, L. E., & Stanley, J. C. (2005). Youths who reason exceptionally well mathematically and/or verbally: Using the MVT:D4 model to develop their talents. In R. J. Sternberg & J. E. Davidson (Eds.), *Conceptions of giftedness* (2nd ed., pp. 20–37). New York, NY: Cambridge University Press.

Colangelo, N., Assouline, S. G., Baldus, C. M., & New, J. K. (2003). Gifted education in rural schools. In N. Colangelo & G. A. Davis (Eds.) *Handbook of gifted education* (3rd ed., pp. 572–581). Boston, MA: Allyn & Bacon.

Colangelo, N., Assouline, S. G., & Gross, M. U. M. (2004). *A nation deceived: How schools hold back America's students* (Vol. 1). Iowa City: University of Iowa, The Connie Belin & Jacqueline N. Blank International Center for Gifted Education and Talent Development.

College Board. (2014). *The 10th annual AP report to the nation.* Retrieved from http://files.eric.ed.gov/fulltext/ED559067.pdf

College Board. (2016). *Annual AP program participation 1956-2016.* Retrieved from https://secure-media.collegeboard.org/digitalServices/pdf/research/2016/2016-Annual-Participation.pdf

Cross, T. L., Andersen, L., & Mammadov, S. (2015). Effects of academic acceleration on the social and emotional lives of gifted students. In S. G. Assouline, N. Colangelo, J. VanTassel-Baska, & A. Lupkowski-Shoplik (Eds.), *A nation empowered: Evidence trumps the excuses holding back America's brightest students* (Vol. 2, pp. 31–42). Iowa City: University of Iowa, The Connie Belin & Jacqueline N. Blank International Center for Gifted Education and Talent Development.

Gold, M. J. (1965). *Education of the intellectually gifted.* Columbus, OH: Merrill.

Hargrove, L., Godin, D., & Dodd, B. G. (2008). *College outcomes comparisons by AP and non-AP high school experiences* (College Board Research Report No. 2008-3). New York, NY: College Board.

Hollingworth, L. S. (1942). *Children above 180 IQ Stanford-Binet: Origin and development.* Yonkers-on-Hudson, NY: World Book.

Keating, D. P. (Ed.). (1976). *Intellectual talent: Research and development.* Baltimore, MD: Johns Hopkins University Press.

Kell, H. J., Lubinski, D., & Benbow, C. P. (2013). Who rises to the top? Early indicators. *Psychological Science, 24,* 648–659.

Keynes, H. B., & Rogness, J. (2011). Historical perspectives on a program for mathematically talented students. *Mathematics Enthusiast, 8,* 189–206.

Lubinski, D. (2004). Long-term effects of educational acceleration. In N. Colangelo, S. G. Assouline, & M. U. M. Gross (Eds.), *A nation deceived: How schools hold back America's brightest students* (Vol. 2, pp. 23–38). Iowa City: University of Iowa, The Connie Belin & Jacqueline N. Blank International Center for Gifted Education and Talent Development.

Lubinski, D., & Benbow, C. P. (2006). Study of Mathematically Precocious Youth after 35 years: Uncovering antecedents for the development of math-science expertise. *Perspectives on Psychological Science, 1,* 316–345.

Lubinski, D., Webb, R. M., Morelock, M. J., & Benbow, C. P. (2001). Top 1 in 10,000: A 10-year follow-up of the profoundly gifted. *Journal of Applied Psychology, 86,* 718.

Lupkowski-Shoplik, A. E., & Assouline, S. G. (1993). Identifying mathematically talented elementary students: Using the lower level of the SSAT. *Gifted Child Quarterly, 37,* 118–123.

Lupkowski-Shoplik, A., Benbow, C. P., Assouline, S. G., & Brody, L. E. (2003). Talent searches: Meeting the needs of academically talented youth. In N. Colangelo & G. A. Davis (Eds.), *Handbook of gifted education* (3rd. ed., pp. 204–218). Boston, MA: Allyn & Bacon.

Lupkowski-Shoplik, A., & Swiatek, M. A. (1999). Elementary student talent searches: Establishing appropriate guidelines for qualifying test scores. *Gifted Child Quarterly, 43,* 265–272.

Ma, J., Pender, M., & Welch, M. (2016). Education pays 2016: The benefits of higher education for individuals and society. *Trends in Higher Education Series.* New York, NY: College Board.

Mattern, K., Marini, J. P., & Shaw, E. J. (2013). *Are AP students more likely to graduate on time?* (College Board Research Report 2013-5). New York, NY: College Board.

McClarty, K. L. (2015). Early to rise: The effects of academic acceleration on occupational prestige, earnings, and satisfaction. In S. Assouline, N. Colangelo, J. VanTassel-Baska, & A. E. Lupkowski-Shoplik (Eds.)., *A nation empowered: Evidence trumps the excuses holding back America's brightest students* (pp. 171–180). Iowa City: University of Iowa, The Connie Belin & Jacqueline N. Blank International Center for Gifted Education and Talent Development.

Mills, C. J., & Barnett, L. B. (1992). The use of the Secondary School Admission Test (SSAT) to identify academically talented elementary school students. *Gifted Child Quarterly, 36,* 155–159.

National Association for Gifted Children. (n.d.). *Acceleration.* Retrieved from http://www.nagc.org/resources-publications/gifted-education-practices/acceleration

National Association for Gifted Children, & Council of State Directors of Programs for the Gifted. (2015). *State of the states in gifted education 2014–2015.* Washington, DC: Authors.

Olszewski-Kubilius, P. (2015). Talent searches and accelerated programming for gifted students. In S. G. Assouline, N. Colangelo, J. VanTassel-Baska, & A. Lupkowski-Shoplik (Eds.), *A nation empowered: Evidence trumps the excuses holding back America's brightest students* (Vol. 2, pp. 111–121). Iowa City: University of Iowa, The Connie Belin & Jacqueline N. Blank International Center for Gifted Education and Talent Development.

Plucker, J. A., & Harris, B. (2015). Acceleration and economically vulnerable children. In S. G. Assouline, N. Colangelo, J. VanTassel-Baska, & A. Lupkowski-Shoplik (Eds.), *A nation empowered: Evidence trumps the excuses holding back America's brightest students* (Vol. 2, pp. 181–188). Iowa City: University of Iowa, The Connie Belin & Jacqueline N. Blank International Center for Gifted Education and Talent Development.

Pressey, S. L. (1949). *Educational acceleration: Appraisals and basic problems.* Bureau of Educational Research Monographs, No. 31. Columbus, OH: Ohio State University Press.

Rogers, K. (2015). The academic, socialization, and psychological effects of acceleration: Research synthesis. In S. G. Assouline, N. Colangelo, J. VanTassel-Baska, & A. Lupkowski-Shoplik (Eds.), *A nation empowered: Evidence trumps the excuses holding back America's brightest students* (Vol. 2, pp. 19–29). Iowa City: University of Iowa, The Connie Belin & Jacqueline N. Blank International Center for Gifted Education and Talent Development.

Siegle, D., Wilson, H. E., & Little, C. A. (2013). A sample of gifted and talented educators' attitudes about academic acceleration. *Journal of Advanced Academics, 24,* 27–51.

Southern, W. T., & Jones, E. D. (2015). Types of acceleration: Dimensions and issues. In S. G. Assouline, N. Colangelo, J. VanTassel-Baska, & A. Lupkowski-Shoplik (Eds.), *A nation empowered: Evidence trumps the excuses holding back America's brightest students* (Vol. 2, pp. 9–18). Iowa City: University of Iowa, The Connie Belin & Jacqueline N. Blank International Center for Gifted Education and Talent Development.

Stanley, J. C. (1996). In the beginning: The Study of Mathematically Precocious Youth. In C. P. Benbow & D. Lubinski (Eds.), *Intellectual talent: Psychometric and social issues* (pp. 225–235). Baltimore, MD: Johns Hopkins University Press.

Stanley, J. C. (2005). A quiet revolution: Finding boys and girls who reason exceptionally well and/or verbally and helping them get the supplemental educational opportunities they need. *High Ability Studies, 16*(1), 5–14.

Stanley, J. C., Keating, D. P., & Fox, L. H. (1974). *Mathematical talent: Discovery, description, and development.* Baltimore, MD: Johns Hopkins University Press.

Steenbergen-Hu, S., Makel, M. C., & Olszewski-Kubilius, P. (2016). What one hundred years of research says about the effects of ability grouping and acceleration on K–12 students' academic achievement: Findings of two second-order meta-analyses. *Review of Educational Research, 86,* 849–899. doi:10.3102/0034654316675417

Subotnik, R. F., Olszewski-Kubilius, P., & Worrell, F. C. (2011). Rethinking giftedness and gifted education: A proposed direction forward based on psychological science. *Psychological Science in the Public Interest, 12*(1), 3–54.

Terman, L. M. (1925). *Genetic studies of genius* (Vol. 1). Stanford, CA: Stanford University Press.

U.S. Department of Agriculture. (2018). *Rural education at a glance, 2017 edition.* Washington, DC: Author. Retrieved from https://www.ers.usda.gov/webdocs/publications/83078/eib-171.pdf?v=42830

Wai, J. (2015). Long-term effects of educational acceleration. In S. G. Assouline, N. Colangelo, J. VanTassel-Baska, & A. Lupkowski-Shoplik (Eds.), *A nation empowered: Evidence trumps the excuses holding back America's brightest students* (Vol. 2, pp. 73–83). Iowa City: University of Iowa, The Connie Belin & Jacqueline N. Blank International Center for Gifted Education and Talent Development.

Warne, R. T. (2017). Research on the academic benefits of the Advanced Placement program: Taking stock and looking forward. *SAGE Open, 7*(1). doi:2158244016682996

Warne, R. T., Larsen, R., Anderson, B., & Odasso, A. J. (2015). The impact of participation in the Advanced Placement program on students' college admissions test scores. *Journal of Educational Research, 108,* 400–416. doi:10.1080/00220671.2014.917253

Wells, R., Lohman, D., & Marron, M. (2009). What factors are associated with grade acceleration?: An analysis and comparison of two U.S. databases. *Journal of Advanced Academics, 20,* 248–273.

CHAPTER 2

Schools Are Places for Talent Development

PROMOTING CREATIVE PRODUCTIVE GIFTEDNESS

Joseph S. Renzulli and Sally M. Reis

As increasing scientific research advances our understanding of how human potential develops over the course of a lifetime, the systems created to enhance that potential (i.e., the education system) must also change to reflect these emerging and contemporary talent development theories. In the field of gifted education over the past several decades, an increasing body of supportive scholarship and research has supported our broadened, expanded conception of giftedness (Dai, 2010; Gardner, 1983; Renzulli, 1978, 2005; Sternberg & Davidson, 2005). Although a thorough review of this research is beyond the scope of this chapter, we do hope to simplify a complex and active debate by stating that very few researchers and theorists continue to believe that an isolated IQ or achievement test score is a valid measure of a child's capacity for producing accomplishments, particularly creative productive accomplishments, over the course of a lifetime. This does not mean that IQ or achievement scores should not be included as *one of the criteria* we consider when we set out to develop gifts and talents, especially creative talents, but rather they should not form *the entire basis* for defining gifts and talents and creating a fair system of identification for gifted and enrichment programs. In this chapter, we discuss the cohesive and critical relationship between definitions, identification systems, and programs for educat-

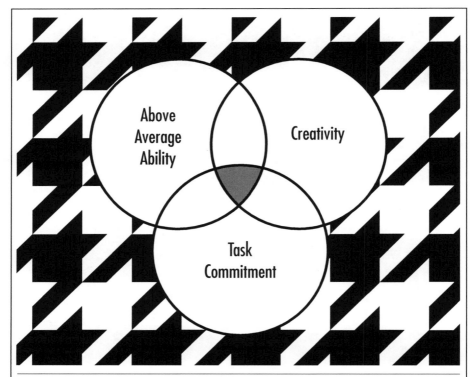

Figure 2.1. The Three-Ring Conception of Giftedness. The houndstooth background represents personality and environment, factors that give rise to the three clusters of traits.

ing talented and high-ability students. We focus on our definition of giftedness/ talent, the Three-Ring Conception of Giftedness; the ways we believe that young people develop their gifts and talents; and finally, our own educational approach, the Schoolwide Enrichment Model, and the body of research that supports its efficacy in the talent development process.

THE THREE-RING
CONCEPTION OF GIFTEDNESS

The Three-Ring Conception of Giftedness, supported by decades of research (Renzulli, 1978, 1986, 2005; see Figure 2.1), was purposefully designed for a programming model that develops both academic or high achieving and creative-productive types of giftedness (Renzulli & Reis, 1994, 1997, 2014), as both of these types of giftedness are important and often interact, and both should be encouraged in special programs. This conception of giftedness identifies three interlocking clusters of abilities, as its name derives from the conceptual framework of the theory—namely, these three interacting clusters of traits: (1) *above average* but not necessarily superior ability as measured by cognitive ability and achievement tests, (2) *task commitment*, and (3) *creativity*. The model emphasizes the relationship of these clusters in the development of what we prefer to call "gifted behaviors," which is the overlap between and among these clusters.

Perhaps the most salient aspect of this theory is that it is the *interaction* between and among these clusters of traits brought to bear upon a particular problem situation and/or performance area that creates the conditions for the creative productive process to begin and flourish. Additionally, these clusters of traits emerge in certain people, at certain times, and under certain circumstances. The Enrichment Triad Model (Reis & Renzulli, 2003; Renzulli, 1977, 1988) is the compatible learning theory from which we promote educational circumstances that create the conditions for stimulating interaction between and among the three rings as described below.

Above average ability encompasses both general (e.g., verbal and numerical reasoning, spatial relations, memory) and specific (e.g., chemistry, ballet, musical composition, experimental design) performance areas and is the most constant of the rings. That is, any student's performance within the parameters of this ring is minimally variable, as it is linked most closely with traditional cognitive/intellectual traits. The reason that this ring makes reference to "above average ability" (as opposed to, for example, "the top 5%" or "exceptional ability") derives from research suggesting that, beyond a certain level of cognitive ability, real-world achievement is less dependent upon ever-increasing performance on skills assessments than upon other personal and dispositional factors (e.g., task commitment and creativity; Renzulli, 1978, 1986, 2005). The sole use of intelligence tests, aptitude, and/or achievement tests to identify candidates for "gifted programs" has been universally discussed and dismissed in the field.

Task commitment represents a nonintellective cluster of traits found consistently in creative productive individuals (e.g., perseverance, determination, willpower, positive energy), and what some contemporary authors (Duckworth, 2009) are currently calling *grit*. It may best be summarized as a focused or refined form of motivation—energy brought to bear on a particular problem or specific performance area. The significance of this cluster of traits in any definition of giftedness derives from myriad research studies, as well as autobiographical sketches of creative productive individuals. (Reis & Renzulli, 2011; Renzulli, 2002, 2012). Simply stated, one of the primary ingredients for success among persons who have made important contributions to their respective performance areas is their ability to immerse themselves fully in a problem or area for an extended period of time and to persevere even in the face of obstacles that may inhibit others.

Creativity is that cluster of traits that encompasses curiosity, originality, innovation, imagination, ingenuity, and a willingness to challenge convention and tradition. For example, there have been many gifted scientists throughout history, but the scientists whose work we revere, whose names have remained recognizable in scholarly communities and among the general public, are those scientists who used their creativity to envision, analyze, and ultimately help resolve scientific questions in new, original ways.

A frequently raised question relates to whether creativity and task commitment must be present in order for a person to be considered "gifted." In the study of human abilities, traditionally measured achievement tends to remain constant over time (indeed, this is the reason for the high reliability of cognitive ability and achievement tests). Task commitment and creativity, on the other hand, are not always present or absent; rather, they emerge and are developed within certain contexts and circumstances that are the result of experiences and effective teaching to promote them. Creativity and task commitment, unlike traditionally measured academic achievement traits included in the above average ability circle, are developmental and therefore subject to the kinds of experiences provided for both young people and adults. They are the result of the opportunities, resources, and encouragement that are provided to spark a creative idea or develop the motivation that causes a person or group to want to follow through on the idea.

In many cases, creativity and task commitment "feed" upon one another. For example, a person notices a problem that needs to be solved (e.g., bullying in a school). She becomes interested and develops the task commitment to do something about it. She may then begin to explore various creative ways to start an awareness campaign, complete a questionnaire study about bullying, obtain a video to be shown to the students in their school, or prepare some posters or discussion groups that address this issue.

The reciprocal relationship between creativity and task commitment may also work in the opposite direction. A group of students may, for example, have a creative idea about starting a local museum on their town's history. They must now develop their task commitment and executive functioning skills to actually get the job done. Task commitment requires the time, energy, and the organizational and management skills necessary for their creative idea to become a reality.

The Three-Ring Conception of Giftedness is based on an overlap and interaction between and among these three clusters of traits that create the conditions for developing and applying gifted behaviors. Giftedness is not viewed as an absolute or fixed state of being (i.e., "you have it or you don't have it"). Rather, it is viewed as a developmental set of behaviors that can be applied to creative endeavors and problem-solving situations. Varying kinds and degrees of gifted behaviors can be developed and displayed in certain people, at certain times, under certain circumstances, and within certain domains or contexts. In a certain sense, we might view the most important role of teachers as to provide young people with the opportunities, resources, and encouragement to generate creative ideas and the skills necessary to follow through on their ideas. In other words, in individuals with above-average ability, our most important goal is to create the creativity and task commitment traits specified in the Three-Ring Conception of Giftedness and to bring the circles together to enable gifted behaviors to coalesce and activate. This concept is a cornerstone of the corresponding Renzulli Identification System for Gifted Program Services (RIS/GPS; Renzulli & Reis, 2012).

To best support effective implementation of gifted programming, internal consistency and congruence should exist among the criteria used in the identification process and the goals and types of services that constitute the day-to-day gifted program's activities in which students will be involved. There should also be a link between a broad range of services and teaching practices that are specifically designed to develop a variety of talents in young people. We also believe that we should label the services rather than the students, enabling teachers to document specific strengths and to use this information to make decisions about the types of activities and the levels of challenge that should be made available.

Our identification system (RIS/GPS; Renzulli & Reis, 2012) incorporates these important factors, recognizes students with undiscovered potential, and provides opportunities to develop their talents through an integrated continuum of special services. This approach enables the identification of students who would benefit from services that recognize both academic and creative-productive giftedness. A key feature within this identification system is the formation of a Talent Pool that includes students who have been identified by both test and nontest criteria. The system includes students who earn high scores on traditional measures, but also leaves room for students who show their potentials in other ways or those who have high academic potential but underachieve in school. In districts where this system has been implemented, students, parents, teachers, and administrators have expressed high degrees of satisfaction with this approach. By eliminating many of the problems usually associated with the identification of gifted students, we can expand general enrichment opportunities to students below the top few percentile levels usually admitted into special programs and those students who gain entrance by nontest criteria. This more flexible and open approach enables us to eliminate the often times justifiable criticism about failures to identify students who are in need of special opportunities, resources, and encouragement.

HOW DO PEOPLE DEVELOP
THEIR GIFTS AND TALENTS?

Young people identified as gifted and talented are as diverse and eclectic as the paths they take to develop their gifts and talents. They exhibit a wide range of characteristics in ability and achievement, temperament, and effort invested in reaching goals. No clear standard pattern or path of talent development exists among gifted individuals, but rather qualities that can be developed are the key components of creative productive giftedness. Abilities, task commitment, and creativity can be applied to areas of interest or passion over time. The development of above-average abilities is accomplished when individuals begin the process of developing their academic abilities and interests both in and out of school. The development of task commitment and creativity is accomplished when individuals find an area in which they desire and choose to develop these skills, usually when an interest is activated. We believe that when children experience and enjoy creative and productivity experiences, such as independent or small-group investigative projects, they will be more likely to seek additional creative and productive experiences later in life. These projects are called Type III Enrichment in the Enrichment Triad Model (Renzulli, 1977). Type III Enrichment casts the young learner in the role of thinking, feeling, and doing like the practicing professional, even if he or she is operating at a more junior level than adult professionals. The traditional models of education that focus on compliance, rote memorization, and test preparation are now giving way to approaches that emphasize thinking skills and the application of knowledge that reflect what professionals do in their daily work. The theory of knowledge (Renzulli, 2016) underlying this approach is designed to guide teachers in how students can use received and analyzed knowledge in applied ways to produce Type III outcomes that approximate the work of persons who use an investigative approach and creative mindset to become producers rather than consumers of knowledge. The theory also makes distinctions between presented knowledge that typifies the traditional curriculum and the "just in time" knowledge needed by professionals to address a problem or project of current interest.

Recently, we interviewed a university student who had participated in an SEM program in elementary and middle school, and he described the intensity of his interests he experienced when working on creative projects. He shared the memories of his excitement about developing a creative invention in elementary school and the passion he felt when doing something that helped others. He is currently an engineering major who hopes to continue these types of opportunities in his career, and he explained that the experience of his creative productive work in elementary and secondary school gifted programs enabled him to identify a college major and pursue it with intensity, as he craved the opportunity to complete creative projects in college and in his subsequent career. We believe that early creative productive experiences in elementary or secondary school enable some academically talented students to learn to relish the creative experiences and become more likely to pursue these options in their adult lives, leading to a more creative and productive personal life, regardless of the work and career they select.

Each of us has also pursued our own interests in additional research about talent development over the lifespan. Sally has studied talented girls and women in all domains across the life spans (Reis, 1996, 2002, 2005), elaborating on the Three-Ring Conception of Giftedness. She defines feminine talent development as occurring when women with high intellectual, creative, artistic, or leadership ability or potential achieve in an area they choose and when they make contributions that they consider meaningful to society. These contributions are further enhanced when these talented women pursued what they believed to be important work that made the world a healthier, more beautiful, and more peaceful place in which diverse expressions of art and humanity are celebrated.

Joe has continued his fascination with the scientific components that give rise to socially constructive giftedness, leading him to examine the personal attributes that explain the interconnected "houndstooth" pattern that forms the background of the Three-Ring Conception of Giftedness. After a comprehensive review of the literature (Renzulli, 2002), he identified six components that explained the environmental and personality characteristics of the background, as described briefly below.

➤ *Optimism.* Optimism includes cognitive, emotional, and motivational components and reflects the belief that the future holds good outcomes. Optimism may be thought of as an attitude associated with expectations of a future that is socially desirable, to the individual's advantage, or to the advantage of others. It is characterized by a sense of hope and a willingness to accept hard work.

➤ *Courage.* Courage is the ability to face difficulty or danger while overcoming physical, psychological, or moral fears. Integrity and strength of character are typical manifestations of courage, and they represent the most salient marks of those creative people who actually increase social capital.

➤ *Romance with a topic or discipline.* When an individual is passionate about a topic or discipline, a true romance, characterized by powerful emotions and desires, evolves. The passion of this romance often becomes an image of the future in young people and provides the motivation for a long-term commitment to a course of action.

➤ *Sensitivity to human concerns.* This trait encompasses the abilities to comprehend another's affective world and to accurately and sensitively communicate such understanding through action. Altruism and empathy, aspects of which are evident throughout human development, characterize this trait.

➢ *Physical/mental energy.* All people have this trait in varying degrees, but the amount of energy an individual is willing and able to invest in the achievement of a goal is a crucial issue in high levels of accomplishment. In the case of eminent individuals, this energy investment is a major contributor to task commitment. Charisma and curiosity are frequent correlates of high physical and mental energy.

➢ *Vision/sense of destiny.* Complex and difficult to define, vision or a sense of destiny may best be described by a variety of interrelated concepts, such as internal locus of control, motivation, volition, and self-efficacy. When an individual has a vision or sense of destiny about future activities, events, and involvements, that vision serves to stimulate planning and to direct behavior; it becomes an incentive for present behavior.

These "co-cognitive factors" interact with and enhance the cognitive traits that are ordinarily associated with success in school and with the overall development of human abilities. The literature reviews and empirical research that resulted in the identification of these components, along with a graphical representation of Operation Houndstooth, focus primarily on clarifying definitions and identifying, adapting, and constructing assessment procedures that have extended our understanding of the components, especially as they are exhibited by young people. A major assumption underlying this project is that all of the components defined in our background research are subject to modification, for us, by the implementation of the Schoolwide Enrichment Model (SEM).

TALENT DEVELOPMENT IN SCHOOL: USING THE SEM

The process of talent development in children within and across specific domains has fascinated us for more than four decades. How is it that some extremely smart students drop out of high school and fail to realize their promise and potential, while others excel? Why is it that some extremely talented individuals grow up to be quite average in the very fields in which they showed such promise when they were young children? Why are the co-cognitive traits mentioned above so important in talent development in addition to having potential and talent in a particular domain? Our research interests have focused most often on the program that we developed, the Schoolwide Enrichment Model (described in this section), and evolving over 40 years of research. Although it is impossible to summarize four decades of research and development (Gubbins, 1995; Reis & Renzulli, 2003; Renzulli & Reis, 1994) that contributed to the development of this approach, one of the guiding principles that summarizes our work is our belief that the creative and productive experiences of children who complete and enjoy Type III experiences will lead them to further develop and seek additional creative and productive experiences later in life. That is, we believe that students who experience the joys and challenges and intensities of creative productive work in elementary and secondary school, and indeed even in college, will be more likely to continue to pursue it in their adult lives. This, in turn, will lead them to a more creative and productive personal life, regardless of what domain, interest, or career they choose.

The SEM has been implemented in school districts worldwide, and extensive evaluations and research studies indicate the effectiveness of the model, which VanTassel-Baska and Brown (2007) called one of the mega-models in the field. Prior research suggests that the model is effective at serving high-ability students in a variety of educational settings and works well in schools that serve diverse ethnic and socioeconomic populations, exactly the population targeted by this school (Reis & Renzulli, 2003; Renzulli & Reis, 1994).

The SEM combines the previously developed Enrichment Triad Model (Renzulli, 1977) with a more flexible approach to identifying high-potential students (see Figure 2.2). Research on the SEM has been conducted in schools with widely differing socioeconomic levels and program organizational patterns and has shown consistently positive results (Reis & Renzulli, 2003; Renzulli & Reis, 1994). In the SEM, a talent pool of 15%–20% of above-average ability/high-potential students is identified through a variety of measures, including achievement tests, teacher nominations, assessment of potential for creativity, and task commitment, as well as alternative pathways of entrance (self-nomination, parent nomination, etc.).

In the SEM, students receive several kinds of services. First, interest, learning styles, and product style assessments are conducted with Talent Pool students using the program Renzulli Learning (http://www.renzullilearning.com). Each student creates a profile that identifies his or her unique strengths and talents, and teachers can identify patterns of student's interests, products, and learning styles across the three classes. These methods are being used to both identify and create students' interests and to encourage students to develop and pursue these interests in various ways. Learning style preferences assessed include projects, independent study, teaching games, simulations, peer teaching, programmed instruction, lecture, drill and recitation, and discussion. Product style preferences include the kinds of products students like to do, such as those that are written, oral, hands-on, artistic, displays, dramatization, service, and multimedia.

The curriculum/instructional focus in the SEM for all learning activities is the Enrichment Triad Model (Renzulli, 1977), which was initially implemented

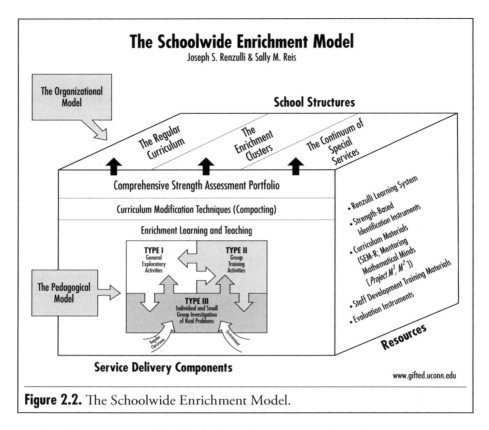

Figure 2.2. The Schoolwide Enrichment Model.

in school districts as a gifted and talented program, and is often now integrated into whole-school programming. Research on the use of the Enrichment Triad Model and its integration into the SEM has consistently shown the positive outcomes of the use of this approach with urban students, finding that the enriched and accelerated content can reverse underachievement and increase achievement (Baum, 1988; Baum, Renzulli, & Hébert, 1994; Delcourt, 1993; Hébert, 1993). The Enrichment Triad Model is designed to encourage creative productivity on the part of students by exposing them to various topics, areas of interest, and fields of study, and to further train them to *apply* advanced content, process-training skills, and methodology training to self-selected areas of interest. Accordingly, three types of enrichment are included in the Enrichment Triad Model. In order for enrichment learning and teaching to be applied systematically to the learning process of all students, it must be organized in a way that makes sense to teachers and students, and the Enrichment Triad Model can be used for this purpose. The Enrichment Triad Model is based on the ways in which people learn in a natural environment rather than the artificially structured environment that characterizes most classrooms. External stimulation, internal curiosity, necessity, or combinations of these three starting points cause people to develop an interest in a topic, problem, or area of study. Children are, by nature, curious and they enjoy the use of problem solving, but in order for them to act upon a problem or interest with some degree of commitment and enthusiasm, the interest must be sincere and they must feel a personal reason for taking action. In the Enrichment Triad Model, the *interaction* among the following three types of enrichment is as important as any single type of enrichment (Type I, II, or III).

Curriculum Compacting

Curriculum compacting (Reis, Renzulli, & Burns, 2016) is also offered and provided to all eligible Talent Pool students in the SEM. Compacting enables classroom teachers to modify the regular curriculum by eliminating portions of previously mastered content when students show content strengths. Research on compacting has consistently demonstrated that academically talented students can have up to 50%–75% of their regular curriculum eliminated or streamlined to avoid repetition of previously mastered work, guaranteeing mastery, while simultaneously substituting more appropriately challenging activities (Reis & Purcell, 1993; Reis, Westberg, Kulikowich, & Purcell, 1998). Compacting enables teachers to document the content areas that have been compacted and the alternative, more interesting, and engaging work that has been substituted.

Enrichment

The Enrichment Triad Model underlies all enrichment in the SEM (see Figure 2.3). Most Type I and II Enrichment are considered appropriate for all students, as the more advanced Type III Enrichment is usually considered appropriate for students who are capable of developing gifted and creative behaviors. Type I consists of general exploratory experiences, such as guest speakers, field trips, demonstrations, interest centers, and the use of audiovisual materials and technology (such as webinars) designed to expose students to new and exciting topics, ideas, and fields of knowledge not ordinarily covered in the regular curriculum. Type II Enrichment includes instructional methods and materials purposefully designed to promote the development of thinking, feeling, research, communication, and methodological processes. Type II training, usually carried out both in classrooms and in enrichment programs, includes the development of creative thinking and problem solving, critical thinking, and affective processes; a variety of specific learning-how-to-learn skills; skills in the appropriate use of advanced-level reference materials; and written, oral, and visual communication skills. Most Type II activities are appropriate for all students, as few would argue against all students learning problem solving, creative thinking, and reference and communication skills. It is the specific skills within these categories, such as advanced training in statistics or in methodological skills, such as robotics, or advanced historical

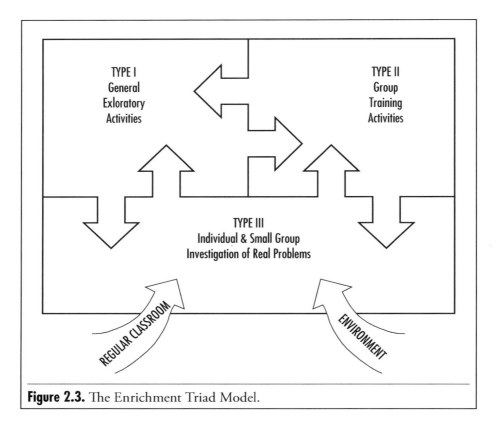

Figure 2.3. The Enrichment Triad Model.

documentation, that are reserved for more advanced students whose interests in a topic cause these skills to be necessary for their Type III work.

Type III Enrichment is the most advanced level in the Enrichment Triad Model. Although Types I and II Enrichment and curriculum compacting should be provided on a regular basis to talent pool students, the ability to revolve into Type III Enrichment depends on an individual's interests, motivation, and desire to pursue advanced level study. Type III Enrichment is defined as investigative activities and artistic productions in which the learner assumes the role of a first-hand inquirer thinking, feeling, and acting like a practicing professional, with involvement pursued at as advanced or professional level as possible given the student's level of development and age. The most important feature of the model is the "flow" or connection among the experiences. Each type of enrichment is viewed as a component part of a holistic process that blends present or newly developed interests (Type I) and advanced-level thinking and research skills (Type II) with application situations based on the modus operandi of the firsthand inquirer (Type III).

Renzulli Learning

Students in SEM programs also have access to Renzulli Learning System, another research supported component (Field, 2009). Field studied the use of Renzulli Learning, an innovative online enrichment program based on the Enrichment Triad Model, finding that gifted and nongifted students who participated in this enrichment program for 2–3 hours each week demonstrated significantly higher growth in reading comprehension than control group students who did not participate in the program.

Four steps enable students to have access to enrichment during the day as well as after school and at home if the technology is available in their homes. The first step consists of a computer-based diagnostic assessment that creates a profile of each student's academic strengths, interests, learning styles, and preferred modes of expression. The online assessment, which takes about 30 minutes, results in a personalized profile that highlights individual student strengths and sets the stage for step two of the RLS. The profile serves as a compass for the second step, which is a differentiation search engine that examines thousands of resources that relate specifically to each student's profile. A project management tool guides students and teachers to use specifically selected resources for assigned curricular activities, independent or small-group investigative projects, and a wide variety of challenging enrichment experiences. Another management tool enables teachers to form instructional groups and enrichment clusters based on interests and learning style preferences. Teachers have instant access to student profiles, all websites visited, and the amount of time spent in each activity. Parents may also access their child's profile and web activities. In order to promote parent involvement, we suggest that students work on some of their favorite activities with their parents.

Next, the differentiation search engine matches student strengths and interests to an enrichment database of 50,000 enrichment activities, materials, resources, and opportunities for further study that are grouped into the following categories: virtual field trips, real field trips, creativity training, critical thinking, projects and independent study, contests and competitions, websites, fiction and nonfiction books, summer programs, online activities, research skills, and high-interest videos and DVDs. Many of these resources provide the methods of inquiry, advanced-level thinking and creative problem-solving skills, and investigative approaches. Students are guided toward the *application of knowledge* to the development of original research studies, creative projects, and action-oriented undertakings that put knowledge to work in personally meaningful areas of interest, and provide students with suggestions for outlets and audiences for their creative products. The resources available in step two also provide students with opportunities to pursue advanced-level training in their strength areas and areas of personal interest.

The third part of Renzulli Learning for students is a project organization and management plan called the Wizard Project Maker. Using this project planner, teachers can help students target their web-based explorations to undertake original research, investigative projects, and the development of a wide variety of creative undertakings. The sophisticated software used in this tool automatically locates potentially relevant web-based resources that can be used in connection with the student's investigative activity. This management device is designed to fulfill the requirements of a Type III Enrichment experience, which is the highest level of enrichment described in our discussion of the Enrichment Triad Model.

The final step in the Renzulli Learning System is an automatic compilation and storage of all student activity from steps one, two, and three into an ongoing student record called the Total Talent Portfolio. A management tool allows students to evaluate each site visited and resource used, students can complete a self-assessment of what they derived from the resource, and if they choose they can store favorite activities and resources in their portfolio. This feature allows easy-return-access to ongoing work. The portfolio can be reviewed at any time by teachers and parents through the use of an access code, which allows teachers to give feedback and guidance to individual students and provides parents with information about students' work and opportunities for parental involvement. The Total Talent Portfolio can travel with students throughout their school years to serve as a reminder of previous activities and creative accomplishments that they might want to include in college applications. It also is an ongoing record that can help students, teachers, guidance counselors, and parents make decisions about future educational and vocational plans. Teacher resources in Renzulli Learning enable teachers to differentiate assignments, and send tiered and compacted assignments to students by placing them in their electronic talent portfolio. Teachers can also use Renzulli Learning to group students based on their interests, learning, and expression or product styles.

The SEM-R

A newer component of the SEM is the Schoolwide Enrichment Model in Reading, also supported by extensive research showing its success with differentiating challenge and engagement for all readers (Reis, Eckert, McCoach, Jacobs, & Coyne, 2008; Reis et al., 2007; Reis, McCoach, Little, Muller, & Kaniskan, 2011). This approach, developed by Sally Reis and a team of reading and gifted education specialists, focuses on reading acceleration and enrichment for the development of talent in readers through engagement in challenging, self-selected reading, accompanied by instruction in high-level thinking and reading strategy skills. A second core focus of the SEM-R is differentiation of reading content and strategies, coupled with more challenging reading experiences and advanced opportunities for metacognition and self-regulated reading. In other words, the SEM-R program challenges and prepares students who are talented in reading to begin reading more challenging books in school and to continue this reading at home.

The goals of the SEM-R approach are to encourage children to begin to enjoy the reading process by giving them access to high-interest, self-selected books that they can read for periods of time at school and at home; to develop independence and self-regulation in reading through the selection of these books as well as the opportunity to have individualized reading instruction; and, finally, to enable all students to improve in reading fluency and comprehension through the use of reading comprehension strategies.

The SEM-R intervention includes three phases. During Phase 1, the "exposure" phase, teachers present short read-alouds from high-quality, engaging literature to introduce students to a wide variety of titles, genres, authors, and topics. Along with these read-alouds, teachers provide instruction through modeling and discussion, demonstrating reading strategies and self-regulation skills and using higher order questions to guide discussion. Early in the implementation of the SEM-R, these Phase 1 activities lasted about 20 minutes per day; Phase 1 decreased in length over the course of the year when students could spend more time on Phase 2, usually resulting in all students reading appropriately challenging self-selected content for about 50–60 minutes each day.

Phase 2 of the SEM-R emphasized the development of students' ability to engage in supported independent reading (SIR) of self-selected, appropriately challenging books, with differentiated instructional support provided through conferences with the teacher or another adult. During Phase 2, students selected books that were at least 1 to 1.5 grade levels above their current reading levels. Students learned strategies for recognizing appropriately challenging books, and they were guided and encouraged to select challenging books in their areas of interest to promote engagement. Over the course of the intervention, students initially read for 5–15 minutes a day during Phase 2; over time they extended SIR to 20–25 minutes, and finally to almost an hour each day. During this in-class reading time, students participate in individualized reading conferences with their teachers; on average, each student participated in one to two conferences per week, and conferences usually lasted about 5–7 minutes. In these conferences, teachers and instructional aides assessed reading fluency and comprehension and provided individualized instruction in strategy use, including predicting, using inferences, and making connections. For more advanced readers, conferences focused less on specific reading strategies and more on higher order questions and critical concepts.

In Phase 3, students are encouraged to move from teacher-directed opportunities to self-choice activities over the course of the intervention. Activities include (but are not limited to) opportunities to explore new technology, discussion groups, practice with advanced questioning and thinking skills, creativity training in language arts, learning centers, interest-based projects, free reading, and book chats. These experiences provide time for students to pursue areas of personal interest through the use of interest development centers and the Internet to learn to read critically and to locate other reading materials, especially high-quality, challenging literature. Options for independent study using Renzulli Learning are also made available for students during Phase 3. The length of Phase 3 varies with the length of the other phases, with more or less time devoted to Phase 3 on particular days based on progress in independent reading and need for time to be devoted to independent projects and activities.

All teachers received approximately 350 high-interest books across several reading levels to support their SEM-R implementation, and the teachers have augmented their collections as needed, choosing literature based on students' interests and experiences. Teachers also use sets of bookmarks with higher order questions that are free and available for download at http://www.gifted.uconn. edu/semr. Each bookmark includes a series of questions addressing a particular literary element, theme, genre, or other area of study and is tied to advanced reading strategies as well as state standards. Teachers use the bookmarks in both Phase 1 discussions and Phase 2 conferences to promote higher order thinking. Using the SEM-R, students also complete advanced writing selections on a weekly basis. Based on almost a decade of research, the SEM-R has been found to be effective at increasing achievement in reading and encouraging talented readers to read more challenging material for longer periods of time (Reis et al., 2008; Reis et al., 2007; Reis et al., 2011).

Research on the SEM

Gifted education programs based on the SEM have been found to have specific benefits for gifted and talented students, helping students increase aspirations for college and careers, determine postsecondary and career plans, and develop creativity and motivation that was applied to later work (Delcourt, 1993; Hébert, 1993). Hébert (1993) and Delcourt (1993) found that gifted programs using the Triad/SEM approach (Renzulli, 1977; Renzulli & Reis, 1985, 1997, 2014) helped focus students' interest development and productivity in areas of interest, had a positive effect students' subsequent interests, and positively affected postsecondary plans; Renzulli and Reis (2014) also learned that that early advanced project work in gifted programs served as important training for later productivity. Hébert (1993) also observed that nonintellectual characteristics, such as creativity, interests, and task commitment, remain consistent in gifted and talented students over time. Westberg (1999), investigating longitudinal findings of students who participated in the same type of program, found that students maintained interests and were still involved in both interests and creative productive work after they finished college and graduate school. Delcourt (1993) identified benefits of gifted programs, including students' ability to maintain interests over time and continue to be involved in creative productive work.

In summary, both qualitative and quantitative longitudinal studies of SEM gifted programs demonstrate positive outcomes in cognitive, affective, and social development of participating students. The participants increased their college and work aspirations, and maintained interests and creative productive work that begin in gifted programs after they finished college and graduate school. It is our hope that more schools and districts will continue to implement talent development programs based on the SEM in the years to come, whether as part of gifted or enrichment programs, magnet or theme schools, or as a part of a general education program. During the last decade, several Renzulli Academies, schools based on the SEM using the SEM-based strategies and methods described in this chapter, have been developed, focusing on the pedagogy described in this chapter for high-potential students. These schools have been successful at ensuring academic achievement as well as many opportunities for creative productivity (Reis & Taylor, 2011). Also, additional new resources have been published or are in press focusing on implementing the SEM philosophy in science (Heilbronner & Renzulli, 2015), technology (Housand, Housand, & Renzulli, 2017), and in social studies and mathematics (expected to be published in 2018).

CONCLUSION

Our recommendations for developing gifted behaviors and talents in young people differ from traditional ways in which programs for gifted students are usually conceived and organized. Our identification system is and has always been more flexible than most traditional identification systems, and we have always advocated providing general enrichment (Type I and II Enrichment) for all students. Our focused efforts on talent development result from our consistent attempts to change the culture of schools by creating an organized and systemic set of opportunities for talent development. Schools with educators who focus on talent development differ fundamentally from schools that focus on compliance, test preparation, and a prescribed curriculum. Many SEM schools with goals related to talent development offer a special haven for creative and talented students who want to learn in an active and engaging way, pursue their interests, and complete products that are personally meaningful. In a 25-year follow-up study of students who participated in a school based on our SEM model (Booji, Hann, & Plug, 2016), three Dutch economists reported that participating students obtained higher grades, followed a more science-intensive curriculum (most notably for girls), and reported stronger beliefs about their academic abilities. They also found that the positive SEM program effects persisted in university, where students chose more challenging fields of study with, on average, higher returns. They also entered career tracks at higher levels of challenge and financial rewards. Together, these results are consistent with our human capital interpretation of a SEM program that promotes both academic excellence and creative productivity.

Complex organizations like schools and school systems are not easy to change. An emphasis on compliance, test preparation, and a host of state and federal regulations present challenges that make even the smallest attempts to promote the kinds of talent development discussed in this chapter possible. It's one thing to come up with an idea about improving a school or school district but quite another to engineer the day-to-day practices, teacher training requirements, and categorically recommended resources that will make the type of learning described here work in the real world. Most importantly, if SEM sustainability is to occur over an extended period of time, the teachers who are expected to use an approach to learning that focuses on talent development must view the intended change positively. In other words, using the SEM should instill in teachers the same kind of enjoyment, engagement, and enthusiasm for learning that we expect our students to experience.

The research that we have conducted over the last few decades has been an important part of the evolution and change process in the SEM, as has our summer institute, Confratute, which has provided opportunities for professional development in the SEM. Both Confratute and our strong body of research have helped to convince sometimes skeptical administrators about the value of moving beyond traditional memory-oriented forms of learning. But visitations to best-case examples of schools that have implemented our model have also been a powerful force in persuading others to examine the possibilities of infusing more engaging forms of learning into their schools. We are grateful to the administrators and teachers using our model for the many innovative ideas they have shared with us and that we have, in turned, shared with others. We are grateful that these teachers and administrators demonstrated the courage and focus to use their creativity and task commitment to use a talent development approach to enhance learning for all students. Our work and research has convinced us that the enjoyable creative productive experiences that young people have in school can and will increase the likelihood that they will seek these opportunities in their subsequent work and personal lives. And when they do, the world will benefit from their creative and personally meaningful contributions.

Major Takeaways

- The SEM is based on more than four decades of research and experience in developing programs for high-potential and talented students and is derived from Renzulli's Three-Ring Conception of Giftedness and Enrichment Triad.

- The SEM is a talent development approach that has resulted from our consistent attempts to change the culture of schools by creating an organized and systemic set of opportunities for talent development, and these are the services in the model. The SEM has been implemented in thousands of schools across the world as a gifted and talented program, an enrichment program, or a school-based theme that delivers services to all students.

- The enjoyable creative productive experiences that young people have in school will increase the likelihood that they will seek these opportunities in their subsequent work and personal lives. In fact, in a recent interview with a college student who participated in an SEM program, he explained, "I was in an SEM program and remember Future Problem Solving and the projects we did. I created several inventions (Type III's). Even now, I get through my classes and do enough to have a decent GPA, but I can't wait to do the creative stuff. I love coding on a Friday night and creating new ideas and new products."

- Creativity and task commitment, unlike traditionally measured academic achievement traits included in the above average ability circle, are developmental and therefore subject to the kinds of experiences provided for both young people and adults. Creativity and task commitment develop as a result of the opportunities, resources, and encouragement that are provided to spark a creative idea or develop the motivation that causes a person or group to want to follow through on the idea, helping to reverse underachievement in some talented students.

RECOMMENDED READING

Reis, S. M., & Renzulli, J. S. (2011). Intellectual giftedness. In R. J. Sternberg & S. B. Kaufman, S. B. (Eds.), *The Cambridge handbook of intelligence* (pp. 235–252). New York, NY: Cambridge University Press.

Reis, S. M. (2005). Feminist perspectives on talent development: A research based conception of giftedness in women. In R. J. Sternberg & J. E. Davidson (Eds.), *Conceptions of giftedness* (2nd ed.). Boston, MA: Cambridge University Press.

Renzulli, J. S., & Reis, S. M. (2014). *The Schoolwide Enrichment Model: A how-to guide for talent devlopment* (3rd ed.). Waco, TX: Prufrock Press.

Renzulli, J. S. (2012). Reexamining the role of gifted education and talent development for the 21st century: A four-part theoretical approach. *Gifted Child Quarterly, 56,* 150–159.

REFERENCES

Baum, S. M. (1988). An enrichment program for gifted learning disabled students. *Gifted Child Quarterly, 32,* 226–230.

Baum, S. M., Renzulli, J. S., & Hébert, T. P. (1994). Reversing underachievement: Stories of success. *Educational Leadership, 52*(3), 48–52.

Booji, A., Hann, F., & Plug, E. (2016). *Enriching students pays off: Evidence from an individualized gifted and talented program in secondary education.* University of Amsterdam, Discussion Paper No. 9757.

Dai, D. Y. (2010). *The nature and nurture of giftedness: A new framework for understanding gifted education.* New York, NY: Teachers College Press.

Delcourt, M. A. B. (1993). Creative productivity among secondary school students: Combining energy, interest, and imagination. *Gifted Child Quarterly, 37,* 23–31.

Duckworth, A. L. (2009). Backtalk: Self-discipline is empowering. *Phi Delta Kappan, 90,* 536.

Field, G. B. (2009). The effects of using Renzulli Learning on student achievement: An investigation of Internet technology on reading fluency, comprehension, and social studies. *International Journal of Emerging Technology, 4,* 29–39.

Gardner, H. (1983). *Frames of mind.* New York, NY: Basic Books.

Gubbins, E. J. (Ed.). (1995). *Research related to the enrichment triad model* (RM95212). Storrs: University of Connecticut, The National Research Center of the Gifted and Talented. Retrieved from http://nrcgt.uconn.edu/wp-content/uploads/sites/953/2015/04/rm95212.pdf

Hébert, T. P. (1993). Reflections at graduation: The long-term impact of elementary school experiences in creative productivity. *Roeper Review, 16,* 22–28.

Heilbronner, N., & Renzulli, J. S. (2015). *The Schoolwide Enrichment Model in science: A hands-on approach for engaging young scientists.* Waco, TX: Prufrock Press.

Housand, A. M., Housand, B. C., & Renzulli, J. S. (2017). *Using the Schoolwide Enrichment Model with technology.* Waco, TX: Prufrock Press.

Reis, S. M. (1996). Older women's reflections on eminence: Obstacles and opportunities. In K. Arnold, K. Noble, & R. Subotnik (Eds.), *Remarkable women: Perspectives of female talent development* (pp. 149–168). Cresskill, NJ: Hampton Press.

Reis, S. M. (2002). Toward a theory of creativity in diverse creative women. *Creativity Research Journal, 14,* 305–316.

Reis, S. M. (2005). Feminist perspectives on talent development: A research-based conception of giftedness in women. In R. J. Sternberg & J. E. Davidson (Eds.), *Conceptions of giftedness* (2nd ed.). Boston, MA: Cambridge University Press.

Reis, S. M., Eckert, R. D., McCoach, D. B., Jacobs, J. K., & Coyne, M. (2008). Using enrichment reading practices to increase reading fluency, comprehension, and attitudes. *Journal of Educational Research, 101,* 299–314.

Reis, S. M., McCoach, D. B., Coyne, M., Schreiber, F. J., Eckert, R. D., & Gubbins, E. J. (2007). Using planned enrichment strategies with direct instruction to improve reading fluency, comprehension, and attitude toward reading: An evidence-based study. *The Elementary School Journal, 108,* 3–24.

Reis, S. M., McCoach, D. B., Little, C. M., Muller, L. M., & Kaniskan, R. B. (2011). The effects of differentiated instruction and enrichment pedagogy on reading achievement in five elementary schools. *American Educational Research Journal, 48,* 462–501.

Reis, S. M., & Purcell, J. H. (1993). An analysis of content elimination and strategies used by elementary classroom teachers in the curriculum compacting process. *Journal for the Education of the Gifted, 16,* 147–170.

Reis, S. M., & Renzulli, J. S. (2003). Research related to the Schoolwide Enrichment Triad Model. *Gifted Education International, 18*(1), 15–40.

Reis, S. M., & Renzulli, J. S. (2011). Intellectual giftedness. In R. J. Sternberg & S. B. Kaufman (Eds.), *The Cambridge handbook of intelligence* (pp. 235–252). New York, NY: Cambridge University Press.

Reis, S. M., Renzulli, J. S., & Burns, D. E. (2016). *Curriculum compacting: A guide to differentiating curriculum and instruction through enrichment and acceleration* (2nd ed.). Waco, TX: Prufrock Press.

Reis, S. M., & Taylor, M. M. (2011). From high potential to gifted performance: Encouraging academically talented urban students. *Gifted Child Today, 33*(4), 28–38.

Reis, S. M., Westberg, K. L., Kulikowich, J. M., & Purcell, J. H. (1998). Curriculum compacting and achievement test scores: What does the research say? *Gifted Child Quarterly, 42,* 123–129.

Renzulli, J. S. (1977). *The Enrichment Triad Model: A guide for developing defensible program for the gifted and talented.* Mansfield Center, CT: Creative Learning Press.

Renzulli, J. S. (1978). What makes giftedness? Re-examining a definition. *Phi Delta Kappan, 60,* 180–184.

Renzulli, J. S. (1986). The Three-Ring Conception of Giftedness: A developmental model for creative productivity. In R. J. Sternberg & J. E. Davidson (Eds.), *Conceptions of giftedness* (pp. 332–357). New York, NY: Cambridge University Press.

Renzulli, J. S. (Ed.). (1988). *Technical report of research studies related to the enrichment triad/revolving door model* (3rd ed.). Storrs: University of Connecticut.

Renzulli J. S. (2002). Expanding the conception of giftedness to include co-cognitive traits and to promote social capital. *Phi Delta Kappan, 84,* 33–40, 57–58.

Renzulli, J. S. (2005). The Three-Ring Conception of Giftedness: A developmental model for promoting creative productivity. In R. J. Sternberg & J. Davidson (Eds.), *Conceptions of giftedness* (2nd ed., pp. 217–245). Boston, MA: Cambridge University Press.

Renzulli, J. S. (2012). Reexamining the role of gifted education and talent development for the 21st century: A four-part theoretical approach. *Gifted Child Quarterly, 56,* 150–159.

Renzulli, J. S. (2016). The role of blended knowledge in the development of creative productive giftedness. *International Journal for Talent Development and Creativity, 4*(1), 13–24.

Renzulli, J. S., & Reis, S. M. (1985). *The Schoolwide Enrichment Model: A comprehensive plan for educational excellence.* Mansfield Center, CT: Creative Learning Press.

Renzulli, J. S., & Reis, S. M. (1994). Research related to the Schoolwide Enrichment Triad Model. *Gifted Child Quarterly, 38,* 7–20.

Renzulli, J. S., & Reis, S. M. (1997). *The Schoolwide Enrichment Model: A how-to guide for educational excellence* (2nd ed.). Mansfield, CT: Creative Learning Press.

Renzulli, J. S., & Reis, S. M. (2012). Defensible and do-able: A practical, multiple criteria gifted program identification system. In S. L. Hunsaker (Ed.), *Identification: The theory and practice of identifying students for gifted and talented education services* (pp. 25–56). Waco, TX: Prufrock Press.

Renzulli, J. S., & Reis, S. M. (2014). *The Schoolwide Enrichment Model: A how-to guide for talent development* (3rd ed.). Waco, TX: Prufrock Press.

Sternberg, R. J. (1985). *Beyond IQ: A triarchic theory of human intelligence.* Cambridge, England: Cambridge University Press.

Sternberg, R. J., & Davidson, J. E. (Eds.). (2005). *Conceptions of giftedness* (2nd ed.). New York, NY: Cambridge University Press.

VanTassel-Baska, J., & Brown, E. F. (2007). Toward best practice: An analysis of the efficacy of curriculum models in gifted education. *Gifted Child Quarterly, 51,* 342–358.

Westberg, K. L. (1999, Summer). What happens to young, creative producers? *NAGC: Creativity and Curriculum Divisions' Newsletter, 3,* 13–16.

CHAPTER 3

Meeting the Individual Educational Needs of Students by Applying Talent Search Principles to School Settings

Linda E. Brody

P arents of bright and inquisitive children, even some parents of 2- and 3-year-olds, eagerly turn to educators and psychologists wanting to know if their child is gifted. Their request becomes more urgent when schools begin to divide children into two groups, the students who are chosen for special programs for gifted and talented students and the students whose classes consist of the regular program, and the parents fear that their child's abilities may not be recognized if they fail to qualify for the gifted programming. Meanwhile, school administrators struggle to find a defensible identification strategy or tool that can determine which students within their population are truly gifted and warrant inclusion in their programs for gifted learners.

Unfortunately, an approach to talent identification that suggests that individuals either are or are not gifted fails to recognize the complex nature of cognitive abilities and the many factors that influence the development of those abilities in children and adolescents. Although talent search programs do require certain scores for eligibility for their programs, the purpose of the talent search assessment is not to determine who is gifted, but to provide insight into students' abilities so that academic needs can be met in school and elsewhere through appropriate programmatic options. There is much in this approach to talent identification and development that schools might replicate as they seek to address the needs of students who exhibit advanced academic abilities and/or achievement.

WHAT IS THE TALENT SEARCH?

Talent search testing is domain-specific, the ceiling is raised for students who excel beyond their age group so that the full range of their abilities can be assessed, and reassessment over time is encouraged out of recognition that students' cognitive abilities may not all develop at the same rate. The goal is to identify students whose educational needs may not be adequately met by the age-in-grade instruction and/or gifted and talented programs typically offered in schools and to provide them with opportunities to be optimally challenged.

Although more information about students' content knowledge is needed to determine their appropriate placement in classes, the information gleaned from above-grade-level reasoning tests is extremely helpful for calling attention to abilities that might otherwise remain unrecognized. In particular, performance on these assessments differentiates high-ability students who exhibit the reasoning abilities of older, more advanced students and may be ready for accelerated content from those who perform at a lower level on the above-grade-level assessments and may be adequately challenged by an honors-level curriculum with age peers. Since the founding of the first talent search centers in the late 1970s and early 1980s, millions of students have availed themselves of the opportunity to take above-grade-level talent search tests, and many thousands of eligible students take courses or participate in other opportunities each year offered by the talent search centers (Lee, Matthews, & Olszewski-Kubilius, 2008).

Early History: The Study of Mathematically Precocious Youth

The Talent Search model has its roots in the work of the late Professor Julian Stanley at Johns Hopkins University. After intervening on behalf of several highly precocious students so that they could enroll as undergraduates at Johns Hopkins at extremely young ages, Stanley became intrigued with the possibility that there might be other students with extraordinary potential who were languishing unchallenged in age-in-grade classes and might need help to advance their educational progress. In 1971, he established the Study of Mathematically Precocious Youth (SMPY) to "find [more] youths who reason exceptionally well mathematically and to provide the special, supplemental, accelerative smorgasbord of educational opportunities they sorely need and richly deserve for their own optimal development and the good of society" (Stanley, 2005, p. 9).

Throughout the 1970s, SMPY sponsored talent searches where seventh and eighth graders took the SAT as an above-grade-level test of mathematical reasoning. Those who earned high scores were invited to take additional assessments so that the researchers could learn more about them. Many more students performed well on these tests than were expected, but the researchers also found that the mathematically talented students were quite heterogeneous in many ways—in their specific ability patterns, knowledge of math and science topics, interests, willingness to work hard, and in the available resources in their schools (e.g., see Keating, 1976). Consequently, it was clear that there were many students in need of intervention, but it was also clear that, with such diverse characteristics, the students had differing needs and no one-size-fits-all program could address them.

Stanley and the SMPY staff studied the research literature on acceleration, reviewed the backgrounds of eminent individuals, became knowledgeable about program models and strategies that might be effective for serving advanced learners, and experimented with offering programs of their own, especially fast-paced math classes. Their methods were viewed as quite radical at the time, but SMPY's research validated a variety of accelerative strategies for serving students with advanced academic abilities (e.g., Benbow & Stanley, 1983; Brody & Benbow, 1987; George, Cohn, & Stanley, 1979; Southern, Jones, & Stanley, 1993). Stanley (1979a, 1979b) ultimately embraced the concept of offering students a "smorgasbord of opportunities," from which the most appropriate options could be selected to meet their individual needs, and he advocated for curricular flexibility in schools whereby a student's educational needs, rather than age or grade, should determine placement. SMPY's approach was to identify students, learn more about them, try intervention strategies, evaluate their effectiveness, modify the approach if needed, and share the results of SMPY's research with others. These steps are described in the literature as the D^4 Model of Talent Development: Discovery, Description, Development, and Dissemination (Brody, 2009a; Brody & Stanley, 2005). Follow-up studies of SMPY talent search participants support the effectiveness of identifying students on the basis of above-level mathematical and/or verbal reasoning abilities, although spatial abilities, interests and values, and special educational opportunities have also been shown to play a role in the development of their talents (Lubinski, 2016; Lubinski & Benbow, 2006; Lubinski, Benbow, & Kell, 2014).

Talent Search Programs Today

Talent search programs utilizing this model today are based at the Center for Talented Youth (CTY) at Johns Hopkins University, the Center for Talent

Development (CTD) at Northwestern University, and the Talent Identification Program (TIP) at Duke University, as well as the Center for Bright Kids in Denver, the Belin-Blank Center at the University of Iowa, and elsewhere. It has also been applied in other countries, notably the Irish Centre for Talented Youth at Dublin City University (O'Reilly, 2012). These centers offer above-grade-level assessments for the purpose of identifying advanced reasoning abilities in domain-specific areas (verbal, mathematical, and/or spatial aptitude) and provide challenging academic programs and services to the students they identify. Recent research continues to support SMPY's longitudinal findings that talent search assessments effectively predict high achievement later in adults (Makel, Kell, Lubinski, Putallaz, & Benbow, 2016).

Among the talent search offerings is a 3-week residential summer program, a programmatic model that was developed from Julian Stanley's recommendation that academically advanced students need access to accelerated coursework in a setting that allows them to interact with age peers who share their interests and abilities. Stanley was well aware of the importance of fostering students' psychosocial as well as academic development, and he believed that providing access to intellectual peers is vitally important. The summer programs have proven to be highly successful in achieving their academic and social goals. Notably, studies have shown that summer program participants can master considerable advanced content in a short period of time (e.g., Stanley & Stanley, 1986), and participants have indicated that the rigorous residential programs enhance their self-confidence and help them build positive relationships with peers (Lee, Olszewski-Kubilius, Makel, & Putallaz, 2015; Mickenberg & Wood, 2009).

A Counseling Model: The Study of Exceptional Talent

In addition to establishing programs to serve advanced learners, SMPY, under Julian Stanley's direction, individually counseled many students to help them find the resources they needed to excel. Intending for school counselors and others to use a similar approach with their academically advanced students, SMPY disseminated its ideas and recommendations widely with the intent to impact "not only the SMPY participants, their teachers, and their parents, but also other brilliant students, their teachers, and their parents who reside outside SMPY's own geographical area" (Stanley & George, 1978, p. 11).

The Study of Exceptional Talent (SET) is an outgrowth of SMPY's efforts to provide counseling to top-scoring talent search participants. Based at CTY, SET's counselors work with students individually to identify their strengths, weaknesses, interests, and other characteristics; evaluate their circumstances and needs; and recommend in-school and out-of-school options for meeting those needs. For students with such advanced abilities, acceleration of school content is often necessary, and supplemental courses, summer programs, and extracurricular activities extend their learning opportunities and support their psychosocial development in crucial ways. In addition, the staff's ongoing interaction with students allows it to evaluate the efficacy of particular intervention strategies and programs for meeting the needs of talented students.

In contrast to the early SMPY students who felt forced to enter college radically early in order to be challenged because there were few alternatives, programmatic opportunities have increased dramatically so that it is possible for students today to find the resources they need to be challenged through high school. For the most part, SET has been highly successful in helping students who attend all kinds of schools create the learning environments they need to achieve their full potential (Brody, 2007), and many of the recommendations for schools included in this chapter have evolved from SET's work with students and their schools.

With their SET counselors serving as knowledgeable advocates for differential programming, most SET students leave high school having completed extensive college-level coursework earned through Advanced Placement, International Baccalaureate, dual enrollment, or online programs. Those who participate in residential summer programs have the opportunity to take advanced courses and live on college campuses with peers who share their interests and abilities; still others may find a compatible peer group in their school or through their activities. In general, SET students' accomplishments outside of school are exceptional. Many win awards in math competitions or participate in internships side-by-side with scientists in labs and submit their work to prestigious science competitions. Others pursue the arts at high levels, find ways to publish their writing, or engage in entrepreneurial or community service initiatives. What these students have in common is taking full advantage of the opportunities that their schools offer and supplementing them with out-of-school options that allow students to pursue their interests in greater depth.

Like SMPY, SET disseminates information about its approach to talent development in an effort to encourage a broader segment of the gifted student population to pursue challenging opportunities. SET's publications include professional articles (e.g., Brody, 2007, 2009b; Muratori et al., 2006), newsletters for SET students and their parents, and *Imagine* magazine, which is available by subscription and describes challenging resources and opportunities for motivated middle and high school students.

WHAT DOES IT MEAN TO BE GIFTED?

SET does not call the students it works with "gifted," nor did SMPY, and the term is avoided by most of the talent search programs. Notably, Julian Stanley referred to the students he identified as "youths who reason extremely well mathematically," deferring any recognition of giftedness to others to evaluate based on achievement over time. But it is incorrect to suggest that there is no conception of giftedness behind talent search identification (Brody & Stanley, 2005).

This conception is grounded in a belief in the psychology of individual differences. It assumes that individuals differ from each other in a wide range of specific abilities; also, it is not a matter of having a specific ability or not having it, but rather that human abilities lie along a continuum. Having a higher level of a particular ability is likely to promote achievement in the relevant domain, but it is never clear how much is necessary to achieve at a particular level, so strict cutoff-scores for programs do not make sense, and factors other than ability also contribute to determining what individuals achieve. Nonetheless, it is important to identify students who appear to exhibit exceptional abilities within a domain and to nurture those talents to the extent possible in order to help students achieve their potential. Identification should be domain-specific, and the talent searches, believing that students who exhibit advanced reasoning abilities are likely to be most in need of services, focus on identifying precocious reasoning within domains.

In this view, students do not have to be advanced in all areas to be considered gifted. They can have extraordinary strengths in a particular area, but also have significant weaknesses in other areas, although the weaknesses could have an impact on achievement if not addressed. It is understood that an individual student's developmental trajectory may be atypical so no single assessment is intended to be definitive, and it is assumed that the development of talent occurs over time in response to the opportunities that are provided.

In addition to the role that ability plays in talent development, the Talent Search model assumes that psychosocial factors are important for defining giftedness and determining achievement, and their programs have been designed to have a positive impact on the participants' psychological well-being and social development. Investigations into personality characteristics, interests, and values as concomitants to academic talent were important avenues of research when SMPY was first established (Stanley, Keating, & Fox, 1974), and, since then, talent search researchers have continued to investigate a variety of psychological and social characteristics in the students they serve, thereby shedding much light on the special needs of the students. In particular, they have studied personality traits (e.g., Olszewski-Kubilius & Kulieke, 1989; Olszewski-Kubilius, Lee, & Thomson, 2014; Parker & Stumpf, 1998), learning styles (Mills, 1993), self-concepts (e.g.,

Brounstein, Holahan, & Dreyden, 1991; Makel, Lee, Olszewski-Kubilius, & Putallaz, 2012), perfectionism (Ablard & Parker, 1997; Parker & Mills, 1996), social competencies (Luthar, Zigler, & Goldstein, 1992), and peer relationships (Lee, Olszewski-Kubilius, & Thomson, 2012). Gender differences in achievement have also been explored and been shown to be at least partially explained by differences in interests, values, and other noncognitive traits (Fox & Denham, 1974; Robertson, Smeets, Lubinski, & Benbow, 2010).

In the minds of many, giftedness is also equated with creativity, and Julian Stanley aimed to develop the talents of students who would ultimately make creative and innovative contributions to society. However, his interventions focused more on developing content knowledge rather than on creativity because Stanley believed that creativity must occur within a domain and that mastering significant content was necessary before creative output could be expected. The talent search programs continue to emphasize content in their courses, and Mills and Brody (2012) defended the position of placing the instructional emphasis for gifted students on advanced and accelerated curricular content rather than on creativity exercises in a point-counterpoint discussion with creativity experts who feel otherwise. Notably, the longitudinal studies that are tracking the adult accomplishments of high-scoring SMPY talent search participants, who received much support for their abilities, show that they have produced patents, publications, and other creative earmarks of success at much greater rates than comparison subjects (Lubinski, 2016; Lubinski, Webb, Morelock, & Benbow, 2001; Makel et al., 2016).

HOW ARE GIFTS AND TALENTS DEVELOPED?

There has been a long-standing debate about the role that nature and nurture each play in the development of talent and in determining who excels in a particular field. Increasingly, we have begun to realize that it is the *interaction* of the two (i.e., of numerous personal traits influencing and being influenced by a variety of experiences) that leads to high achievement (Anastasi, 1958; Kaufman, 2013). Clearly, talent search initiatives support this perspective, as their assessments serve to identify high ability, while their programs foster the cognitive and psychosocial traits that enhance those abilities and lead to higher levels of achievement.

In an attempt to learn more about the experiences that contribute to the development of talent, numerous researchers have studied the lives of eminent individuals. Bloom's (1985) retrospective study of adults who achieved high levels of recognition in the arts, athletics, mathematics, and science is particularly informative because he observed that exceptional ability, intrinsic interest, and parental support led to intensive study and much hard work but also that motivating educational opportunities, especially those experienced outside of school, provided the fuel for stimulating interest and spurring an eagerness to achieve at high levels. In particular, the mathematicians and scientists attributed much importance to their involvement in outside-of-school opportunities during high school for stimulating their interest in these fields, specifically to math teams and science clubs, contests and competitions, and summer and Saturday programs (Bloom, 1985). Bloom concluded that:

> Precociousness in a talent field is not to be dismissed, but . . . no matter how precocious one is at age ten or eleven, if the individual doesn't stay with the talent development process over many years, he or she will soon be outdistanced by others who do continue. A long term commitment to the talent field and an increasing passion for the talent development are essential if the individual is to attain the highest levels of capability in the field. (p. 538).

Research on former talent search participants has also found participation in stimulating activities during high school to be relevant to their achievement as adults. In fact, the number of special opportunities and activities—what the researchers termed the "dose"—seemed to be important for developing their talents (Wai, Lubinski, Benbow, & Steiger, 2010). Particular activities have also been highlighted in anecdotal comments by former talent search participants. For example, a mathematician recalled that: "It was the competitions that really introduced the fun side of math to me . . . [and they] also contributed quite a bit to my social life . . . I could hang out with kids with similar interests" (Muratori et al., 2006, p. 316–317). Another mathematician, commenting anonymously during a panel discussion at the Symposium on Math Talent Development at the Center for Talented Youth, said that "the summer programs when I was in high school were integral to my development as a mathematician, and I value the community I met there as much as the research experiences that I had." He added that, "I can't imagine how many otherwise brilliant scientists or mathematicians we lose because they never find a community that understands or values them."

Talent development is a complex process that occurs over the life of an individual, and many intrinsic and extrinsic factors are involved. However, the precollege years seem to be a particularly important time for students to develop their abilities and define their interests so that they are ready to take them to the next level. Such optimal development is unlikely to result unless students are exposed to stimulating experiences that leave them wanting more.

HOW SCHOOLS FAIL GIFTED STUDENTS

Early in American history, students were educated at home or in small schools that allowed them to progress at their own pace. Relatively few of those students enrolled in college, but those who did were typically quite a bit younger than students who enter college today, having been allowed to progress as rapidly as they wished through the precollege curriculum. As the student population grew and universal education became the goal, schools were organized into grades on the basis of age so that larger numbers of students could be educated in an organized way. But the assumption that students of the same age should all learn the same content at the same pace is faulty; a grade spans an age range of a full 12 months or more resulting in students who are just hours apart in age finding themselves assigned to different grades solely because of their birthdates. This formula also denies individual differences in cognitive abilities, learning rates, and content knowledge within an age group, and students who process information faster than their age peers can quickly outpace the curriculum if no accommodations are made.

In an effort to try to address the needs of advanced learners, well-intentioned schools have developed special programs for the students they designate as gifted and talented. However, whether they consist of pull-out programs, a somewhat differentiated curriculum in the regular classroom, or more advanced sections of certain classes, the commitment to age-in-grade instruction is still a strong factor in the composition of these opportunities. For example, a school may offer an instructional program for a group of first graders reading on a second- to third-grade level, a G/T pullout enrichment option for fourth graders, and an algebra class for seventh graders—all options that offer more advanced instruction than the participants would get in their regular classes. But they were all designed for students within a particular age/grade level and are narrow in their scope. They do not meet the needs of the first grader reading on a middle school level, the fourth grader who needs advanced math and not just general enrichment, or the seventh grader who mastered algebra a long time ago and needs access to high school level math.

Some whole-school models have emerged to serve gifted students, including selective magnet schools. Highly desirable, they provide rigorous curricular options, relevant extracurricular activities, and peer groups with somewhat compatible interests and/or abilities. However, even these schools can get caught up in the age-in-grade mindset. For example, a student who enrolled in a particularly prestigious magnet high school was required to take Algebra II and physics upon entry, the prescribed ninth-grade courses, even though he was much more advanced in both subjects and had scored high on the SAT Math II and Physics achievement tests while in middle school. Although this high-quality school serves many academically advanced students well, it was unwilling to address the unique needs of this individual student. We can only truly meet the needs of advanced students if we break away from the assumption that students must be grouped in classes according to their age.

APPLYING TALENT SEARCH PRINCIPLES AND PRACTICES TO SCHOOLS

Early in SMPY's history, Julian Stanley argued against hiring special teachers of the gifted, suggesting that they could not be trained to adequately teach all of the subject matter that advanced students might need. Clearly a field that was training teachers to fill this role did not want to hear this, but he believed that highly knowledgeable subject matter specialists should teach content and what schools needed were counselors that he called "Coordinators of Special Experiences" (Stanley, 1979b). Schools might consider employing such individuals, particularly for working with advanced students.

These counselors could help students identify their strengths and interests, and they could work with them to define their individual goals and develop plans to achieve them. They could arrange for flexible placement and find opportunities to augment school offerings as needed. This is the SET model; it assures that students are taking full advantage of opportunities in school and outside of school to maximize their talent development. Of course, any efforts to optimally meet students' individual needs require getting to know the students well, and that begins with assessment.

Assessment

Above-grade-level assessments are the hallmark of the talent searches, having successfully raised the ceiling to identify advanced reasoning abilities. Schools should be aware of the value and importance of using above-level assessments with students who top out on in-level tests. Of course, standardized tests, regardless of level, are not placement tests. Assessment of actual content knowledge is important for determining placement, and pretesting of skills before beginning new units of instruction can prevent students from having to work on skills that they may already have mastered. Tests, teacher evaluations, and student products all provide relevant data about performance in the classroom. In general, assessments should primarily be for the purpose of gathering information about students' achievement levels and learning needs, rather than for judging performance; in fact, if students are appropriately placed, there is really no need for grading students, as they all should be achieving goals that are appropriate for them, or placement should be reconsidered.

Students' interests should also be considered when determining the direction their educational programs might take. Interest and career inventories can be helpful, but students should also share their thoughts with their counselor, as they work together to identify opportunities in their areas of interest. In addition, any students with signs of possibly being twice-exceptional (i.e., having undiagnosed learning disabilities) warrant full psychoeducational assessments to identify the cause(s) of their issues, and schools should take responsibility for assuring that this is done.

For all students, it must be recognized that cognitive development may not be linear or typical, and that their specific abilities and learning levels could unexpectedly leap ahead of others'. Thus, reassessment of aptitude and performance should be done at regular intervals, as well as assessments to determine changing interests and readiness for new opportunities as they arise. In addition, if students lack clear qualifications for certain opportunities but are highly motivated, have strong work ethics, and are eager to participate, schools should be flexible about their criteria and offer students a chance to demonstrate their readiness.

Accelerative Strategies and Flexible Placement

Students who exhibit above-grade-level reasoning abilities, learn at a faster rate, and/or exhibit advanced content knowledge compared to age peers may need accelerative strategies that allow them to access more advanced content and/or progress through content more quickly. There are many ways to accelerate students in grade placement or subject matter that have been outlined in numerous publications (e.g., Southern & Jones, 2015; Southern et al., 1993), and there is a vast amount of research that supports the efficacy of acceleration for academically talented students (Assouline, Colangelo, VanTassel-Baska, & Lupkowski-Shoplik, 2015; Steenbergen-Hu, Makel, & Olszewski-Kubilius, 2016).

The need for acceleration was amplified in a recent study that revealed that large numbers of students appear to be performing above-grade level in core content areas, yet these students are assigned to classes in their schools where instruction is on grade level (Peters, Rambo-Hernandez, Makel, Matthews, & Plucker, 2017). Among talent search participants, increasing numbers of students are electing to advance their learning outside of school through online courses, summer classes, and other opportunities. Yet these students often face resistance when they request the differential placement in their schools appropriate for their more advanced levels of knowledge. The reluctance of schools to recognize above-grade-level achievement and to grant credit for learning that occurs outside of school sends the very negative message to students that their efforts and eagerness to learn are not valued, and being forced to repeat content already mastered assures that a student is likely to be bored and unhappy in the classroom.

Some educators today are encouraging "personalized learning," an initiative that appears to have goals similar to those outlined above (i.e., to place students at their level in content areas and allow them to progress through the curriculum at their own pace). In practice, unfortunately, much personalized learning tends to be heavily centered on computer-based instruction that focuses on mastering the skills necessary to excel on standardized tests. Learning in this context can be a rather lonely and not particularly challenging or inspiring experience, especially for gifted students. Schools should be open to a variety of options for placing students in appropriate learning environments and not rely on computer-based instruction as the sole vehicle for providing advanced content to gifted students.

Julian Stanley advocated for longitudinal K–12 teaching teams in content areas, especially in math, although he believed that it could also be applied to other subject areas. In such teams, teachers work together to assure that each student moves ahead at his or her own pace and makes continuous progress in that subject. Students could still learn in groups, but the groups are based on students' content knowledge, and teachers with the stronger backgrounds teach the more advanced topics (Stanley, 1979b). Presumably, these teachers would also be knowledgeable about ways to extend students' learning in their content area outside of the classroom through extracurricular activities and summer programs, and could facilitate finding adult mentors that might work with students when they are ready for that experience.

While individualization is important, placing high-ability students together in a classroom to allow for enhanced discussion and group work with peers can also be advantageous at times. Although grouping students together based on ability fell into disfavor for many years, it has been shown to be effective when it is combined with clear educational and/or social goals (Steenbergen-Hu et al., 2016).

Curricular Modifications

The suggestions above relate mostly to taking advantage of existing opportunities and placing students where they need to be within the school system, a highly cost-effective approach to meeting their needs, as it requires little new curricular development. However, schools should also examine their offerings to determine if they are adequately meeting the talent development needs of their students or whether additional courses or modification of existing ones might be warranted.

For example, would it be helpful to add elective math classes like statistics or cryptology for math-talented students who are accelerating rapidly through the regular curriculum? Should a research internship track be introduced for high school students who are completing AP work well before senior year? Are the arts or languages adequately represented among the offerings to address students' specific interests and talents in these areas? Are students getting an adequate background in technology to meet their needs in today's world or enough experience with lab-based science to be prepared to potentially be a STEM major in college? If adding courses seems daunting to small schools, either for financial reasons or because they do not have enough students to support so much variety, consider cross-grouping across schools to create courses. For gifted students who progress quickly through the curriculum, provisions for more advanced courses at the upper end are necessary. A dual enrollment program with a local college, access to an online program, and/or early graduation from high school are options to consider.

Within classes, project-based learning, an emphasis on creative and critical thinking and writing, and in-depth discussions allow students to work at their own levels even in a somewhat heterogeneous setting. In addition, extended field trips to historical sites and museums, as well as other experiential and applied learning options, can enhance the learning experiences of all students, including advanced learners.

Extracurricular Activities

Schools must recognize that learning need not be confined to the classroom; in fact, it is through their freely chosen activities that students can extend their learning in meaningful ways that are important to them. Extracurricular activities allow students to define their interests, develop their talents, provide opportunities for leadership, and offer ways for students to interact with peers who share their interests and abilities. Selective colleges have come to recognize extracurricular initiatives as indicative of a student's commitment to an interest area and of his or her motivation to work hard beyond what is required, and admissions officers believe they can be predictive of future achievement. Thus, admissions officers look for this involvement among their applicants, and students who lack extracurricular experiences tend to be at a disadvantage in the college admissions process.

Most middle and high schools offer students opportunities to write for the school newspaper, participate in a student government, and be active in musical groups and sports. But some schools offer much more, such as foreign language clubs, community outreach options, debate and math teams, robotics, and science research opportunities. Unfortunately, with budget cutbacks, some schools have turned many of their extracurricular activities into courses (e.g., the newspaper may be a journalism class that requires a full class period, or the school orchestra may be a music class offered during the school day), making participation difficult for academically motivated students with full academic course loads. In many schools, sports teams receive considerably more funding and recognition than academic extracurricular offerings.

In response to student demand for activities that they cannot access in school, many students look outside of school for opportunities. For example, students may take art classes, join a community theatre group, or find a LEGO League meeting in their town. They may engage in a community service initiative, submit their writing to a local newspaper for publication, or pursue an internship. They may join a Math Circle, get involved in scouting, or join a community orchestra. Although these out-of-school programs offer opportunities to students whose schools have few extracurricular offerings, taking advantage of such activities is often restricted to students who know about them and can access them, which raises additional equity issues for those students who lack these advantages.

Schools need to recognize that optimally developing students' interests and talents requires extending learning opportunities beyond the school day. They should offer as broad an array of school-based clubs and activities as possible, and counselors should help students access any out-of-school offerings that are appropriate for their particular needs and interests. For gifted students who excel in particular initiatives, participation that takes them to higher levels should be encouraged, such as progressing in science fairs and math competitions from school and local contests, to regional and state competitions, and possibly even to national or international levels of recognition. Many gifted students are also eager to participate in internships during high school and their schools can build relationships with universities and corporations that will facilitate this option for them.

Summer Programs and Opportunities

In addition to helping students extend their learning opportunities into after-school hours, schools should help students identify ways to make the most out of their summers. Although there has long been evidence to suggest that a lack of academic activity in the summer leads to a loss of knowledge and skills, particularly among low-income students, many students still lack access to summer learning opportunities (Alexander, Entwisle, & Olson, 2007). Among gifted students, with an increasing number of students participating in meaningful summer opportunities such as those offered by the talent search programs, differential participation by certain students could be a contributing factor to what has been termed the *excellence gap* (i.e., the disparities in performance among subgroups of high-ability students; Plucker & Peters, 2016).

Unfortunately, few schools see providing their students with summer learning opportunities as their responsibility. Finding meaningful summer activities is pretty much left up to parents in most communities, and their knowledge of options, and the ability of their children to access them, may be limited. School systems should provide classes during the summer that allow students to accelerate their learning or to take electives that they do not have time to take during the school year. Extracurricular activities, such as musical and theatrical groups practicing and performing together, students working on projects, and older students tutoring younger students might also continue into the summer under school supervision.

In addition, school counselors should provide information about summer opportunities outside of school, including local camps and programs in the community and residential programs elsewhere that might be appropriate for the students' particular interests. If necessary, they should be helped with applications and informed of scholarship options. Whatever path is chosen by the individual students, schools should take steps to assure that students have access to summer learning opportunities that allow them to continue to develop their interests and talents.

Evaluation

Each student's talent development goals should be clearly stated in his or her individual learning plans, and progress toward achieving them should be evaluated by his or her counselor. With an individualized approach where students of the same age are working at many different levels, traditional evaluative tools such as standardized achievement tests that compare performance to grade-level standards or grades that compare students to age peers are not particularly helpful. Rather, performance should be compared to the student's goals. When tests are used, they should be appropriate for the content learned, such as letting students take AP tests whenever they are ready, even if the students are much younger than is typical for most students taking these exams.

Students' products and accomplishments such as science projects, artwork, written reports, awards, and leadership roles should be assessed as to whether they are measuring up to expectations. The students should also be asked to self-assess their enthusiasm for the level of challenge their current academic program provides, the degree to which they believe it is helping them achieve their academic goals, and whether they are getting enough support for participation in out-of-school programs.

For the school as a whole, its climate should be assessed to determine whether it is meeting the needs of all its students. Through surveys and focus groups, answers to the following questions should be sought. Does the staff feel supported and successful in meeting the needs of individual students? Is the school a happy place where students want to go? Are advanced students being challenged, and do they feel comfortable if they must follow a unique program, such as taking classes with older students or classes outside of school? Is there a smorgasbord of in-school and out-of-school options available for meeting the needs of all students? Are students fully engaged in afterschool and summer opportunities, and are these options available to all students regardless of their socioeconomic status? Do students, parents, and teachers feel comfortable making suggestions for change to the administrative staff? Finally, does the school feel like all stakeholders are connected as a community that is working together for the success of all individuals, including helping students with advanced abilities achieve at levels beyond their age peers?

CONCLUSION

In reflecting on his work, Julian Stanley noted that he did not initially work with school systems because the students SMPY served came from too many different schools to influence them all directly. Rather, his goal was to "to burrow up under school systems to coerce changes there in curricular flexibility and articulation of in-school with out-of-school educational experiences" (Stanley, 2005, p. 11), and he hoped that someday school policies would change to reflect this goal. Many students are pursuing the path that Stanley and the talent search programs have recommended—they are taking challenging courses and supplementing them with stimulating extracurricular activities and summer programs. But for the most part, they are doing it on their own, without a great deal of school support, and these opportunities are not available to all students who might benefit from them.

As we look to the future, it is more important than ever that we help promising innovators and creators find their passions, develop their abilities, and be prepared to apply their creativity to solve society's most complex problems. But students are unlikely to have the background to find solutions to tough issues if they sit in age-in-grade classes exposed to content they have already mastered or if their desire to probe a topic more deeply is ignored. Schools must do a better job of identifying talent; they must acknowledge, and respond to, individual differences in students' learning levels and educational needs; and they must help students access the extensive smorgasbord of learning opportunities that can develop their talents and keep their hunger for learning alive.

Major Takeaways

- The more talented/advanced a student is, the more likely a differentiated program will be needed.

- Above-grade-level tests are crucial for estimating a high-performing student's true level of ability or achievement.

- Schools can enhance their educational programs to meet the needs of advanced students with curricular flexibility and accelerative strategies.

- Learning can be extended in important ways through extracurricular activities, summer programs, and other outside-of-school opportunities.

- Academically talented students need opportunities to interact with peers who share their interests and abilities.

RECOMMENDED READING

Assouline, S. G., Colangelo, N., VanTassel-Baska, J., & Lupkowski-Shoplik, A. (2015). *A nation empowered: Evidence trumps the excuses holding back America's brightest students* (Vol. 2). Iowa City: University of Iowa, The Connie Belin & Jacqueline N. Blank International Center for Gifted Education and Talent Development

Johns Hopkins Center for Talented Youth. *Imagine* magazine. Retrieved from http://cty.jhu.edu/imagine

VanTassel-Baska, J. (Ed.). (2007). *Serving gifted learners beyond the traditional classroom.* Waco, TX: Prufrock Press.

REFERENCES

Ablard, K. E., & Parker, W. D. (1997). Parents' achievement goals and perfectionism in their academically talented children. *Journal of Youth and Adolescence, 26,* 651–667.

Alexander, K. L., Entwisle, D. R., & Olson, L. S. (2007). Summer learning and its implications: Insights from the beginning school study. *New Directions for Youth Development, 114,* 11–32.

Anastasi, A. (1958). Heredity, environment, and the question "how?" *Psychological Review, 65,* 197–208.

Assouline, S., Colangelo, N., VanTassel-Baska, J., & Lupkowski-Shoplik, A. (Eds.). (2015). *A nation empowered: Evidence trumps the excuses that hold back America's brightest students* (Vol. 2). Iowa City: University of Iowa, The Connie Belin & Jacqueline N. Blank International Center for Gifted Education and Talent Development.

Benbow, C. P., & Stanley, J. C. (Eds.). (1983). *Academic precocity: Aspects of its development*. Baltimore, MD: Johns Hopkins University Press.

Bloom, B. S. (1985). *Developing talent in young people*. New York, NY: Ballantine Books.

Brody, L. E. (2007). Counseling highly gifted students to utilize supplemental educational opportunities: Using the SET program as a model. In J. L. VanTassel-Baska (Ed.), *Serving gifted learners beyond the traditional classroom* (pp. 123–143). Waco, TX: Prufrock Press.

Brody, L. E. (2009a). The Johns Hopkins talent search model for identifying and developing exceptional mathematical and verbal abilities. In L. V. Shavinina (Ed.), *International handbook on giftedness* (pp. 999–1016). New York, NY: Springer.

Brody, L. E. (2009b). Personalized programs for talent development: The Johns Hopkins model for meeting individualized needs. In B. MacFarlane & T. Stambaugh (Eds.), *Leading change in gifted education: The festschrift of Dr. Joyce VanTassel-Baska* (pp. 93–105). Waco, TX: Prufrock Press.

Brody, L. E., & Benbow, C. P. (1987). Accelerative strategies: How effective are they for the gifted? *Gifted Child Quarterly, 31,* 105–110.

Brody, L. E., & Stanley, J. C. (2005). Youths who reason exceptionally well mathematically and/or verbally: Using the MVT:D^4 model to develop their talents. In R. J. Sternberg & J. E. Davidson (Eds.), *Conceptions of giftedness* (pp. 20–37). New York, NY: Cambridge University Press.

Brounstein, P. J., Holahan, W., & Dreyden, J. (1991). Change in self-concept and attributional styles among academically gifted adolescents. *Journal of Applied Social Psychology, 21,* 198–218.

Fox, L. H., & Denham, S. A. (1974). Values and career interests of mathematically and scientifically precocious youth. In J. C. Stanley, D. P. Keating, & L. H. Fox (Eds.), *Mathematical talent: Discovery, description, and development* (pp. 140–175). Baltimore, MD: Johns Hopkins University Press.

George, W. C., Cohn, S. J., & Stanley, J. C. (Eds.). (1979). *Educating the gifted: Acceleration and enrichment*. Baltimore, MD: Johns Hopkins University Press.

Kaufman, S. B. (Ed.). (2013). *The complexity of greatness*. New York, NY: Oxford University Press.

Keating, D. P. (Ed.). (1976). *Intellectual talent: Research and development*. Baltimore, MD: Johns Hopkins University Press.

Lee, S.-Y., Matthews, M. S., & Olszewski-Kubilius, P. (2008). A national picture of talent search and talent search educational programs. *Gifted Child Quarterly, 52,* 55–69.

Lee, S.-Y., Olszewski-Kubilius, P., Makel, M. C., & Putallaz, M. (2015). Gifted students' perception of an accelerated summer program and social support. *Gifted Child Quarterly, 59,* 265–282.

Lee, S.-Y., Olszewski-Kubilius, P., & Thomson, D. (2012). Academically gifted students' perceived interpersonal competence and peer relationships. *Gifted Child Quarterly, 56,* 90–104.

Lubinski, D. (2016). From Terman to today: A century of findings on intellectual precocity. *Review of Educational Research, 86,* 900–944.

Lubinski, D., & Benbow, C. P. (2006). Study of Mathematically Precocious Youth after 35 years: Uncovering antecedents for the development of math-science expertise. *Perspectives on Psychological Science, 1,* 316–345.

Lubinski, D., Benbow, C. P., & Kell, H. J. (2014). Life paths and accomplishments of mathematically precocious males and females four decades later. *Psychological Science, 25,* 2217–2232.

Lubinski, D., Webb, R. M., Morelock, M. J., & Benbow, C. P. (2001). Top 1 in 10,000: A 10-year follow-up of the profoundly gifted. *Journal of Applied Psychology, 86,* 718–729.

Luthar, S. S., Zigler, E., & Goldstein, D. (1992). Psychosocial adjustment among intellectually gifted adolescents: The role of cognitive-developmental and experiential factors. *Journal of Child Psychology and Psychiatry, 33,* 361–375.

Makel, M. C., Kell, H. J., Lubinski, D., Putallaz, M., & Benbow, C. P. (2016). When lightning strikes twice: Profoundly gifted, profoundly accomplished. *Psychological Science, 27,* 1004–1018.

Makel, M. C., Lee, S.-Y., Olszewski-Kubilius, P., & Putallaz, M. (2012). Changing the pond, not the fish: Following high ability students across different educational environments. *Journal of Educational Psychology, 104,* 778–792

Mickenberg, K., & Wood, J. (2009). *Alumni program satisfaction and benefits of CTY summer programs* (Technical Report No. 29). Baltimore, MD: Johns Hopkins Center for Talented Youth.

Mills, C. J. (1993). Personality, learning style, and cognitive style profiles of mathematically talented students. *High Ability Studies, 4,* 70–85.

Mills, C. J., & Brody, L. E. (2012). Should the primary focus of gifted education be on teaching advanced and accelerated curricular content? In A. J. Eakle (Ed.), *Curriculum and instruction* (pp. 162–168). Los Angeles, CA: SAGE.

Muratori, M., Stanley, J. C., Gross, M. U. M., Ng, L., Tao, T., Ng, J., & Tao, B. (2006). Insights from SMPY's former child prodigies: Drs. Terrence (Terry) Tao and Lenhard (Lenny) Ng reflect on their talent development. *Gifted Child Quarterly, 50,* 307–324.

Olszewski-Kubilius, P., & Kulieke, M. J. (1989). Personality dimensions of gifted adolescents. In J. L. VanTassel-Baska & P. Olszewski-Kubilius (Eds.), *Patterns of influence on gifted learners* (pp. 125–145). New York, NY: Teachers College Press.

Olszewski-Kubilius, P., Lee, S.-L., & Thomson, D. L. (2014). Family environment and social development in gifted students. *Gifted Child Quarterly, 58,* 119–216.

O'Reilly, C. (2012). Gifted education in Ireland. *Journal for the Education of the Gifted, 36,* 97–118.

Parker, W. D., & Mills, C. J. (1996). The incidence of perfectionism in gifted students. *Gifted Child Quarterly, 40,* 194–199.

Parker, W. D., & Stumpf, H. (1998). A validation of the five-factor model of personality in academically talented youth across observers and instruments. *Personality and Individual Differences, 25,* 1005–1025.

Peters, S. J., Rambo-Hernandez, K., Makel, M.C., Matthews, M. S., & Plucker, J. A. (2017). Should millions of students take a gap year? Large numbers of students start the school year above grade level. *Gifted Child Quarterly, 61,* 229–238.

Plucker, J. A., & Peters, S. J. (2016). *Excellence gaps in education.* Cambridge, MA: Harvard Education Press.

Robertson, K. F., Smeets, S., Lubinski, D., & Benbow, C. P. (2010). Beyond the threshold hypothesis: Even among the gifted and top math/science graduate students, cognitive abilities, vocational interests, and lifestyle preferences matter for career choice, performance, and persistence. *Current Directions in Psychological Science, 19,* 346–351.

Southern, W. T., & Jones, E. D. (2015). Types of acceleration: Dimensions and issues. In S. G. Assouline, N. Colangelo, J. VanTassel-Baska, & A. Lupkowski-Shoplik (Eds.). *A nation empowered: Evidence trumps the excuses holding back America's brightest students* (Vol. 2, pp. 9–18). Iowa City: University of Iowa, The Connie Belin & Jacqueline N. Blank International Center for Gifted Education and Talent Development.

Southern, W. T., Jones, E. D., & Stanley, J. C. (1993). Acceleration and enrichment: The content and development of programs. In E. A. Heller, F. K. Mönks, & A. H. Passow (Eds.), *International handbook of research and development of giftedness and talent* (pp. 387–409). New York, NY: Pergamon Press.

Stanley, J. C. (1979a). The study and facilitation of talent for mathematics. In A. H. Passow (Ed.), *The gifted and the talented: Their education and development. The 78th yearbook of the National Society for the Study of Education* (pp. 169–185). Chicago, IL: University of Chicago Press.

Stanley, J. C. (1979b, October). *Educating the gifted.* Paper presented at meeting of the National Academy of Education, Boston, MA.

Stanley, J. C. (2005). A quiet revolution: Finding boys and girls who reason exceptionally well mathematically and/or verbally and helping them get the supplemental educational opportunities they need. *High Ability Studies, 16,* 5–14.

Stanley, J. C., & George, W. C. (1978). Now we are six: The ever-expanding SMPY. In *G/C/T, 1* (1), 9–11, 43–44, 50–51.

Stanley, J. C., Keating, D. P., & Fox, L. H. (Eds.). (1974). *Mathematical talent: Discovery, description, and development.* Baltimore, MD: Johns Hopkins University Press.

Stanley, J. C., & Stanley, B. S. K. (1986). High-school biology, chemistry, or physics learned well in three weeks. *Journal of Research in Science Teaching, 23,* 237–250.

Steenbergen-Hu, S., Makel, M. C., & Olszewski-Kubilius, P. (2016). What one hundred years of research says about the effects of ability grouping and acceleration on K–12 students' academic achievement: Findings of two second-order meta-analyses. *Review of Educational Research, 86,* 849–899.

Wai, J., Lubinski, D., Benbow, C. P., & Steiger, J. H. (2010). Accomplishment in science, technology, engineering, and mathematics (STEM) and its relation to STEM educational dose: A 25-year longitudinal study. *Journal of Educational Psychology, 102,* 860–871.

CHAPTER 4

Using Cluster Grouping to Improve Student Achievement, Equity, and Teacher Practices

Marcia Gentry and Juliana Tay

Consider a program developed to meet the needs of students with gifts and talents implemented school wide and focused on the performance of all students and the composition of all teachers' classrooms. Imagine an elementary school with a program that results in more students achieving at higher levels and fewer students achieving at lower levels and in which the achievement of all students improves over time. Picture the students who become high achieving or who leave behind low achievement as students from traditionally underserved populations, including students from low-income families; students from Black, Latinx, or Native American racial groups; students who are learning to speak English; or students who have disabilities. Finally, envision all teachers using strategies from gifted education with their students—focused on students' strengths, interests, and talents, involving them in enriched learning experiences often reserved only for students identified as gifted. A growing body of research supports the use of Total School Cluster Grouping (TSCG; Gentry, 2014) to help achieve these outcomes in elementary schools for the benefit of all students and their teachers.

Traditional gifted education programs are often implemented and designed with only the students they serve in mind. Few programs for youth with gifts and talents consider how the program affects the other students and teachers in the school. Further, many of these programs can be isolated from the rest of the school day. A typical pull-out program serves students for fewer than 3 hours per week, yet students have advanced educational needs for the rest of the week (Siegle et al., 2017). Having separate, even isolated, gifted programs puts the programs at risk for lacking understanding by most educators and for lacking cohesion with the general education program (Gentry, 2009). As a result, gifted programs are often the first programs to be cut in times of financial challenges. Therefore, it is desirable to marry programs that provide separate special services to students with gifts and talents to full-time programs such as TSCG and thereby provide full-time and special services in a comprehensive, supportive program that everyone understands and supports.

Education for students with gifts and talents has often been influenced by policies and regulations enacted for general education students. When resources are limited, support to one group of students is often made at the expense of another group of students. In situations like this, students with gifts and talents often pay the price (Moon, 2009). Despite evidence from researchers showing how students with gifts and talents need support and challenges to help them work to their potential and develop their talents, these students are seldom given adequate support (Cooper, 2009; Hertberg-Davis, 2009). With calls for accountability and to close the achievement gap among the different groups of students, the situation for students with gifts and talents is unlikely to improve. Although it is important to ensure that lower achieving students have the support they need to close the achievement gap, the needs of students with gifts and talents should not be ignored. As such, it is important to consider what can be done within current educational frameworks, using existing resources to ensure that students with gifts and talents receive the services they need, while also addressing the needs of students who struggle.

Grouping used by teachers to address the diverse needs of their students and with aim to close the achievement gaps has become more popular recently (Loveless, 2013) and is one set of education strategies. Grouping can be used in schools to meet the needs of students with gifts and talents without incurring additional cost (Gentry & Owen, 1999; Hertberg-Davis, 2009). However, grouping, and specifically, ability grouping, has been the subject of much and heated debate during the past three decades (e.g., Kulik & Kulik, 1992; Loveless, 2013; Nomi, 2010; Oakes, 1985; Olszewski-Kubilius, 2013; Slavin, 1988; Tieso, 2003). Researchers from both sides of the ability grouping debate continue to discuss the pros and cons of its application in schools. As such, not all educators support the use of grouping, and further, not all forms of grouping strategies bring about the same results. For grouping strategies to appropriately meet the needs of students with gifts and talents, there are more factors to consider than simply putting students of similar levels of academic achievement together. Namely, curriculum and instruction has to be adjusted to accommodate the needs of these students, and care must be taken to ensure that other students receive appropriately enriched instruction and interesting curriculum so that they have a high-quality education that promotes academic growth and achievement.

WHAT DOES IT MEAN TO BE GIFTED?

According to the federal government (U.S. Department of Education [USDOE], 1993), children and youth with gifts and talents are those who exhibit exceptional performance or potential when compared with others similar in age, experience, and environment, and they come from all cultural groups and exist across all economic strata and in every area of human endeavor. Renzulli (1986) described giftedness as a behavior rather than a state of being, and explained that this behavior occurs "in certain people, at certain times, and under certain circumstances" (p. 7) when above-average ability (in an area of human endeavor) comes together with task commitment and creativity. We believe the most import-ant thing educators can do is create learning environments in which students can discover, develop, and reveal their gifts and talents. As the late scholar A. Harry Passow explained, "schools ought to be places for talent development, it is that simple" (A. Harry Passow, personal communication, November 3, 1994). Some argue that being gifted comes with an obligation to make a contribution, to be ethical, and to make the world a better place. We believe these are noble goals and that giftedness, creativity, and talents must be properly nurtured, cultivated, and balanced between what the student can do and who she is as a human being. Compassion, ethics, care, and empathy are as important as academic accomplish-ments. So to be gifted involves behaviors and beliefs, actions and contributions, ability and effort, ethics and values, and unique accomplishments. As we label and serve these youth, we can no longer turn a blind eye to students from groups who for decades have been woefully underrepresented in gifted programming. Namely, these are the students who come from low-income families; those who come from Black, Latinx, and Native American racial and cultural groups; those who are learning the English language; and those who have disabilities. We must stop blindly following the results of ability testing based on national norms that yield disparate results and begin to examine dynamic and local group norms as well as develop alternate pathways into program (Peters & Engerrand, 2016; Peters & Gentry, 2010). Standardized scores should not be the only, nor the most important, way into a program for youth with gifts and talents. We must recog-nize discrepancies in opportunities and in social capital and put programs and services in place that help discover and nurture talents among youth from all of these groups. Nothing less is defensible.

Students with gifts and talents in some ways are not a unique group of students. Like their age peers, they have social-emotional needs, and they experience challenges and issues in their learning process (Moon, 2009; Peterson, 2009). However, it is often too easy to set them aside and focus on the rest of class, as students with gifts and talents generally perform better academically than their peers, and they typically experience fewer problems in schools. Yet, this does not mean their needs are being met. Researchers have found that students with gifts and talents placed in regular classrooms where the lessons are pitched at the level of average students experience boredom and suffer from a lack of challenges (Robinson, Reis, Neihart, & Moon, 2002). Students with gifts and talents need to experience appropriate rigor in their learning to stretch and develop their potential. Furthermore, they need help to connect what they are learning to their interests and to their needs (Sousa, 1998; Tomlinson; 2014). With a wide array of students replete with unique challenges and needs, teachers may find it overwhelming to meet these very diverse needs in a heterogeneously grouped classroom.

GROUPING

Grouping is one set of strategies teachers may use in the classroom to help to address the diverse needs of their students. Grouping is not new; teachers' use of grouping in the classroom can be traced back to 1900s (Slavin, 1988). Over the years, the use of ability grouping has been controversial, with many researchers investigating the effects of various forms of ability grouping with mixed findings. At least 13 meta-analyses have been conducted on the use of ability grouping since the early 1980s (i.e., Goldring, 1990; Henderson, 1989; C. Kulik, 1985; C. Kulik & J. Kulik, 1982, 1984; J. Kulik & C. Kulik, 1987, 1992; Lou et al., 1996; Mosteller, Light, & Sachs, 1996; Noland & Taylor, 1986; Slavin, 1987, 1990, 1993), and most researchers agree that grouping benefits students in the higher groups, but findings are mixed for students in the lower groups. Specifically, when curriculum and instruction are adjusted to the skill level of the students, all students benefit from grouping; however, when students in lower groups receive inferior curricula, less-qualified teachers, and low expectations, outcomes for them are poor, as would be expected. In fact, recent research by Kalogrides and Loeb (2013) revealed a trend of lower quality and more novice teachers being assigned to students with low performance as well as these classrooms having fewer resources. The takeaway here is that any time programming is put into place grouping students with high ability, educators must also consider how this grouping affects other students and teachers, and they must design services for all students that are enriched, enhanced, and that offer all students the best chance of success and growth (Gentry, 2014). In this chapter, we focus on the Total School Cluster Grouping model and the key components of its implementation. We also discuss benefits of the TSCG model and how the successful implementation of the model can be measured. TSCG is a system that when used appropriately helps teachers address the needs of *all* students, including those with gifts and talents, without incurring additional costs.

TOTAL SCHOOL CLUSTER GROUPING

Total School Cluster Grouping operates on the premise that the gifted education program will enhance the entire school. As noted by Tomlinson and Callahan (1992), Renzulli (1994), Reis, Gentry, and Park (1995), and the U.S. Department of Education (1993), the use of gifted education "know-how" has the potential to improve general education practices. Gubbins and a team of researchers from the National Research Center on the Gifted and Talented (2002) found that when teachers integrated strategies typically used in gifted programs, students' academic needs were more likely to become the focus of the curriculum rather than topical themed units common in many classrooms. Cluster grouping, when designed appropriately, can simultaneously address the needs of high-achieving students *and* the needs of other students.

Cluster grouping is a widely recommended and often used strategy for meeting the needs of high-achieving students in the regular elementary classroom. Its use has gained popularity in recent years because of the move toward inclusive education, budget cuts, and heterogeneous grouping policies that have eliminated programs for gifted students (National Association for Gifted Children [NAGC] & Council of State Directors of Programs for the Gifted [CSDPG], 2015; Purcell, 1994; Renzulli, 2005). When viewed in the larger context of school reform and extending gifted education services to more students, cluster grouping can reach and benefit teachers and students beyond those in traditional gifted programs. And in doing so, it serves as a talent development model, helping more students achieve at higher levels.

Cluster grouping is generally defined as placing a group of students who are gifted, high achieving, or who have high ability in an elementary classroom with other students. Many experts in the field of gifted education recommend this approach (e.g., NAGC, 2017; Renzulli & Reis, 2014; Rimm, Siegle, & Davis, 2017). They may even suggest a specific number of high-ability children to comprise the cluster and specify that the rest of the class should be heterogeneous. Further, many applications of cluster grouping are often only concerned with the children identified as high-ability and what occurs in their classroom. Composition of and practices within the other classrooms are frequently ignored, as the perceived purpose of cluster grouping is to serve the identified children.

However, because cluster grouping places the highest achieving students in one classroom and affects the composition of all other classrooms, it affects all students and teachers in the school. Therefore, cluster grouping should not be viewed as only a program for students with gifts and talents, but as a total school program. Through staff development, flexible placement, and grouping integrated with the regular school structure, cluster grouping offers a means for improving curriculum, instruction, and student achievement.

Total School Cluster Grouping is a specific form of cluster grouping that has a research base, theoretical rationale, and model for successful implementation in schools. Total School Cluster Grouping is guided by the following four goals:

1. Provide full-time services to high-achieving elementary students.
2. Help all students improve their academic achievement and educational self-efficacy.
3. Help teachers more effectively and efficiently meet the diverse needs of all of their students.
4. Weave gifted education and talent development "know-how" into the fabric of all educational practices in the school.

Total School Cluster Grouping considers the placement and performance of *every* student in the school together with the students who might traditionally be identified as gifted, and students are placed in the clusters within the classroom to minimize the number of instructional levels. In TSCG, the achievement levels of all elementary students (gifted/high, above-average, average, low-average, or low achieving)[1] in the school are identified for the purposes of classroom placement and curricular modification. TSCG involves the following specific conditions:

1. Identification occurs yearly on the basis of student performance, with the expectation that student achievement will increase as students grow, develop, and respond to appropriately differentiated curriculum.
2. Identification encompasses the range of low-achieving to high-achieving students, with all student achievement levels identified.

---

1   These identification categories are defined as follows: *high achieving*—students who are great at math and reading when compared to their age peers; *above-average achieving*—students who are great at math or reading or are pretty good at math and reading but not as advanced as students identified as high achieving; *average achieving*—students who achieve in the middle when compared to others in their grade level (in an impoverished area, they might be achieving below grade level, but at an average level for the school population); *low-average achieving*—students may struggle with math or reading, or be slightly behind their peers in both areas; *low achieving*—students who struggle with school and face the risk of failure in school.

3. The classroom(s) that contain clusters of high achievers contain no above-average achieving students, as these students are clustered into the other classrooms.

4. Some classrooms may contain clusters of special needs students with assistance provided to the classroom teacher.

5. Teachers may flexibly group between classes or among grade levels as well as use a variety of flexible grouping strategies within their classrooms.

6. All teachers receive professional development in gifted education strategies and have the opportunity for more advanced education in gifted education and talent development through advanced workshops, conferences, and coursework.

7. The teacher whose class has the high-achieving cluster is selected by his or her colleagues and provides differentiated instruction and curriculum to these students as needed to meet their educational needs. (Gentry, 2014, p. 9)

Researchers have noted benefits from grouping gifted students. These benefits include improved academic achievement (Brulles, Peters, & Saunders, 2012; Brulles, Saunders, & Cohn, 2010; Gentry, 1999; Matthews, Ritchotte, & McBee, 2013; Pierce et al., 2011; Tieso, 2005), accurate perception of abilities when compared to peers (Marsh, Chessor, Craven, & Roche, 1995), appropriate levels of challenge (Gentry, 1999; J. Kulik, 2003; Rogers, 2002), ability for teachers to address unique social and emotional needs of gifted students (Peterson, 2003), and the ability of the teacher to better address individual strengths and weakness with a more focused range of ability levels (Gentry, 2013; Moon, 2003). Cluster grouping can offer these and other benefits to students and their teachers.

Additionally, researchers have identified several major benefits of cluster grouping:

1. Gifted students regularly interact both with their intellectual peers and their age peers (Delcourt & Evans, 1994; Rogers, 2002; Slavin, 1987);

2. Cluster grouping provides full-time services for gifted students without additional cost (Gentry & Owen, 1999; Hoover, Sayler, & Feldhusen, 1993; LaRose, 1986);

3. Curricular differentiation is more efficient and likely to occur when a group of high-achieving students is placed with a teacher who has expertise, training, and a desire to differentiate curriculum than when these students are distributed among many teachers (Brulles et al., 2010; Bryant, 1987; Kennedy, 1995; J. Kulik, 1992; Rogers, 2002; Schroth, 2007);

4. Removing the highest achievers from most classrooms allows other achievers to emerge and gain recognition (Gentry & Owen, 1999; Kennedy, 1995);

5. Student achievement increases when cluster grouping is used (Brulles et al., 2010; Brulles et al., 2012; Gates, 2011; Gentry & Owen, 1999; Pierce et al., 2011);

6. Over time, fewer students are identified as low achievers and more students are identified as high achievers (Brulles et al., 2012; Gentry, 1999, 2011, 2013); and

7. Cluster grouping reduces the range of student achievement levels that must be addressed within the classrooms of all teachers (Coleman, 1995; Delcourt & Evans, 1994; Gentry, 1999; Nomi, 2011; Rogers, 1993). (Gentry, 2014, p. 14)

In addition, the professional development component of this model had positive effects not only on the students, but also on the teachers who felt that they received both the instructional and collegial support that allowed them to become leaders in their schools (Gentry & Keilty, 2004). Staff development opportunities afforded teachers opportunities to explore instructional strategies that can be implemented successfully in cluster-grouped classrooms. Through integrating higher order thinking skills, developing critical thinking skills, compacting curriculum, using open-ended questions, accelerating students in content areas, and using several other instructional strategies, teachers reported being able to address the specific needs of their students (Gentry & Owen, 1999).

Thus, Total School Cluster Grouping provides an organizational model that places students into classrooms on the basis of achievement, flexibly groups and regroups students as needed for instruction (based on interests and needs), and provides appropriately challenging learning experiences for all students. TSCG offers districts a method of placing students in classrooms in a manner that can help teachers better meet their academic needs and help all of their students achieve at higher levels.

TCSG Achievement, Ability, Class Assignments, and Grouping

Superior performance in schoolwork is not the only indicator of giftedness. In the past, teachers often focused on students' academic achievement or IQ scores when grouping them into ability groups (Slavin, 1988). However, the field of education has changed, and grouping in today's context consists of more than just grouping students by ability. In the TSCG model we refer to *achievement grouping* and emphasize that it is flexible. Students are grouped based on their achievement within a subject or unit with the intention of modifying the curricula, the instruction, and the pace to meet the students' needs (Tieso, 2003). Additionally, the term *ability*, often viewed as a fixed construct, is not well aligned with the talent development perspective that giftedness can be developed. As such, we prefer the term *achievement grouping* instead of *ability grouping* (Gentry, 2014). However, we do include students with high ability scores in the top cluster group whether or not they achieve at high levels. This is done in an effort to develop achievement and to mitigate early underachievement.

Ability is a latent construct that underlies achievement; whereas, achievement is a manifestation of ability. As such, we have developed a comparison of how ability and achievement differ, as depicted in Figure 4.1. We only see ability when students present it. It is possible to have high ability but not to show it, so we caution educators not to assume that a child who achieves at average or even low levels has low ability, but rather to work to develop achievement by maintaining high expectations, offering interesting curricula, and engaging in meaningful learning experiences with all students. Similarly, we believe any student who achieves at a high level has the *ability* to do so; and thus we do not distinguish between "truly gifted" and "only high achieving." High-achieving students have high ability, and to diminish their high achievement as just due to hard work diminishes their ability and potential. In the TSCG model, students with high test scores are identified as high achievers regardless of whether they produce in the classroom (this ensures that underachievers are identified), and students who achieve at high levels, but who may not test exceptionally high, are identified as high achieving by their teachers. This two-pronged approach ensures that students have multiple pathways into the program. Coupled with yearly identification, this model accommodates student growth and change over time.

For achievement grouping to be effective as a strategy to meet the needs of students with gifts and talents, the teachers must be able to adjust the curricula or modify the pace of instructions to provide appropriate challenges to the specific group of learners. This means that the teachers continually consider the varying levels of achievement of the students in their classrooms. Sorenson and Hallinan (1986) examined 48 classes of elementary students and found when teachers group the students by ability, they were able to provide the individual groups of students with the pace of instruction and appropriate materials for their learning. Additionally, by working with smaller groups of students each time, teachers were also able to pay more attention to the students in the group and create a more conducive environment for learning. By applying flexible grouping within the classroom, the teachers can work with smaller groups of students and have better control over their learning process.

We encourage teachers to consider their daily knowledge of students' work in addition to how students perform on standard achievement or ability measures. Worrell (2009) highlighted the limited validity of a single test score in identifying students for gifted services. The same idea was applied in the TSCG model in which test scores are only one pathway to identification as high achieving.

Achievement	Ability
Observable, manifest	Latent
Variable	Fixed
Develops	Something one "has"
Readily accepted concept	Can bring out biases
Can be influenced by education	A predetermined quality

Figure 4.1. Achievement and ability comparison.

Teachers who work closely with the students often have a better understanding of the students' potential and performance than may be indicated on a single test. Furthermore, there is also the need to consider the performance of students who do not achieve well across all subjects or who have other learning difficulties that may mask their potential. In such cases, the teachers may have a better sense of the students' potential than test scores may indicate.

With the TSCG model, teachers and administrators work together to group students into different classes across each elementary grade level. Armed with information about the students' academic performance, social-emotional needs, and other pertinent knowledge of the students, teachers work as a team to organize students into different classrooms by considering students identified as high achieving, above-average achieving, average achieving, low-average achieving, and low achieving (Gentry, 2014). Major differences between cluster grouping and tracking are numerous and include the flexibility of these groups and reidentification and placement that occurs yearly. Additionally, tracking was done based on ability testing with secondary students. TSCG uses student performance and teacher perceptions of elementary students to reduce the range of achievement levels within classrooms, thereby enabling teachers to better target individual students' readiness and achievement levels for optimal learning opportunities. Further, the identification of achievement levels is done for the purposes of placement within classrooms, rather than for inflexible instructional groups. With tracking, students were grouped into certain tracks based on their measured ability, and they generally remained in the assigned track for the rest of their education (Renzulli & Reis, 1991; Slavin, 1988; Tieso, 2003). However, with TSCG students are assessed/identified yearly to facilitate careful placement into classrooms. This procedure enables educators to respond to students' growth over a year based on the changes to the students' academic performance. This practice is in line with current thinking in the field of gifted education, in which scholars have highlighted the influence of environment and opportunities on the manifestation of gifted behaviors in students (e.g., Gagné, 2010; Renzulli, 2002). As such, by providing a system in which teachers and administrators can come together and review the students' progress and reassign students to the appropriate classrooms, the needs of students are better addressed. See Gentry (2014) for a full discussion of the various forms of grouping and their definitions, which are depicted in Figure 4.2.

It is important to note that grouping students does not stop once students are assigned to their respective classes. Teachers are encouraged to use flexible grouping strategies within and among classes. The TSCG model allows teachers to consider different aspects of the students' development, skills, and readiness during group assignments and not rely solely on their test scores. Flexible grouping supports growth in student achievement.

Purposeful and Flexible Grouping to Meet the Needs of All Students

Teachers often have students with a wide range of performance levels, diverse interests, and different needs in their classrooms. This is a situation that can be mediated if the teachers have some control over the range of achievement levels of the students they have in their classroom. With the TSCG model, students with gifts and talents are not simply put into classes with students of varying levels of achievement. Instead there is a conscious effort to reduce the range of achievement levels within a classroom by selecting specific groups of students and putting them into one classroom (Brulles et al., 2012; Gentry, 2014). This involves *not* grouping the students with the highest achievement together with above-average achieving students and low achieving students in the same classroom. Rather, above-average students become the top students clustered in the *other* classrooms. This not only helps to reduce the amount of lesson preparation the teachers have to do for their classes, but also allows teachers to meet the needs of the students more effectively (Gentry, 2014; Tieso, 2003). It also provides the opportunities needed by the above-average students to develop their own potential and strengths without continual comparison to the highest achievers. Finally, it reduces the differentiation stretch in the classroom because the lowest achievers' needs are met in the other classrooms. This way, each teacher has fewer achievement levels for which to plan and deliver instruction, and students have peers who achieve at their same levels within their classes.

TSCG as a Tool to Mitigate Underrepresentation

Nationally, students from low-income families and students from culturally and linguistically diverse (CLD) backgrounds remain underidentified, underrepresented, and underserved in gifted and talented programs (Bernal, 2007; Worrell, 2007; Wyner, Bridgeland, & DiIulio, 2009; Yoon & Gentry, 2009). Despite

Term	Definition
Cluster Grouping	The placement of several high-achieving, high-ability, or gifted students in a regular classroom with other students and a teacher who has received training or has a desire to differentiate instruction for these "target" students.
Total School Cluster Grouping	Cluster grouping model that takes into account the achievement levels of all students and places students in classrooms yearly in order to reduce the number of achievement levels in each classroom and facilitate teachers' differentiation of curriculum and instruction for all students and (thus increase student achievement).
Ability Grouping	Students are grouped for the purpose of modification of pace, instructions, and curriculum. Groups can be flexible and arranged by subject, within classes, or between classes.
Achievement Grouping	Focuses on demonstrated levels of achievement by students and is viewed as something dynamic and changing. Groups can be arranged by subject, within classes, or between classes.
Between-Class Grouping	Students are regrouped for a subject area (usually within an elementary grade level) based on ability or achievement. Teachers instruct students working at similar levels with appropriately challenging curricula, at an appropriate pace, with methods most suited to facilitate academic gain.
Within-Class Grouping	Different arrangements teachers use within their classes. Groups may be created by interest, skill, achievement, job, ability, self-selection—either heterogeneous or homogeneous—and can include various forms of cooperative learning grouping arrangements. Groups are intended to be flexible.
Flexible Grouping	The use of various forms of grouping for instruction, pacing, and curriculum in such a manner to allow for movement of students between and among groups based on their progress and needs.
Tracking	The full-time placement of students into ability groups for instruction—usually by class and at the secondary level. Little opportunity exists to move between tracks.

Figure 4.2. Grouping terminology summary. Adapted from *Total School Cluster Grouping and Differentiation: A Comprehensive Research-Based Plan for Raising Student Achievement and Improving Teacher Practices* (p. 12), by M. Gentry (with K. A. Paul, J. McIntosh, C. M. Fugate, and E. Jen), 2014, Waco, TX: Prufrock Press. Copyright 2014 by Prufrock Press. Adapted with permission.

attempts to develop alternative identification procedures, the problem remains severe and pervasive (Borland, 2008; Ford, 2007; Miller, 2004; U.S. Office of Civil Rights, 2002; Wyner et al., 2009). Excellence gaps exist between higher income White and Asian students and their lower income Black and Hispanic peers (Plucker, Hardesty, & Burroughs, 2013; Plucker & Peters, 2016). The excellence gaps exist for Native American students as well (Wu & Gentry, 2017). Further exacerbating the problem are district personnel improperly implementing assessment and identification systems (McBee, Peters, & Waterman, 2014), failing to assess if proportional representation occurs, and unnecessarily limiting the number of students identified and served in gifted programs (Peters, Matthews, McBee, & McCoach, 2014). This results in the systematic exclusion from gifted programming of students who come from poverty or CLD families, or who have parents unable or unwilling to advocate for their identification and service. In simple terms, these students need access to enriched programming, teachers with skills in developing and recognizing their strengths, and opportunities for academic success. Providing this access requires a total school approach to talent development—an approach that TSCG takes.

Our original quasi-experimental research showed that, over time, more students were identified as high achieving (+50% to +100%), fewer students were identified as low achieving (-66% to -100%), student achievement increased compared to control-school students, and teachers' practices improved as they implemented strategies in general classrooms often reserved for students in gifted programs (Gentry & Owen, 1999). More recent quasi-experimental research has revealed similar findings and has shown that TSCG resulted in larger numbers of students from traditionally underrepresented groups being identified as gifted and that these students experience achievement growth (Brulles et al., 2012; Brulles et al., 2010; Collins & Gan, 2013; Gates, 2011; Gentry & McDougall, 2008; Matthews et al., 2013; Pierce et al., 2011). Additionally, these researchers found no negative effects of cluster grouping on any children—so lower performing children were not harmed, and in some cases were helped, by grouping high-achieving students in a clustered model. In fact, Matthews et al. (2013) found that TSCG positively influenced math achievement for gifted and for typical learners. Brulles et al. (2012) found that typical learners experienced similar growth in mathematics regardless of whether they were grouped with high-achieving students. Pierce et al. (2011) examined math achievement for gifted and typical students in total school applications of cluster grouping and found performance gains for both groups of students in mathematics. Gentry and MacDougall (2008) found increased representation rates for students with free or reduced lunch assistance (+33%), English language learners (+10%), and students from underrepresented racial/ethnic groups (African American, +12%; Latinx, +10%) after just one year of TSCG programming. A controlled evaluation study of a 3-year implementation of TSCG in an urban area revealed average Normal Curve Equivalent (NCE) achievement gains across five treatment schools in reading (+3.28) and math (+7.07) for all students, gains among students identified as high achieving in reading (+7.31) and in math (+8.32), and treatment schools outperforming their matched comparison schools in achievement.[2] This evaluation study also revealed an increase in the number of students from low-income (+24%) and Black (+21%) families identified as high achieving and an increase in the number of students from underserved populations who qualified as gifted under state guidelines (+100% on average at each school). Currently TSCG is the subject of a 5-year, federally funded study being implemented nationally in more than 100 schools. Early results show similar trends in identification data as reported above (Gentry, 2017).

In the TSCG model, students initially identified as above average frequently come from underserved groups, including students from low-income families; students from Black, Latinx, or Native American racial/cultural groups; and students learning the English language. Over time, more of these students move into high achievement and others from these groups move out of low achievement, with TSCG resulting in more equitable recognition of students from traditionally underserved groups as high achieving (Gentry & McDougall, 2008).

Common Arguments Against Grouping

Self-concept. One criticism of achievement grouping is that separating the gifted students into a different class lowers self-concepts (Oakes, 1985) and reduces learning opportunities (Lleras & Rangel, 2009) of students in other classes. However, researchers have found that when high-achieving students were separated from low-achieving students, the latter group developed a better sense of self-concept without the pressure of being judged by their higher achieving peers (C. Kulik & J. Kulik, 1982). Additionally, Brulles and her colleagues (2012) found that by using a cluster grouping model, average- to low-achieving students also showed gains in their math achievement levels. This could be due to the increased amount of dedicated time and opportunities teachers had to work with these students, developing their skills.

No classroom leaders or role models for other students. Another common argument against grouping is that by removing the gifted students from a classroom, the rest of the students do not have role models to emulate and no leaders remain in the classroom. This perspective, of course, assumes that students with gifts and talents are actually the role models and leaders. Schunk (1987), in his review of 29 studies, found that low-achieving students do not adopt gifted students as role models in terms of learning strategies and behaviors. In fact, Schunk found that, for the low-achieving students, a more effective role model is a fellow peer. Seeing students of similar achievement level completing the learning tasks increased the students' sense of self-efficacy. As such, by separating students with

---

2   *Editor's note.* NCEs are similar to percentile scores, in that they range from 0–100, with the advantage that they represent equal-interval scores (e.g., a five-point NCE difference represents the same size difference regardless of where the two scores are in the score distribution).

gifts and talents, other students have more opportunities to demonstrate mastery and to serve as role models for their peers. This allows students who otherwise may be overshadowed by their peers with gifts and talents to step up as leaders and role models (Gentry & Owen, 1999; Kennedy, 1995). Further, students with gifts and talents are not necessarily leaders and should not be expected to be leaders, tutors, and role models for others.

Teachers and Gifted Education Strategies Are Critical and Necessary

TSCG is not a miracle cure for the woes of gifted education; for this model to be effective in serving the needs of the gifted students, teachers must actively engage in differentiation. In some states, teachers assigned to work with students who have gifts and talents need additional professional development and/or licensure to teach (NAGC & CSDPG, 2015; VanTassel-Baska & Stambaugh, 2005). Components of such professional development often include learning about the characteristics of gifted students; their academic and social-emotional needs, as well as teaching strategies such as differentiation and curriculum modification. Additionally, professional development should include an emphasis on the understanding and implementation of culturally responsive practices (Gay, 2010). This professional development helps to increase teachers' awareness of the wide range of students' characteristics and how they can address the students' interests and needs through differentiating the curricula or learning tasks. However, researchers have found differentiation is a difficult and time-consuming process, in which many teachers do not engage (Hertberg-Davis, 2009). Further, some researchers found that when teachers do differentiate, the focus is more likely to be on the low-achieving students than on those with gifts and talents (Brighton, Hertberg, Callahan, Tomlinson, & Moon, 2005; Westberg & Daoust, 2004). This highlights the current focus of education in which the spotlight is on the low-achieving students in an effort to close the achievement gaps, while setting aside the needs of students with gifts and talents.

Some researchers considered gifted strategies such as grouping and differentiation to be elitist, thereby widening the gap between the different groups of students (Oakes, 1985). However, this is not the case. Researchers have shown that teaching strategies that worked with gifted students were also useful with other students (Gentry & Owen, 1999; Tomlinson & Callahan, 1992). Beecher and Sweeny (2008) worked with an elementary school staff to close the achievement gap and improve the students' academic performance. As part of the school improvement process, all teachers were trained in differentiation and enrichment strategies. After 8 years of working with the school, Beecher and Sweeny found improvement in students' academic performances and narrowed achievement gaps between the different groups of students. This showed that benefits from strategies that were developed in the field of gifted education were not limited to only students with gifts and talents.

In addition, for cluster grouping to be effective, teachers must be committed to making changes to the materials, instructional strategies, and learning tasks for students of all achievement levels and from all cultural, language, and economic groups. They need to have a strong understanding of the curricular content, instructional objectives, and the needs of their students to make suitable modifications to the curricula for students of varying achievement levels (Callahan, 2001; Hertberg-Davis, 2009; VanTassel-Baska & Stambaugh, 2005). Additionally, they must hold high expectations for all students to achieve, grow, and learn. Critics of grouping often cite researchers who found grouping deprived certain groups of students from rich learning experiences because teachers used materials that were either too simple or focused mainly on drill and practice (Oakes, 1992; Slavin, 1988). In the TSCG model, all teachers are expected to receive professional development on gifted education pedagogy including curricular and instructional differentiation, project-based learning, curriculum compacting, and addressing student interests, strengths, and talents. Although not all teachers work with students who achieve at the highest levels, all teachers have students who achieve at above-average levels, and professional development is essential to creating learning environments in which all students can develop their strengths, skills, and talents (Brulles et al., 2012; Gentry, 2014; J. Kulik & C. Kulik, 1992).

EVALUATION OF SUCCESS

It is unwise, and some might suggest, even unethical to implement any program without evaluating it for effectiveness, successes, and failures. Only through thoughtful and informed evaluation can educators understand whether and how a program is working, and its effects on students and their teachers. Additionally, as issues of equity and accountability continue to exert pressure on the field of education, it is important to measure the effectiveness and success of any program or intervention. The use of TSCG is no exception. The success of the model can be measured simply by examining the students' academic achievement and changes in their identification categories over time. These data can be further examined for proportional representation changes among students from low-income families and students who come from culturally and linguistically diverse families. Researchers who have studied the implementation of the TSCG in schools have reported improvement on students' test scores and other measures of academic achievement (Beecher & Sweeny, 2008; Brulles et al., 2010; Brulles et al., 2012;

Collins & Gan, 2013; Gates, 2011; Gentry & McDougall, 2008; Gentry & Owen, 1999; Matthews et al., 2013; Pierce et al., 2011). The positive performance is not restricted only to students who achieve at high levels, as students from the other achievement levels have also shown improvement. Equally important is that these researchers have reported no negative effects of implementing this model on any students achieving at any level.

In addition to individual students' academic achievement, another measure of success for the cluster grouping model would include examining the achievement gaps between various groups of students. Critics of the cluster grouping model have commented on its possible negative influence in widening the achievement gaps among students of different ethnicities and socioeconomic statuses. However, no such evidence exists in the literature. TSCG has as a goal improving access and services to students traditionally underserved in gifted education programs, and has steps in place to help this happen over time, such as ongoing identification, enrichment for all students, and training in gifted education pedagogy for all teachers. Conversely, researchers have demonstrated that by educating teachers about the characteristics of students with gifts and talents, helping teachers understand how to implement culturally responsive practices, and helping them apply differentiation strategies in their teaching, teachers could better identify and address the needs of their students and help them develop their potentials (e.g., Beecher & Sweeny, 2008; Gay, 2010). As a result, more students progressed to the next achievement level and fewer students were identified as low achieving (Gentry, 2017; Gentry & Owen, 1999). This trend may actually help reduce the achievement gaps among the students, but more research is needed.

Apart from academic achievement, another method to evaluate the success of the program is to consider the teachers' and students' satisfaction. Beecher and Sweeny (2008) wrote about the change in school climate in their study, where students were more engaged in their learning and were positive about school. Gentry and Owen (1999) highlighted the positive change in attitudes of the students as they received appropriate curriculum and instruction from their teachers, enhancing their academic success. In addition, researchers also reported on the increased level of satisfaction reported by teachers who acknowledged that the professional development they received helped them understand the diverse needs of their students and learn different strategies they could use to meet their students' needs (Beecher & Sweeny, 2008; Gentry & Owen, 1999). Do teachers improve their culturally responsive practices as they develop the potentials of students from traditionally underserved groups? Finally, these practices and attitudes can be quantified and changes in instructional repertoires can be investigated.

CONCLUSION

Ability grouping is commonly used in today's schools (Loveless, 2013). Repeating mistakes from the past in which some forms of ability grouping effectively denied certain groups of students access to quality teachers, instruction, and curriculum cannot be allowed. Common identification practices have overlooked and marginalized students from low-income families; students from Black, Latinx, and Native American racial/cultural backgrounds; and students learning to speak English. These practices cannot continue. No longer can educators turn a blind eye to equity in gifted programs and hide behind measures that for whatever reason yield disparate results of identified students from cultural, income, and language groups. Efforts must be made that address (not simply "try to address") issues of inequity among students who achieve at high levels and those who do not. These efforts include putting into place a continuum of services to address as many talent areas as possible (Gentry, 2009); using multiple measures, multiple pathways, and local group norms to mitigate inequities in identification practices (Peters & Engerrand, 2016); creating access to high-quality, enriched programming for all students as well as access for all teachers on how to teach students as if they are gifted (Gentry, 2014); and implementing programs that have promising evidence of meeting the needs of students with gifts and talents while also developing strengths and talents among student with potential, including those from traditionally underserved populations. Further, programs need to be comprehensive, responsive to students' needs, integrated with the general education program, and provide services on a regular, even full-time, basis. TSCG is one program that addresses these issues for elementary school children and their teachers. It works in conjunction with other programs on a continuum of services, and we believe that a mounting body of evidence shows that it effectively addresses many of the concerns about ability grouping.

Major Takeaways

- Total School Cluster Grouping used in conjunction with challenging instruction and high teacher expectations may improve how teachers view their students with regard to ability and achievement, resulting in an increased number of students, including those from underserved populations, identified as high achieving.

- Cluster grouping may positively influence the achievement of all students due to its approach as a talent development model.

- The use of gifted education "know-how" has the potential to improve general education practices; therefore, professional development in gifted education should not be restricted to just those teachers responsible for students identified as gifted.

- A well-developed cluster grouping program can offer gifted education services to high-achieving students while helping teachers better meet the needs of all students.

- Placing the high achievers in one classroom can increase the chance that their needs will be met while offering the opportunity for talent to emerge in the other classrooms, while restricting the range of achievement levels in elementary classrooms can help teachers better address individual needs.

RECOMMENDED READINGS

Gay, G. (2010). *Culturally responsive teaching: Theory research, and practice* (2nd ed.). New York, NY: Teachers College Press.

Gentry, M., Pereira, N., Peters, S., McIntosh, J., & Fugate, C. M. (2015). *HOPE teacher rating scale: Involving teachers in equitable identification of gifted and talented students in K–12.* Technical manual. Waco, TX: Prufrock Press.

Gentry, M. (with K. A. Paul, J. McIntosh, C. M. Fugate, & E. Jen). (2014). *Total school cluster grouping and differentiation: A comprehensive research-based plan for raising student achievement and improving teacher practices* (2nd ed.). Waco, TX: Prufrock Press.

Peters, S. J., Matthews, M., McCoach, D. B., & McBee, M. (2014). *Beyond gifted education: Designing and implementing advanced academic programs.* Waco, TX: Prufrock Press.

Wyner, J. S., Bridgeland, J. M., & Dilulio, J. J., Jr. (2009). *Achievement trap: How America is failing millions of high-achieving students from low-income families* (Rev. ed.). Lansdowne, VA: Jack Kent Cooke Foundation Civic Enterprises.

REFERENCES

Beecher, M., & Sweeny, S. M. (2008). Closing the achievement gap with curriculum enrichment and differentiation: One school's story. *Journal of Advanced Academics, 19,* 502–530. doi:10.4219/jaa-2008-815

Bernal, E. M. (2007). The plight of the culturally diverse student from poverty. In J. VanTassel-Baska & T. Stambaugh (Eds.), *Overlooked gems: A national perspective on low-income promising learners* (pp. 27–41). Washington, DC: National Association for Gifted Children.

Brighton, C., Hertberg, H., Callahan, C., Tomlinson, C., & Moon, T. (2005). *The feasibility of high-end learning in academically diverse middle schools* (RM 05210). Storrs: University of Connecticut, National Research Center on the Gifted and Talented.

Borland, J. (2008). Identification. In J. Plucker & C. Callahan (Eds.), *Critical issues and practices in gifted education: What the research says* (pp. 261–280). Waco, TX: Prufrock Press.

Brulles, D., Peters, S. J., & Saunders, R. (2012). Schoolwide mathematics achievement within the gifted cluster grouping model. *Journal of Advanced Academics, 23,* 200–216. doi:10.1177/1932202X12451439

Brulles, D., Saunders, R., & Cohn, S. (2010). Improving performance for gifted students in a cluster grouping model. *Journal for the Education of the Gifted, 34,* 327–350.

Bryant, M. A. (1987). Meeting the needs of gifted first grade children in a heterogeneous classroom. *Roeper Review, 9,* 214–216. doi:10.1080/02783198709553054

Callahan, C. M. (2001). Fourth down and inches. *Journal of Secondary Gifted Education, 12,* 148–156.

Coleman, M. R. (1995). The importance of cluster grouping. *Gifted Child Today, 18,* 38–40.

Collins, C. A., & Gan, L. (2013). *Does sorting students improve scores? An analysis of class composition.* (National Bureau of Economic Research Working Paper 18848). Retrieved from http://www.nber.org/papers/w18848

Cooper, C. R. (2009). Myth 18: It is fair to teach all children the same way. *Gifted Child Quarterly, 53,* 283–285. doi:10.1177/0016986209346947

Delcourt, M. A. B., & Evans, K. (1994). *Qualitative extension of the learning outcomes study.* Storrs: University of Connecticut, National Research Center on the Gifted and Talented.

Ford, D. Y. (2007). Diamonds in the rough: Recognizing and meeting the needs of gifted children from low SES backgrounds. In J. VanTassel-Baska & T. Stambaugh (Eds.), *Overlooked gems: A national perspective on low-income promising learners* (pp. 63–37). Washington, DC: National Association for Gifted Children.

Gagné, F. (2010). Motivation within the DMGT 2.0 framework. *High Ability Studies, 21,* 81–99. doi:10.1080/13598139.2010.525341

Gates, J. (2011). *Total school cluster grouping model: An investigation of student achievement and identification and teachers classroom practices* (Doctoral dissertation, Purdue University). Available from ProQuest Dissertations and Theses database. (UMI No. 3479482)

Gay, G. (2010). *Culturally responsive teaching: Theory research, and practice* (2nd ed.). New York, NY: Teachers College Press.

Gentry, M. (1999). *Promoting student achievement and exemplary classroom practices through cluster grouping: A research-based alternative to heterogeneous elementary classrooms* (RM99138). Storrs: University of Connecticut, National Research Center on the Gifted and Talented.

Gentry, M. (2009). Myth 11: A comprehensive continuum of gifted education and talent development services: Discovering, developing, and enhancing young people's gifts and talents. *Gifted Child Quarterly, 53,* 262–265. doi:10.1177/0016986209346937

Gentry, M. (2011). *Total School Cluster Grouping National Scale-up project. Year 2 report.* West Lafayette, IN: Purdue University.

Gentry, M. (2013). Cluster grouping. In C. M. Callahan & J. Plucker (Eds.), *Critical issues and practices in gifted education* (2nd ed., pp. 107–115). Waco, TX: Prufrock Press.

Gentry, M. (with K. A. Paul, J. McIntosh, C. M. Fugate, & E. Jen). (2014). *Total school cluster grouping and differentiation: A comprehensive research-based plan for raising student achievement and improving teacher practices* (2nd ed.). Waco, TX: Prufrock Press.

Gentry, M. (2017). *TSCG Javits Grant. Year 3 report.* West Lafayette, IN: Purdue University.

Gentry, M., & Keilty, B. (2004). Rural and suburban cluster grouping: Reflections on staff development as a component of program success. *Roeper Review, 26,* 147–155. doi:10.1080/02783190409554260

Gentry, M., & MacDougall, J. (2009). Total school cluster grouping: Model, research, and practice. In J. S. Renzulli, E. J. Gubbins, K. S. McMillen, R. D. Eckert, & C. A. Little (Eds.), *Systems and models for developing programs for the gifted and talented* (2nd ed., pp. 211–234). Waco, TX: Prufrock Press.

Gentry, M., & Owen, S. V. (1999). An investigation of total school flexible cluster grouping on identification, achievement, and classroom practices. *Gifted Child Quarterly, 43,* 224–243. doi:10.1177/001698629904300402

Goldring, E. B. (1990). Assessing the status of information on classroom organizational frameworks of gifted students. *Journal of Educational Research, 83,* 313–326. doi:10.1080/00220671.1990.10885977

Gubbins, E. J., Westberg, K. L., Reis, S. M., Dinnocenti, S., Tieso, C. M., Muller, L. M., . . . Burns, D. E. (2002). *Implementing a professional development model using gifted education strategies with all students* (RM02172). Storrs: University of Connecticut, The National Research Center on the Gifted and Talented.

Henderson, N. D. (1989). *A meta-analysis of ability grouping achievement and attitude in the elementary grades* (Unpublished doctoral dissertation). Mississippi State University, Starkville.

Hertberg-Davis, H. (2009). Myth 7: Differentiation in the regular classroom is equivalent to gifted programs and is sufficient: Classroom teachers have the time, the skill, and the will to differentiate adequately. *Gifted Child Quarterly, 53,* 251–253. doi:10.1177/0016986209346927

Hoover, S., Sayler, M., & Feldhusen, J. F. (1993). Cluster grouping of elementary students at the elementary level. *Roeper Review, 16,* 13–15. doi:10.1080/02783199309553527

Kalogrides, D., & Loeb, S. (2013). Different teachers, different peers: The magnitude of student sorting within schools. *Educational Researcher, 42,* 304–316. doi:10.3102/0013189X13495087

Kennedy, D. M. (1995). Teaching gifted in regular classrooms: Plain talk about creating a gifted-friendly classroom. *Roeper Review, 17,* 232–234. doi:10.1080/02783199509553669

Kulik, C.-L. C. (August, 1985). *Effects of inter-class ability grouping on achievement and self-esteem.* Paper presented at the 93rd Annual Convention of the American Psychological Association, Los Angeles, CA.

Kulik, C., & Kulik J. (1982). Effects of ability grouping on secondary school students: A meta-analysis of evaluation findings. *American Educational Research Journal, 19,* 415–428. doi:10.3102/00028312019003415

Kulik, C.-L. C., & Kulik, J. A. (1984). *Effects of ability grouping on elementary school pupils: A meta-analysis.* Paper presented at the annual meeting of the American Psychological Association, Toronto, ON. (ERIC Document Reproduction Service No. ED 255329)

Kulik, J. A. (1992). *An analysis of the research on ability grouping: Historical and contemporary perspectives.* Storrs: University of Connecticut, The National Research Center on the Gifted and Talented.

Kulik, J. A. (2003). Grouping and tracking. In N. Colangelo & G. Davis (Eds.), *Handbook of gifted education* (pp. 268–281). Boston, MA: Allyn & Bacon.

Kulik, J. A., & Kulik, C.-L. C. (1987). Effects of ability grouping on student achievement. *Equity & Excellence in Education, 23,* 22–30. doi:10.1080/1066568870230105

Kulik, J. A., & Kulik, C-L. C. (1992). Meta-analytic findings on grouping programs. *Gifted Child Quarterly, 36,* 73–77.

LaRose, B. (1986). The lighthouse program: A longitudinal research project. *Journal for the Education of the Gifted, 9,* 224–232. doi:10.1177/016235328500900306

Lleras, C., & Rangel, C. (2009). Ability grouping practices in elementary school and African American/Hispanic achievement. *American Journal of Education, 115,* 279–304. doi:10.1086/595667

Lou, Y., Abrami, P. C., Spence, J. C., Poulsen, C., Chambers, B., & d'Apollonia, S. (1996). Within-class grouping: A meta analysis. *Review of Educational Research, 66,* 423–458. doi:10.3102/00346543066004423

Loveless, T. (2013). *The resurgence of ability grouping and persistence of tracking.* Washington, DC: Brookings Institution, Brown Center on Education Policy. Retrieved from http://www.brookings.edu/research/reports/2013/03/18-tracking-ability-grouping-loveless

Marsh, H. W., Chessor, D., Craven, R., & Roche, L. (1995). The effects of gifted and talented programs on academic self-concept: The big fish strikes again. *American Educational Research Journal, 32,* 285–319. doi:10.3102/00028312032002285

Matthews, M. S., Ritchotte, J. A., & McBee, M. T. (2013). Effects of school-wide cluster grouping and within-class ability grouping on elementary school students' academic achievement growth. *High Ability Studies, 24,* 81–97. doi:10.1080/13598139.2013.846251

McBee, M. T., Peters, S. J., & Waterman, C. (2014). Combining scores in multi-criteria assessment systems: The impact of the combination rule. *Gifted Child Quarterly, 58,* 69–89. doi:10.1177/0016986213513794

Miller, L. S. (2004). *Promoting sustained growth in the representation of African Americans, Latinos, and Native Americans among top student in the United States at all levels of the education system* (RM04190). Storrs: University of Connecticut, The National Research Center on the Gifted and Talented.

Moon, S. M. (2003). Personal talent. *High Ability Studies, 14,* 5–21.

Moon, S. M. (2009). Myth 15: High-ability students don't face problems and challenges. *Gifted Child Quarterly, 53,* 274–276. doi:10.1177/0016986209346943

Mosteller, F., Light, R. J., & Sachs, J. A. (1996). Sustained inquiry in education: Lessons from skill grouping and class size. *Harvard Educational Review, 66,* 797–842.

National Association for Gifted Children. (2017). *Grouping.* Retrieved from https://www.nagc.org/resources-publications/gifted-education-practices/grouping

National Association for Gifted Children, & Council of State Directors of Programs for the Gifted. (2015). *2014-2015 state of the states in gifted education: Policy and practice.* Washington, DC: Authors.

Noland, T. K., & Taylor, B. L. (1986). *The effects of ability grouping: a meta-analysis of research findings.* Paper presented at the 70th Annual meeting of the American Educational Research Association, San Francisco, CA. (ERIC Document Reproduction Service No. ED 269541)

Nomi, T. (2010). The effect of within-class ability grouping on academic achievement in the early elementary years. *Journal of Research on Educational Effectiveness, 3,* 56–92. doi:10.1080/19345740903277601

Oakes, J. (1985). *Keeping track: How schools structure inequality.* New Haven, CT: Yale University Press.

Oakes, J. (1992). Can tracking research inform practice? Technical, normative, and political considerations. *Educational Researcher, 21,* 12–21.

Olszewski-Kubilius, P. (2013). Setting the record straight on ability grouping. *Education Week.* Retrieved from http://www.edweek.org/tm/articles/2013/05/20/fp_olszewski.html

Peters, S. J., & Engerrand, K. G. (2016). Equity and excellence: Proactive efforts in the identification of underrepresented students for gifted and talented services. *Gifted Child Quarterly, 60,* 159–171. doi:10.1177/0016986216643165.

Peters, S. J., & Gentry, M. (2010). Multi-group construct validity evidence of the *HOPE Scale*: Instrumentation to identify low-income elementary students for gifted programs. *Gifted Child Quarterly, 54,* 298–313. doi:10.1177/0016986212469253.

Peters, S. J., Matthews, M., McCoach, D. B., & McBee, M. (2014). *Beyond gifted education: Designing and implementing advanced academic programs.* Waco, TX: Prufrock Press.

Peterson, J. S. (2003). An argument for proactive attention to affective concerns to gifted students. *The Journal of Secondary Gifted Education, 15,* 62–70. doi:10.4219/jsge-2003-419

Peterson, J. S. (2009). Myth 17: Gifted and talented individuals do not have unique social and emotional needs. *Gifted Child Quarterly, 53,* 280–282. doi:10.1177/0016986209346946

Pierce, R., Cassady, J., Adams, C., Neumeister, K., Dixon, F., & Cross, T. (2011). The effects of clustering and curriculum on the development of gifted learners' math achievement. *Journal for the Education of the Gifted, 34,* 569–596. doi:10.1177/016235321103400403

Plucker, J., Hardesty, J., & Burroughs, N. (2013). *Talent on the sidelines: Excellence gaps and America's persistent talent underclass.* Retrieved from http://cepa.uconn.edu/mindthegap

Plucker, J. A., & Peters, S. J. (2016). *Excellence gaps in education: Expanding opportunities for talented students.* Cambridge, MA: Harvard Education Press.

Purcell, J. (1994). *The status of programs for high ability students* (CRS94306). Storrs: University of Connecticut, The National Research Center on the Gifted and Talented.

Reis, S. M., Gentry, M., & Park, S. (1995). *Extending the pedagogy of gifted education to all students* (RM95118). Storrs: University of Connecticut, The National Research Center on the Gifted and Talented.

Renzulli, J. S. (1986). The Three-Ring Conception of Giftedness: A developmental model for creative productivity. In R. J. Sternberg & J. Davidson (Eds.), *Conceptions of giftedness* (53–92). New York, NY: Cambridge University Press.

Renzulli, J. S. (1994). *Schools for talent development: A comprehensive plan for total school improvement.* Mansfield Center, CT: Creative Learning Press.

Renzulli, J. S. (2002). Emerging conceptions of giftedness: Building a bridge to the new century. *Exceptionality, 10*(2), 67–75. doi:10.1207/S15327035EX1002_2

Renzulli, J. S. (2005, May). A quiet crisis is clouding the future of R & D. *Education Week, 24,* 32–33, 40.

Renzulli, J. S., & Reis, S. M. (1991). The reform movement and the quiet crisis in gifted education. *Gifted Child Quarterly, 35,* 26–35. doi:10.1177/001698629103500104

Renzulli, J. S., & Reis, S. M. (2014). *The Schoolwide Enrichment Model: A comprehensive plan for talent development* (3rd ed.). Waco, TX: Prufrock Press.

Rimm, S. B., Siegle, D., & Davis, G. A. (2017). *Education of the gifted and talented* (7th ed.). New York, NY: Pearson.

Robinson, N. M., Reis, S. M., Neihart, M., & Moon, S. M. (2002). Social and emotional issues facing gifted and talented students: What have we learned and what should we do now? In M. Neihart, S. M. Reis, N. M. Robinson, & S. M. Moon (Eds.), *The social and emotional development of gifted children: What do we know?* (pp. 267–289). Waco, TX: Prufrock Press.

Rogers, K. B. (1993). Grouping the gifted and talented: Questions and answers. *Roeper Review, 24,* 103–107.

Rogers, K. B. (2002). *Re-forming gifted education.* Scottsdale, AZ: Great Potential Press.

Schunk, D. (1987). Peer models and children's behavioral change. *Review of Educational Research, 57,* 149–174. doi:10.3102/00346543057002149

Schroth, S. T. (2007). Levels of service. In C. M. Callahan & J. A. Plucker (Eds.), *Critical issues and practices in gifted education* (pp. 281–294). Waco, TX: Prufrock Press.

Siegle, D., Puryear, J. S., Estepar-Garcia, W., Callahan, C. M., Gubbins, E. J., McCoach, D. B., & Amspaugh, C. M. (2017, April). *Gifted education structures in elementary schools and their connections to program focus.* Paper presented at the annual meeting of the American Educational Research Association, San Antonio, TX.

Slavin, R. E. (1987). Ability grouping and student achievement in elementary schools: A best-evidence synthesis. *Review of Educational Research, 57,* 293–336. doi:10.3102/00346543057003293

Slavin, R. E. (1988). Synthesis of research on grouping in elementary and secondary schools. *Educational Leadership, 46,* 67–77.

Slavin, R. E. (1990). Achievement effects of ability grouping in secondary schools: A best-evidence synthesis. *Review of Educational Research, 60,* 471–499. doi:10.3102/00346543060003471

Slavin, R. E. (1993). Ability grouping in the middle grades: Achievement effects and alternatives. *The Elementary School Journal, 93,* 535–552.

Sorensen, A., & Hallinan, M. (1986). Effects of ability grouping on growth in academic achievement. *American Educational Research Journal, 23,* 519–542. doi:10.3102/00028312023004519

Sousa, D. A. (1998). Is the fuss about brain research justified? *Education Week, 18*(16), 35–52.

Tieso, C. L. (2003). Ability grouping is not just tracking anymore. *Roeper Review, 26,* 29–36. doi:10.1080/02783190309554236

Tieso, C. L. (2005). The effects of grouping practices and curricular adjustments on achievement. *Journal for the Education of the Gifted, 29,* 60–89. doi: 10.1177/016235320502900104

Tomlinson, C. A. (2014). *Differentiated classroom: Responding to the needs of all learners.* Alexandria, VA: ASCD.

Tomlinson, C. A., & Callahan, C. M. (1992). Contributions of gifted education to general education in a time of change. *Gifted Child Quarterly, 36,* 183–189. doi:10.1177/001698629203600403

United States Department of Education. (1993). *National excellence: A case for developing America's talent.* Washington, DC: United States Government Printing Office.

U.S. Office of Civil Rights. (2002). *2002 elementary and secondary civil rights compliance report. National and state projections.* Washington, DC: U.S. Department of Education, Office of Civil Rights.

VanTassel-Baska, J., & Stambaugh, T. (2005). Challenges and possibilities for serving gifted learners in the regular classroom. *Theory Into Practice, 44,* 211–217. doi:10.1207/s15430421tip4403 5

Westberg, K., & Daoust, M. E. (2004). *The results of the replication of the classroom practices survey replication in two states.* Storrs: University of Connecticut, The National Research Center on the Gifted and Talented.

Worrell. F. C. (2007). Identifying and including low-income learners in programs for the gifted and talented: Multiple complexities. In J. VanTassel-Baska & T. Stambaugh (Eds.), *Overlooked gems: A national perspective on low-income promising learners* (pp. 47–51). Washington, DC: National Association for Gifted Children.

Worrell, F. (2009). Myth 4: A single test score or indicator tells us all we need to know about giftedness. *Gifted Child Quarterly*, *53,* 242–244. doi:10.1177/0016986209346828

Wu, J., & Gentry, M. (2017). *NAEP Excellence gap scores among ethnic groups including Native American youth.* Manuscript in preparation.

Wyner, J. S., Bridgeland, J. M., & Dilulio, J. J., Jr. (2009). *Achievement trap: How America is failing millions of high-achieving students from low-income families* (Rev. ed.). Lansdowne, VA: Jack Kent Cooke Foundation Civic Enterprises.

Yoon, S., & Gentry, M. (2009). Racial and ethnic representation in gifted programs: Current status of and implications for gifted Asian American students. *Gifted Child Quarterly, 53,* 121–136. doi:10.1177/0016986208330564

CHAPTER 5

The Autonomous Learner Model

HONORING AND NURTURING THE WHOLE GIFTED CHILD

George T. Betts, Robin J. Carey, and Blanche M. Kapushion

INTRODUCTION

During the 1970s many high schools in the United States were finding that traditional methods of curriculum and instruction were not sufficient. For example, Arvada West High School, in Colorado's Jefferson County Public Schools, was determined to provide alternative learning environments for students. At first this was not seen as a movement for gifted students, but rather an option for all students whose cognitive, emotional, and social needs were not being met. "A major question that emerged was, 'Are the students failing?' or 'Is the system failing the students?'" (Betts & Kercher, 2009, p. 51). The principal and teachers provided a school climate that welcomed formal and informal forums for discussion about change. When change occurs, it is necessary that students should be part of the process and part of the plan. "The gifted are but one category of students that are capable of participating in the development of their own education" (Betts, 1986, p. 33).

These informal discussions paved the way to the more organized discussions and seminars that were the first steps toward developing what is known today as the "Autonomous Learner Model." It was immediately decided, by the *learners,* that this approach would become a program for the gifted and talented. Why? In the process of research, focus groups, informal discussions, and review of research, presentations to the faculty indicated that one group of students that was being ignored in the school system was the gifted.

Yes, there were other groups of students who also needed assistance and change, but for a group of 10 teachers at this high school, the gifted were the ones they wanted to serve. To begin with, there was no gifted education model at the school. It would be several years before new approaches and models would be completely developed. The school was dedicated to meeting all students' needs and dedicated to the process of change. The change that did happen at Arvada West impacted not only the gifted and talented, but also vocational students, potential dropouts, bored and withdrawn students, and students that just basically did not fit in at the school. School should be a place that lets you be, lets you experience, and allows you input into your education!

The Autonomous Learner Model incorporates the needs of the whole gifted child, looking at giftedness and potential. This model moves beyond the label of "gifted and talented" to understanding giftedness as an integral part of who the learner truly is. Let's look at how we describe and define the essence of "autonomous learners":

> Autonomous learners perceive learning and living as two main components of their ongoing development of potential in the cognitive, emotional, social and physical domains. Their motivation comes from within, they internalize skills, and passion learning is their driving force. Autonomous learners are never satisfied, for they perceive their needs for a nourishing life, as well as the greater needs of society. (Betts, Carey, & Kapushion, 2017, p. 2)

Figure 5.1 shows the five dimensions of the model: Orientation, Individual Development, Enrichment, Seminars, and In-Depth Study along the perimeter. At the center lie the four domains at the heart of the model: Emotional, Social, Intellectual/Cognitive, and Physical (Health). A brief description of the model's five dimensions and four domains follows. These dimensions will be discussed in detail in the application section of this chapter.

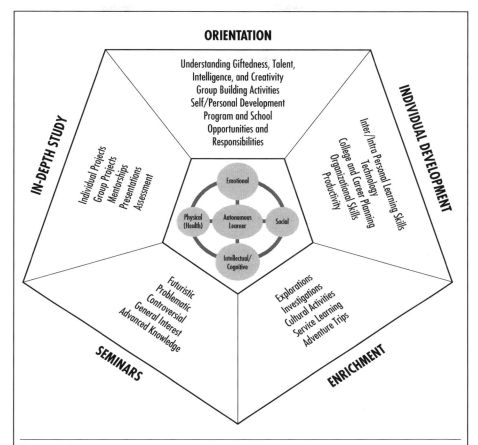

Figure 5.1. Autonomous Learner Model. From *Autonomous Learner Model Resource Book* (p. 2), by G. T. Betts, R. J. Carey, and B. M. Kapushion, 2017, Waco, TX: Prufrock Press. Copyright 2017 by Prufrock Press. Reprinted with permission.

THE FIVE DIMENSIONS OF THE AUTONOMOUS LEARNER MODEL

The Autonomous Learner Model (ALM) for the Gifted and Talented was developed specifically to meet the diversified cognitive, emotional, and social needs of learners. The model is currently implemented at all grade levels in many diversified settings with the gifted and talented. Many learners do not remain in grade-level courses but pursue upper level courses, mentorships, in-depth studies, university courses, and opportunities to work with entrepreneurs. The Autonomous Learner Model for the Gifted and Talented is the result of observing and focusing on the problem of the lack of a challenging and motivating curriculum and the absence of a "place to belong" for many gifted students. "The goal of the model is to facilitate the growth of the students as independent, self-directed learners, with the development of the skills, concepts and positive attitudes within the cognitive, emotional and social domains" (Betts, 1986, p. 34).

All students begin with Orientation, most students continue on to Individual Development, while other students participate in activities in Enrichment, Seminars, or In-Depth Studies. The ALM is not a sequential model built on stages; rather, it is responsive to the needs and readiness of each individual student.

Dimension One: Orientation

The *Orientation Dimension* of the ALM provides learners, teachers, administrators, and parents the opportunity to develop a foundation of the concepts of giftedness, talent, intelligence, creativity, and the development of potential. Learners discover more about themselves, their abilities, and what the ALM has to offer. Activities are presented to give learners an opportunity to work together as a group, to learn more about group process and interaction, and to learn more about the other people in the program.

As learners engage in the Orientation Dimension of the ALM, they are beginning to understand their giftedness, talents, potential, and cognitive intelligence, as well as their emotional intelligence. The understanding of self is obtained through a variety of individual and group activities that enhance the formal and informal settings in the learners' lives. The Orientation Dimension is foundational and should not be ignored or skimmed over. One of the first foundational activities of Orientation is the Pre/Post Knowledge Assessment. Personal growth and data supporting change over time are concepts embedded in the ALM. Creating a personal action plan for academic and affective growth is incorporated in most Orientation activities. Many teachers at the elementary level find it easy to integrate activities from the Orientation Dimension in class meetings, opening or closing activities, or during brain breaks. As learners engage in the Orientation Dimension at the middle or high school level, they become the leaders or mentors for other learners in their grade level, or learners who are new to the ALM as they begin their journey to autonomy. A middle school gifted education center teacher explained it this way: "I appreciate the fact that the elementary level GT feeder school implements the ALM. The differences I see in the GT students as they enter middle school are vastly different. They are confident, self-assured, and ready to tell me what they need from me! I can tell the students have engaged in the first three ALM dimensions!" Over time, we have conjectured that when students engage in the ALM as youngsters, they are better prepared and more resilient when they transition into the next levels of their educational journey.

Dimension Two: Individual Development

The *Individual Development Dimension* of the model provides learners with the opportunity to develop the cognitive, emotional, social, and physical skills, concepts, and attitudes necessary for lifelong learning. In other words, learners are preparing to become autonomous in their learning.

Areas within the dimension include opportunities for the inter-/intrapersonal development of learners, the appropriate learning skills for lifelong learning, and the area of technology. The learners also participate in college and career planning, the development of organizational skills, and the acquisition of productivity skills. Formal and informal activities are essential for the teaching of the skills, concepts, and attitudes for lifelong learning.

Dimension Three: Enrichment

The *Enrichment Dimension* of the ALM is developed to provide learners with opportunities to explore content and curriculum that is usually not part of the prescribed school curriculum. The highest level of learning is manifested when learners have the freedom to select and pursue content or curriculum in their own style. Curriculum differentiation by the learners begins with Explorations, where the goal is to "discover" what is out there. Students become explorers and find new and unique knowledge in a variety of methods. The second type of learner differentiation is Investigations. These are more in-depth than Explorations and require the learners to design, implement, complete, and present a project with a product. Learners take part in Cultural Activities in the community, and Service Learning is an essential component of this dimension.

When learners engage in the Enrichment Dimension, they have explored their giftedness through the Orientation Dimension and have a foundational understanding of who they are as learners through activities in the Individual Development Dimension. Within the Enrichment Dimension, teachers transition into the role of facilitators of learning, and students transition into learners, as illustrated in Table 5.1.

Dimension Four: Seminar

The *Seminar Dimension* of the model is designed to give learners, in groups of three to five, opportunities to research a topic, present it as a Seminar to the rest of the class and other interested people, and assess it by criteria selected and developed by the learners. A Seminar is essential because it allows each student to move from the role of student to that of learner. If students are to truly become learners, they must experience guided independent learning by developing a Seminar in a structure that promotes new knowledge.

TABLE 5.1
Teacher/Facilitator; Student/Learner

Teacher/Student (Orientation Dimension)	Student/Teacher (Individual Development Dimension)	
	Learner/Facilitator (Enrichment Dimension)	Learner/Facilitator (Seminar Dimension) (In-Depth Study Dimension)
• Curriculum designed by the teacher • ALM is taught to students • Learner begins to develop Personal Growth Plans with input from the teacher	• Learner develops Personalized Learning Plan with input from facilitator • Learner skill development is enhanced with input from facilitator • Learner presents Personalized Learning Plan to develop skills, concepts, and attitudes • Learner engages in Explorations and Investigations	• Learner assesses, modifies, and implements Personalized Learning Plan with emphasis on demonstration of learning • Learner designs and completes a culminating demonstration of learning (i.e., capstone project) and presents to authentic audience • Learner engages in assessment and self-reflection of the learning experience

As learners engage in the Seminar Dimension, they are not only diving into an area that is of interest to the members of the group, they are also engaging in preparation for productively and collaboratively engaging in the workforce:

> Employers are looking for candidates that on their own are able to identify a driving question, determine a team they need to help answer that question, able to effectively work with that team, execute and manage the project—through multiple iterations with lots of feedback—and then reflect and evaluate their work. (Vander Ark & Liebtag, 2016, para. 7)

Typically, Seminars are completed by collaborative groups with a common passion or interest. Learners experience the power of teamwork, interconnected collaboration, cognitive struggle, compromise, and sense of completion. Seminars engage learners in critical, strategic, and creative thinking. Within the ALM, the Seminar Dimension is divided into four different categories:

➢ Problematic
➢ Controversial
➢ General Interest
➢ Advanced Knowledge

In the Seminar Dimension, specific activities have been created to support the facilitator and the learners as they research and prepare for the Seminar experience. The defined support activities include:

➢ defining the four categories,
➢ brainstorming and selecting a topic within the categories,
➢ steps and procedures in defining the Seminar,
➢ planning documents,
➢ self- and group evaluation tools and rubrics, and
➢ reflective activity that helps the learners take a stand in the seminar.

Dimension Five: In-Depth Study

The *In-Depth Study Dimension* of the ALM empowers learners to pursue long-term in-depth studies in their area(s) of passion. Learners determine what and how they will learn, how it will be presented, and what facilitation will be necessary by the teacher and mentor. These plans are then implemented and completed by the learners, with presentations being made at appropriate times until the completion of the project. Final presentations and assessments are given to all who are involved and interested.

As learners and facilitators engage in the five dimensions of the model, they are simultaneously discovering and experiencing the domains, too. The dimensions and domains are interconnected, just as in our daily life experiences, knowledge, skills, concepts, and ideas are born out of our emotional, social, intellectual/cognitive, and physical (health) being.

One of the goals of the ALM is for learners to attain skills, attitudes, and the desire to be lifelong learners so that the learning will add to new experiences in their lives. In-Depth Studies tend to be lifelong passions. Sometimes these passions are developed through the Exploration and Investigation process carried forward from the Enrichment Dimension, sometimes they are passions from environmental or familial interests or experiences. Learners might dive into an In-Depth Study and carry on the research for 1 or 2 years and feel satisfied with what they have experienced after they have shared their research, engaged in evaluation, and reflected upon the processes. Some learners will dive in, research, create, present, evaluate, and reflect and then after a long period of time, let the study go for awhile before coming back to the topic to continue on the next phase of the study.

As learners engage in the In-Depth Study process, they are supported through several resources, including:

➣ proposal process for a topic with an individual or group,
➣ planning process for the research,
➣ self- and group evaluation forms and rubrics, and
➣ authentic audience evaluation forms.

The richness of an In-Depth Study is that it is learner-driven through a proposal process, and the facilitator coaches the learner while the research is conducted. Depending on the topic of study, career or business mentors may be included so that true hands-on and experiential learning through an apprenticeship is experienced as a key component. Finding and including a mentor involves greater commitment, proposal, and follow through on the part of the learner. The In-Depth Study is really passionate learning, and the learners live for this! When the study topic is chosen and approved, and learners have completed required assignments, they can go to this passion-learning project and engage in the In-Depth Study.

THE FOUR DOMAINS OF THE AUTONOMOUS LEARNER

In the formal school setting, teachers focus on the intellectual/cognitive domain of learning, but if we are looking at the whole child, it is necessary to tend

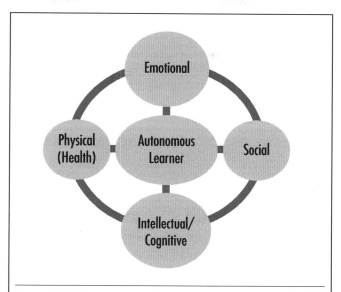

Figure 5.2. Autonomous Learner Model domains. From *Autonomous Learner Model Resource Book* (p. 12), by G. T. Betts, R. J. Carey, and B. M. Kapushion, 2017, Waco, TX: Prufrock Press. Copyright 2017 by Prufrock Press. Reprinted with permission.

to the emotional, social, intellectual/cognitive, and physical (health) domains of learning. If one or more of the domains are not addressed, learners may miss the opportunity to find balance and cope in today's world.

The four domains of the Autonomous Learner Model (Figure 5.2) include emotional, social, intellectual/cognitive, and physical (health). These domains are not separate; rather, they are fluid and interact with each other, influencing learner development. Betts, Carey, and Kapushion (2017) defined the four domains as:

- ➤ *Emotional Domain*: Experiencing the emotions and feelings of everyday living and the awareness of the emotions on self and others.
- ➤ *Social Domain*: Awareness of how one interacts or behaves with others and the effect of the interactions on self and others.
- ➤ *Intellectual/Cognitive Domain*: Ability to obtain or create new knowledge through critical thinking, problem solving, application, and synthesis.
- ➤ *Physical (Health) Domain*: Ability to understand and practice appropriate habits that support positive physical, mental, social, and emotional development through nutrition and movement. (p. 12)

The integration of the four domains within the five dimensions of the ALM enhances the growth and development of the learners who then become self-directed and autonomous. For example, in the activity Retreat in the Orientation dimension, the learners experience not only the group building area of the dimension, but also tap into the social, emotional, intellectual/cognitive, and physical (health) domains through various activities conducted at the retreat. Multiple opportunities are included for the learners to experience all four of the domains through other activities such as Secret Friends, Talent Show, Buddy Walks, and Pass the Gavel (Betts et al., 2017).

A strong foundation is necessary to begin the journey to becoming a life-long learner. The ALM Process Standards shown in Table 5.2 include the elements essential in providing this foundation. The process standards encompass the "concepts, skills, attitudes, and behaviors necessary for the fully functioning autonomous learner" (Betts et al., 2017, p. 15). These standards, first developed by learners and teachers, have and will continue to evolve and change over time as our learners, educational settings, and society do the same.

HOW ARE AUTONOMOUS LEARNERS DEVELOPED?

One incredible aspect of the Autonomous Learner Model is the flexibility in its usage. It can be implemented grades K–12, in all content areas, in gifted education programs and programming, as well as in mixed-ability classrooms. As students develop a foundation through activities in the Orientation and Individual Development Dimensions of the model, they are able to fully take charge of their learning and transition from *students* to *learners*. As experienced in the "Introductory Activity," teachers will learn to shift from *leading*, to the role of *facilitating*, providing students with the autonomy to transition to *learners* (Figure 5.3).

The *Autonomous Learner Model Resource Book* (Betts et al., 2017) includes more than 40 activities to solidify this shift from teachers to facilitators, and students to learners, such as:

➢ Learner's Needs Assessment
➢ "I Am" Poems
➢ Individual Explorations
➢ Group Explorations
➢ Night of the Notables
➢ Learner-Designed Adventure Trip

This list is a small sample of the activities designed to strengthen facilitation and learning.

TABLE 5.2

ALM Process Standards

Dimension	Process Standards
Orientation	Autonomous learners will be able to: • comprehend their own abilities in relationship to self, society, and global needs; • develop more positive self-concepts and self-esteem (development of the whole self); and • become responsible, creative, independent, lifelong learners.
Individual Development	Autonomous learners will be able to: • comprehend their own abilities in relationship to self, society, and global needs; • develop more positive self-concepts and self-esteem (development of the whole self); • develop skills to interact effectively with peers, siblings, parents, and other adults; • develop critical and creative thinking skills; • develop decision-making and problem-solving skills; • integrate activities that facilitate responsibility for own learning in and out of the school setting; and • become responsible, creative, independent, lifelong learners.
Enrichment	Autonomous learners will be able to: • develop skills to interact effectively with peers, siblings, parents, and other adults; • increase knowledge in a variety of areas; • develop critical and creative thinking skills; • develop decision-making and problem-solving skills; • integrate activities that facilitate responsibility for own learning in and out of the school setting; • discover and develop individual passion area(s) of learning; and • become responsible, creative, independent, lifelong learners.
Seminars	Autonomous learners will be able to: • develop critical and creative thinking skills; • develop decision-making and problem-solving skills; • integrate activities that facilitate responsibility for own learning in and out of the school setting; • discover and develop individual passion area(s) of learning; and • become responsible, creative, independent, lifelong learners.
In-Depth Study	Autonomous learners will be able to: • develop critical and creative thinking skills; • develop decision-making and problem-solving skills; • integrate activities that facilitate responsibility for own learning in and out of the school setting; • discover and develop individual passion area(s) of learning; and • become responsible, creative, independent, lifelong learners.

Note. From *Autonomous Learner Model Resource Book* (p. 20), by G. T. Betts, R. J. Carey, and B. M. Kapushion, 2017, Waco, TX: Prufrock Press. Copyright 2017 by Prufrock Press. Reprinted with permission.

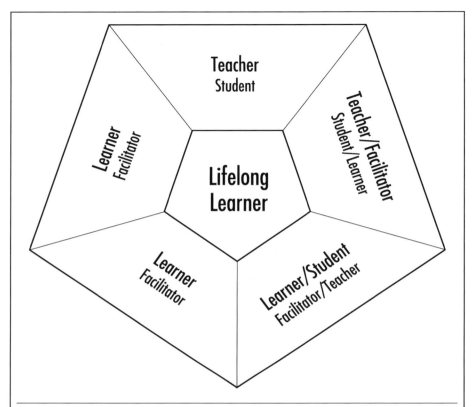

Figure 5.3. From *Autonomous Learner Model Resource Book* (p. 7), by G. T. Betts, R. J. Carey, and B. M. Kapushion, 2017, Waco, TX: Prufrock Press. Copyright 2017 by Prufrock Press. Reprinted with permission.

It is important to emphasize that not all learners are the same, nor are all identified gifted learners the same. Each individual learner has strengths, preferences, and instructional needs. Within the ALM the understanding of these differences can be found in *The Profiles of the Gifted* by Betts and Neihart (1988) and the *Revised Profiles of the Gifted* (Betts & Neihart, 2010). The six types of gifted learners are shown in Table 5.3.

The ALM includes differentiation, not only by the teachers, but by *the learners* as well. The highest level of learning is passion-based, *learner-differentiated* learning, both in a formal school setting and also out of a formal school setting—informal, life settings that include the home and community. Informal learning is more important than formal learning because the learner goes beyond the classroom, asks more questions, seeks new knowledge, and creates his or her own self-directed projects, which then influences how he or she lives his or her life. In an environment where the ALM is in place, learners are in charge of their educational pathways. They are able to truly have learner-based curriculum, instruction, and

TABLE 5.3
Profiles of the Gifted (Betts & Neihart, 1988; Betts & Neihart, 2010)

Profile	Attributes
The Successful	Complacent learners who tend to do well in the current structures of the academic system
The Creative	Highly creative learners who are easily bored and become frustrated with the structures of a traditional school setting
The Underground	Learners who desire to belong socially and may see some of their academic achievements as a betrayal of the social group; may dumb down or hide their abilities, gifts, and talents
The At-Risk	Learners who present as resentful, angry, or depressed and may connect with an antisocial subgroup
The Twice- or Multi-Exceptional	Learners who have identified area(s) of strength, as well as a learning disability or weakness that is documented in an IEP or 504 Plan
The Autonomous Learner	Self-confident, self-accepting, and intrinsically motivated learners who may not view academics as their highest priority

assessment that is personalized to their needs, interests, and passions. This has been the case through the implementation of the ALM in a variety of settings and at all grade levels in the United States and internationally since 1976.

How do we learn to develop our gifts and talents? Today we spend most of our time as educators and researchers in the development of learning in school without including learning outside of the school, in the home and community. It is essential to realize that formal learning usually occurs at school, but informal learning takes place outside of school. As a teacher who has implemented the model for a number of years indicated, "The ALM creates the independent learner who is responsible, focused, and driven to achieve and be successful. The ultimate goal of the ALM is that the students become the learners on their own, and they create their own path through exploration of self."

Besides learning, educators and parents must include the concept of living. How can we separate learning and living? Is there one right pathway? Several? Besides learning how to develop gifts and talents, it is essential to discover and develop that which is within, the "giftedness" of the child. For some, this is still potential, while for others giftedness provides daily opportunities to comprehend, incorporate, and develop their own form of learning and living.

Several different approaches may be discovered and used by the learner. Some people learn early on to be independent. They work best if others leave them alone to develop their ideas and create their own path. Others have a need to work alone but sometimes they seek out two to three people who are like themselves.

They may learn in the same manner and/or share the same interests and passions. They discover the art of learning independently, how to learn collaboratively, and how to become productive producers of knowledge. Besides learning, they strive to have a fulfilling life through developing a healthy, functioning lifestyle that includes accepting self and others; finding others with the same values, interests, and passions; and going beyond what others expect of them to create a positive, nourishing world.

Others are still functioning as students and don't comprehend the roles of the learner. They are dependent on the teacher, but the teacher doesn't have all of the answers—or will not give the answers. The students become frustrated, and without more guidance from the teacher, will not move in the direction of autonomy. Until teachers understand the role of being facilitators of learning, students will not move toward becoming learners and they may not discover the empowerment of autonomous learning.

Another group of individuals that are emerging very quickly in our schools are entrepreneurs. Unless we, as teachers, know the autonomous learner process, we will continue to lag behind them. Entrepreneurs need more freedom to try to experiment, fail, and succeed. The most important thing a teacher can do is to watch how the students learn, how they find resources, how they discover problems, and how they are able to solve them. Only through watching this unique approach will teachers truly be able to facilitate growth, understand what it means to facilitate learning, and get out of students' way.

Students have the potential to become learners! So, no, please don't rescue them; support them, and let them find their own paths of learning. When students experience cognitive struggle, they become learners and begin to make sense of autonomous learning. With understanding and enthusiasm, they engage in the learning process and experience the joy of lifelong learning.

The emphasis in the ALM is more on what the learner can "become" rather than a focus on identifying or labeling the learner. The autonomous learner has the potential to "be." According to Heather Gingerich, Program Coordinator for College Spark Washington, entities involved in college and career readiness are "more interested in how effective instructional strategies help students become 'learners' in ways that extend beyond any one particular class or point in time" (as cited in Vander Ark & Ryerse, 2017). This is exactly what participants in the ALM are engaged in through exploration, involvement, interests, and passions that encompass life beyond the four walls of school.

APPLYING THE AUTONOMOUS LEARNER MODEL

Within each dimension and domain of the Autonomous Learner Model, learners participate in a variety of activities designed to address essential questions that support them on the journey to becoming independent, self-directed, lifelong learners. All of the activities within the ALM are designed to increase the affective, as well as the cognitive, growth and development of the learners. In our work with teachers and learners over time, many have shared the impact of the model on their lives. As one teacher pointed out,

> The social-emotional awareness of the gifted child is so intense and so great—it (the ALM) allows them to breathe and to be calm while they allow the weight of the world to drift away. It gives them a time to focus on the present and to express their emotions while trusting that no judgment will occur. It is a very raw experience to have at such a young age of 6 or 7, and then allows them to grow emotionally, cognitively, and as a whole child who is more willing to open up and share their gifts with the world.

In the first two dimensions of the ALM, the majority of activities are developed by teachers. By the third, fourth, and fifth dimensions, the learners develop, participate in, and assess the activities. By now, activities are not developed for a large group, but by individuals and small groups, according to the needs, abilities, skills, and passions of the learners.

The implementation and integration of the ALM can be done in a variety of ways depending on the school setting (i.e., urban, suburban, or rural), structure, schedule, or level. One example of implementation, and probably the most common, is a typical general education classroom with gifted and talented learners included in the composition of the class. In this situation, the ALM is integrated into 10% of the daily schedule, and the Orientation and Individual Development Dimensions are the focus. In this setting, Orientation activities such as "Temperature Reading" or "Creative Quotes" can be integrated into daily class meetings at the beginning or end of the day. Activities like the "Lifelong Notebook" can be easily integrated into learning centers. One classroom teacher shared,

> I believe the ALM helps to develop the student's minds to grow and self-reflect on their creative ideas and learning. The ALM reminds each child they can decipher how they learn, what their

learning experience is, and how far beyond the realm of thinking and doing is within their control.

As the learners gain self-direction and self-confidence in their learning potential and passion, the Enrichment Dimension can be introduced within specific content such as science and social studies. When, as the teacher previously stated, learners begin to "decipher how they learn," they can then advocate for their exploration and investigation topics, complete their learning contracts, and articulate their desired learning outcomes, which tend to be far more complex and in depth than the grade-level standards they are sometimes held accountable for demonstrating.

Another setting might be a self-contained gifted classroom. In this setting, all of the above-mentioned implementation ideas can be employed, but with greater depth and complexity or advanced pace, depending on the learners. In self-contained gifted learner classrooms, standards and benchmarks are covered at a more rapid pace, providing the teacher/facilitator with an opportunity to integrate and implement the ALM for 20%–25% of the scheduled day. A gifted education self-contained classroom teacher shared,

> I am a second-grade gifted and talented educator, so I use a lot of the primary (ALM) resources to support my gifted students. In the classroom, as we are building community, writing personal narratives, we use "I AM" poems to support who we are and who we want to share with the world. When the gifted children talk about feelings and go more in-depth within their creative minds, they develop the whole child and discover *who* they are!

For gifted learners, the development of the affective domains is critical. When they "discover who they are" as learners and grow to self-acceptance and the acceptance of others, the cognitive domain is more open to learn new content, create new knowledge, reason with ease, and problem solve at higher, more complex levels.

Orientation

In the fall of each school year, learners and facilitators from middle and high school levels engage in an activity called Retreat. These retreats have taken place in Arizona, Colorado, Wyoming, New Mexico, Iowa, Illinois, Texas, and in several other countries. Retreats have been experienced in many locations from inner-city Chicago to farms and retreat centers in Iowa and Colorado. Overnight retreats have also taken place in school gymnasiums. Mary Irvine from the University of Waikato in New Zealand talks about the power of ALM retreats in gifted programming. She indicates, "Time away from the school environment with like-minded peers offers an opportunity for students with special abilities to develop positive self-concepts and self esteem. It allows for development in understanding what it means to have special gifts and talents, and the responsibilities associated with these gifts and talents" (Irvine, n.d.). As she noted, the learning retreat has become an important part of gifted programming in the Waikato region.

At the Wheat Ridge High School GT Center program in Wheat Ridge, CO, upperclassmen take responsibility for the planning of the Retreat. Each year the retreat is held in the mountains of Colorado at the YMCA of the Rockies camp in Estes Park. The planning committee, consisting only of learners, is in charge of determining a theme for the weekend, delegating the planning of the agenda, and the activities that will fill the agenda. Activities may include:

- Communication Center
- Learner-directed and leaner-created activities like:
  - Murder mystery theater
  - Night hike
  - Bonfire with songs, stories, and reflection

- Buddy Walks each morning for small-group reflection and processing
- Pass the Gavel or Friendship Circle—end of retreat reflection

What is the role of the facilitator in the Retreat activity, you might ask? The facilitators oversee the planning process, drive the cars, and assure group safety. The rest is the responsibility of the learners, and they can be successful!

Again, we believe the Orientation Dimension is foundational in establishing the lifelong ALM journey. It is the discovery and acceptance of self and others that connects the present to the future and all the possibilities yet to come.

Individual Development

The Individual Development Dimension of the ALM is dynamic. As students engage in Individual Development they explore their:

- inter-/intrapersonal self,
- learning skills,
- use of ever-evolving technology,
- college and career planning, and
- organizational skills and strategies.

When students begin to discover who they are, why they are, and what they can become, a sense of individuality and potential evolves. Students begin this dimension as *students* and leave this dimension as *learners*. Teachers facilitate the students in this journey of self-advocacy and discovery. A community begins to form. A sense of empowerment in both the academic and affective realms permeates the learning environment. A few of the activities that support the transition include:

➢ Journey Into Self: An Experience in Personal Growth
➢ Personalized Learner Plan
➢ Decision Making
➢ Keeping Up-to-Date! (with technology)
➢ College and Career Planning: A Choice for the Future
➢ Life Management Wheel

As students engage in the activities and share what they discover about themselves, confidence and self-assurance begins to solidify. Members of the learning community, adults and students alike, begin to connect with each other as they discover common interests, passions, and ideas.

When teachers guide the students through the Individual Development Dimension, they begin to see who is gaining the self-confidence and assurance to transition into the role of learner. The transition from student to learner varies for each individual. Some students make this personal discovery more quickly than others. The teacher has to become flexible, as some students move into this realm more readily, while others need more time. It is at this point that the classroom teacher might take on two roles: the teacher who continues to instruct some students on their journey to becoming a learner, and the facilitator who is guiding some learners on their continued pathway to autonomy. The possibilities are endless and exciting for everyone.

Enrichment

An activity that can be completed within this dimension at any level or in any setting, including with adult learners, is the First Exploration. This activity provides learners a personal experience in what others in their class like to do outside of the school setting that may not emerge from formal academic activities, supporting the emotional and social domains. Explorations, as a general rule, should be frequent, ungraded, and shared with others, including a reflection on what was learned and if further research will be conducted or the topic will be shelved. Support materials to assist learners and facilitators in this process include:

➢ Individual Exploration planning forms
➢ Group Exploration planning forms

Facilitators are encouraged and expected to engage in the exploration process, sharing and reflecting to both build and increase their knowledge base, but to also model the process of lifelong learning. Explorations can be shared during class meetings or at the opening or closing activities of each day. When learners report on their exploration, they share verbally, and should include an artifact to support the learning. The sharing should take 3–5 minutes per student and include the title of the topic, what was learned, and whether further exploration will take place. One young man shared, "For every exploration and investigation we do, it is always interesting to me. I am able to see the big picture. I can see other's ideas . . . every exploration that I have seen is good, I learn and can make connections."

When teachers take the role of facilitator and students engage in content as learners, the world of knowledge expands to unlimited possibilities. As previously shared, learning becomes bigger, broader, meaningful, and connected for all. Another learner shared her excitement about the opportunity to engage in explorations for a personal reason. She said, "I want to do an exploration on fibromyalgia because my mom has it and I need to gain a better understanding of what we will have to do to support her and what we will have to do to change the way we function as a family." Learning new knowledge in a formal setting to impact the informal setting is deeply connected learning and the motivation, in this case, comes from within the learner and is personal and inspirational. Because of the personal connection to the topic, this learner also indicated a desire to take the topic of fibromyalgia into an investigation. Imagine how deeply the learner will take this study, how motivated she is to research, read, comprehend, and share, not only with her classmates, but also with her family.

Investigations are the second level of study in the Enrichment Dimension. The learners typically engage in an Investigation for a minimum of one month and go deeper into the topic until they have reached a level of understanding that meets their needs. When a learner invests this amount of time and effort, it is important to present to an authentic audience a formal or structured presentation of the new knowledge. If the topic continues to be of interest and there is still motivation, the investigation can then become an In-Depth Study, the highest level of learning within the ALM.

Within the Enrichment Dimension, when teachers have transitioned into facilitators and students have become learners, they will not only engage in explorations, investigations, and in-depth studies, but also various Cultural Activities, Service Learning projects, and Adventure Trips. All of these opportunities can be connected to formal and informal settings, enhancing the learner's journey to discovery, authentic engagement, connections to community, and autonomy. The content knowledge, skills, new knowledge, and evaluative processes that are experienced within the Enrichment Dimension are high level in their depth, complexity, and engagement. Imagine the possibilities and learning produced within this dimension. The passion for learning has been ignited!

Seminars

One example of a Seminar topic selection process that occurred organically was the need to come together to advocate for a school's gifted and talented program. A group of learners decided this was a controversial issue that needed to be addressed in a short time frame with a specific outcome. The learners approached their facilitators and shared their desire to advocate for their program in front of their principal and the Board of Education. The learners and facilitators of the GT program had learned of the school district's proposal to close their program, so they knew that they needed to act quickly to do their research, decide who was going to write letters, who was going to speak to the principal, who was going to speak at public forums, and who was going to speak in front of the Board of Education. This Seminar group needed to be identified as a community in solidarity with purpose, so they designed a T-shirt to wear when they spoke to the principal and Board of Education. The group presented its argument and research to its class, a small group of parents, its administrative team, and the Board of Education. (It is important that the Seminar be presented to multiple authentic audiences.) As a result of the group's Seminar preparation, participation, and presentations, the Board of Education agreed to support the GT Center program for another school year.

In talking with the learners who were engaged in this specific Seminar process, they agreed that when this particular controversial and authentic topic arose, their foundational experiences within the ALM prepared them to come together as a group and collaborate quickly, with focus and purpose. They created and submitted a proposal that identified the topic and need, as well as the desired outcome for which they were advocating. One learner, who spoke in front of the Board of Education as well as more than 300 members of the audience, shared that he was most proud of his ability to stand up and advocate for *his* GT program (Schmike, 2017). This student's sense of self-confidence has been a journey of self-actualization, which in turn has led him to become autonomous. He openly shared that he has ADHD, and sufferers from anxiety and depression. The inner strength and confidence that this student found within himself was important to him "because I have 'a family' of people like me, who understand me . . . and when I am in the ALM (class) I can figure out ways to counteract and balance the effects with these illnesses . . . I can adapt to new situations, the ALM helps me with relationships, to manage stress and helps me find new ways to do new things."

When learners engage in the Seminar Dimension of the ALM, they learn key skills, clarify attitudes and beliefs, and learn to advocate proactively and creatively for what they believe. As indicated previously, 21st-century employers are keen on these skills, attitudes, and beliefs for the current postsecondary workforce. Our evolving and complex society needs autonomous learners who are creative problem solvers and people who can create new knowledge and perspectives.

In-Depth Study

An example of an In-Depth Study from one learner stemmed from a genealogy project. During the prior school year, the facilitator introduced a genealogy project as an Exploration option. Some learners chose to engage in this Exploration option at a basic level, completing only the required components. Some learners completed the basic components and then decided to go further in their research and engage in an Investigation of deeper genealogy topics and research related to their family. One learner, a senior, wanted to complete the Exploration components and chose to go further into the Investigation phase, and is now in the In-Depth Study phase.

This senior's journey in this lifelong project had to do with researching his father and his paternal lineage. He shared that during the Exploration phase of the genealogy project he learned about his maternal heritage and was excited to learn more about his mother and grandmother; however, he became curious about his father, whom he did not know well and vaguely remembered. During the Investigation phase of his genealogy research, he investigated his paternal lineage. He learned that his father made some bad choices, was incarcerated for a while, and eventually died of a drug overdose. In his research, this learner obtained arrest, medical, and prison records pertinent to his father. He shared that without his facilitators' help and support it would have been difficult for him to continue. His genealogy interests have turned into an In-Depth Study. He has chosen to connect with family members who were disconnected in the past due to the difficult family circumstances. This learner shared that because of this study, he has grown to be more empathetic and has connected with his mother on a more compassionate level. He said he has learned from the past mistakes of his father and become a better adult. The student said this study has changed him, and he will put it aside for now due to the intensity and difficult emotional toll, but he knows this topic will be a lifelong passion for him.

Passion learning is the highest form of learning, and contributes to healthy, lifelong habits and attitudes. As the ALM continues to be implemented and experienced in schools, it is clear that "learners, given the opportunity, will discover the skills, concepts, attitudes, and abilities necessary for lifelong, autonomous learning" (Betts et al., 2017, p. 1).

CONCLUSION

Autonomous learners strive to make positive contributions to society. When we have self-directed and confident autonomous lifelong learners, our collective global community benefits. A teacher shared,

> I feel so passionately about what the ALM does for the gifted learner that I have made it part of my learning, my life. I want my students to have independent thoughts . . . to step outside the realm of possibilities and to reach far beyond this galaxy; they have the innocence to do this with their whole hearts and to explore the world with the gifts that illuminate them.

We know the Autonomous Learner Model is successful and has impacted many lives over the past 40 years; we are committed to the growth and development of the ALM in the future. The following poem conveys the many facets of an autonomous learner. As you begin working with your students and learners, please share it to encourage discussion about how some people learn and grow.

SOME PEOPLE

Some people have the ability
to create excitement in their lives.
They are the ones who strive,
who grow,
who give and share,
They are the ones who love . . .
for themselves, others,
Nature and experiences.
They have the ability
to see beyond today,
to rise above the hectic pace,
to strive for their own perfection . . .
And they are gentle,
for they love themselves,
and they love others.
Through their living
they create peace and contentment.
At the same time,

they create excitement,
for there is always another mountain,
A deeper joy,
A new dawn . . .

George Betts

Major Takeaways

The Autonomous Learner Model:

- provides a safe and nurturing environment for learners to explore their cognitive, emotional, social, and physical selves;

- values acceptance of others through engagement in high levels of cooperation and collaboration;

- encourages in-school and out-of-school learner-differentiated curriculum and promotes passion learning;

- reinforces the development of the skills, concepts, and attitudes necessary for lifelong learning; and

- fosters independent, self-directed, autonomous learners.

RECOMMENDED READING

Betts, G. T., Carey, R. J., & Kapushion, B. M. (2017). *Autonomous learner model resource book*. Waco, TX: Prufrock Press.

Betts, G. T., & Neihart, M. (1988). Profiles of the gifted and talented. *Gifted Child Quarterly, 32,* 248–253.

Betts, G. T., Kapushion, B. M., & Carey, R. J. (2016). The autonomous learner model: Supporting the development of problem finders, creative problem solvers, and producers of knowledge to successfully navigate the 21st century. In D. Ambrose & R. J. Sternberg (Eds.), *Giftedness and talent in the 21st century* (pp. 201–220). The Netherlands: Sense.

Betts, G. T., & Kercher, J. J. (1999). *Autonomous learner model: Optimizing ability*. Greeley, CO: ALPS.

Betts, G. T., & Kercher, J. K. (2009). The autonomous learner model for the gifted and talented. In J. Renzulli (Ed.), *Systems and models for developing programs for the gifted and talented* (2nd ed., pp. 49–100). Waco, TX: Prufrock Press.

REFERENCES

Betts, G. (1986). The autonomous learner model for the gifted and talented. In J. S. Renzulli (Ed.), *Systems and models for developing programs for the gifted and talented* (pp. 27–56). Mansfield Center, CT: Creative Learning Press.

Betts, G. T., Carey, R. J., & Kapushion, B. M. (2017). *Autonomous learner model resource book.* Waco, TX: Prufrock Press.

Betts, G. T., & Kercher, J. K. (2009). The autonomous learner model for the gifted and talented. In J. Renzulli (Ed.), *Systems and models for developing programs for the gifted and talented* (2nd ed., pp. 49–100). Waco, TX: Prufrock Press.

Betts, G. T., & Neihart, M. (1988). Profiles of the gifted and talented. *Gifted Child Quarterly, 32,* 248–253.

Betts, G. T., & Neihart, M. (2010). *Revised profiles of the gifted and talented.* Retrieved from http://www.ingeniosus.net/archives/dr-george-betts-and-dr-maureen-neihart-share-revised-profiles-of-gifted

Irvine, M. (n.d.). *The learning retreat: An innovative way of nurturing talent and unlocking potential.* Retrieved from http://hkage.org.hk/en/events/080714%20APCG/05-%20Open/5.13%20Irvine_The%20Learning%20Retreat-%20An%20Innovative%20Way%20of%20Nurtu.pdf

Schimke, A. (2017). Gifted and talented center at Wheat Ridge High School on chopping block as part of Jeffco budget cuts. *Chalkbeat.* Retrieved from http://www.chalkbeat.org/posts/co/2017/02/08/gifted-and-talented-center-at-wheat-ridge-high-school-on-chopping-block-as-part-of-jeffco-budget-cuts

Vander Ark, C. & Ryerse, M. (2017). 10 reasons why lifelong learning is the only option. *Getting Smart.* Retrieved from http://www.gettingsmart.com/2017/01/10-reasons-why-lifelong-learning-is-the-only-option

Vander Ark, T. & Liebtag, E. (2016). Developing self-directed learners. *Getting Smart.* Retrieved from http://www.gettingsmart.com/2016/12/developing-self-directed-learners

CHAPTER 6

Athletic Talent Development From Theory to Practice

THE SELF-REGULATED TALENT DEVELOPMENT PROCESS

Steve Portenga

A thletic talent development typically follows a similar path (often conceptualized as a pyramid) regardless of the sport of interest. At the base, we find children engaged in play or recreation, with local clubs and high school sports typically forming the next level. Some young athletes are identified for entry into elite programs, such as traveling teams or Olympic development programs. From there, athletes join regional or college teams. Next may come a pre-elite level. Finally, the tip of the pyramid is the elite level comprised of professional and Olympic athletes. To understand effective talent development, it is important to first take a critical look at this traditional pathway.

ASSESSING THE TRADITIONAL ATHLETIC TALENT DEVELOPMENT PATHWAY

Talent identification is the process of distinguishing which athletes in a sport have the potential to become elite. Talent development is the process of providing the right coaching, opportunities, resources, and environment to actualize this potential (Vaeyens, Lenoir, Williams, & Philippaerts, 2008). Typical athlete development pipelines are built upon the notions of talent identification and talent development. They illustrate a sequential pathway of identifying the right athletes to move into the next level where their talent will be further developed. If the athletes are unable to develop enough, then their journey toward becoming an elite athlete typically comes to an end.

Unfortunately, there is low predictive ability to the talent identification process. The pyramid type talent development model oversimplifies the typical developmental trajectory by offering only "up" or "out" pathways (Green, 2005; Gulbin, Oldenziel, Weissensteiner, & Gagné, 2010). Evaluations of different national support systems' talent development programs find that only up to 2% of the young athletes attain international senior success (Ackerman, 2014; Güllich, 2014; Güllich & Cobley, 2017; Vaeyens, Güllich, Warr, & Philippaerts, 2009; Weissensteiner, 2017a).

Several conclusions can be drawn from nearly three decades of research on athletic talent development. First, there is little conclusive research on the process of talent identification. Physical factors dominate most of this research, with little attention to psychological factors. Second, it is unfortunate that even what we do know about successful talent identification is not consistently integrated into practice (Gulbin et al., 2010; Vaeyens et al., 2009). Third, for all of the money, time, and effort invested in talent identification, the inability to consistently and accurately identify talent is disappointing (e.g., Koz, Fraser-Thomas, & Baker, 2012). For example, Güllich and Emrich (2012, 2014) examined the developmental training histories of 1,558 world and national level athletes. Long-term senior elite performance was not associated with early youth sports success. The more successful senior athletes typically had a later age of specialization and later onset of deliberate training (Weissensteiner, 2017a). There are three additional broad issues that make talent identification difficult, which will be explained in further detail.

Problems With Talent Identification: Issues Related to Age and Maturation

Talent identification assumes that characteristics of success identified in youth will predictably relate to the characteristics of success needed in a senior athlete. However, this approach ignores the inherent challenges of puberty and maturation (Vaeyens et al., 2008). Kids grow in unpredictable ways as they mature and prepubertal characteristics do not always translate into elite senior performance (Abbott & Collins, 2002; Ackland & Bloomfield, 1996).

We know that chronological age and biological maturity rarely progress at the same rate (Katzmarzyk, Malina, & Beunen, 1997). We also know body size (height and weight) is related to sports performance, particularly in youth sports (Figueiredo, Gonçalves, Coelho-e-Silva, & Malina, 2009). Therefore, it is an advantage to mature early instead of late (Coelho-e-Silva et al., 2010). This advantage applies most in direct competitions, such as when scores on performance tests are compared to chronological age-specific norms. Additionally, the early maturing athletes commonly benefit from the enriched practice opportunities that come from these selection policies (Vaeyens et al., 2008). However, early maturity is only a temporary advantage, as the differences in performance characteristics, such as muscular strength, muscular endurance, aerobic power, motor skill execution, and general intelligence, often disappear as the late maturing athletes go through puberty and sexual maturation (Elferink-Gemser, Jordet, Coelho-e-Silva, & Visscher, 2011; Jones, Hitchen, & Stratton, 2001). Recent findings suggest that some athletes who achieve success at junior level through early selection may struggle at the senior level when late maturers catch up (Vaeyens et al., 2008).

Problems With Talent Identification: Issues Related to Criteria

Talent identification research has significantly relied upon cross-sectional design instead of longitudinal design. The ability to make accurate predictions based on results from this type of research design requires that the performance indicators of success in adult performance are evident in youth athletes. However, success at difference age groups often is dependent on different task demands (Pienaar & Spamer, 1998; Vaeyens et al., 2006). For example, this difference is evident in team sports such as soccer, where there is a significant increase in tempo at higher levels of play (Williams, Lee, & Reilly, 1999).

The changes that occur with development lead to a system that rarely identifies youth athletes as talented based on their future level of performance. The criteria commonly used for selection are more related to performance characteristics than to actual future potential. Thus, youth athletes are selected based on their existing level of performance. It is possible, and quite likely, that these programs fail to select athletes who may not be the best performers presently, yet have tremendous future potential (Elferink-Gemser et al., 2011).

This process of talent identification creates a dilemma for young athletes who must balance the demands of outperforming their peers while also working to develop their potential. They need to work to improve the characteristics that will allow them to compete at a high level currently. They also need to develop the characteristics that will help them reach senior competitive levels (Jonker, Elferink-Gemser, Tromp, Baker, & Visscher, 2015).

Problems With Talent Identification: Issues Related to Developmental Level

We know that maturation effects mean the performance characteristics we measure in youth may have little resemblance to what they will possess as an adult. We also know that the characteristics for superior performance as a youth may not match the characteristics needed as a senior athlete. To add to the challenge of talent identification, we know that it may not be until late adolescence that some of these characteristics needed as an adult actually become apparent (French & McPherson, 1999; Simonton, 1999; Tenenbaum, Sar-El, & Bar-Eli, 2000).

Additionally, we must keep in mind that there is rarely one specific set of skills or physical attributes needed for success as a senior. Sport is filled with a variety of examples of elite athletes. There are many unique combinations of skills, attributes, and capabilities that may lead one to become an elite athlete (Vaeyens et al., 2008). The success of athletes who do not fit the "traditional" profile within a sport is a common enough event that it has been termed the "compensation phenomenon," meaning that strengths in one area of performance may compensate for deficiencies in others (Williams & Ericsson, 2005).

Therefore, talent identification should include several interactive criteria related to physiology, psychology, and sport technique, along with developmental background (Weissensteiner, 2017a). A growing number of reviews of talent identification models has illustrated that potentially important psychological characteristics (e.g., personality, predictors of learning and performance improvement, perceptual-cognitive skills) are frequently ignored in talent identification models and programs (Abbott, Button, Pepping, & Collins, 2005; Abbott & Collins, 2004; Durand-Bush & Salmela, 2001; MacNamara & Collins, 2013; Ward, Belling, Petushek, & Ehrlinger, 2017).

GIFTS AND TALENTS IN THE ATHLETIC DOMAIN

In many domains, the terms *giftedness* and *talented* may be used synonymously. Talent development assumes that whatever potential a young person has, it must somehow be furthered to actualize that potential. In addition to cognitive development, there is an aspect of physical development in sports that is confounded by the maturation process and puberty. Therefore, to understand the necessary elements of athletic talent development, one must separate giftedness, talent, and exceptional performance.

Definition of Giftedness

Gagné (2015) defined giftedness as the possession of natural abilities or aptitudes to a degree that places individuals among the top 10% of their peers. This concept of giftedness is challenging to apply to athletic talent development due to the concept of maturation. Does giftedness apply to a young athlete's current abilities and aptitudes or does it apply to what will be present as a senior? Trying to define giftedness in the athletic domain could be quite a challenge, given the previously mentioned difficulties with talent identification. Perhaps though, including the ability to learn and develop in defining athletic giftedness may lead to a better prediction of potential.

The pace of progress with which people acquire new competencies has been noted as the hallmark of giftedness. Gifted athletes either develop a given amount of expertise in less time or develop more expertise in the same amount of time. Simonton (2017) highlighted this by including deliberate practice as a mediating variable between physical abilities and psychological traits and athletic performance. Thus, giftedness can be recognized by the rate of learning instead of current ability level.

Definition of Talent

Gagné (2015) defined talent as systematically developed knowledge and skills to a "degree that places an individual at least among the top 10% of 'learning peers' (those having accumulated a similar amount of learning time from either current or past training)" (p. 15). Talents are the well-trained and systematically developed competencies that emerge from natural abilities or gifts. Although it has been estimated that 66% of the differences in elite athletic ability are explained by genetic factors (Quijada, 2016), these factors do not guarantee success without proper development (Tucker & Collins, 2012).

Definition of Exceptional Performance

Across the range of sports, the hallmark of exceptional performance is consistency. Exceptional performers are those who can deliver the skills and abilities they have developed on a regular basis. A key aspect of the ability to perform in the upper range of one's abilities consistently is mental resourcefulness, which is the ability to manage performance pressure and stay focused on their performance plan regardless of events in the performance venue. Resourcefulness requires awareness and understanding of emotion to be able to process the information within it.

HOW DO YOUNG ATHLETES DEVELOP THEIR GIFTS INTO TALENTS?

This next section provides an overview of the elements involved in the process of helping young athletes develop their gifts and talents. It will start with a brief theoretical overview of the athletic talent development process, highlighting the role of practice. Next, it will explore the pathways to exceptional performance. Finally, it will examine the importance of self-regulation and talent development.

The Role of Practice in the Athletic Talent Development Process

The outstanding skills witnessed in sport are developed through a process of learning and training, which takes place through practice. Practice is paramount to skill acquisition, and the level of attainment in sports is related to accumulated practice (Baker & Young, 2014; Tedesqui & Young, 2016; Vaeyens et al., 2008). Ericsson and colleagues (Ericsson & Charness, 1994; Ericsson, Krampe, & Tesch-Römer, 1993) concluded that the achievement of expertise across various domains requires the accumulation of sufficient amounts of Deliberate Practice (about 10,000 hours). They defined Deliberate Practice as a particular kind of practice, one that requires physical and cognitive effort; is done with the purpose of improvement; does not lead to immediate personal, social, or financial rewards; and may not be enjoyable. Deliberate practice requires the athlete to have a well-defined task to work on, explicit feedback, the mental energy to correct errors and work on weaknesses, and the willingness to explore strategies to accomplish the difficult parts of the task (Araújo, 2016). However, research has also shown that the 10,000-hour mark is not absolute. Some athletes develop expertise, achieve national team selection, or compete at an international level with only 4,000 to 6,000 hours (Baker, Côté, & Abernethy, 2003; Baker & Young, 2014; Coutinho, Mesquita, & Fonseca, 2016). Other activities and experiences beyond deliberate practice contribute to the development of expertise in sport (MacNamara, Hambrick, & Oswald, 2014).

There are three types of constraints a developing athlete must manage to acquire sufficient hours: motivation, resources, and physical and mental effort (Baker & Young, 2014). Motivation is especially important, because the reward for this practice is not immediate. Athletes that are motivated for enjoyment or social reasons may not find particular value in engaging in deliberate practice (Côté, Baker, & Abernethy, 2003; Hayman, Polman, Taylor, Hemmings, & Borkoles, 2011).

PATHWAYS TO EXCEPTIONAL PERFORMANCE

The Developmental Model of Sport Participation (DMSP) shares three possible pathways for talent development (Côté & Vierimaa, 2014; Coutinho et al., 2016). The first pathway addresses those who stay at a recreational level of participation. The other two address the development of elite athletes, either through early specialization or early diversification (i.e., late specialization). The DMSP recognizes that the peak performance age is younger in some sports than others, so early specialization is necessary to acquire enough hours to transform gifts into talents by the time the athlete reaches the peak age.

Both of the DSMP elite pathways include Deliberate Play at an early age. Deliberate Play has been described as having an important function in children's development (Baker & Young, 2014). It provides opportunities for children to develop enthusiam for the sport, gain a sense of autonomy, and learn a range of movement and psychosocial skills.

In addition to Deliberate Play at a young age, there is substantial evidence for the value of diversified early sport experiences (e.g., Hayman et al., 2011; Memmert, Baker, & Bertsch, 2010). Children who participate in a variety of sports are exposed to a range of different cognitive, affective, and physical experiences. As a result, these athletes typically have increased autonomous motivation for sport as a result of the enjoyment and competencies they develop in these varied environments. The skills developed through this diversified sport experience transfer to the sport in which the athlete eventually specializes, particularly the psychosocial skills. There is a significant, and growing, amount of evidence demonstrating that athletes can achieve an elite level of performance, not just in spite of, but because of this early diversified sport experience (Coutinho et al., 2016).

What is consistent in the trajectories of developing athletes is that athletes' development is a dynamic and complex process (Webb, Collins, & Cruickshank, 2016). If athletes are to realize their potential, they will have to manage multiple transitions. They will have to adapt positively to a variety of setbacks. They will have to be ready to capitalize on unique opportunities. They will have to adjust to differing coaching styles and team environments. The athletes' ability to successfully navigate this dynamic and complex process is as important as their accumulation of hours of deliberate practice (MacNamara, Button, & Collins, 2010b).

The dynamic and complex nature of most talent development trajectories means that successful talent development programs need to ensure young athletes have the skills and ability to progress through these pathways (Vaeyens et al., 2008). Successful programs certainly need to focus on the development of the skills that are important at the senior level. Additionally, they would be wise to also focus on the skills that help the athletes through this process, such as their ability to learn and adapt. Programs must find a balance between current performance and the athletes' longer term development.

Self-Regulation as a Part of Talent Development

Psychologists use the phrase *self-regulation* to describe the process when one compares his or her current state with a target state and is then motivated to take actions that attempt to remove the discrepancy he or she perceives between the two (Goetz, Nett, & Hall, 2013). Self-regulation is more commonly referred to by terms such as discipline, commitment, grit, or resilience—all qualities associated with elite athletes. Thus, it should be of no surprise that elite senior athletes use more self-regulatory skills than nonelite athletes (Cleary & Zimmerman, 2001; Kitsantas & Zimmerman, 2002).

A great deal of variety exists as to how some of the more common theoretical models of talent development explore and explain this process (Côté & Vierimaa, 2014; Ericsson & Charness, 1994; Gulbin, Croser, Morley, & Weissensteiner, 2013; Stambulova, 1994; Wylleman, Alfermann, & Lavallee, 2004). They all acknowledge the need for motivational and self-regulatory skills for the athlete to develop to elite status (Elbe & Wikman, 2017). Once adolescent athletes decide to specialize, they must have the discipline to commit to high amounts of practice and resist distracting alternatives (Côté, Baker, & Abernethy, 2003; Tedesqui & Young, 2015, 2016).

The nature of the practice needed to develop into an elite athlete imposes the constraints mentioned previously (Ericsson et al., 1993). If these constraints limit the amount of practice an athlete can undertake, developing athletes need to make decisions that maximize how much they get out of their training (Baker & Young, 2014). They need to understand what is needed at the senior level so they can adequately plan the activities, resources, and training they need to get there. Researchers have validated these ideas, finding that the athletes who achieve elite status seem to gain more from hours of training in a similar context than less successful ones (Elferink-Gemser, Visscher, Lemmink, & Mulder, 2007; Elferink-Gemser et al., 2011; Elferink-Gemser et al., 2015). Developing athletes who make more decisions to optimize their training and who use more frequent self-motivational processes have been found to get more out of their practice and achieve higher levels of sport performance (Toering, Elferink-Gemser, Jordet, & Visscher, 2009; Young & Medic, 2008; Young & Starkes, 2006). These self-regulation skills seem to be particularly helpful in navigating the dynamic and complex developmental trajectories (Webb et al., 2016).

TALENT DEVELOPMENT AS A FORM OF SELF-REGULATED LEARNING

Talent development is a process of learning. Self-regulation is important to talent development. So, there seems to be some connection between these constructs. The concept of self-regulated learning has a long history in academic settings. The basics of self-regulated learning will be introduced here along with some research about its use in sports.

Self-Regulated Learning

Self-regulated learning is a process of learning in which the learners are engaged and self-motivated (Zimmerman, 2015). Learners take ownership of their developmental goals and learning strategies by comparing their current skills and abilities with their target skills and abilities. This comparison highlights the process of regulation: reducing the discrepancy between the learner's current state and the target learning state. Actively managing this discrepancy may be regarded as the most basic principle of self-regulated learning. Self-regulated learners want to improve. To reach their goals, they must know which aspects of their current knowledge, skills, and abilities need improvement and how the improvement can be accomplished.

Four competencies have been suggested for self-regulated learning to be successful (Goetz et al., 2013). First, learners need diagnostic skills to accurately determine the difference between their current knowledge and skills and their target learning goals. This includes paying attention to the rate of progress in achieving their learning goals. They must know how much further they need to progress for upcoming evaluation points, such as high-stakes testing or try-outs. Second, they need the ability to establish appropriate learning goals. They must understand quality goal setting, account for the time they have available for learning, and consider the type of learning necessary to reach their goal. Third, they need to have knowledge about strategies to help them reduce the discrepancy between the current and target learning states. This includes planning ability, understanding learning strategies, and knowing which strategies to use when. Finally, they must have the motivation to use these competencies to maintain their learning throughout their development (Jonker, Elferink-Gemser, & Visscher, 2010; Zimmerman, 2015). They must understand how their values, goals, and emotions play out throughout the learning process. To engage in effective self-regulated learning, they must be willing to put sustained effort in their development, have persistence with effective learning strategies, and have the ability to disengage from strategies that are unproductive (Jonker, Elferink-Gemser, & Visscher, 2011). Learners must also believe that they have the potential to organize and execute the required actions (i.e., self- efficacy; Bandura, 1997; Hong & O'Neill, 2001; Zimmerman, 1990).

Students' efforts to self-regulate their learning have been described in terms of three cyclical phases that happened before, during, and after efforts to learn (Zimmerman, 2015). The initial phase is the Forethought Phase, or planning stage, which refers to the processes that proceed efforts to learn. The learner must set goals appropriately, identify aspects of performance that need improvement, and plan practice strategies. The second phase is the Performance Phase, when the learner engages in processes to optimize their learning efforts. During the learning tasks, self-monitoring occurs to evaluate how well the learning process is going. The Self Reflection Phase follows, during which learners evaluate each learning session and the associated learning outcomes to determine whether the strategies they used were effective. In addition to evaluating any individual learning session after it occurs, self-regulated learners reflect constantly on the cycles of planning, monitoring, and evaluation. This reflection enables them to use their prior knowledge and strategies in subsequent Forethought Phases to adjust ensuing learning activities.

Research suggests that the possession and use of self-regulatory skills predicts academic achievement (Nota, Soresi, & Zimmerman, 2004). Meta-analyses of studies that teach self-regulated learning report gains in academic performance, motivation, and strategic functioning (Dignath & Büttner, 2008; Dignath, Büttner, & Langfeldt, 2008). Training programs that address metacognitive strategies (e.g., learning to control, monitor, regulate, and reflect on learning) and motivational feedback regarding learning yield the largest improvements (Zimmerman, 2015). Self-regulation has also been related to effective time management (Brettschneider, 1999), which is particularly important for teenage athletes as these years involve significant investments of time in sport training in combination with their academic responsibilities (Jonker, Elferink-Gemser, & Visscher, 2010).

Self-regulatory skills may arise as early as 6 years of age (McCabe, Cunnington, & Brooks-Gunn, 2004; Veenman & Spaans, 2005). From 12 years on, these skills develop further and start to transfer across performance domains (Van der Stel & Veenman, 2008; Veenman & Spaans, 2005). It also appears that children after 12 years of age are better able to balance their motivation to succeed and are better at interpreting their capabilities (Boekaerts, 1997). Even though self-regulatory skills may start to develop at a young age, research suggests they typically do not develop on their own (Boekaerts, 1997). Children develop their self-regulatory skills best with guidance in a positive, goal-oriented environment (Boekaerts & Corno, 2005; Pintrich & Zusho, 2002).

Self-Regulated Learning in Sport

Practice and learning are key elements of athletic talent development, thus maximizing the outcomes of training is an important goal to help young athletes reach their potential. Given the positive impact of self-regulated learning on academic achievements, it is worth exploring the possibility of integrating these processes into sport. A few researchers have started investigating just this.

Compared to sub-elite athletes, elite athletes have been found to set more specific practice goals (Cleary & Zimmerman, 2001), have greater structure in their daily practice plans (Kitsantas & Zimmerman, 2002), and have an increased awareness of a task's demands prior to its execution (Jonker et al., 2011). Expert volleyball players are more likely to self-reflect during athletic practice sessions (Kitsantas & Zimmerman, 2002). Athletes competing at junior international level appear to learn more by reflecting on their previous learning tasks than their junior national peers (Jonker et al., 2011). Elite athletes report higher self-efficacy for learning and put in more effort to succeed at achieving their goals (Bartulovic, Young, & Baker, 2017; Cleary & Zimmerman, 2001; Jonker et al., 2011). Because elite athletes may try harder to succeed when performing tasks, even in adverse conditions, they may learn more than nonelite players (Toering et al., 2009). Elite adolescent athletes may benefit from higher levels of self-regulated learning skills to manage sport and academic development (Jonker, Elferink-Gemser, Toering, Lyons, & Visscher, 2010; Jonker et al., 2011).

Collectively, the research suggests athletes engaged in self-regulated learning gain valuable information about their training goals, learning strategies, and practice efforts (Baker & Young, 2014). Through an improved ability to prioritize what they need to learn and how it must be learned, they can optimize their time spent on learning (Toering et al., 2009). Self-regulated learning processes help elite athletes optimally adapt aspects of their practice to get the most out of their training (Bartulovic et al., 2017). In summary, it appears that self-regulatory skills help athletes to learn more efficiently; the hallmark of gifted athletes (Jonker et al., 2015). Thus, self-regulated learning should be a cornerstone of athletic talent development.

THEORY INTO ACTION:
SELF-REGULATED TALENT DEVELOPMENT

Most athletic talent development models focus primarily on the trajectories or pathways from youth to elite status. Although they make note of the need for a few psychosocial characteristics to navigate this pathway, such as motivation and persistence, they do not fully address the ideal process along the pathway. Most of these models are descriptive in nature. They are a roadmap of how one may get from point A to point B. What they do not typically do is provide much insight to the experiences while traveling on the road from point A to point B.

Self-regulation is the extent to which athletes exert control over their own development to improve and master specific knowledge, skills, and abilities. Athletes who incorporate self-regulated learning into their development are active, strategic, self-aware, reflective, and motivationally driven in pursuing their development goals. Self-regulated learners plan their training in advance, monitor whether they are still on track during practice, and evaluate their practice outcomes afterward.

The Self-Regulated Talent Development (SRTD) process looks at athletic development from a long-range perspective. It recognizes that developing athletes must both develop their talent and the ability to perform. Developing athletes need to increase their knowledge, skills, and abilities. At points along the development pathway, young athletes need to switch from a focus on development to a focus on performing. Performing means being able to use what they have developed through their training in competition. Thus, SRTD addresses psychosocial characteristics related to performing to the self-regulated learning model previously used in sport research.

As mentioned, little research on the psychosocial aspects of talent development has been conducted. The most comprehensive studies are those by MacNamara and colleagues whose retrospective studies of elite sport performers identified psychological factors that helped athletes realize their potential. MacNamara, Button, and Collins (2010a, 2010b) described these factors as Psychological Characteristics of Developing Excellence (PCDEs). This term encompasses both the trait characteristics (the tendency to . . .) and the state skills (the ability to . . . when . . .) they found involved in the realization of potential. The psychological characteristics they identified were far more comprehensive than the mental skills typically addressed in sport psychology research. The PCDEs included attitudes, emotions, and desires such as commitment and motivation. Of note, they observed that learning strategies such as goal setting, planning, and realistic performance evaluations were important for athletes to get the maximum benefit from their training and practice (MacNamara & Collins, 2012). They concluded that the systematic development of these psychological characteristics should be a formal part of talent development programs. MacNamara et al. (2010b) took a self-regulation perspective to describe the effectiveness of the psychological characteristics. The characteristics they identified in this research fit well with the self-regulated learning ideas of planning, self-monitoring, managing emotions, focusing on self-improvement, and seeking guidance from others. Unfortunately, their list was solely based on athlete interviews without a theoretical basis.

Performance is a unique aspect of sport that differentiates it from academic talent development and should be addressed in any athletic talent development model. Learning can be thought of as a process of developing knowledge, skills, and abilities. Performance can be thought of as a process of delivering what an athlete has already learned and developed (Portenga, Aoyagi, & Cohen, 2016). Hence, practice is a process of getting in and performance is a process of getting out. These two different purposes suggest two different, but overlapping, models of psychological characteristics. Zimmerman (2015) previously discussed self-regulation of performance. He described it as "personal efforts to control adverse behaviors and/or emotions during learning, such as impulsivity or anxiety" (p. 541). This definition fails to recognize learning and performance as two different processes. This definition also assumes that the focus of performance is avoiding negative behaviors. Expert performers need to focus primarily on the execution of the skills related to their performance. The inability to control emotions or actions, such as impulsivity, certainly have a negative impact on performance. However, the idea that learning is simply acquiring positive behaviors and performance is avoiding negative ones misses critical aspects of the psychology of high performance. Although there is a place for integrating self-regulation into a model of performance, there are key aspects of such a model that would differ from self-regulated learning. Because young athletes must balance the dual goals of developing skills while at the same time being capable of delivering those skills in performance settings, Self-Regulated Talent Development must address the development of both of these goals.

Building off the model of self-regulated learning used in previous research and the expert learning model by Ertmer and Newby (1996), Self-Regulated Talent Development has five different phases to it. These phases cover not just the learning cycle that happens in individual training sessions, but also the processes involved in managing learning cycles over the full developmental timeframe. The Forethought Phase is broken into a Foundational Planning Phase and a Training Preparation Phase. The Foundational Planning Phase includes issues related to long-term developmental planning. The Training Preparation Phase can be thought of as a practice planning phase. This phase is involved in the more detailed aspects of training and practice on a micro level. What has previously been referred to as the Performance Phase is renamed the Training Action Phase. This change addresses the differences between learning and performance mentioned above. It also signifies the importance of action in any training session. Finally, the Self-Evaluation Phase is broken down into a Training Evaluation Phase and a Development Reflection Phase. The Training Evaluation Phase encompasses the processes related to evaluating an individual training session. The Development Reflection Phase is related to the processes involved in a big picture analysis of the athlete's overall development. Thus, the Foundational

Planning Phase sets the stage for the athletes' overall training goals and individual practices. Athletes maximize their development in practices by undertaking the processes in the Training Preparation, Training Action, and Training Evaluation Phases. As athletes progress through their training, they need to bring in processes from the Development Reflection Phase to ensure that daily practices are continuing to move them toward their long-term developmental goals.

Foundational Planning Phase

The Foundational Planning Phase considers issues related primarily to identity and commitment. Identity includes all of the aspects of our self, such as values and self-esteem. Commitment refers to the things that we truly put ourselves toward.

Our identity determines how we make sense of and what we think about ourselves, others, and the world around us (Carver & Scheier, 1990). It is a lens through which we focus our attention on our world and make meaning of it (Oyserman, 2007). Our identity determines our thoughts, our emotions, and our actions. Identity has been described as a self-regulatory system that functions to "direct attention, filter or process information, manage impressions, and select appropriate behaviors" (Adams & Marshall, 1996, p. 433). The values and beliefs underlying our identity help define what is important to us, how we go about making decisions in the world, what we pursue, and how we go about pursuing it.

There are two main ways identity influences how we see ourselves (Serafini & Maitland, 2013). First, there are certain aspects or components that we ascribe to our identity. We may decide that being gifted is a part of our identity. We then make judgments about the fact that this component is a part of our identity. Second, we also view ourselves on our status within each component. For every aspect of our identity, we judge the discrepancy between what we view as our current self and our ideal self.

When we feel a component or status within a component is threatened, decreasing the perceived threat takes precedence in our lives. Psychological and performance pressure build from these perceptions of threat. When we are engaged in something meaningful and we feel that our identity is threatened by how we do in this endeavor, we feel pressure.

Identity influences important definitions related to the process of performance (Portenga, in press). How we define what constitutes success, failure, and adversity, along with the consequences of failure, are all driven by aspects of our identity. These definitions affect what we commit to and determine the things that we perceive as threatening to our sense of self. The nature of sports, with constant quantification and the celebration of success, make it likely young athletes learn to identify through their sport. Their desire to develop may lead to unrealistic expectations related to success and thus increase perceptions of threat and pressure.

Athletes who report high levels of pressure tended to pursue goals and strategies that have negative impacts on talent development (Conroy & Elliot, 2004). These athletes have increased experiences of stress and anxiety due to the emotional cost of ongoing pressure. Excessive pressure or fear of failure can have a negative behavioral impact for young athletes in the talent development process due to underutilization of effective learning strategies.

It is important that an athlete's performance identity is integrated with his or her personal identity. Although this process may happen effectively on its own, this process deserves to be facilitated deliberately. Young athletes should be helped to develop an identity that is based upon celebrating effort in process and progress beyond just outcomes (positive effort is more than putting in hard physical work; it should also include elements from Self-Regulated Talent Development). If a positive integrated identity is developed in adolescence, the athletic talent development process is likely to be positively facilitated for the rest of the athlete's career (MacNamara & Collins, 2015; Portenga, in press).

Commitment is connected to an athlete's overall development-related motivation. Commitments athletes make influence how they choose their learning goals, how they understand the value and importance they attach to these goals, and how they make decisions about the personal resources they spend trying to achieve these goals (Boekaerts, 1999). Commitment is related to the decisions athletes make to select their current and future activities that best fit their desires, needs, expectations, and resources. Athletes need to make commitments that help initiate positive development activities and protect their motivation to complete these activities against competing influences not related to their goals.

There are some key self-motivation beliefs that help inform the process of commitment. Sustained effort, goal attainment, and increases in well-being are more likely to happen when goals are pursued for reasons that have an internal perceived locus of causality and because of self-identified personal convictions (Sheldon & Elliot, 1999; Sheldon, Ryan, Deci, & Kasser, 2004). Goals that are consistent with core values lead to greater changes in well-being when they are accomplished (Zimmerman, 2005). When the overall goals an athlete pursues are aligned with important aspects of his or her identity, his or her commitment is strengthened (Crocetti, Sica, Schwartz, Serafini, & Meeus, 2013). Athletes who focus first on committing to meaningful outcomes related to their sense of self will be far more successful at setting goals along the way and planning the appropriate actions and learning strategies necessary to meet those goals (Sheldon & Elliot, 1999; Sheldon et al., 2004).

When athletes become motivated to avoid failing in front of others, they may use more superficial learning strategies (Goetz et al., 2013; MacNamara & Collins, 2015). In this case, athletes may find themselves more focused on minimizing threats to their sense of self, than on achieving valued outcomes. When they're focused on minimizing threats and avoiding fear of failure, their choices very rarely help maximize the development of their potential. However, when athletes expect positive emotions from the learning experience, deeper, more strategic learning strategies are likely to be used (Bonneville-Roussy & Bouffard, 2015).

Another important aspect of the commitment process is self-efficacy, which refers to the evaluations an athlete makes of his or her own capacity to learn or perform a particular task effectively (Bandura, 1997). A self-efficacious athlete increases his or her efforts when initial attempts at obtaining a goal fail, whereas athletes who doubt themselves are more likely to give up. Additionally, goal attainment can give feedback to self-efficacy. Self-regulated learners increase their feelings of self-efficacy when they achieve goals within the plans they have laid out for themselves. Seeing steps within a larger plan accomplished leads to immediate satisfaction rather than having to wait for the final outcome.

Training Preparation Phase

With an appropriate foundation of a performance identity and commitments that support the process of achievement, developing athletes should prepare the steps that allow their vision to be actualized. The Preparation Phase is concerned with the planning needed to select the appropriate activities to achieve their developmental goals (Zimmerman, 2005). The result of this phase is a detailed action plan to guide their development and manage their investment of the limited resources of their time and energy. This process includes goal setting to identify the key aspects that need improvement and the strategic planning of specific practice strategies.

Goal setting refers to the process of deciding the specific outcomes of training and practice (Zimmerman, 2005). Many athletes are great at setting goals, then forgetting them as they go through their training. Goal setting should not be a process that occurs at the beginning and then again at the end of a season.

The concept of action planning better captures the spirit of this process. Athletes need to have certain indicators of success that they're working toward throughout their developmental journey. It is important, however, that they know the things they need to be working on to get to the desired outcomes. Thus, action plans should provide a roadmap about what they want to have happen and the things they need to work on to make those outcomes occur. An ideal developmental plan helps clarify for athletes their physical, technical, tactical, and mental goals for the season. These goals should be broken down into the steps that are needed to make these outcomes happen and should lead to weekly plans. Every week, and every practice session, athletes should have a clear sense not only of what they want to work on, but also how these activities fit into the larger picture. The primary purpose of this action planning is to direct an athlete's attention to the importance of everyday practice sessions and how they connect back to his or her big picture developmental goals.

Ultimately, the effectiveness of an athlete's development will depend on how well he or she manages his or her learning process in day-to-day practices.

Elements of MacNamara's et al.'s (2010a, 2010b) research on the Psychological Characteristics of Developing Excellence help inform how this action planning and goal-setting process should occur. One of the key elements discussed is that developing athletes should have a vision of what it takes to be successful, which informs the goals and actions they choose to put into their plan. They should recognize that successful development will require a willingness to push oneself and step out of one's comfort zone. Developing athletes need to recognize the importance of looking beyond just the physical components of talent. They need to understand the importance of developing positive performance mindset. MacNamara et al. (2010a, 2010b) also highlighted the importance of working on weaknesses. This depends first on accurate self-awareness. It also depends on the nature of young athletes' identities, which informs their tolerance for undertaking activities and practice that may risk initial failure. Finally, MacNamara et al. (2010a, 2010b) shared important qualities of effective goal setting and action planning. The athletes who develop the most effectively are the ones who can translate the drills and activities set up by their coaches into the specific attributes they need to focus on within those drills.. Although many coaches are wonderful at deliberate planning for developmental purposes, coaches with more than one athlete may find it difficult to make sure every practice session is individually optimized.

The importance of having an action plan to guide athletes' practice and training should not be undervalued. In the absence of a good action plan, athletes too often focus on protecting their self-esteem instead of developing their potential (Boekaerts, 1999; Boekaerts & Cascallar, 2006). When this priority becomes activated, athletes operate in a mode where their choice of strategies are redirected and opportunities to develop are set aside. A good action plan connects the importance of daily activities to valued long-term outcomes, preventing the protection of self-esteem from becoming a priority. An action plan should connect activities that may involve the perceptions of failure to valued outcomes and reframe them as important elements of the learning process. The importance of protecting self-esteem, particularly in young athletes, should not be underestimated. It is wise to realize that most learning involves tension between these priorities (Winne, 2015).

The second aspect of the preparation phase involves strategic planning of learning. Self-regulation learning strategies are purposeful actions directed at acquiring the skill. When athletes select appropriate strategies, they enhance their learning by focusing their thoughts, controlling their affect, and directing their actions. Strategic planning is an ongoing process of selecting the activities and strategies that best suit the athlete. As a result of ongoing development and change, athletes must continuously adjust their goals and choice of strategies. This need for adjustment may happen when athletes get new coaches, move to a new team, or join a new club.

Too many young athletes approach learning by showing up to practice and working hard, but essentially going through the motions. To develop effectively and efficiently, athletes need to be active participants in their learning process. Few athletes are as actively engaged in the learning that occurs during practice as they might be in academic settings. Academic learning strategies such as highlighting, taking notes, creating flashcards, or reviewing with a partner are commonly used without full appreciation for the breadth of learning strategies they are incorporating. For athletes to learn as much as possible in the sport setting, they would be wise to take as much individual responsibility for their learning. Learning strategies helpful in the sports domain include training journals, mental rehearsal, and having intentional learning goals when watching videos.

Another aspect of importance for action planning is the nature of the knowledge about development that young athletes hold. For practice to be focused and efficient, developing athletes need to have prior knowledge of the areas in which they need to improve. This includes general knowledge of their sport and the specifics for their own position and skill set. An appreciation of what is required to excel is another factor of the Psychological Characteristics of Developing Excellence (MacNamara et al., 2010b). Athletes who excelled in the developmental process were aware of the developmental pathway they needed to undertake and aware of the next stage in their own personal development. They had awareness of the processes required to progress to the next level and felt that lack of awareness at times was responsible for slowing the progress.

There are several facets of knowledge that help inform goal setting and action planning (Weinstein, Husman, & Dierking, 2000). Declarative knowledge is an understanding of *what* is important in a given setting, such as knowledge about one's skills, abilities, and the current state of one's knowledge (Ertmer & Newby, 1996). Procedural knowledge is knowledge about *how* to make decisions and select appropriate actions that use athletes' skills and abilities most effectively within the context of their sport (Elferink-Gemser, Kannekens, Lyons, Tromp, & Visscher, 2010; Schorer & Elferink-Gemser, 2013).

Another essential form of knowledge that is often ignored is tacit knowledge (Olszewski-Kubilius, Subotnik, & Worrell, 2015). This kind of knowledge is often considered the "insider knowledge" that often gets passed on by mentors (e.g., coaches or elite athletes), but is not a formal part of development (Subotnik, Olszewski-Kubilius, & Worrell, 2011). This type of knowledge includes knowledge of how to navigate sport systems, who to know, what to avoid, and, unfortunately an all-too important part of athletic talent development, the politics of sport development. Young athletes should be encouraged to actively seek knowledgeable mentors with the goal of making this tacit knowledge explicit

(Olszewski-Kubilius et al., 2015). Self-regulated talent development should be considered a process where young athletes are deliberately taught declarative, procedural, and tacit knowledge related to their sport (Button, 2011; Collins, 2011; MacNamara et al., 2010b).

It is important, and quite interesting, to note that beyond the benefit of action planning to develop intentional practice, there is also a negative effect to practicing mindlessly. A recent study found that the amount of time spent practicing without clear goals and learning strategies was negative related to performance (Bonneville-Roussy & Bouffard, 2015). These results seem to suggest practice that does not involve goal direction, focused attention, and self-regulation strategies may actually be detrimental to talent development.

Finally, goal setting and strategic planning can be a helpful part of the process of building self-efficacy and autonomous motivation to continue (Zimmerman, 2005). The clearer the athletes can lay out their development process, the more consistent feedback they get about their success in meeting goals and their overall development. The process of moving through this developmental pathway can become intrinsically motivating in its own right and provides a sense of fulfillment in balance with the overall outcome goals (Bandura & Schunk, 1981; Goetz et al., 2013).

Training Action Phase

After planning, it is time for action. The Action Phase covers the behaviors, thoughts, and emotions that occur in practice. This phase is where the rubber meets the road. There are two major types of control processes that are related to the action phase: self-control and self-observation.

Self-control processes refer to how well athletes keep their focus on learning objectives without being distracted by task irrelevant thoughts or by environmental factors (Zimmerman, 2005). Self-control is the essence of grit, the ability to persist and stay on task (Duckworth, Peterson, Matthews, & Kelly, 2007). Self-control processes, such as self-instruction, mental rehearsal, and task strategies, help athletes stay focused on practice tasks to optimize their efforts. Self-instruction involves describing how to proceed as one executes a drill. When athletes have a sense not only of the outcomes of their movements, but what they must focus on to make those outcomes happen, their learning is improved. Mental rehearsal helps the athlete stay focused by setting the stage, allowing them to gain a clear picture of what to do, and allowing them to get additional learning, particularly of a sequence of actions. Task strategies are those that help athletes reduce the task to its essential parts. Although many of these control processes may seem common in sport, to maximize self-regulated learning these processes should be intentionally taught to young athletes.

Even with a variety of self-control processes at their disposal, athletes may not always make commitment-directed decisions during training due to the confounding role of emotions (Carver & Scheier, 2009). People typically pursue many goals simultaneously. Only one can have top priority at any given moment. There are changes over time in which goal has the top priority. It has been proposed that strong emotions interfere with this prioritization process (Carver & Scheier, 2009). Emotions related to a goal may arise outside of awareness and drive people to interrupt what they are doing to give the goal underlying the emotion higher priority (Boekaerts & Niemivirta, 2005). The stronger the emotion, the more likely the underlying goal takes priority. As discussed previously, threats to sense of self, fear of embarrassment, and fear of failure are all underlying emotions that can shift a prioritization of actions and thoughts within practice away from talent development and toward self-protection. Developing robust self-control processes help protect an athlete by maintaining focus on whatever task development goals should have priority. It is important when athletes are off task to determine whether this blip is a result of them not understanding the essential elements of the task or if something else, such as self-protection, has taken priority.

The second type of control processing involves self-observation, which refers to the checking in and monitoring of training, the conditions that surround it, and the effects that it produces (Bartulovic et al., 2017; Zimmerman, 2005). Although this process may seem simple, it can be challenging for young athletes to effectively self-monitor due to the amount of information involved in typical training activities. Experts are better able to track themselves selectively through a detailed process when necessary.

Research has shown self-monitoring to be one of the most important aspects of the self-regulated learning cycle for athletes (Jonker et al., 2010; Jonker et al., 2011; Jonker, Elferink-Gemser, de Roos, & Visscher, 2012). Self-monitoring is an athlete's ongoing assessment of his or her learning process and enhances an athlete's awareness of his or her actions during practice. Self-monitoring helps athletes focus on information relevant to assessing their progress during a task. Athletes should also self-monitor the personal effort they are putting forth physically and into the learning strategies. Self-monitoring should be used to determine sources of confusion, error, or inefficiency in learning throughout a practice.

There are a few elements of self-monitoring that can influence its effectiveness (Zimmerman, 2005). The timing of one's self-observations is an important variable. Self-feedback that comes after a training session precludes the athlete from taking any action during practice. A second element of quality self-monitoring relates to the quality of information in the feedback. The more knowledge an athlete has about what he or she is trying to develop, what effective use of a skill or ability looks like, and how to go about learning, the more he or she gets from the self-monitoring process. A third feature involves the accuracy of self-monitoring.

Athletes must be able to accurately observe and assess their functioning. A fourth feature involves the nature of the behaviors being monitored. Athletes who focus only on behaviors they wish to avoid may end up diminishing their motivation to self-regulate these activities. It is better for athletes to focus their self-monitoring on actions, behaviors, or thoughts that they wish to accomplish.

Another valuable self-observational technique that increases the proximity, instructiveness, accuracy, and behavioral direction of feedback is self-recording (Zimmerman & Kitsantas, 1996). Self-recording is a process of actively writing down in a training journal predetermined elements of the practice related to learning. Predetermining elements to record provides a meaningful structure without the athlete having to remember what to observe. Self-recording is helpful for athletes to notice recurring patterns and how they approach practice. It is rare for athletes to completely remember learning elements from practice to practice.

Another valuable self-observational technique is self-experimentation (Bandura, 1991). Self-experimentation offers a way to systematically learn how they learn best and a way around perceptions of failure. The idea of an experiment implies some things will work and some things won't work. The process of going through an experiment is to try and identify which elements do work and those that don't. Thus, athletes go into experiments with an explicit understanding that some aspects of what they are about to do may, and likely will, fail. Knowing ahead of time that some aspects of what they are going to do will be a failure puts the blame for those failures on the processes themselves and not on the athlete as a person. The explicit use of "experiments" can help athletes start to separate failures in learning from failures in their own personal identity.

Training Evaluation Phase

After a training session, athletes need to assess how well the strategies they used met their goals for the day (Kitsantas & Zimmerman, 2002). They need to self-evaluate their learning process and attribute causes to their results (Goetz et al., 2013). Self-evaluation can lead to adjustments for the next training session. Self-evaluation refers to comparing information from self-monitoring with the standards or goals they had for the training session. Causal attributions about these results reflect the decisions athletes make about whether the results are due to abilities, plans, strategies, or effort. These attributions are important to the learning cycle because attributions of negative results to aspects of the athlete that are fixed lead to negative reactions and discouragement.

After completing a training session, the progress achieved is evaluated in reference to the initial learning goals. There are three factors that may inform how athletes evaluate a training session (Goetz et al., 2013): (1) the quantitative factors, such as the number of reps or drills completed; (2) the qualitative factors, such as how well a new skill was learned or elaborated upon; and (3) the subjective factors that are emotionally related, such as feelings of satisfaction or pride. The standards used to evaluate performance can be individually referenced, such as personal improvement compared to past attempts at the skill, or externally defined, such as meeting a pre-established age group score. The outcome of this evaluation impacts future training sessions. If athletes are satisfied with the day's outcome, then a similar approach to practice and learning will be used again. The strategies athletes used for self-regulation to maximize the learning process will also be repeated. In contrast, poor results should prompt athletes to change their learning strategies. They may slow down the learning process to better identify roadblocks. They may choose to set more realistic goals, try different learning strategies, or decide they need to put in more effort.

Development Reflection Phase

In addition to evaluating each training session, a regular process of analyzing the overall preparation, action, and evaluation cycle should be planned. Although the Evaluation Phase is focused on how well athletes met the goals for individual training sessions, the Reflection Phase is focused on how well athletes are developing toward their long-term developmental goals.

Self-reflective analysis is linked to the causal attributions athletes make about their progress (Zimmerman, 2005). Athletes have a tremendous amount of latitude to interpret for themselves why their learning has been successful or unsuccessful (Bandura, 1991). Athletes who have plans to use specific strategies during training are more likely to attribute failures in learning to those strategies, rather than to low ability (Zimmerman & Kitsantas, 1996, 1997). Because learning strategies can be perceived as correctable causes, attributing failure to the strategies protects the athletes against negative self-reactions. These attributions help with maintaining motivation and persistence during periods of subpar performance and help foster a strategically advantageous and adaptive future course of action.

Self-reflective and attributional self-judgments lead to important self-reactions: self-satisfaction and adaptive inferences (Zimmerman, 2005). Self-satisfaction involves athletes' perceptions of satisfaction or dissatisfaction with their developmental progress and the associated emotions. This is an important concept because people follow courses of action that result in satisfaction and positive affect (Bandura, 1991). We avoid pathways that lead to dissatisfaction and negative affect, such as anxiety, doubt, and worry. When athletes find self-satisfaction in reaching stepping-stone goals, they give direction to their actions and create incentives to continue their developmental efforts. In this way, athletes find motivation.

Adaptive or defensive inferences are the conclusions athletes draw about their need to alter their learning approaches during future training sessions

(Zimmerman, 2005). Adaptive inferences direct athletes to new and potentially better forms of self-regulated learning, such as shifting goals in their action plan or choosing more effective learning strategies (Zimmerman & Martinez-Ponz, 1992). Defensive inferences, such as procrastination, task avoidance, cognitive disengagement, or apathy, serve the primary purpose of protecting the athlete from future dissatisfaction and the negative affect that goes along with it. These defensive reactions have been described as self-handicapping strategies because they ultimately limit athletic development (Garcia & Pintrich, 1994).

It is important to note that athletes without an action plan will still seek to explain their development. Athletes with action plans are able to proactively reflect on their development, whereas athletes without a plan must rely on reactive self-reflection (Zimmerman, 2005). Athletes without a clear developmental plan have no process goals or baseline information to guide their reflection. Athletes who reflect reactively tend not to see success as connected to the specific efforts that they put in. Reactive methods of self-regulation are typically ineffective because the athletes are unable to strategically analyze goals, plans, and their planned investment of effort. They typically end up using social comparison to evaluate their outcomes. These comparisons are frequently unfavorable and often lead to causal attributions that are personalized, defense inferences, and self-dissatisfaction. These reactions lead reactive self-regulators to experience a loss of self-efficacy and a decline in autonomous motivation (Zimmerman & Kitsantas, 1996). Instead of having a plan that allows them an opportunity to evaluate what is working or not working, these athletes typically label themselves as untalented, leading to a higher chance for dropout.

The process of self-reflection effects Foundational Planning and Preparation Phase processes, consequently impacting future courses of action. Enhanced self-motivational beliefs (i.e., self-satisfaction, adaptive inferences) increase the athletes' sense of agency and reinforces continued use of the self-regulated learning principles (Jonker et al., 2015). In contrast, reactions of self-dissatisfaction may diminish perceptions of self-efficacy and motivation to continue along their development. Athletes with increased self-motivational beliefs are able to channel their efforts toward valued goals and keep their attention away from their deepest fears. Therefore, this overall cycle explains elements of persistence and the sense of fulfillment of athletes who achieve elite status.

It appears that to perform at an international level, above-average investment in reflection is necessary (Jonker et al., 2011). Self-reflection helps athletes to better understand the knowledge, skills, and abilities that they have acquired (Jonker et al., 2010). Elite youth athletes learn more from past experiences, are better able to put that knowledge into action and apply what they have learned in the past to future situations (Bartulovic et al., 2017; Toering et al., 2009). Thus, this process of self-reflection helps athletes know which task characteristics they are required to perform, how to set goals regarding their improvement, and how to reach these goals in an effective manner.

PRACTICAL INSIGHTS FOR DEVELOPING TALENT

There are a few practical insights that emerge from this exploration of athlete talent development. The first is that for athletes to progress through athletic talent development pathways in a way that maximizes their potential, they must continue to stay involved in sports. This is an incredibly simple observation. Yet, it is one that is often overlooked. Athletes who are not involved in sports will not be able to develop their talent. A primary goal of programs in the athlete talent development pipeline should be maintaining the interests of those athletes. Above all else, athletes need to want to continue along the athletic development pathway.

Another practical insight is the need for people in athletic talent development programs to be mindful of the impact of maturation and puberty. These processes significantly change elements related to criteria for athlete identification and selection. Unfortunately, too many athletes are misidentified or deselected due to criteria that are not related to achieving elite athlete status. Along with first insight, this means it is in the athletes', and the sports', best interest to keep as many kids involved and interested as possible until the effects of puberty have finished.

Understanding the development of self-regulation yields another practical insight. Self-regulation skills and self-regulated learning processes need to be explicitly taught and developed (Boekaerts & Corno, 2005; Pintrich & Zusho, 2002). The research on self-regulation highlights that before an athlete can be self-regulated, he or she must be "other regulated" (Jonker et al., 2010). Self-regulation skills are developed through the instructions and feedback athletes receive from others, such as coaches and parents, and should be just as deliberately developed as any other technical or tactical skill (Jonker et al., 2011). Athletes commonly set goals and receive feedback in the sports environment, but this alone is not self-regulated learning. Too often, these goals are set by coaches or set by athletes sharing what they expect the coach wants to hear. Most goal-setting programs stop at setting goals. They do not progress to the action planning stage, where they have a systematic and sequential plan of development for how those goals will be achieved. Athletes typically do not learn how to evaluate and reflect in a way that supports their progress instead of leading to negative emotions. It is also important to note that for athletes to learn self-regulation skills, they must be provided opportunities in which to actually self-regulate. This means they must be afforded opportunities to use the self-regulated learning processes, even though this may appear to slow down learning. Once these skills are learned, they will more than make up for any delay in skill development.

In addition to teaching young athletes how to develop regulation skills, it is paramount that athletic development also systematically teach athletes how to perform (Baker & Young, 2014). Developing athletes must navigate the dual challenges of developing toward elite athlete status while also having to prove themselves in competitive situations along the pathway. Learning how to learn is a different process from learning how to compete. The cognitive demands and emotion involved in training differ from performance settings. This capability to compete needs to be taught. Often, competition itself may be the only place young athletes learn how to compete. Most athletes are very reluctant to try something new in competition. It is important then to find opportunities for athletes to learn and test their ability to perform. These opportunities may be intentional competitive settings in a practice format, such as scrimmaging against another team. Or they could be legitimate competitions that are purposefully selected as opportunities for athletes to experiment with new ways of competing, because they have little significance to the athletes' overall developmental process. In these opportunities, athletes then have the freedom to try new ways of managing their thoughts and emotions during the competitive process.

Finally, numerous transitions occur throughout the developmental process. These may be times when young athletes get new coaches, move to new teams, or move to increased levels of competition. Research exploring antecedents to later senior expertise find that athletes are often unprepared for many of the transitions that occur (Weissensteiner, 2017b). Particular transitions for which to prepare are the junior-to-senior transition and first-time senior competitive experiences. Research shows that senior performance leaders and coaches often find athletes are not ready for the transition to the senior competition (Webb et al., 2016). Anticipating these transitions by developing athletes' psychological characteristics in advance should be an integral, intentional aspect of the athletic talent development pipeline (MacNamara & Collins, 2011).

Major Takeaways

- Due to the challenges in predicting elite talent at a younger age, the capability of young athletes to engage in self-regulated learning may be one of the best indicators of senior success.

- Concerned adults in the talent development environment should include the teaching of self-regulated talent development as an outcome of a youth or adolescent talent development program.

- Young athletes should be encouraged to develop an integrated identity that protects against fear of failure or embarrassment becoming prioritized over the risk-taking and experimentation needed to develop one's potential.

- Young athletes should be taught how to self-monitor their progress during practice sessions so they can adjust their learning strategies as needed.

- Young athletes should be taught how to reflect on their development to use progress to strengthen motivation and self-efficacy.

RECOMMENDED READINGS

Bartulovic, D., Young, B. W., & Baker, J. (2017). Self-regulated learning predicts skill group differences in developing athletes. *Psychology of Sport and Exercise, 31,* 61–69.

Jonker, L. J., Elferink-Gemser, M. T., Tromp, E. J. Y., Baker, J., & Visscher, C. (2015). Psychological characteristics and the developing athlete: The importance of self-regulation. In J. Baker & D. Farrow (Eds.), *Routledge handbook of sport expertise* (pp. 317–328). London, England: Routledge.

MacNamara, Á. (2011). Psychological characteristics of developing excellence. In D. Collins, H. Richards, & A. Button (Eds.), *Performance psychology: A practitioner's guide* (pp. 47–64). London, England: Elsevier.

Zimmerman, B. J. (2015). Self-regulated learning: Theories, measures, and outcomes. In J. D. Wright (Ed.), *International Encyclopedia of the Social & Behavioral Sciences* (2nd ed., pp. 541–546). London, England: Elsevier.

REFERENCES

Abbott, A., Button, C., Pepping, G. J., & Collins, D. (2005). Unnatural selection: Talent identification and development in sport. *Nonlinear Dynamics, Psychology, and Life Sciences, 9*(1), 61–88.

Abbott, A., & Collins, D. (2002). A theoretical and empirical analysis of a 'state of the art' talent identification model. *High Ability Studies, 13,* 157–178.

Abbott, A., & Collins, D. (2004). Eliminating the dichotomy between theory and practice in talent identification and development: Considering the role of psychology. *Journal of Sports Sciences, 22,* 395–408.

Ackerman, P. L. (2014). Nonsense, common sense, and science of expert performance: Talent and individual differences. *Intelligence, 45,* 6–17.

Ackland, T. R., & Bloomfield, J. (1996). Stability of human proportions through adolescent growth. *Australian Journal of Science and Medicine in Sport, 28*(2), 57–60.

Adams, G. R., & Marshall, S. K. (1996). A developmental social psychology of identity: Understanding the person-in-context. *Journal of Adolescence, 19,* 429–442.

Araújo, M. V. (2016). Measuring self-regulated practice behaviours in highly skilled musicians. *Psychology of Music, 44,* 278–292.

Baker, J., Côté, J., & Abernethy, B. (2003). Learning from the experts: Practice activities of expert decision-makers in sport. *Research Quarterly for Exercise and Sport, 74,* 342–347.

Baker, J., & Young, B. (2014). 20 years later: Deliberate practice and the development of expertise in sport. *International Review of Sport and Exercise Psychology, 7*(1), 135–157.

Bandura, A. (1991). Self-regulation of motivation through anticipatory and self-reactive mechanisms. In R. A. Dienstbier (Ed.), *Nebraska symposium on motivation* (pp. 69–164). Lincoln: University of Nebraska Press.

Bandura, A. (1997). The nature and structure of self-efficacy. In A. Bandura (Ed.), *Self-efficacy: The exercise of control* (pp. 36–78). New York, NY: Freeman.

Bandura, A., & Schunk, D. H. (1981). Cultivating competence, self-efficacy, and intrinsic interest through proximal self-motivation. *Journal of Personality and Social Psychology, 41,* 586–598.

Bartulovic, D., Young, B. W., & Baker, J. (2017). Self-regulated learning predicts skill group differences in developing athletes. *Psychology of Sport and Exercise, 31,* 61–69.

Boekaerts, M. (1997). Self-regulated learning: A new concept embraced by researchers, policy makers, educators, teachers, and students. *Learning and Instruction, 7,* 161–186.

Boekaerts, M. (1999). Self-regulated learning: Where we are today. *International Journal of Educational Research, 31,* 445–457.

Boekaerts, M., & Cascallar, E. (2006). How far have we moved toward the integration of theory and practice in self-regulation? *Educational Psychology Review, 18,* 199–210. doi:10.1007/s10648-006-9013-4

Boekaerts, M., & Corno, L. (2005). Self-regulation in the classroom: A perspective on assessment and intervention. *Applied Psychology, 54,* 199–231.

Boekaerts, M., & Niemivirta, M. (2005). Self-regulated learning: Finding a balance between learning goals and ego-protective goals. In M. Boekaerts, P. Pintrich, R., & M. Zeidner (Eds.), *Handbook of self-regulation* (pp. 417–450). San Diego, CA: Elsevier Academic Press.

Bonneville-Roussy, A., & Bouffard, T. (2015). When quantity is not enough: Disentangling the roles of practice time, self-regulation and deliberate practice in musical achievement. *Psychology of Music, 43,* 686–704.

Brettschneider, W. D. (1999). Risk and opportunities: Adolescents in top-level sport growing up with the pressures of school and training. *European Physical Education Review, 5,* 121–133.

Button, A. (2011). Aims, principles and methodologies in talent identification and development. In D. Collins, A. Abbott, & H. Richards (Eds.), *Performance psychology: A practitioner's guide* (pp. 9–29). San Diego, CA: Elsevier Academic Press.

Carver, C., & Scheier, M. (1990). Principles of self-regulation: Action and emotion. In E. T. Higgins & R. M. Sorrentino (Eds.), *Handbook of motivation and cognition: Vol. 2. Foundations of social behavior* (pp. 3–52). New York, NY: Guilford Press.

Carver, C. S., & Scheier, M. F. (2009). Action, affect, multitasking, and layers of control. In J. P. Forgas, R. F. Baumeisters, & D. M. Tice (Eds.), *Psychology of self-regulation: Cognitive, affective, and motivational processes* (pp. 109–128). New York, NY: Psychology Press.

Cleary, T. J., & Zimmerman, B. J. (2001). Self-regulation differences during athletic practice by experts, non-experts, and novices. *Journal of Applied Sport Psychology, 13,* 185–206.

Coelho-e-Silva, M. J., Carvalho, H. M., Goncalves, C. E., Figueiredo, A. J., Elferink-Gemser, M. T., Philippaerts, R. M., & Malina, R. M. (2010). Growth, maturation, functional capacities and sport-specific skills in 12–13 year old basketball players. *Journal of Sports Medicine and Physical Fitness, 50,* 174–181.

Collins, D. (2011). Implications and applications In D. Collins, A. Abbott, & H. Richards (Eds.), *Performance psychology: A practitioner's guide* (pp. 85–94). San Diego, CA: Elsevier Academic Press.

Conroy, D. E., & Elliot, A. J. (2004). Fear of failure and achievement goals in sport: Addressing the issue of the chicken and the egg. *Anxiety, Stress, and Coping, 17,* 271–285.

Côté, J., Baker, J., & Abernethy, B. (2003). From play to practice: A developmental framework for the acquisition of expertise in team sports. In J. L. Starkes & K. A. Ericsson (Eds.), *Expert performance in sports: Advances in research on sport expertise* (pp. 89–110). Champaign, IL: Human Kinetics.

Côté, J., & Vierimaa, M. (2014). The developmental model of sport participation: 15 years after its first conceptualization. *Science & Sports, 29,* S63–S69.

Coutinho, P., Mesquita, I., & Fonseca, A. M. (2016). Talent development in sport: A critical review of pathways to expert performance. *International Journal of Sports Science & Coaching, 11,* 279–293.

Crocetti, E., Sica, L. S., Schwartz, S. J., Serafini, T., & Meeus, W. (2013). Identity styles, dimensions, statuses, and functions: Making connections among identity conceptualizations. *European Review of Applied Psychology/Revue Européenne De Psychologie Appliquée, 63*(1), 1–13.

Dignath, C., & Büttner, G. (2008). Components of fostering self-regulated learning among students. A meta-analysis on intervention studies at primary and secondary school level. *Metacognition and Learning, 3,* 231–264.

Dignath, C., Büttner, G., & Langfeldt, H. (2008). How can primary school students learn self-regulated learning strategies most effectively? A meta-analysis on self-regulation training programmes. *Educational Research Review, 3,* 101–129.

Duckworth, A. L., Peterson, C., Matthews, M. D., & Kelly, D. R. (2007). Grit: Perseverance and passion for long-term goals. *Journal of Personality and Social Psychology, 92,* 1087–1101.

Durand-Bush, N., & Salmela, J. H. (2001). The development of talent in sport. In R. N. Singer, H. A. Hausenblas, & C. M. Janelle (Eds.), *Handbook of sport psychology* (2nd ed., pp. 269–289). New York, NY: Wiley.

Elbe, A.-M., & Wikman, J. M. (2017). Psychological factors in developing high performance athletes. In J. Baker, S. Cobley, J. Schorer, & N. Wattie (Eds.), *Routledge handbook of talent identification and development in sport.* London, England: Routledge.

Elferink-Gemser, M. T., De Roos, I., Torenbeek, M., Fokkema, T., Jonker, L., & Visscher, C. (2015). The importance of psychological constructs for training volume and performance improvement. A structural equation model for youth speed skaters. *International Journal of Sport Psychology, 46,* 726–744.

Elferink-Gemser, M. T., Jordet, G., Coelho-e-Silva, M. J., & Visscher, C. (2011). The marvels of elite sports: How to get there. *British Journal of Sports Medicine, 45,* 683–684.

Elferink-Gemser, M. T., Kannekens, R., Lyons, J., Tromp, Y., & Visscher, C. (2010). Knowing what to do and doing it: Differences in self-assessed tactical skills of regional, sub-elite, and elite youth field hockey players. *Journal of Sports Sciences, 28,* 521–528.

Elferink-Gemser, M. T., Visscher, C., Lemmink, K. A., & Mulder, T. (2007). Multidimensional performance characteristics and standard of performance in talented youth field hockey players: A longitudinal study. *Journal of Sports Sciences, 25,* 481–489.

Ericsson, K. A., & Charness, N. (1994). Expert performance: Its structure and acquisition. *American Psychologist, 49,* 725–747.

Ericsson, K. A., Krampe, R. T., & Tesch-Römer, C. (1993). The role of deliberate practice in the acquisition of expert performance. *Psychological Review, 100,* 363–406.

Ertmer, P. A., & Newby, T. J. (1996). The expert learner: Strategic, self-regulated, and reflective. *Instructional Science, 24,* 1–24.

Figueiredo, A. J., Gonçalves, C. E., Coelho-e-Silva, M. J., & Malina, R. M. (2009). Characteristics of youth soccer players who drop out, persist or move up. *Journal of Sports Sciences, 27,* 883–891.

French, K. E., & McPherson, S. L. (1999). Adaptations in response selection processes used during sport competition with increasing age and expertise. *International Journal of Sport Psychology, 30,* 173–193.

Gagné, F. (2015). From genes to talent: The DMGT/CMTD perspective. *Revista de Educación, 368,* 12–37.

Garcia, T., & Pintrich, P. R. (1994). Regulating motivation and cognition in the classroom: The role of self-schemas and self-regulatory strategies. In D. H. Schunk & B. J. Zimmerman (Eds.), *Self-regulation of learning and performance: Issues and educational applications* (pp. 127–153). Hillsdale, NJ: Erlbaum.

Goetz, T., Nett, U. E., & Hall, N. C. (2013). Self-regulated learning. In N. C. Hall & T. Goetz (Eds.), *Emotion, motivation, and self-regulation: A handbook for teachers* (pp. 123–166). Bingley, England: Emerald.

Green, B. C. (2005). Building sport programs to optimize athlete recruitment, retention, and transition: Toward a normative theory of sport development. *Journal of Sport Management, 19,* 233–253.

Gulbin, J. P., Croser, M. J., Morley, E. J., & Weissensteiner, J. R. (2013). An integrated framework for the optimisation of sport and athlete development: A practitioner approach. *Journal of Sports Sciences, 31,* 1319–1331.

Gulbin, J. P., Oldenziel, K. E., Weissensteiner, J. R., & Gagné, F. (2010). A look through the rear view mirror: Developmental experiences and insights of high performance athletes. *Talent Development & Excellence, 2,* 149–164.

Güllich, A. (2014). Selection, de-selection and progression in German football talent promotion. *European Journal of Sport Science, 14,* 530–537.

Güllich, A., & Cobley, S. (2017). On the efficacy of talent identification and talent development programmes. In J. Baker, S. Cobley, J. Schorer, & N. Wattie (Eds.), *Routledge handbook of talent identification and development in sport* (pp. 80–98). London, England: Routledge.

Güllich, A., & Emrich, E. (2012). Individualistic and collectivistic approach in athlete support programmes in the German high-performance sport system. *European Journal for Sport and Society, 9,* 243–268.

Güllich, A., & Emrich, E. (2014). Considering long-term sustainability in the development of world class success. *European Journal of Sport Science, 14*(Suppl. 1), S383–S397.

Hayman, R., Polman, R., Taylor, J., Hemmings, B., & Borkoles, E. (2011). Development of elite adolescent golfers. *Talent Development & Excellence, 3,* 249–262.

Hong, E., & O'Neill, J., H. F. (2001). Construct validation of a trait self-regulation model. *International Journal of Psychology, 36,* 186–194.

Jones, A. M., Hitchen, P. J., & Stratton, G. (2001). The importance of considering biological maturity when assessing physical fitness measures in girls and boys aged 10 to 16 years. *Annals of Human Biology, 27*(1), 57–65.

Jonker, L., Elferink-Gemser, M. T., Toering, T. T., Lyons, J., & Visscher, C. (2010). Academic performance and self-regulatory skills in elite youth soccer players. *Journal of Sports Sciences, 28,* 1605–1614.

Jonker, L., Elferink-Gemser, M. T., & Visscher, C. (2010). Differences in self-regulatory skills among talented athletes: The significance of competitive level and type of sport. *Journal of Sports Sciences, 28,* 901–908.

Jonker, L., Elferink-Gemser, M. T., & Visscher, C. (2011). The role of self-regulatory skills in sport and academic performances of elite youth athletes. *Talent Development & Excellence, 3,* 263–275.

Jonker, L., Elferink-Gemser, M. T., de Roos, I. M., & Visscher, C. (2012). The role of reflection in sport expertise. *The Sport Psychologist, 26,* 224–242.

Jonker, L. J., Elferink-Gemser, M. T., Tromp, E. J. Y., Baker, J., & Visscher, C. (2015). Psychological characteristics and the developing athlete: The importance of self-regulation. In J. Baker & D. Farrow (Eds.), *Routledge handbook of sport expertise* (pp. 317–328). London, England: Routledge.

Katzmarzyk, P. T., Malina, R. M., & Beunen, G. P. (1997). The contribution of biological maturation to the strength and motor fitness of children. *Annals of Human Biology, 24,* 493–505.

Kitsantas, A., & Zimmerman, B. J. (2002). Comparing self-regulatory processes among novice, non-expert, and expert volleyball players: A microanalytic study. *Journal of Applied Sport Psychology, 14,* 91–105.

Koz, D., Fraser-Thomas, J., & Baker, J. (2012). Accuracy of professional sports drafts in predicting career potential. *Scandinavian Journal of Medicine and Science in Sports, 22,* e64–e69.

MacNamara, Á., Button, A., & Collins, D. (2010a). The role of psychological characteristics in facilitating the pathway to elite performance. Part 1: Identifying mental skills and behaviors. *The Sport Psychologist, 24,* 52–73.

MacNamara, Á., Button, A., & Collins, D. (2010b). The role of psychological characteristics in facilitating the pathway to elite performance. Part 2: Examining environmental and stage related differences in skills and behaviors. *The Sport Psychologist, 24,* 74–96.

MacNamara, Á., & Collins, D. (2011). Development and initial validation of the Psychological Characteristics of Developing Excellence Questionnaire. *Journal of Sports Sciences, 29,* 1273–1286.

MacNamara, Á., & Collins, D. (2012). Building talent systems on mechanistic principles: Making them better at what makes them good. In J. Baker, S. Cobley, & J. Schorer (Eds.), *Talent identification and development in sport: International perspectives* (pp. 25–38). London, England: Routledge.

MacNamara, Á., & Collins, D. (2013). Do mental skills make champions? Examining the discriminant function of the psychological characteristics of developing excellence questionnaire. *Journal of Sports Sciences, 31,* 736–744.

MacNamara, Á., & Collins, D. (2015). Profiling, exploiting, and countering psychological characteristics in talent identification and development. *The Sport Psychologist, 29*(1), 73–81.

MacNamara, B. N., Hambrick, D. Z., & Oswald, F. L. (2014). Deliberate practice and performance in music, games, sports, education, and professions: A meta-analysis. *Psychological Science, 25,* 1608–1618.

McCabe, L. A., Cunnington, M., & Brooks-Gunn, J. (2004). The development of self-regulation in young children: Individual characteristics and environmental contexts. In R. F. Baumeister & K. Vohs (Eds.), *Handbook of self-regulation: Research, theory and applications* (pp. 340–356). New York, NY: Guilford Press.

Memmert, D., Baker, J., & Bertsch, C. (2010). Play and practice in the development of sport-specific creativity in team ball sports. *High Ability Studies, 21,* 3–18.

Nota, L., Soresi, S., & Zimmerman, B. J. (2004). Self-regulation and academic achievement and resilience: A longitudinal study. *International Journal of Educational Research, 41,* 198–215.

Olszewski-Kubilius, P., Subotnik, R. F., & Worrell, F. C. (2015). Antecedent and concurrent psychosocial skills that support high levels of achievement within talent domains. *High Ability Studies, 26,* 195–210.

Oyserman, D. (2007). Social identity and self- regulation. In A. W. Kruglanski & E. T. Higgins (Eds.), *Social psychology: Handbook of basic principles* (2nd ed., pp. 432–453). New York, NY: Guilford Press.

Pienaar, A. E., & Spamer, E. J. (1998). A longitudinal study of talented young rugby players as regards their rugby skills, physical and motor abilities and anthropometric data. *Journal of Human Movement Studies, 34*(1), 13–32.

Pintrich, P. R., & Zusho, A. (2002). The development of academic self-regulation. The role of cognitive and motivational factors. In A. Wigfield & J. S. Eccles (Eds.), *Development of achievement motivation* (pp. 249–284). San Diego, CA: Academic Press.

Portenga, S. T. (in press). Psychosocial skills in the world of sport inside and outside of schools. In P. Olszewski-Kubilius, R. F. Subotnik, & F. C. Worrell (Eds.), *Talent development as a framework for gifted education: Implications for best practices and applications in schools*. Waco, TX: Prufrock Press.

Portenga, S. T., Aoyagi, M. W., & Cohen, A. B. (2016). Helping to build a profession: A working definition of sport and performance psychology. *Journal of Sport Psychology in Action, 8*(1), 1–13.

Quijada, M. R. (2016). Is the successful athlete born or made? A review of the literature. *Apunts: Educació Física i Esports, 123,* 7–12.

Schorer, J., & Elferink-Gemser, M. T. (2013). How good are we at predicting athletes' futures? In D. Farrow, J. Baker, & C. MacMahon (Eds.), *Developing sport expertise: Researchers and coaches put theory into practice* (pp. 30–44). London, England: Routledge.

Serafini, T. E., & Maitland, S. B. (2013). Validating the Functions of Identity Scale: Addressing methodological and conceptual matters. *Psychological Reports, 112*(1), 160–183.

Sheldon, K. M., & Elliot, A. J. (1999). Goal striving, need satisfaction, and longitudinal well-being: The self-concordance model. *Journal of Personality and Social Psychology, 76,* 482–497.

Sheldon, K. M., Ryan, R. M., Deci, E. L., & Kasser, T. (2004). The independent effects of goal contents and motives on well-being: It's both what you pursue and why you pursue it. *Personality and Social Psychology Bulletin, 30,* 475–486.

Simonton, D. K. (1999). Talent and its development: An emergenic and epigenetic model. *Psychological Review, 106,* 435–457.

Simonton, D. K. (2017). Does talent exist? Yes! In J. Baker, S. Cobley, J. Schorer, & N. Wattie (Eds.), *Routledge handbook of talent identification and development in sport* (pp. 11–18). London, England: Routledge.

Stambulova, N. B. (1994). Developmental sports career investigations in Russia: A post-perestroika analysis. *The Sport Psychologist, 8,* 221–237.

Subotnik, R. F., Olszewski-Kubilius, P., & Worrell, F. C. (2011). Rethinking giftedness and gifted education: A proposed direction forward based on psychological science. *Psychological Science in the Public Interest, 12*(1), 3–54.

Tedesqui, R. A. B., & Young, B. W. (2015). Perspectives on active and inhibitive self-regulation relating to the deliberate practice activities of sport experts. *Talent Development & Excellence, 7*(1), 29–39.

Tedesqui, R. A. B., & Young, B. W. (2016). Associations between self-control, practice, and skill level in sport expertise development. *Research Quarterly for Exercise and Sport, 88*(1), 108–113.

Tenenbaum, G., Sar-El, T., & Bar-Eli, M. (2000). Anticipation of ball location in low and high-skill performers: A developmental perspective. *Psychology of Sport and Exercise, 1*(2), 117–128.

Toering, T. T., Elferink-Gemser, M. T., Jordet, G., & Visscher, C. (2009). Self-regulation and performance level of elite and non-elite youth soccer players. *Journal of Sports Sciences, 27,* 1509–1517.

Tucker, R., & Collins, M. (2012). What makes champions? A review of the relative contribution of genes and training to sporting success. *British Journal of Sports Medicine, 46,* 555–561.

Vaeyens, R., Güllich, A., Warr, C. R., & Philippaerts, R. (2009). Talent identification and promotion programmes of Olympic athletes. *Journal of Sports Sciences, 27,* 1367–1380.

Vaeyens, R., Lenoir, M., Williams, A. M., & Philippaerts, R. M. (2008). Talent identification and development programmes in sport. *Sports Medicine, 38,* 703–714.

Vaeyens, R., Malina, R. M., Janssens, M., Van Renterghem, B., Bourgois, J., Vrijens, J., & Philippaerts, R. M. (2006). A multidisciplinary selection model for youth soccer: The Ghent Youth Soccer Project. *British Journal of Sports Medicine, 40,* 928–934.

Van der Stel, M., & Veenman, M. V. J. (2008). Relation between intellectual ability and metacognitive skillfulness as predictors of learning performance of young students performing tasks in different domains. *Learning and Individual Differences, 18,* 128–134.

Veenman, M. V. J., & Spaans, M. A. (2005). Relation between intellectual and metacognitive skills: Age and task differences. *Learning and Individual Differences, 15,* 159–176.

Ward, P., Belling, P., Petushek, E., & Ehrlinger, J. (2017). Does talent exist? A re-evaluation of the nature-nurture debate. In J. Baker, S. Cobley, J. Schorer, & N. Wattie (Eds.), *Routledge handbook of talent identification and development in sport* (pp. 19–34). London, England: Routledge.

Webb, V., Collins, D., & Cruickshank, A. (2016). Aligning the talent pathway: Exploring the role and mechanisms of coherence in development. *Journal of Sports Sciences, 34,* 1799–1807.

Weinstein, C. E., Husman, J., & Dierking, D. R. (2000). Self-regulation interventions with a focus on learning strategies. In M. Boekaerts, P. Pintrich, & M. Zeidner (Eds.), *Handbook of self-regulation* (pp. 727–747). San Diego, CA: Academic Press.

Weissensteiner, J. R. (2017a). How contemporary international perspectives have consolidated a best-practice approach for identifying and developing sporting talent. In J. Baker, S. Cobley, J. Schorer, & N. Wattie (Eds.), *Routledge handbook of talent identification and development in sport* (pp. 51–68). London, England: Routledge.

Weissensteiner, J. R. (2017b). Method in the madness: Working towards a viable 'paradigm' for better understanding and supporting the athlete pathway. In J. Baker, S. Cobley, J. Schorer, & N. Wattie (Eds.), *Routledge handbook of talent identification and development in sport* (pp. 133–149). London, England: Routledge.

Williams, A. M., & Ericsson, K. A. (2005). Perceptual-cognitive expertise in sport: some considerations when applying the expert performance approach. *Human Movement Science, 24,* 283–307.

Williams, A. M., Lee, D., & Reilly, T. (1999). *A quantitative analysis of matches played in the 1991–92 and 1997–98 seasons.* London, England: The Football Association.

Winne, P. H. (2015). Self-regulated learning. In J. D. Wright (Ed.), *International encyclopedia of the social & behavioral sciences* (2nd ed., pp. 535–540). San Diego, CA: Elsevier Academic Press.

Wylleman, P., Alfermann, D., & Lavallee, D. (2004). Career transitions in sport: European perspectives. *Psychology of Sport and Exercise, 5*(1), 7–20.

Young, B. W., & Medic, N. (2008). The motivation to become an expert athlete: How coaches can promote long-term commitment. In D. Farrow, J. Baker, & C. MacMahon (Eds.), *Developing elite sports performers: Lessons from theory and practice* (pp. 43–59). New York, NY: Routledge.

Young, B. W., & Starkes, J. L. (2006). Measuring outcomes of swimmers' non-regulation during practice: Relationships between self-report, coaches' judgments, and video-observation. *International Journal of Sport Science and Coaching, 1,* 131–148.

Zimmerman, B. J. (1990). Self-regulated learning and academic achievement: An overview. *Educational Psychologist, 25,* 3–17.

Zimmerman, B. J. (2005). Attaining self-regulation: A social cognitive perspective. In M. Boekaerts, P. R. Pintrich, & M. Zeidner (Eds.), *Handbook of self-regulation* (pp. 13–39). San Diego, CA: Elsevier Academic Press.

Zimmerman, B. J. (2015). Self-regulated learning: Theories, measures, and outcomes. In J. D. Wright (Ed.), *International encyclopedia of the social & behavioral sciences* (2nd ed., pp. 541–546). San Diego, CA: Elsevier Academic Press.

Zimmerman, B. J., & Kitsantas, A. (1996). Self-regulated learning of a motoric skill: The role of goal setting and self-monitoring. *Journal of Applied Sport Psychology, 8,* 69–84.

Zimmerman, B. J., & Kitsantas, A. (1997). Developmental phases in self-regulation: Shifting from process to outcome goals. *Journal of Educational Psychology, 89,* 29–36.

Zimmerman, B. J., & Martinez-Pons, M. (1992). Perceptions of efficacy and strategy use in the self-regulation of learning. In D. H. Schunk & J. Meece (Eds.), *Student perceptions in the classroom: Causes and consequences* (pp. 185–207). Hillsdale, NJ: Erlbaum.

CHAPTER 7

The Integrative Model of Talent Development (IMTD)

FROM THEORY TO EDUCATIONAL APPLICATIONS

Françoys Gagné

Scholars and educational practitioners almost unanimously acknowledge that the term *giftedness* designates two distinct realities: early emerging forms of giftedness with strong biological roots, as opposed to fully developed adult forms of giftedness. They express that distinction through associated pairs of terms, like potential/realization, aptitude/achievement, and promise/fulfillment. That dichotomy surfaces in countless popular expressions, such as "education's goal is to maximize each student's potential," or "realizing her potential is each person's lifelong challenge." It also manifests itself in many practical situations, for instance, in the way most school districts select students for their gifted programs. They use two main sources of information: (a) group IQ tests that measure intellectual abilities, and (b) school grade results (exams or tests) that assess academic performance (Cox, Daniel, & Boston, 1985; Johnsen, 2009). Thanks to these ubiquitous tools, they select students who possess both outstanding *potentialities* and outstanding *achievements*; in other words, they manifest at the same time "gifted" aptitudes and "gifted" achievements. This practice is so common that it led me to describe gifted program participants as IGAT students: Intellectually Gifted and Academically Talented (Gagné, 2007). The IGAT acronym conveys that idea of "bright achievers," an expression that merges (confuses?) both meanings of the giftedness label.

What does this dual meaning tell us about gifted underachievers? Professionals commonly describe underachievement "as a discrepancy between expected performance (ability or potential) and actual performance (achievement)" (Siegle & McCoach, 2013, p. 377). According to that definition, gifted underachievers become, at the same time, gifted (high potential) and nongifted (average or low achievement)—a clear oxymoron! Similarly, when advocates for the gifted insist that all of these children should be able to fulfill their potential, they are in fact demanding special educational services that will help the gifted become gifted!

Our field lived with that conceptual incoherence until the publication (Gagné, 1985) of the Differentiating Model of Giftedness and Talent (DMGT, initially identified as *Differentiated*). The DMGT introduced a clear conceptual differentiation between the two labels *giftedness* and *talent*. Even more, it used that differentiation as the foundation for a detailed theory of talent development. The editor of the journal in which the DMGT first appeared hailed that article as "the best discussion of giftedness and talent presented in the last decade" (Feldhusen, 1985, p. 99). And Borland (1989) stated in his handbook:

> Gagné's use of the terms *giftedness* and *talent* appears to be the least arbitrary and the most useful of those proposed thus far. The distinction between competence and performance is a real and meaningful one, and it allows for the building of a model that permits the operationalization of the concepts. (p. 23)

Unfortunately, in spite of these early laudatory comments, the DMGT approach remains to this day a marginal perspective—the biconceptual use of the term *gifted* continues to reign in our professional literature; ensconced habits are hard to break!

Thanks to a major update (Gagné, 2013) that included the creation of the Developmental Model for Natural Abilities (DMNA), both the DMNA and the DMGT were recently merged into the Integrative Model of Talent Development (IMTD; see Figure 7.1). In this chapter, the IMTD, and especially its DMGT component, will serve as the conceptual framework to answer the five following questions: (1) How does the DMGT distinguish gifts from talents? (2) How does the DMGT describe the talent development process? (3) Where do gifts come from; are they innate? (4) How can we best foster academic talent development (ATD)? (5) What makes the DMGT/IMTD unique?

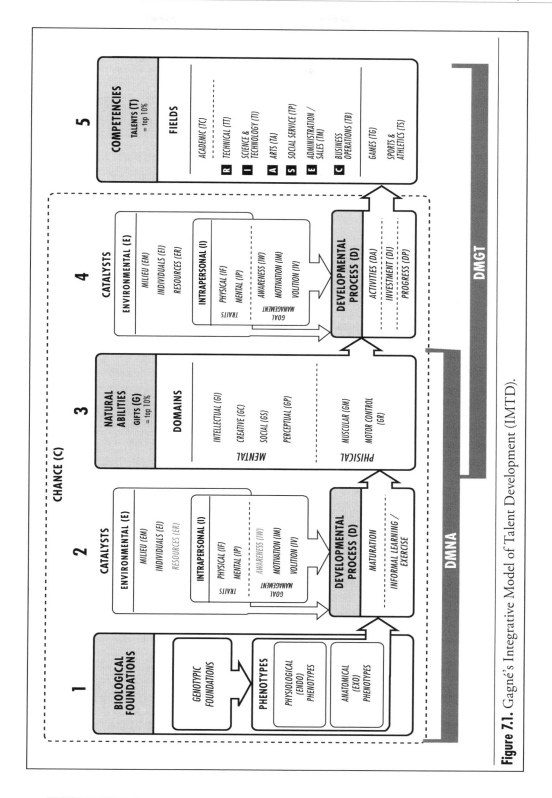

Figure 7.1. Gagné's Integrative Model of Talent Development (IMTD).

HOW DOES THE **DMGT** DISTINGUISH GIFTS FROM TALENTS?

The DMGT's crucial differentiation has its roots in two observations I made when I entered this field in the late 1970s: (a) the presence of two distinct concepts subsumed under the single label of giftedness, and (b) the gross underuse of a readily available label, namely the term *talent*. Wouldn't we eliminate unnecessary conceptual ambiguity if we adopted distinct labels when referring to aptitudes as opposed to achievements? This is exactly what the DMGT proposed: Adopt the term gifted to convey a potential anchored in biological and genetic foundations, and the term talent to represent outstanding systematically developed competencies. Thus were born the two basic definitions that constitute the core of the DMGT framework.

> *Giftedness* designates the possession and use of biologically anchored and informally developed outstanding natural abilities or aptitudes (called gifts), in at least one ability domain, to a degree that places an individual at least among the top 10% of age peers.

> *Talent* designates the outstanding mastery of systematically developed competencies (knowledge and skills) in at least one field of human activity to a degree that places an individual at least among the top 10% of "learning peers" (those having accumulated a similar amount of learning time from either current or past training).

Note how the DMGT clearly separates the concepts of giftedness, potential, aptitude, and natural abilities on the one hand, from those of talent, performance, achievement, and systematically developed abilities, as well as expertise, eminence, and prodigiousness; it is one of the DMGT's unique qualities. Note also that the term *ability* is used here as an umbrella construct; it covers both natural abilities (aptitudes) and systematically developed abilities (competencies). Beyond offering differentiated definitions, the DMGT proposes a detailed theory of talent development (see Figure 7.2). It has five major structures called *components*: gifts (G), talents (T), talent development process (D), and two types of catalysts, intrapersonal (I) and environmental (E). Each component is subdivided into *subcomponents,* just like the domains of giftedness and fields of talent we have mentioned above. And all subcomponents harbor subdivisions called *facets;* they are so numerous that the DMGT identifies just some of them as illustrative examples. The DMGT uses three-letter

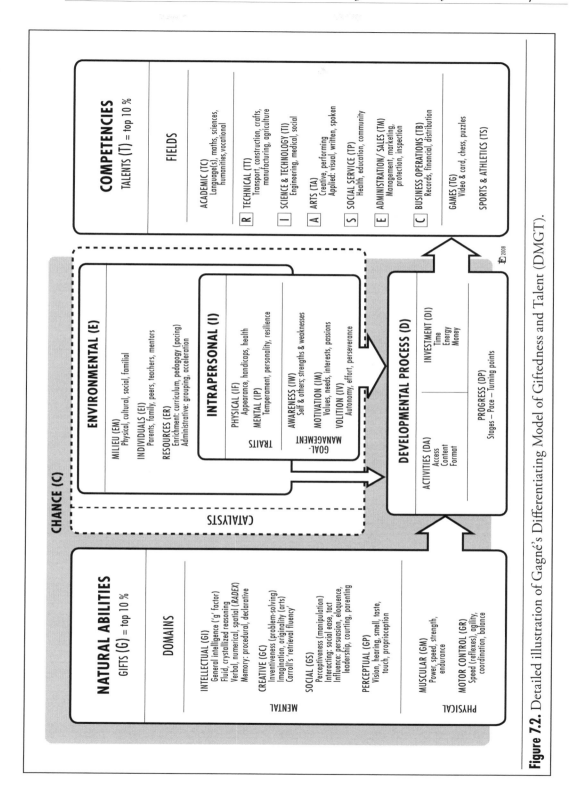

Figure 7.2. Detailed illustration of Gagné's Differentiating Model of Giftedness and Talent (DMGT).

codes to represent all of its constitutive elements; the first letter identifies the component, the second represents the subcomponent, and the third a particular facet. Let's begin with the first two components: gifts (G) and talents (T).

Giftedness and Talent

The *DMGT* identifies six natural ability *domains*, or subcomponents, of the Giftedness (G) component. Four of them belong to the mental realm (intellectual–*GI*, creative–*GC*, social–*GS*, perceptual–*GP*), and the other two to the physical realm (muscular–*GM,* motor control–*GR*). Each subcomponent comprises more specific natural abilities called *facets* (see Figure 7.2). Note that in our field the term *gifted* designates almost exclusively outstanding intellectual or cognitive natural abilities (GI). Natural abilities are not innate; as we will discuss in Part III, they do develop, especially during childhood, through maturational processes and informal exercise. Yet, that development and the level of expression are substantially controlled by the individual's genetic endowment. We observe major individual differences in natural abilities in the daily lives of all children, both at home and at school. For instance, think of the intellectual abilities needed to learn to read, speak a foreign language, or understand new mathematical concepts; the creative abilities that help solve different types of problems and produce original work in the visual and performing arts, in literature, and in science; the physical abilities involved in sports, music, and sculpture; the social abilities essential when interacting with classmates, teachers, and parents. Gifts can be observed more easily and directly in young children because environmental influences and systematic learning have not yet exerted their moderating influences in a significant way. However, they still show themselves in older children, even in adults, through the facility and speed with which individuals acquire new competencies in any field of human activity. Said differently, ease and speed in learning are the trademarks of giftedness: they contribute significantly to every learner's pace of progress.

Talents (T) belong to the performance pole of a potential-performance continuum; they represent the outcome of any outstanding talent development process. Talent fields can be extremely diverse; the *International Standard Classification of Occupations* (ISCO; see https://en.wikipedia.org/wiki/International_Standard_ Classification_of_Occupations) reveals that there are literally thousands of distinct occupations, and we can find talented individuals in each of them. Figure 7.2 shows nine talent subcomponents of the T component, each with a series of more specific facets. Six of them have their source in Holland's RIASEC classification of work-related personality types: Realistic, Investigative, Artistic, Social, Enterprising, Conventional (alternatively Doer, Thinker, Creator, Helper, Persuader, Organizer; see Anastasi & Urbina, 1997). Three additional subcomponents complement the RIASEC taxonomy: preoccupational academic (K–12) subjects, games, and sports. A particular natural ability can express itself in many different ways depending on the field(s) of occupation adopted by an individual. For example, motor control (GR) can be modeled into the particular skills of a pianist, a painter, or a video game player. Similarly, cognitive processes can be modeled into the scientific reasoning of a chemist, the memorization and game analysis of a chess player, or the strategic planning of an athlete.

The Prevalence of Gifted and Talented Individuals

How many people are gifted and/or talented? As shown in both definitions above, the DMGT offers a clear answer to the prevalence question: "outstanding" means individuals who belong to the top 10% of the relevant reference group in terms of natural ability (for giftedness) or achievement (for talent). This generous choice for the initial threshold is counterbalanced by the recognition of levels of giftedness or talent; the DMGT's metric-based (MB) system of levels constitutes an intrinsic constituent of the DMGT. It has four hierarchically superposed levels, each of them comprising the top 10% of the preceding one; you can be either simply (no label) gifted or talented (top 10%), *highly* G or T (top 1%), *exceptionally* G or T (top 1: 1,000), or *extremely/profoundly* G or T (1:10,100). These levels apply to every domain of giftedness and every field of talent. Why 10%? I could answer "Why not?" because the prevalence question has no absolute answer; nowhere will we find a magical number that automatically separates those labeled gifted or talented from the rest of the population. In other words, giftedness and talent are not qualitative distinctions.

The choice of a proper threshold requires that professionals come to a consensus, just like nutritionists did when they established the various category thresholds for the body mass index (BMI). Unfortunately, no such consensus has yet been achieved in the various fields of talent development. Yet, the prevalence question is crucial for both theoretical and practical reasons. From a theoretical standpoint, a prevalence estimate represents an important contribution toward a more precise definition of any *normative* construct (e.g., poverty, tallness, weight, most neurotic syndromes) that targets, as is the case with giftedness and talent, a marginal subgroup within a population. Practically speaking, adopting, for instance, a threshold of 10% instead of 1%—a *tenfold* difference in estimated prevalence—has a huge impact on selection practices and talent development services (Gagné, 1998). For example, the availability of clear thresholds and labels facilitates not only the selection process and the description of study samples, but also the comparison of results from different studies. Moreover, the MB system of levels should remind educators that the vast majority of gifted or talented individuals (90%) belong to the lowest—mild—category, and that only a tiny fraction of those identified as gifted or talented in their youth will ever achieve eminence in their chosen field.

How Does the DMGT Describe the Talent Development Process?

Although talent development is not a new concept in our field, it acquired its popularity mostly in the present century. Indeed, if we go back just a few decades, the talent development label disappears from the titles of books or chapters, as well as subject indexes (e.g., Barbe & Renzulli, 1975; Passow, 1979). The expression slowly took flight in the 1980s, helped possibly by the immense popularity of Bloom's (1985) *Developing Talent in Young People*. Soon after, Renzulli and Reis (1991) ended a politically oriented article as follows: "Talent development is the 'business' of our field, and we must never lose sight of this goal, regardless of the direction that reform efforts might take" (p. 34). Unfortunately, they did not specify what they meant by talent development. From the 1990s onward, the number of publications that included "talent development" in their title grew steadily. A cursory look at the tables of contents and subject indexes of recent handbooks (e.g., Balchin, Hymer, & Matthews, 2009; Callahan & Hertberg-Davis, 2013; Colangelo & Davis, 2003; Dixon & Moon, 2006; Kerr, 2009; MacFarlane & Stambaugh, 2009; Plucker & Callahan, 2008; Renzulli, Gubbins, McMillen, Eckert, & Little, 2009; Shavinina, 2009; Sternberg & Davidson, 2005) confirms its more frequent use by academics. But, as I argued elsewhere (Gagné, 2015b), the DMGT alone analyzes in depth the various influences that affect the talent development process, from the first struggles of novices to the full-time investment of world-level performers in academia, arts, or sports.

The Talent Development Process

The G-T-D components constitute the core of the DMGT; they express a basic premise of the DMGT's view of talent development: talents result from the progressive transformation of outstanding aptitudes, or gifts, into equally outstanding competencies, or talents. Thus, natural abilities or aptitudes serve as the "raw materials," or constitutive elements, of talents; they act through the talent development process. I created the neologism *talentee* to label any individual, child or adult, actively involved in a systematic talent development process, whatever the field. Talentees coordinate the various elements of that process, which is subdivided into three subcomponents: activities (DA), investment (DI), and progress (DP), each of them subdivided again into multiple facets (Figure 7.2). Talent development begins when a child or adult gains access (DAA), through an identification/selection process, to a systematic program of specialized activities. They include a specific content (DAC), the curriculum, offered within a specific learning environment (DAF or format). The investment (DI) subcomponent quantifies the intensity of the talent development process in terms of time (DIT), psychological energy (DIE), or money (DIM). Ericsson's (2006) concept of deliberate practice combines the DIT and DIE facets. Finally, the progress (DP) of talentees from initial access to peak performance can be broken down into a series of stages (DPS; e.g., novice, advanced, proficient, expert). Its main quantitative representation is pace (DPP), or how fast—compared to learning peers—talentees are progressing toward their predefined excellence goal. The long-term developmental course of most talentees will be marked by a series of crucial turning points (DPT; e.g., being spotted by a teacher or coach, receiving an important scholarship, suffering a major accident as an athlete, having difficulty overcoming the death of a parent).

The "Supporting Cast" of I and E Catalysts

The large sets of *intrapersonal* (I) and *environmental* (E) catalysts affect the talent development process either positively or negatively. The I component comprises five subcomponents grouped into two main dimensions, namely stable traits (physical–IF, mental–IP), and goal management processes (self-awareness–IW, motivation–IM, and volition–IV). Within the mental or personality (IP) category, the concept of temperament refers to behavioral predispositions with strong biological and hereditary underpinnings, whereas the term *personality* encompasses a large diversity of positive or negative acquired styles of behavior (Rothbart, 2012). The most widely accepted structure for personality attributes is called the Five-Factor Model; research has shown each factor to possess significant biological roots (McCrae, 2009). The term *motivation* usually brings to mind both the idea of what motivates us (IM) and how motivated (IV) we are, that is, how much effort we are ready to invest in order to reach a particular goal. Within the framework of their Action Control Theory, two German scholars (Kuhl & Beckmann, 1985; see also Corno, 1993) proposed to differentiate the global goal-seeking process into (a) distinct goal-setting activities, which would receive the label motivation (IM), and (b) goal-attainment activities, which they labeled volition or willpower (IV). Talentees will first examine their values and their needs (IW), as well as determine their interests or be swept by a sudden passion; these will serve to identify the specific talent goal they will be aiming for (IM). The loftier that goal, the more efforts talentees will need to put forth in order to reach it (IV). Long-term goals placed at a very high level will require intense dedication, as well as daily acts of willpower to maintain investment in practice (the DI subcomponent) through obstacles, boredom, and occasional failure.

The E component appears partially hidden behind the I component (Figures 7.1 and 7.2). This partial overlap signals the crucial filtering role that the I component plays with regard to environmental influences. The bulk of environmental stimuli have to pass through the analytical sieve—conscious or subconscious—of an individual's needs, interests, or personality traits; talentees continually pick and choose which stimuli will receive their attention. The E component comprises three subcomponents that refer to distinct environmental perspectives: social, psychological, and educational. The first one, called *milieu* (EM), includes a diversity of influences, from physical ones (e.g., climate, rural vs. urban living) to social, political, financial, or cultural ones. The second subcomponent focuses on the psychological influence of significant *individuals* (EI) in the talentees' immediate environment. It includes, of course, parents and siblings, but also the larger family, teachers and trainers, peers, mentors, and even public figures adopted as role models by talentees. The third subcomponent covers all forms of talent development *resources* (ER), among them adapted curricula, special courses or schools, advanced teams in sports, and so forth.

The Chance Factor

Chance represents the *degree of control* talentees have over the various causal factors affecting their talent development. Atkinson (1978) affirmed: "all human accomplishments can be ascribed to two crucial 'rolls of the dice' over which no individual exerts any personal control: the accidents of birth and background" (p. 221). Indeed, we do not control the genetic endowment received at conception; yet, it affects both our natural abilities (G component), our temperament (IP), as well as other elements of the I component (IM + IV). Moreover, we do not choose or control the family (EI) or social environment (EM) in which we are raised. These two sources alone give chance much power in sowing the bases of a person's talent development possibilities. Because of its polyvalent role as an *éminence grise* throughout the model, I have chosen to illustrate its influence as a background halo covering the components it influences (Figures 7.1 and 7.2).

Dynamic Interactions

All five components of the DMGT entertain a large diversity of complex dynamic interactions, both among themselves and between specific facets within each of them. Space does not allow a detailed survey, but consider, for example, that all efforts by teachers or parents to modify the characteristics of children and students (e.g., interests, personality, beliefs, deviant behavior) illustrate E → I influences; of course, you can easily imagine influences in the opposite direction (e.g., students' passions influencing the behavior of parents or teachers). The most fundamental pattern of interactions defines the DMGT's view of the talent development process, namely the long-term transformation of outstanding potentialities into equally outstanding competencies, thanks to the constant mediating effect of both groups of catalysts. Even talent, the outcome, can have a motivating impact on students: Success breeds success! It can also influence environmental sources, parents as well as teachers. In summary, no causal component stands alone; they all interact with each other and with the learning process in very complex ways, and these interactions will differ significantly from one person to the next.

The G into T transformation process needs nuances; strictly speaking, that definition is incomplete. If we consider that individual differences in achievement have many other sources than just G, it means that students with aptitudes below the top 10% gifted level can still achieve above the talent threshold (also top 10%) thanks to the positive influence of high levels of influences from either D, or I, or E (or all of them!). Of course, as the level of aptitudes decreases, the probability of talent will also decrease sharply, so much so that there is only a small probability that students with average cognitive aptitudes will reach talent level performances (Gottfredson, 1997; Herrnstein & Murray, 1994). Conversely, gifted level aptitudes do not guarantee the emergence of talent, as evidenced by the well-known phenomenon of underachievement.

Even though all four causal components are constantly active, it does not mean that they are equally powerful as agents of talent emergence. This is no doubt a truism at the individual level because each talented person follows a unique path toward excellence. But what can we say about averages? Are some factors *generally* recognized as stronger predictors of outstanding performance? For all those involved in the talent development of gifted individuals, this is *the* ultimate question both theoretically and practically. Most of us harbor a personal "implicit theory" about the causal origins of academic talent, and a major characteristic of these personal—or more scientific—views is the tendency to privilege one key influence of success. That key influence may reside within the family or in the school environment, be identified as amount of study, determination and willpower, motivation and passion, cognitive aptitudes, and so forth. I have labeled that question "What makes a difference?" Its extensive discussion represents another unique characteristic of the DMGT. Unfortunately, space does not allow a presentation of that analysis (see Gagné, 2004), but allow me a teaser. For the specific case of academic achievement, I proposed in that article the following decreasing hierarchy of influence for the four causal components: (a) intellectual giftedness (GI); (b) intrapersonal catalysts, especially IM and IV; (c) developmental activities, especially investment in energy (DIE); and (d) environmental influences.

The above discussion leads to the following *theoretical* definition of academic talent development (ATD) within the DMGT/IMTD framework:

> Academic talent development (ATD) corresponds to the progressive transformation through a long-term learning process of biologically anchored, informally developed, and mostly cognitive outstanding natural abilities (the gifts) into equally outstanding

systematically developed academic competencies (knowledge and skills) (the talents), thanks to constant moderating interactions with two large groups of catalysts, intrapersonal characteristics and environmental influences.

Practical Usefulness of the Differentiation

Here is one example among many of the potential usefulness of the DMGT's differentiation between giftedness and talent. The vast majority of studies that compare gifted students with nongifted peers use "convenience" samples, usually participants in gifted programs. Recall that these "gifted" students have been selected, most of the time, with measures of both intellectual giftedness and academic talent; as I mentioned early in this chapter, they are IGAT students. Researchers use such comparison groups to examine the relationship between intelligence and a diversity of other personal characteristics (e.g., motivation, perseverance, personality traits, psychopathology, and so forth). But, these researchers do not realize that their so-called gifted samples are conceptually tainted; the inclusion of achievement data makes them more than just intellectually gifted. Keep in mind that academic talent results from the complex influence of multiple causal factors from the D, the I, and the E subcomponents, not just the GI subcomponent. Individual differences in valid academic achievement measures faithfully reflect these complex influences: differences in level of intrinsic motivation, in family support, in personality traits like anxiety, in peer influences, in study time, and so forth. Consequently, we should not be surprised that the high achievers typically selected for gifted programs will prove themselves, on average, somewhat more motivated, socially adept, or psychologically stable than average peers (Neihart, Pfeiffer, & Cross, 2016). As a case in point, at the end of their comparative analysis of the psychopathological characteristics of "gifted" versus average students, Francis, Hawes, and Abbott (2016) observed:

> It is possible that the nature of the gifted program selection process results in members who are functioning well in school (academically, behaviorally, and socially), potentially leading to participant selection bias in studies that underestimates the prevalence of intellectually gifted children with behavioral or other difficulties. (p. 295)

Could it be that their knowledge of the DMGT prompted that very relevant observation emphasizing the DMGT difference between giftedness and talent?

Where Do Gifts Come From; Are They Innate?

In the first part of the chapter, we defined natural abilities as having significant biological roots; these roots manifest themselves in many ways, for instance, anatomical or morphological characteristics, neurophysiological activity in the brain and body, gene expression, and countless other forms discussed in the scientific literature on talent development (Geake, 2009). Unfortunately, the DMGT framework presented leaves no room for these distal sources of talent emergence. In order to offer a comprehensive view of the talent development process, I judged it imperative to find a way to integrate these causal influences.

Biological Foundations of Gifts and Talents

Science has adopted a hierarchical organization of explanations, moving progressively from behavioral phenomena, down to physiology, microbiology, chemistry, and then physics. For instance, Plomin, DeFries, Craig, and McGuffin (2003) described functional genomics as "a bottom-up strategy in which the gene product is identified by its DNA sequence and the function of the gene product is traced through cells and then cell systems and eventually the brain" (p. 14). The expression "bottom-up" makes clear that such biological underpinnings would occupy some underground level under the strictly behavioral DMGT framework. A brief examination of the literature did suggest that three underground levels would create an acceptable vertical differentiation (see Column 1 in Figure 7.1). The bottom *chemical* basement is reserved for genotypic foundations (e.g., gene identification, mutations, gene expression, epigenetic phenomena, protein production, and so forth). The next one, the *physiological* basement, covers microbiological and (neuro)physiological processes; it moves us from genotypic to phenotypic phenomena, but their hidden nature, at least to the naked eye, explains their label of *endophenotypes*: They correspond to "physical traits—phenotypes—that are not externally visible but are measurable" (Nurnberger & Bierut, 2007, pp. 48–49). Finally, the upper *morphological* basement includes anatomical characteristics that have been shown to impact abilities or intrapersonal catalysts. Most of these characteristics are observable *exophenotypes*, either directly (e.g., tallness in basketball, physical template in gymnastics) or indirectly (e.g., brain size through neuroimaging, muscle type through biopsy). Both endophenotypes and morphological traits are part of the complex hierarchical causal chain joining genes to physical or mental abilities, and ultimately to systematically developed skills.

The Proper Meaning of "Innate"

The Developmental Model for Natural Abilities (DMNA) aimed to integrate these biological foundations as building blocks in the development of natural abilities and gifts. It also aimed to respond to scholars who question the relevance of the concept of giftedness, and correct the misunderstanding transmitted by well-meaning users of the DMGT who simplistically describe gifts as innate and talents as acquired. That simplistic bipolar view is wrong. As already pointed out, gifts are not innate; they develop during the course of childhood, and sometimes continue to do so during adulthood. Of course, this developmental view of natural abilities has to fight its way through a host of common language expressions that maintain the ambiguity, like "She is a born musician," "It's God's gift," or "Either you have it or you don't!"

If these uses of the label *innate* are incorrect, what does innateness really mean? When we say that young Mary is a "born" pianist, we are certainly not implying that she began playing the piano in the nursery, or that she was able to play a concerto within weeks of beginning her piano lessons. Describing her talent as innate makes sense only metaphorically. It will convey the idea that Mary progressed rapidly and seemingly without effort through her music curriculum, at a much more rapid pace than that of her learning peers. The same applies to any natural ability. Intellectually precocious children do not suddenly manifest an exceptional vocabulary or logical reasoning processes; their cognitive development goes through the same stages as any other child. The difference resides in the ease and speed with which they advance through these successive stages. The term *precocious* says it all: They reach a given level of knowledge and reasoning *before* the vast majority of their learning peers. Researchers in behavioral genetics have given the term *innate* a very specific definition. At the behavioral level, it implies

> hard-wired, fixed action patterns of a species that are impervious to experience. Genetic influence on abilities and other complex traits does not denote the hard-wired deterministic effect of a single gene but rather probabilistic propensities of many genes in multiple-gene systems. (Plomin, 1998, p. 421)

So, when people use the term innate to qualify the DMGT's natural abilities, they spread two false interpretations, namely that the observed individual differences are immutable, and that they are present at birth or, if not, appear suddenly with minimal training. Because of its restricted meaning, few scientists use the term innate to describe any type of natural ability or temperamental characteristic.

If natural abilities cannot be considered innate as defined above, where does the "gift" in giftedness reside? Certainly not in the upper basement identified above, because these morphological structures require extensive development; most do not achieve maturity until adolescence or even adulthood. If we go one basement down to the physiological level, we might be in a gray zone where it becomes difficult to separate innate processes, like maturation, from environmentally influenced developmental activities. For example, genetic agents govern most stages of embryogenesis. If the development was strictly maturational, then we could probably speak of innateness. It is clear, however, that the lowest basement, devoted to gene activity, is almost completely—but not totally, according to the new field of epigenetics—under inborn control.

Introducing the DMNA

How does the development of natural abilities proceed? Figure 7.1 shows that process through the DMNA. At first glance, it appears similar to its right side counterpart, the DMGT, but a closer look shows major differences between them, both at the component and the subcomponent levels. The main difference is, of course, a transfer of the G component from the left side (DMGT) to the right side (DMNA); aptitudes—and their outstanding expression as gifts—are now the outcome of this particular developmental process. Here, the three levels of biological underpinnings, structural elements as well as processes, play the role of building blocks for the phenotypic natural abilities. The developmental process specific to the DMNA appears here in summary form, with just two macroprocesses identified. Maturation, of course, covers a diversity of biological processes at each of the three basement levels, from embryogenesis upward, that govern the growth of mental and physical abilities. These maturational processes have no direct relationship with the talent development process itself; their role is to mold the natural abilities that will become, in turn, the building blocks of talents. As for the learning subcomponent, it is called informal because it lacks the structured organization (e.g., curriculum, access rules, systematic schedule, formal assessment) typical of talent development activities. It takes the form of spontaneous learning and practice, acquired mostly subconsciously and automatically, without regular attention to its growth.

Every developmental process requires catalytic influences, both intrapersonal and environmental. These two sets of catalysts appear here structurally identical to their DMGT counterparts. The exact contents within each element will differ, as well as their relative causal significance. Two subcomponents, self-awareness (IW) and resources (ER), appear in lighter font because they play a much more modest causal role than in the DMGT; we cannot expect, for instance, young children to show the same level of awareness (IW) toward their strengths and weaknesses as older individuals, but no doubt that interests and passions (IM) can manifest themselves very early (Gagné & McPherson, 2016). Similarly, within the realm of mental traits (IP), large individual differences appear as soon as we start assessing any of them. With respect to motivational issues, children express very early their desire—or lack of it!—to engage in all kinds of daily activities: physical exercise, reading, learning to play a musical instrument, video games, playing with friends, and so forth. To some extent, their level of interest will influence the amount of their short-term or long-term investment, as well as their potential decision to participate in a talent development program and to maintain their involvement in it. Environmental catalysts also play a significant role in fostering or hindering the development of human aptitudes, and all three subcomponents are involved, except that formal resources play a minimal causal role.

Here are just a few examples. With regard to the Milieu (EM) subcomponent, recent studies (e.g., Harden, Turkheimer, & Loehlin, 2007) suggested that the degree of heritability (H) of cognitive abilities varies with the socioeconomic level of the families; the H component's importance decreases significantly in low-income families. In fact, the whole area of gene by environment interactions belongs to the E component (Plomin, 1994). With regard to the Individuals (EI) subcomponent, interventions by parents to create a specific family environment, propitious either to general knowledge learning, to musical activities, or to athletic ones, could impact the development of related natural abilities. In the case of the Resources (ER) subcomponent, government programs developed to improve the school preparedness (a.k.a. cognitive abilities) of at-risk children (te Nijenhuis, Jongeneel-Grimen, & Kirkegaard, 2014) represent interesting efforts to build these natural abilities. In sum, natural abilities proceed through a developmental process somewhat similar to the talent development process. The same basic "ingredients" are involved in fostering or hindering their growth. Of course, as Angoff (1988) perceptively highlighted, the most significant distinction between gifts and talents remains the amount of direct genetic contribution. The DMNA makes that point clear in its choice of building blocks.

Introducing the IMTD

As soon as the DMNA was conceived, it became clear that joining the two developmental models into an Integrative Model of Talent Development (IMTD) would bring closure to these theoretical musings. Figure 7.1 illustrates the result, with the G component's central position ensuring the linkage between the DMNA's build-up of outstanding natural abilities on the left side and the DMGT's talent development process on the right side. The IMTD shows how talent development has its distal origins in the progressive emergence of natural abilities, as early as through the complex process of embryogenesis. The maturation process will continue after birth as the various natural abilities, mental and physical, progressively take form at different levels of expression from one individual to the next, thanks to the contribution of the two sets of catalysts, as well as innumerable daily occasions for informal learning and exercise. At some point, usually during childhood or early adolescence depending on the type of talent chosen, some gifted individuals, or those not too far from the DMGT's cutoff threshold of top 10%, will choose a talent field that fits their perceived profile of natural abilities and interests, and begin the long and complex journey leading to eventual top performance, as described in the DMGT model. Some will go far beyond the basic 10% threshold of minimal talent; others will not, and the reasons behind the level of expertise achieved by talentees will be found in the numerous facets that comprise the DMGT.

How Can We Best Foster Academic Talent Development (ATD)?

Most school districts commonly group their special educational provisions for gifted/talented students (the IGAT) under the label "gifted programs." The ATD programmatic approach I will describe here has little in common with the vast majority of these gifted programs. Before going further, let's properly define the concept of *program* I will use here. It originates in a seminal distinction proposed over three decades ago by Tannenbaum (1983); he defined a program as "a comprehensive offering, sequenced over a long period of time, usually designed as a requirement, and very much a major part of the total school curriculum. Thus, the school offers *programs* in mathematics, literature, art, social studies, and the like." (p. 515) On the other hand, provisions were "more fragmentary, an ad hoc offering, relatively brief in duration, often designed by an individual teacher with special abilities rather than by a curriculum committee, and supplemental to the major offerings, not integral with them" (Tannenbaum, 1983, p. 515). Borland (1989) endorsed and expanded Tannenbaum's distinction. Although he considered "that there is nothing at all wrong with provisions for the gifted," and that they "may be among the most valuable [opportunities] offered to students in their school careers" (Borland, 1989, p. 44), he judged these provisions to have major drawbacks. He stated, for instance, that "whereas provisions are fragmentary, programs have well-articulated sequences of goals, skills, and content. Whereas provisions are extracurricular, programs consist of activities that constitute a prescribed part of the course of study of identified gifted students" (Borland, 1989, p. 44). Note that programs and provisions do not represent qualitatively distinct categories, but rather opposite poles on a continuum. Thus, some educational resources could possess characteristics that place them somewhere between these two poles. Both scholars considered that most existing gifted programs at that time belonged much more to the provision than to the program pole. As we will see later, I consider that judgment to apply equally well to current gifted programs. Sadly, that seminal conceptual distinction has had literally no impact on the terminological habits of scholars and educators; terminological fuzziness remains one major differentiating characteristic between the social and natural sciences! To allow for easier reading, I will keep using the expression "gifted programs" to refer to the same ensemble of provisions that this label targets in the gifted education literature.

Moon and Rosselli (2000) proposed to break down talent development programs into three main components: (a) the definition of the program's developmental goals, (b) the identification of the target population, and (c) the contents of the proposed developmental interventions, both in terms of curriculum and administrative parameters. Let's discuss them within the DMGT perspective, because the DMNA component of the IMTD has little relevance here.

Goals of a DMGT-Inspired ATD Program

A DMGT-inspired ATD program aims to foster through the best educational practices available the maximal transfer of high cognitive aptitudes into academic excellence. Keep in mind that the DMGT is a talent development theory, which explains why its key objective is academic excellence. Choosing this particular program goal does not exclude the inclusion of parallel goals within a given ATD program, for instance, developing personal maturity and social conscience, or fostering physical well-being (*mens sana in corpore sano*). But we would have to create a different theoretical structure to present the diverse causal components of each parallel goal. That discussion is not relevant here. My key point is that personal characteristics (the IP subcomponent) appear in the DMGT only because of their potential impact on the developmental (D) process.

Identification of the Target Population

Just as in any talent development program, a DMGT-inspired ATD program aims to select as talentees those students best prepared to profit maximally from the program's content (curriculum and format). Which are the best predictors of academic excellence? Which of them make more of a difference on average? As we discussed in Part II, there are theoretically dozens of potential influences dispersed among the four causal components (G, D, I, E) of the DMGT. But, which among them have revealed better predictive power with respect to academic achievement? Research has shown that current academic achievement outperforms any other predictor of future achievement. For instance, Marques, Pais-Ribeiro, and Lopez (2011) found correlations above .90 between consecutive aggregated subject matter achievements in grades 6 to 8. For his part, Muijs (1997) observed an "extremely strong relationship [between] school achievement in wave 1 [Grade 4] with school achievement in wave 2 [Grade 5], (. . .) a fact borne out by a Pearson correlation of .88 (p < .001) over time" (p. 272). This should surprise no one because successive achievement measures assess exactly the same content; we are in fact just measuring the longitudinal reliability of a given predictor. But there is more to consider. At first glance, indices of academic success appear simple, both at the data collection and interpretation levels. Yet, that easy metric and straight-forward meaning hide a much more complex interpretive power. According to the DMGT, talents (T) result from the progressive transformation of high natural abilities (G) through a long developmental process (D), with the catalytic help of personal characteristics (I) and environmental influences (E). Consequently, measures of academic achievement—indeed of any performance—incorporate the *combined* influences of all these distinct sources (G, I, D, E); they give them very complex roots. They have roots in the genetics of high natural abilities, roots in passion and interest for a field's knowledge and skills, roots in unfailing perse-verance and willpower, roots in parental and teacher support, and, let's not forget, roots in lots of chance, both good and bad luck.

What would be the next best predictor of academic excellence? The answer is clear: intellectual aptitudes. Literally hundreds of predictive studies have con-firmed that IQ scores show impressive correlations with academic achievement; they correlate between .50 and .60 at the elementary level, and between .40 and .50 at the high school level (Jensen, 1980; Macintosh, 2011). This data no doubt explains why, as pointed out earlier, school districts give precedence to these two sources of predictive information in their identification procedures. Beyond these two unavoidable sources of identification, are there any other valuable criteria, sources that might add some specific additional predictive power? The clearest one is the DMGT's subcomponent volition (IV), also called conscientiousness in the Five-Factor model of personality (McCrae, 2009), or grit (Duckworth, Peterson, Matthews, & Kelly, 2007), or "rage to master" (Winner, 1996, p. 3). The main problem with that criterion is the lesser availability of psychometrically valid measures (Gagné & St Père, 2001). Any other criteria (e.g., attention, delib-erate practice) would have to be tried out in specific ATD programs to assess their potential specific contribution to global predictive power.

Seven Essential ATD Characteristics

The search for the essential characteristics of a DMGT-inspired ATD pro-gram began with a survey of our field's professional and scientific literature, tak-ing note of suggestions from various scholars and professionals. I also examined the best recognized practices in other talent development fields, especially the well-structured fields of music and sports. I found there much more convergence and homogeneity in goals and practices; they offered plenty of materials that could be applied in educational settings. A synthesis of that search first took form as the "ten commandments for academic talent development" (Gagné, 2007). They were later condensed (Gagné, 2015a) into the seven following constitutive elements:

1. An enriched K–12 curriculum;
2. Systematic daily enrichment;
3. Full-time ability grouping;
4. Customized/accelerated pacing;
5. Challenging excellence goals;
6. Highly selective access; and
7. Early introduction.

The first four characteristics target Moon and Rosselli's (2000) content/format component, the next one the program's goals, and the last two the talentee population. As a "keystone" characteristic, the first one deserves its first rank hands down; grouping all the others according to program components solved a conundrum, namely trying to create some hierarchy among them. Except for the last one, which sets the point of departure of a structured ATD pathway, I consider the six other constitutive characteristics as necessary components. These seven characteristics lead to the following formal definition of an ATD *program*.

> A DMGT-inspired academic talent development (ATD) program is an early implemented, customized long-term sequence of structured learning activities anchored in a constantly enriched and challenging academic curriculum, directed toward the attainment of high-level excellence goals.

Let's examine in more detail each of these seven constitutive characteristics.

1. An enriched K–12 curriculum. By definition, "academic" talent development programs aim to foster academic excellence, and academic excellence expresses itself as outstanding mastery of the K–12 curriculum; it is that curriculum we must enrich for academic talentees to experience regular learning challenges. The term *curriculum* covers both the content of specific subject matters at a particular grade level and its integrated structure within and between grade levels; it also includes instructional strategies. A provision that does not aim to implement this keystone characteristic cannot receive the DMGT-inspired ATD label. It also constitutes the key element in Tannenbaum's (1983) definition of a proper program for gifted students. As he pointed out, "enrichment for the gifted is as much an educational imperative as is the 'common core' for the general school population" (p. 424). The recently proposed Advanced Academics model (Peters, Matthews, McBee, & McCoach, 2014) recommended a similar curricular priority. I chose the term *enriched* well aware that I was "delinquently" rejecting the choice made by most of my colleagues, who prefer the politically correct term *differentiation* (e.g., French, 2009; Kaplan, 2009; Renzulli, 2009). It is very sad that perceived political pressures or public stereotypes (e.g., a nonenriched curriculum is a poor curriculum) force professionals to put aside proper terminology; its rehabilitation is overdue for the simple reason that the term enriched best describes the type of differentiation *specifically appropriate* for fast learners.

What does an enriched curriculum look like? At the broadest level, that of a structured set of subject matters, it does not differ substantially from the regular curriculum; most adaptations appear to target specific contents at particular grade levels, as well as instructional strategies (e.g., Hertberg-Davis & Callahan, 2013; Tomlinson, 2009; VanTassel-Baska & Little, 2003). For instance, Rogers (2009) identified seven research-based content—and instructional—modifications that provide "significant academic benefits for gifted learners" (p. 264): abstract concepts, complex contents, multidisciplinary themes, sequence reorganization, links with human and social issues, introduction of professional inquiry methods, and subject acceleration. With respect to instructional strategies, I proposed (Gagné, 2007) four different types of enrichment that I labeled the four D's: enrichment in Density, in Difficulty, in Depth, and in Diversity. That particular sequence reflects a *decreasing* order of relevance, thus giving clear priority to enrichment in Density. Also called curriculum condensation or compacting (Reis, Burns, & Renzulli, 1992; Reis, Renzulli, & Burns, 2016), it serves as the pedagogical core of a properly enriched curriculum. Academic talent development specialists should prioritize it over other forms of enrichment because it offers the most relevant response to giftedness' trademark, namely ease/speed in learning. Moreover, the school time liberated through faster mastery of subject matter units creates learning space for additional enrichment.

2. Systematic daily enrichment. This second constitutive element might appear almost tautological, because the adoption of the keystone first element, with its enrichment focused on condensing the regular curriculum, implies its implementation on a daily basis. Yet, I perceived a need for its inclusion because many teachers or school administrators are worried about the—mythic—cataclysmic impact of accelerative measures; these unfounded fears lead them to refuse that their talentees progress too far ahead while still remaining in their regular classroom. Accordingly, after allowing a short burst of enrichment in Density, they will switch to other types of enrichment, like enrichment in Depth (long-term projects) or in Diversity (noncurricular short-term activities). These talentees will progress in brief rapid spurts followed by pauses occupied with "lateral" enrichment, thus ending their school year more or less at the same level of subject matter mastery as their well-performing nontalentee learning peers. Appropriate enrichment must propose instead intellectual challenges on a *daily* basis. Vygotsky's

(1978) concept of *zone of proximal development*, as well as Stanley's Talent Search instructional approach (Brody & Stanley, 2005), aptly convey the need to maintain the talentees' pace at the cutting edge of their learning capacity, neither too slow to force them to idle regularly, nor too fast to create feelings of helplessness. Teachers must look out regularly for signs of unchallenging content; if there is one thing that many high-achieving students resent, it's having to face, day after day, the constant slow and repetitive pace imposed by their learning peers. This particular problem rarely surfaces in sports or arts; their talent development practices almost automatically maintain cutting-edge teaching strategy.

3. Full-time ability grouping. This third constitutive element directly ensues from the preceding one: How can we best deliver daily enrichment to talentees, if not by grouping them with a specially trained ATD teacher (an appellation much more relevant than "gifted teacher"!)? Yet, this administratively sensible solution, especially its full-time variety, touches a very sensitive chord, probably even more sensitive in our field than the subject of academic acceleration (see #4 below). Commonly discussed in gifted education handbooks before the turn of the present century (e.g., Colangelo & Davis, 1997; Davis & Rimm, 1985; Heller, Mönks, & Passow, 1993), the subject of ability grouping has almost disappeared from recent handbooks, not only as a separate chapter on the subject (e.g., Balchin et al., 2009; Callahan & Hertberg-Davis, 2013; Dixon & Moon, 2006; Heller, Mönks, Sternberg, & Subotnik, 2000; MacFarlane & Stambaugh, 2009; Shavinina, 2009), but even as an entry in encyclopedia-type handbooks (e.g., Kerr, 2009; Plucker & Callahan, 2008). I cannot explain that withdrawal; has our field decided to forgo any defense of that essential practice?

It seems to me so easy to justify the full-time grouping of talentees in view of the research evidence on both the positive academic impacts of grouping (Kulik, 2003; Rogers & Span, 1993) and the almost total lack, in regular classrooms, of enrichment activities that specifically target academically talented students. Major evaluation studies (e.g., Archambault et al., 1993; Robinson, 1998) have shown that the vast majority of these provisions offer little more than a lip service response to talented students' needs. The results revealed, among other things, that teachers offered these activities no more than two or three times a month. Even worse, the activities usually targeted the whole classroom, leaving little specific enrichment for talented students. Archambault et al. (1993) concluded that their survey had painted

> a disturbing picture of the types of instructional services gifted students receive in regular classrooms across the United States. It is clear from the results that teachers in regular third and fourth grade classrooms make only minor modifications in the curriculum and their instruction to meet the needs of gifted students. (p. 5)

From these results, one can understand the label of "busywork" Stanley (1979) used with disdain to describe most of what passes for regular classroom enrichment.

At all levels of the K–12 educational system, teachers prioritize students with learning difficulties who stand at the other end of the achievement continuum. Moreover, the curriculum of most preservice teacher training programs reflects the low priority given to talented students' needs. Courses on special populations reserve only a few hours—when they do so!—to the characteristics and educational needs of academically talented students (Croft, 2003). In that context, responding adequately to the special educational needs of fast learners literally becomes a "mission impossible" (Gagné, 2007, p. 110). That inescapable conclusion should lead to the generalization of full-time grouping for talentees as the only effective way to create appropriate classroom conditions for sustained daily enrichment; grouping 30 or so students around a single ATD teacher also provides a very efficient use of limited specialized resources. In a nutshell, full-time grouping answers a full-time need with a full-time solution, facilitates the enrichment of all subject matters in the regular curriculum, and, contrary to most pull-out services, does not require adding a costly specialist teacher to the school faculty. Recent evidence gives additional strength to that solution. An important evaluation study (VanTassel-Baska et al., 2008) confirmed the enormous time and financial resources required to train regular elementary classroom teachers to implement language arts enrichment modules in their classroom. A team of university specialists had to invest hundreds of hours of professional time over a period of 2 years to train just a dozen elementary school teachers to an acceptable level in the proper use of these enrichment materials, which covered about a third of the school year's curriculum in just one subject matter!

4. Customized/accelerated pacing. Grouping talentees to offer an enriched curriculum does not mean that all individual differences in learning pace have disappeared; remaining individual differences produce over time an increasing gap between slower and faster learners, what has been called a "fan spread effect" (Gagné, 2005). Moreover, analyses of achievement test scores, as well as results from talent searches, show the large gap in knowledge and skills between mildly talented students and their exceptionally talented peers (Gagné, 2005; Lupkowski-Shoplik, Benbow, Assouline, & Brody, 2003). Consequently, those who progress significantly faster than peer talentees should be allowed, if they so desire, to move ahead at an accelerated pace. Unfortunately, most accelerative measures face strong resistance from a majority of administrators, teachers, and parents; they ignore or refuse to accept the overwhelming scientific evidence in support of all forms of accelerative enrichment (Assouline, Colangelo, VanTassel-Baska, & Lupkowski-Shoplik, 2015; Rogers, 1991). Borland (1989) elegantly summarized that conundrum: "Acceleration is one of the most curious phenomena in the field of education. I can think of no other issue in which there is such a gulf between what research has revealed and what most practitioners believe" (p. 185).

5. Challenging excellence goals. Four qualifiers (personal, excellence, challenging, long-term) describe the educational goals that talentees would be invited to set for themselves. Excellence goals must be understood normatively, which means in relationship with the expected achievements of learning peers. Of course, as members of a highly selective group (see #3 and #6), their reference base differs from that of regular classroom students. They are no longer "big fish in a little pond" (Marsh & Hau, 2003; Plucker et al., 2004), but have become smaller fish in the bigger pond of talentee classmates. So, these goals should far exceed the level of academic excellence typically expected within the regular curriculum. Obtaining high marks in a regular classroom has nothing to do with academic talent development; most academically talented students can reach such goals much too easily. Note also that their normative status distinguishes these goals from "personal bests," which can apply to the academic goals of all students. The adjective *personal* means that the talentees not only choose these educational goals themselves, but can also revise them periodically; they should have full ownership.

The third adjective, *challenging*, means that these personal excellence goals should incite talentees to leave the security formerly offered by their "big fish" status, and risk testing their learning limits, not only in cognitive terms, but also with respect to their motivation and volition. Finally, the fourth qualifier refers to a goal-setting process that looks ahead far beyond a few weeks or months, trying to encompass at least a full segment (e.g., elementary, middle school, high school) of the K–12 educational trajectory. Consequently, talentees cannot apply to popular activities like summer camps, once a week pull-out classes, or weekend enrichment activities; they need to target main academic objectives relevant to the enriched regular curriculum. They must also involve a substantial investment in time and effort. On the other hand, they need not be ultimate or peak achievement goals, like completing a Ph.D., at least not before entering high school. Of course, if some young talentees entertain with passion long-term career plans, so much the better! But such passionate long-term involvements remain quite rare (see Gagné & McPherson, 2016).

6. Highly selective access. This sixth constitutive element follows directly from the first two defining characteristics: an enriched curriculum offered on a daily basis. Academic talent development requires not only outstanding natural learning abilities, but also, as with any other developmental program, demonstrated probability of future success. Yet, the selection process mentioned above leaves ample room for error; unless the selection ratio is exceedingly high, like top 10% or less of candidates, some selected students will fail to perform at the level expected by the enriched curriculum. It is then tempting to reduce the program's performance requirements to avoid forcing these students to leave. Program administrators should resist that temptation because it marks the beginning of a slippery course toward more mediocre expectations. Instead, all selected students should know when they enter that their membership depends on maintaining adequate academic results. A reduction of the enrichment level will impact the progress and motivation of all other talentees.

7. Early introduction. This final desirable characteristic of DMGT-inspired ATD programs questions a common administrative practice in school districts, namely to delay structured enrichment until at least grades 3 or 4. The justifications given appear associated with worries about (a) less reliable selection procedures with younger children, (b) a still fragile development, and (c) moving too rapidly from the playful early school environment to the more achievement-oriented regular classroom "treadmill" (Rogers, 1991). That postponement policy contradicts a fundamental law of individual differences in development: Precocity manifests itself . . . precociously! Indeed, the popularity of the Wechsler Preschool and Primary Scale of Intelligence (WPPSI-III; Wechsler, 2003) confirms that intellectual precocity becomes easily noticeable by ages 3 or 4. Indeed, many children who enter kindergarten already know the alphabet, can write their name, read some words, and even do simple arithmetic computations. Their intellectual precocity makes them better prepared than the average first grader to tackle the first-grade curriculum.

Dozens of studies have shown that the level of cognitive development measured by IQ and/or school readiness tests predicts academic achievement in the early grades of elementary school much better than students' chronological age. The correlation between chronological age and academic achievement among cohorts of first graders ranges between .10 and .25 (Gagné & Gagnier, 2004), whereas the predictive power increases to .50 or more when using school readiness tests (Jensen, 1980). In terms of explained variance (r^2), the difference between the two predictors amounts to at least a 6:1 ratio! Sadly, although research evidence has shown their numerous benefits, early entrance provisions have never become popular. After examining all 68 evaluative studies of early entrance, Rogers (1991) concluded that it constitutes a very desirable initiative for the vast majority of children. In summary, this seventh constitutive element strongly invites school administrators to make this initial service the cornerstone of their school district's ATD program. Of course, qualifying early entrance as a "cornerstone" implies that it will be followed by the other building blocks of a comprehensive ATD pathway, all the way from kindergarten to college.

Toward ATD pathways. ATD programs could be sequentially structured into comprehensive K–12 ATD pathways. Concretely, it would begin in kindergarten or first grade with an early entrance policy for intellectually precocious children. Beyond that initial cornerstone, academic talentees would follow a parallel, constantly enriched pathway all the way to the end of high school. That pathway would be available to all children manifesting clear indices of future outstanding academic achievement; it would invite these academic talentees to set for themselves challenging academic excellence goals. Full-time ability grouping would not necessarily mean enforcing an enriched age-grade lockstep. Educators would still occasionally allow further acceleration because of remaining large individual differences in learning pace within the talentee population. This comprehensive programming pathway would introduce more relevant designations, replacing the labels "gifted children" and "gifted education" with the more relevant terms *talentee, academically talented*, and *academic talent development*. Educators would still use the gifted label, but in a more specific context; it would refer to natural abilities, for instance, when talking about "gifted learners," exactly as proposed within the DMGT framework. But "academically talented student" or "academic talentee" would become the more common expressions, if only because they represent the main criterion of access to and progress within ADT programs. Teachers endorsed with the responsibility of guiding talentees through the various components of that ATD pathway would be called *ATD teachers.*

I am not aware that such a pathway exists anywhere; most school systems in developed countries do not even succeed in putting into practice the first two key characteristics described above. In fact, the two most popular prototypes currently found in elementary classrooms are pull-out classes and regular classroom enrichment (Callahan, Moon, & Oh, 2017), which has been the case for many decades (Archambault et al., 1993; Cox et al., 1985). Both practices ignore most of the seven key characteristics, especially the crucial principle of daily enrichment of the regular school curriculum. If we encounter virtually no DMGT-based ATD programs in primary schools, we can observe interesting examples of ATD-style academic enrichment at the high school level; for instance the 165 highly selective public high schools—still less than 1% of the U.S.'s 22,568 public high schools— identified by Finn and Hockett (2012) in 30 states, or the network of 50 or so selective high schools in New South Wales, Australia (see https://en.wikipedia.org/ wiki/List_of_selective_high_schools_in_New_South_Wales). Finally, when systematically implemented with a truly enriched curriculum, self-contained honors classes also represent potentially appropriate examples of academic talent development (Kulik, 2003). Note that the highly popular Advanced Placement classes offered in a majority of U.S. high schools *do not* implement the ATD model proposed here. Indeed, although potentially very enriching for the talented students who take them, they are the equivalent of pull-out classes, and consequently affect in no way the slow pace of the regular curriculum. This limited sample of existing programs demonstrates that the DMGT-inspired ATD model can be implemented, if not as a full ATD pathway, at least through partial ATD programs.

These limited examples suggest that extensive dissemination of proper enrichment lies far in the future. Most school systems fall very short of answering the educational needs of their academically talented high school students; they have planned, as their unique pathway, an age-grade lockstep (Stanley, 1979) coupled with a slow-paced curriculum that covers the 13 years from kindergarten to 12th grade. And that harsh judgment of academic monotony extends to almost every developed country. Such slow dissemination should surprise no one; ATD promoters face numerous obstacles. The specter of elitism hangs constantly over their heads, the low priority in most schools of talented students' educational needs remains a serious obstacle to increased public investment, the ambivalent attitudes of many teachers and administrators have deep roots, and resistance toward the two main administrative provisions needed to fully implement the ATD model, namely full-time ability grouping and acceleration, will not disappear easily. Changes in terminology will also happen very slowly; the gifted label is too deeply embedded in our professional lexicon to expect a rapid increase in use for the terms *academically talented* or *talentee*. In summary, just as students do with regard to their educational goals, we should split our ultimate objective into a coordinated series of more modest intermediate goals. At the same time, if we believe in the ATD model, we must maintain constant pressure on educational authorities and the school community.

Major Takeaways

In conclusion, at least nine characteristics distinguish the DMGT/IMTD from competing models. Jointly, they make this theory a distinct and unique conception of talent development.

- The DMGT clearly differentiates the meaning of the field's two key concepts: giftedness and talent. This differentiation between potentialities and realizations makes possible a unique definition of underachievement among gifted individuals; it simply becomes the *non*transformation of high natural abilities into outstanding systematically developed skills.

- The above distinction leads to another clear definition: Talent development becomes a progressive transformation of gifts—or near gifts—in one or more domains into talents in a particular occupational field. The DMGT is unique by making the concept of talent as important as that of giftedness for the developmental understanding of outstanding competencies (knowledge and skills).

- The introduction within the giftedness and talent definitions of prevalence estimates (top 10%) also constitutes a unique contribution of the DMGT. Its metric-based system of five levels that applies to any giftedness domain or talent field helps maintain a constant awareness of differences *within* the subpopulations of gifted and talented individuals.

- Most conceptions focus almost exclusively on intellectual giftedness (GI) and academic talent (TC), as well as academically based professions (e.g., scientists, lawyers, or doctors). By broadening the concepts of giftedness and talent and acknowledging a diversity of manifestations in thousands of occupational fields, the DMGT proposes a uniquely nonelitist view of talent development.

- The DMGT stands almost alone in bringing physical giftedness within the fold of the giftedness construct, defining that domain much more broadly than Gardner's bodily-kinesthetic intelligence (Gardner, 1983). This openness should foster closer ties between professionals who focus on academic talent development and those who devote their energies to the development of athletic or artistic talents.

- The DMGT's complex structure can harbor all potential causal factors of talent emergence. Yet, that structure maintains the individuality of every component, subcomponent, and facet; it also clearly specifies their precise nature and role within this talent development theory. The catalysts are clearly situated outside the giftedness and talent concepts themselves. This sets the DMGT apart from many rival conceptions where disparate elements are included in the giftedness definition itself (e.g., Feldhusen, 1992; Sternberg & Davidson, 2005).

- Only in the DMGT does one find an effort to answer the crucial question: "What makes a difference?" Ranking major causal influences in terms of their relative impact on academic achievement helps acknowledge the crucial role of natural cognitive abilities for the emergence of outstanding academic competencies.

- The newly created DMNA makes it possible to recognize and properly situate structurally the biological and genetic underpinnings of natural abilities and of many intrapersonal catalysts. No other competing model takes into account these more distal causal influences.

- The new IMTD uniquely proposes a fully integrative view of the complex process of talent development, literally "from genes to talents" (Gagné, 2015b).

RECOMMENDED READING

Gagné, F. (1998). A proposal for subcategories within the gifted or talented populations. *Gifted Child Quarterly, 42,* 87–95.

Gagné, F. (2005). From noncompetence to exceptional talent: Exploring the range of academic achievement within and between grade levels. *Gifted Child Quarterly, 42,* 139–153.

Gagné, F. (2007). Ten commandments for academic talent development. *Gifted Child Quarterly, 51,* 93–118.

Gagné, F., & McPherson, G. E. (2016). Analyzing musical prodigiousness using Gagné's Integrative Model of Talent Development. In G. E. McPherson (Ed.), *Musical prodigies: Interpretations from psychology, education, musicology and ethnomusicology* (pp. 3–114). Oxford, England: Oxford University Press.

Gagné, F., & St Père, F. (2001). When IQ is controlled, does motivation still predict achievement? *Intelligence, 30,* 71–100.

References

Anastasi, A., & Urbina, S. (1997). *Psychological testing* (7th ed.). Upper Saddle River, NJ: Prentice-Hall.

Angoff, W. H. (1988). The nature-nurture debate, aptitudes, and group differences. *American Psychologist, 41,* 713–720.

Archambault, F. X., Jr., Westberg, K. L., Brown, S. W., Hallmark, B. W., Emmons, C.L., & Zhang, W. (1993). *Regular classroom practices with gifted students: Results of a national survey of classroom teachers.* Storrs: University of Connecticut, The National Research Center of the Gifted and Talented.

Assouline, S. G., Colangelo, N., VanTassel-Baska, J., & Lupkowski-Shoplik, A. (Eds.). (2015). *A Nation empowered: Evidence trumps the excuses holding back America's brightest students* (Volumes I & II). Iowa City: University of Iowa, The Connie Belin & Jacqueline N. Blank International Center for Gifted Education and Talent Development.

Atkinson, J. W. (1978). Motivational determinants of intellective performance and cumulative achievement. In J. W. Atkinson & J. O. Raynor (Eds.), *Personality, motivation, and achievement* (pp. 221–242). New York, NY: Wiley.

Balchin, T., Hymer, B., & Matthews D. J. (Eds.). (2009). *The Routledge international companion to gifted education.* London, England: Routledge.

Barbe, W. B., & Renzulli, J. S. (Eds.). (1975). *Psychology and education of the gifted* (2nd ed.). New York, NY: Halsted Press.

Bloom, B. S. (Ed.). (1985). *Developing talent in young people.* New York, NY: Ballantine.

Borland, J. H. (1989). *Planning and implementing programs for the gifted.* New York, NY: Teachers College Press.

Brody, L. E., & Stanley, J. C. (2005). Youths who reason exceptionally well mathematically and/or verbally: Using the MVT:D^4 model to develop their talents. In R. J. Sternberg & J. E. Davidson (Eds.), *Conceptions of giftedness* (2nd ed.; pp. 20–37). Cambridge, England: Cambridge University Press.

Callahan, C. M., & Hertberg-Davis, H. L. (2013). *Fundamentals of gifted education.* New York, NY: Routledge.

Callahan, C. M., Moon, T. R., & Oh, S. (2017). Describing the status of programs for the gifted: A call for action. *Journal for the Education of the Gifted, 40,* 20–49. doi:10.1177/0162353216686215

Colangelo, N., & Davis, G. A. (Eds.). (1997). *Handbook of gifted education* (2nd ed.). Boston, MA: Allyn & Bacon.

Colangelo, N., & Davis, G. A. (Eds.). (2003). *Handbook of gifted education* (3rd ed.). Boston, MA: Allyn & Bacon.

Corno, L. (1993). The best-laid plans: Modern conceptions of volition and educational research. *Educational Researcher, 22,* 14–22.

Cox, J., Daniel, N., & Boston, B. O. (1985). *Educating able learners: Programs and promising practices.* Austin, TX: University of Texas Press.

Croft, L. J. (2003). Teachers of the gifted: Gifted teachers. In N. Colangelo & G. A. Davis (Eds.), *Handbook of gifted education* (3rd ed., 558–571). Boston, MA: Allyn & Bacon.

Davis, G. A., & Rimm, S. B. (1985). *Education of the gifted and talented*. Englewood Cliffs, NJ: Prentice-Hall.

Dixon, F. A., & Moon, S. M. (Eds.). (2006). *The handbook of secondary gifted education*. Waco, TX: Prufrock Press.

Duckworth, A. L., Peterson, C., Matthews, M. D., & Kelly, D. R. (2007). Grit: Perseverance and passion for long-term goals. *Journal of Personality and Social Psychology, 92,* 1087–1101.

Ericsson, K. A. (2006). The influence of experience and deliberate practice on the development of superior expert performance. In K. A. Ericsson, N. Charness, P. Feltovich, & R. R. Hoffman (Eds.), *Cambridge handbook of expertise and expert performance* (pp. 685–706). Cambridge, England: Cambridge University Press.

Feldhusen, J. F. (1985). From the editor. *Gifted Child Quarterly, 29,* 99.

Feldhusen, J. F. (1992). *Talent identification and development in education*. Sarasota, FL: Center for Creative Learning.

Finn, C. E., Jr., & Hockett, J. A. (2012). *Exam schools: Inside America's most selective public high schools*. Princeton, NJ: Princeton University Press.

Francis, R., Hawes, D. J., & Abbott, M. (2016). Intellectual giftedness and psychopathology in children and adolescents: A systematic literature review. *Exceptional Children, 82,* 279–302. doi:10.1177/0014402915598779

French, H. M. (2009). Curriculum differentiation. In B. MacFarlane & T. Stambaugh, (Eds.), *Leading change in gifted education: The festschrift of Dr. Joyce VanTassel-Baska* (pp. 351–360). Waco, TX: Prufrock Press.

Gagné, F. (1985). Giftedness and talent: Reexamining a reexamination of the definitions. *Gifted Child Quarterly, 29,* 103–112.

Gagné, F. (1998). A proposal for subcategories within the gifted or talented populations. *Gifted Child Quarterly, 42,* 87–95.

Gagné, F. (2004). Transforming gifts into talents: The DMGT as a developmental theory. *High Ability Studies, 15,* 119–147.

Gagné, F. (2005). From noncompetence to exceptional talent: Exploring the range of academic achievement within and between grade levels. *Gifted Child Quarterly, 42,* 139–153.

Gagné, F. (2007). Ten commandments for academic talent development. *Gifted Child Quarterly, 51,* 93–118.

Gagné, F. (2013). The DMGT: Changes within, beneath, and beyond. *Talent Development and Excellence, 5,* 5–19.

Gagné, F. (2015a). Academic talent development programs : A best practices model. *Asia-Pacific Education Review, 16,* 281–295. doi:10.1007/s12564-015-9366-9

Gagné, F. (2015b). From genes to talent: A DMGT/CMTD perspective. *Revista de Educación, 368,* 12–37. doi:10.4438/1988-592X-RE-2015-368-297

Gagné, F., & Gagnier, N. (2004). The socio-affective and academic impact of early entrance to school. *Roeper Review, 26,* 128–138.

Gagné, F., & McPherson, G. E. (2016). Analyzing musical prodigiousness using Gagné's Integrative Model of Talent Development. In G. E. McPherson (Ed.), *Musical prodigies: Interpretations from psychology, education, musicology and ethnomusicology* (pp. 3–114). Oxford, England: Oxford University Press.

Gagné, F., & St Père, F. (2001). When IQ is controlled, does motivation still predict achievement? *Intelligence, 30,* 71–100.

Gardner, H. (1983). *Frames of mind: The theory of multiple intelligences.* New York, NY: Basic Books.

Geake, J. G. (2009). Neuropsychological characteristics of academic and creative giftedness. In L. V. Shavinina (Ed.), *International handbook on giftedness* (pp. 261–273). Dordrecht, Netherlands: Springer.

Gottfredson, L. S. (1997). Why g matters: The complexity of everyday life. *Intelligence, 24,* 79–132.

Harden, K. P., Turkheimer, E., & Loehlin, J. C. (2007). Genotype by environment interaction in adolescent's cognitive aptitude. *Behavioral Genetics, 37,* 273–283.

Heller, K. A., Mönks, F. J., & Passow A. H. (Eds.). (1993). *International handbook of research and development of giftedness and talent.* Oxford, England: Pergamon Press.

Heller, K. A., Mönks, F. J., Sternberg, R. J., & Subotnik, R. (Eds.). (2000). *International handbook for research of giftedness and talent* (2nd ed.). Oxford, England: Pergamon Press.

Herrnstein, R. J., & Murray, C. (1994). *The bell curve: Intelligence and class structure in American life.* New York, NY: The Free Press.

Hertberg-Davis, H. L., & Callahan, C. M. (2013). Defensible curriculum for gifted students: An introduction. In C. M. Callahan & H. L. Hertberg-Davis (2013), *Fundamentals of gifted education* (pp. 259–262). New York, NY: Routledge.

Jensen, A. R. (1980). *Bias in mental testing.* New York, NY: Free Press.

Johnsen, S. K. (2009). Identification. In B. Kerr (Ed.), *Encyclopedia of giftedness, creativity, and talent* (pp. 439–443). Los Angeles, CA: SAGE.

Kaplan, S. N. (2009). The grid: A model to construct differentiated curriculum for the gifted. In J. S. Renzulli, E. J. Gubbins, K. McMillen, R. D. Eckert, & C. A. Little (Eds.), *Systems and models for developing programs for the gifted and talented* (2nd ed., pp. 235–251). Waco, TX: Prufrock Press.

Kerr, B. (Ed.). (2009). *Encyclopedia of giftedness, creativity and talent.* Los Angeles, CA: SAGE.

Kuhl, J., & Beckmann, J. (Eds.). (1985). *Action control: From cognition to behavior.* New York, NY: Springer-Verlag.

Kulik, J. A. (2003). Grouping and tracking. In N. Colangelo & G. A. Davis (Eds.), *Handbook of gifted education* (3rd ed., pp. 268–281). Boston, MA: Allyn & Bacon.

Lupkowski-Shoplik, A., Benbow, C. P., Assouline, S. G., & Brody, L. E. (2003). Talent searches: Meeting the needs of academically talented youth. In N. Colangelo & G. A. Davis (Eds.), *Handbook of gifted education* (3rd ed., pp. 204–218). Boston, MA: Allyn & Bacon.

MacFarlane, B., & Stambaugh, T. (Eds.). (2009). *Leading change in gifted education: The festschrift of Dr. Joyce VanTassel-Baska.* Waco, TX: Prufrock Press.

Macintosh, N. J. (2011). *IQ and human intelligence* (2nd ed.). Oxford, England: Oxford University Press.

Marques, S. C., Pais-Ribeiro, J. L., & Lopez, S. J. (2011). The role of positive psychology constructs in predicting mental health and academic achievement in children and adolescents: A two-year longitudinal study. *Journal of Happiness Studies, 12,* 1049–1062.

Marsh, H. W., & Hau, K. (2003). Big-fish-little-pond effect on academic self-concept. *American Psychologist, 58,* 364–376.

McCrae, R. B. (2009). The Five-Factor Model of personality traits: Consensus and controversy. In P. J. Corr & G. Matthews (Eds.), *The Cambridge handbook of personality psychology* (pp. 148–161). Cambridge, England: Cambridge University Press.

Moon, S. M., & Rosselli, H. C. (2000). Developing gifted programs. In K. A. Heller, F. J. Mönks, R. J. Sternberg, & R. Subotnik (Eds.), *International handbook for research on giftedness and talent* (2nd ed., pp. 499–521). Oxford, England: Pergamon Press.

Muijs, R. D. (1997). Predictors of academic achievement and academic self-concept: A longitudinal perspective. *British Journal of Educational Psychology, 67,* 263–277.

Neihart, M., Pfeiffer, S. I., & Cross, T. L. (Eds.). (2016). *The social and emotional development of gifted children: What do we know?* (2nd ed.). Waco, TX: Prufrock Press.

Nurnberger, J. I., Jr., & Bierut, L. J. (2007). Seeking the connections: Alcoholism and our genes. *Scientific American, 296*(4), 46–53.

Passow, A. H. (Ed.). (1979). *The gifted and talented: Their education and development.* Chicago, IL: University of Chicago Press.

Peters, S. J., Matthews, M. S., McBee, M. T., & McCoach, D. B. (2014). *Beyond gifted education: Designing and implementing advanced academic programs.* Waco, TX: Prufrock Press.

Plomin, R. (1994). *Genetics and experience: The interplay between nature and nurture.* Thousand Oaks, CA: SAGE.

Plomin, R. (1998). Genetic influence and cognitive abilities. *Behavioral and Brain Sciences, 21,* 420–421.

Plomin, R., DeFries, J. C., Craig, I. W., & McGuffin, P. (2003). *Behavioral genetics.* In R. Plomin, J. C. DeFries, I. W. Craig, & P. McGuffin (Eds.), *Behavioral genetics in the postgenomic era* (pp. 3–15). Washington, DC: American Psychological Association.

Plucker, J. A., & Callahan, C. M. (Eds.). (2008). *Critical issues and practices in gifted education: What the research says.* Waco, TX: Prufrock Press.

Plucker, J. A., Robinson, N. M., Greenspon, T. S., Feldhusen, J. F., McCoach, D. B., & Subotnik, R. F. (2004). It's not how the pond makes you feel, but rather how high you can jump. *American Psychologist, 59,* 268–269. doi:10.1037/0003–066X.59.4.268

Reis, S. M., Burns, D. E., & Renzulli, J. S. (1992). *Curriculum compacting: The complete guide to modifying the regular curriculum for high-ability students.* Waco, TX: Prufrock Press.

Reis, S. M., Renzulli, J. S., & Burns, D. E. (2016). *Curriculum compacting: A guide to differentiating curriculum and instruction through enrichment and acceleration* (2nd ed.). Waco, TX: Prufrock Press.

Renzulli, J. S. (2009). The multiple menu model for developing differentiated curriculum. In J. S. Renzulli, E. J. Gubbins, K. McMillen, R. D. Eckert, & C. A. Little (Eds.), *Systems and models for developing programs for the gifted and talented* (2nd ed., pp. 353–381). Waco, TX: Prufrock Press.

Renzulli, J. S., Gubbins, E. J., McMillen, K. S., Eckert, R. D., & Little, C. A. (2009). *Systems and models for developing programs for the gifted and talented* (2nd ed.). Waco, TX: Prufrock Press.

Renzulli, J. S., & Reis, S. M. (1991). The reform movement and the quiet crisis in gifted education. *Gifted Child Quarterly, 35,* 26–35.

Robinson, G. J. (1998). *Classroom practices with high-achieving students: A national survey of middle school teachers* (Unpublished doctoral dissertation). University of Connecticut, Storrs.

Rogers, K. B. (1991). *A best evidence synthesis of the research on types of accelerative programs for gifted students* (Volumes 1 & 2). Dissertation Abstracts International, no. 9122206. U.M.I. Dissertation Information Service.

Rogers, K. B. (2009). What we now know about appropriate curriculum and instruction for gifted learners. In B. MacFarlane & T. Stambaugh (Eds.), *Leading change in gifted education: The festschrift of Dr. Joyce VanTassel-Baska* (pp. 263–269). Waco, TX: Prufrock Press.

Rogers, K. B., & Span, P. (1993). Ability grouping with gifted and talented students: Research and guidelines. In K. A. Heller, F. J. Mönks, & A. H. Passow (Eds.), *International handbook of research and development of giftedness and talent* (pp. 585–592). Oxford, England: Pergamon Press.

Rothbart, M. K. (2012). Advances in temperament: History, concepts, and measures. In M. Zentner & R. L. Shiner (Eds.), *Handbook of temperament* (pp. 3–20). New York, NY: Guilford Press.

Shavinina, L. (Ed.). (2009). *International handbook on giftedness.* Dordrecht, Netherlands: Springer.

Siegle, D., & McCoach, D. B. (2013). Underachieving gifted students. In C. M. Callahan & H. L. Hertberg-Davis (Eds.), *Fundamentals of gifted education: Considering multiple perspectives* (pp. 377–387). New York, NY: Routledge.

Stanley, J. C. (1979). Educational non-acceleration: An international tragedy. In J. J. Gallagher (Ed.), *Gifted children: Reaching their potential* (pp. 16–43). Jerusalem, Israel: Kollek & Sons.

Sternberg, R. J., & Davidson, J. E. (Eds.). (2005). *Conceptions of giftedness* (2nd ed.). Cambridge, England: Cambridge University Press.

Tannenbaum, A. J. (1983). *Gifted children: Psychological and educational perspectives.* New York, NY: Macmillan.

te Nijenhuis, J., Jongeneel-Grimen, B., & Kirkegaard, E. O. W. (2014). Are Headstart gains on the *g* factor? A meta-analysis. *Intelligence, 46,* 209–215.

Tomlinson, C. A. (2009). The parallel curriculum model: A design to develop potential & challenge high-ability learners. In J. S. Renzulli, E. J. Gubbins, K. McMillen, R. D. Eckert, & C. A. Little (Eds.), *Systems and models for developing programs for the gifted and talented* (2nd ed., pp. 571–597). Waco, TX: Prufrock Press.

VanTassel-Baska, J., & Little, C. A. (Eds.). (2003). *Content-based curriculum for high-ability learners.* Waco, TX: Prufrock Press.

VanTassel-Baska, J., Feng, A. X., Brown, E., Bracken, B., Stambaugh, T., French, H., . . . Bai, W. (2008). A study of differentiated instructional change over 3 years. *Gifted Child Quarterly, 52,* 297–312.

Vygotsky, L. S. (1978). *Mind and society: The development of higher mental processes.* Cambridge, MA: Harvard University Press.

Wechsler, D. (2003). *Wechsler Intelligence Scale for Children* (4th ed.). San Antonio, TX: The Psychological Corporation.

Winner, E. (1996). *Gifted children: Myths and realities.* New York, NY: Basic Books.

CHAPTER 8

Infusing Culture and Equity in Gifted Education for Students of Color

THREE FRAMEWORKS

Donna Y. Ford, Brian L. Wright, Tarek C. Grantham, and James L. Moore III

I t is a grave understatement and injustice to ignore a long-term reality that certain students of color (i.e., Blacks, Hispanics, and Native Americans) have historically been relegated to a footnote and/or second-class status in gifted education definitions, theories, measures, and policies. Early scholarship on intelligence, and, thus, giftedness, all but ignored cultural variables. Hence, many students of color were (and are) significantly underrepresented in gifted education; this is particularly the case for Blacks and Hispanics. Works by Alfred Binet, Lewis Terman, and Arthur Jensen are three examples, with more details and examples shared in Ford (2011, 2013). Federal definitions have been colorblinded and privileged students with the most economic and social capital; there was a noticeable and much needed change in 1993. In this chapter, we present three frameworks to help gifted educators become culturally responsive and equitable: (1) Ford's Venn diagram of culturally responsive gifted education applied to characteristics, referrals, definitions, philosophy, evaluation, and curriculum; (2) an equity formula adopted from the Equal Employment Opportunity Commission; and (3) Ford's revised Bloom-Banks Matrix.

WHY CAN'T I READ BOOKS ABOUT ME?

DeMarkus is a Black student who does well in all subjects (mostly As) and reads two grade levels above his age/grade level. He is the top reader in his third-grade class. He is highly inquisitive, quick to learn, and very thoughtful. DeMarkus is losing interest in reading but was especially excited today to get to his classroom because Ms. Page told them that a new collection of children's books would arrive. As the students enter the classroom, they noticed a big brown box waited for them on the carpet. With anticipation, DeMarkus and classmates attended to their morning "Do Now" work, which was to write three sentences predicting what kinds of books were in the big brown box. Inquisitive as always, DeMarkus asks if the class can predict the content of the books in the box. The teacher agrees, instructing students to raise their hands if they would like to share their prediction. His hand raises high, and he bounces on his crisscrossed legs, until he is called on to share: "I hope the books are about Black and Brown boys." Other children share their predictions. Finally, Ms. Page opens the box and invites students to take a book. Excited, DeMarkus pulls out the first book about a fish. Once all 20 books are out of the box, the children begin reading, except DeMarkus, who just sits with a frown on his face. Ms. Page notices and asks, "Why aren't you reading, DeMarkus?" With a disappointed look on his face, he responds, "Why can't I read books about me? There are no books with Black boys."

I JUST WANT TO READ, BUT I CAN'T

The class of second graders eagerly gather on the carpet for the morning class meeting. One of the most advanced students is Sofía; she is quickly learning English, does well in classes, especially math, and is motivated and eager to learn. Her comments and questions are high level. The school does not have gifted education classes, and none of the teachers have gifted education training. Only a few have bilingual education training. Mr. José announced that today's read-aloud story is *My Name Is María Isabel*. Eager to hear the story of the little girl named María Isabel, Sofía listens attentively. Mr. José reads the line in the story when the teacher says, "We already have two Marías in this class, why don't we call you Mary instead?" This made Sofía and her classmates sad. At the end of the story, Mr. José asks the class to turn and talk to a classmate about how they would feel if their teacher decided to change their name. Sofía's classmates begin to engage in lively conversations about their feelings. Mr. José then instructs them to turn to writing in their journals on the topic of "How would you feel if you were a new student, and what you would do if your teacher decided to change your name?"

Mr. José also announces that copies of the book *My Name Is María Isabel* would be in the class library and the learning centers for all to go re-read the story. Excited, Sofía walks to the class library and stares at the book's cover because the little girl reminded her of herself, then she begins turning the pages. As her classmates enjoyed reading, each taking turns reading to each other and writing in their journals, Sofía sits alone and quietly in the classroom library, staring at the pages of the book. The teacher notices Sofía sitting alone and walks over to ask what she thought of the story. With a quivering lip and tear-filled eyes, she says, "I just want to read, but I can't."

WHAT DOES IT MEAN TO BE GIFTED/ TALENTED VIA A CULTURAL LENS?

Considering children of color like DeMarkus and Sofía (who is also linguistically diverse) and the millions of underidentified students of color who demonstrate high potential, this chapter focuses on the complementary and intersectional nature of gifted education and culturally responsive education in terms of supporting students who are gifted *and* racially and culturally different[1]. We are not offering a new definition of gifted and talented; instead, we are requesting a refinement of definitions and theories via a cultural lens. To do so, we describe a few frameworks from both disciplines to set the foundation for *culturally responsive gifted education*[2], meaning education that is both rigorous and culturally responsive as described and conceptualized by Ford (2010) and Ford and Harris (1999). We declare that the most equitable goals and objectives of gifted education and multicultural education are complementary rather than mutually exclusive. A National Association for Gifted Children (2013) position paper on mandated educational opportunities for gifted students emphasized this complementary and intersectional relationship:

> Education in a democracy must respect the uniqueness of all individuals, the broad range of cultural diversity present in our society, and the similarities and differences in learning characteristics that can be found within any group of students. NAGC is

---

1   We are intentional in using the term *culturally different*, as it supports the reality that all groups have a culture. However, White students are often depicted as not being a cultural group. This is not our position. Thus, the term culturally different means different in reference to the White mainstream culture. We also use the terms *students of color* and *culturally different students* interchangeably.

2   We use the terms *culturally responsive* and *multicultural education* interchangeably.

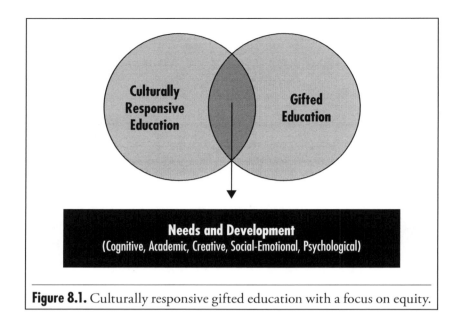

Figure 8.1. Culturally responsive gifted education with a focus on equity.

fully committed to national goals that advocate both excellence
and equity for all students. (p. 1)

Culturally responsive education and gifted education share the mutual goal
of equity for students, as depicted in Figure 8.1. This commonality, illustrated as
a Venn diagram, must be addressed in order to meet the needs of students who
are gifted *and* culturally different from White students. Equity means fairness—
being responsive to students' needs and differences. Gifted education advocates
maintain that students are entitled to learning experiences that meet their cognitive, academic, and creative needs; otherwise inequity is operating. Similarly,
advocates of culturally responsive education contend that education is ineffective
when it is colorblind (fails to and refuses to focus on culture and associated differences, Ford, 2014) and culturally assaultive (e.g., see the works of Alexinia
Baldwin, Ernesto Bernal, Mary Frasier, Martin Jenkins). Gifted education should
support rigor and relevance for the focus of their population. Intersectionality is
in operation—they are students with gifts and talents *and* students of color whose
culture matters. This is not either/or; it is both/and.

Students of color, specifically Black and Hispanic students, are significantly
underrepresented in gifted education—underidentified and underserved. Black
students comprise 19% of U.S. school populations but only 10% of students in
gifted education; Hispanic students represent 25% of school populations but only
16% of gifted education enrollment. In almost every state, district, and building,
underrepresentation exists (Ford, 2013, 2015; U.S. Department of Education,
Office for Civil Rights, 2013). We consider this a national crisis—an erasure of

gifts, talents, and culture with far-reaching implications, such as impacting the achievement gap, increasing underachievement, decreasing access to Advanced Placement (AP) classes, and hindering pathways to the most elite colleges and universities, as well as careers.

APPLYING FORD'S VENN DIAGRAM

In the following sections, we apply the Venn diagram—a dual lens—to referrals, testing, policies and procedures, and curriculum. Our contention is that ignoring, discounting, and misunderstanding students' culture contributes to problems with recruiting and retaining students of color (Ford, 2013). That is, educators must view giftedness through a cultural lens (Sternberg, Jarvin, & Grigorenko, 2010). Sternberg et al. noted that different cultural groups view and value giftedness in different ways. For example, one cultural group may value independence, while another values collaboration; one group may have a high regard for abstract thinking, while another group values tacit intelligence (e.g., concrete thinking, practical thinking, common sense). Important to consider is that a cultural group that values humility may not even want their children to be in gifted education if they consider such programs to be elitist. Essentially, as Gardner (1983) asserted, intelligence is the ability to solve a problem or make something that is valued by a culture.

Educator (Under)Referrals

Although students of color are now half of U.S. students, this diversity is increasing, while teachers and other educators remain extensively White (approximately 85%; McFarland et al., 2017). This mismatch results in cultural clashes. For our purposes herein, this mismatch includes educators' low expectations for Black and Hispanics students, regardless of test and academic performance (Ford, 2013; Ford, Grantham, & Whiting, 2008; Grissom & Redding, 2016). Teacher referrals and nominations are subjective, grounded in philosophy, attitudes, and beliefs. One teacher may think a student is creative, whereas another teacher may think the same student is not. One teacher may consider a student assertive, while another teacher considers the same student to be aggressive. One teacher has patience with highly inquisitive students, while another is annoyed. This influences teachers' referrals and ratings on checklists. A troubling finding by Grissom and Redding is that, even when Black students have the same academic profile as White students, educators underrefer them for gifted education screening and services. This was not found with Hispanic students. The underreferral of Black students by teachers is a long-standing problem that has hindered and jeopardized the academic and vocational experiences, promise, and trajectory of millions of Black and Hispanic students. Ford (2013) estimated that more than 500,000 Black and Hispanic students combined are underidentified as gifted annually.

In most districts, screening for and access to gifted education begins with referrals from educators—teachers, counselors, and administrators. The next step in the process is testing, followed by placement and services. We offer three propositions: (1) the overall gifted education process is grounded in philosophies, views, and definitions of giftedness that infuse culture and equity; (2) this gifted education process is often colorblind or downplays culture; and (3) if the process is not colorblind, then racial prejudice is embedded in philosophy, views, and definitions of giftedness that do not bode well for Black and Hispanic students, such as deficit thinking and negative stereotypes (Ford & Grantham, 2003; Wright, Ford, & Young, 2017).

Referrals are based on perspectives of gifted that are grounded in generic characteristics. We understand this, yet also believe that educators disproportionately focus on gifted characteristics without considering cultural variables. In effect, educational professionals serve as gatekeepers. DeMarkus and Sofía are but two examples of millions. They have potential and should be screened, but are unlikely to be referred based on one who *can* read but won't read due to irrelevance, and one who *can't* read due to lack of bilingual books but wants to read. DeMarkus wants more books with Black characters; Sofía wants more bilingual books. In Figure 8.2, we list a few characteristics frequently associated with gifted students (White and high income). Included are questions that consider culture.

Philosophy, Definitions, and Theories

No federal mandate exists for gifted students at the time of this writing. Developing a definition and a philosophy of gifted education is a challenge for many school districts (see *State of the States in Gifted Education* at http://www.nagc.org/sites/default/files/key%20reports/2014-2015%20State%20of%20the%20States%20%28final%29.pdf). The curriculum and services will depend heavily on educators' beliefs, core values, and commitment to gifted students, inclusive of race and culture. Any statement of curriculum philosophy for gifted students must include three fundamental ideas, according to VanTassel-Baska (1992):

1. Gifted students have a right to an appropriate education grounded in the recognition of individual differences and unique, special, or exceptional learning needs;
2. Gifted students need a curriculum that is responsive to and respectful of their individual learning rate, style, and complexity; and
3. Gifted students learn best in an educational environment that encourages, honors, and nurtures inquiry, flexibility, and divergent thinking. (p. 63)

Generic Gifted Characteristics	Cultural Considerations
Large/extensive vocabulary	What considerations and accommodations are made for students who are not proficient in English, such as Sofía? When such students learn English quickly, is this considered as a gifted characteristic? Also important to consider is how teachers view Black English. Do they evaluate Black students low when they do not speak mainstream English? How do they perceive Black English? Do teachers understand that we all speak a variety of the English language that depends on geographical location, dialects, and accents?
Reads widely in area(s) of giftedness; enjoys reading	Few authentic multicultural books exist accounting for less than 10% of all children's books*. Thus, some students, like DeMarkus, who can read may not like to read (i.e., aliteracy). How do educators take this into consideration? Just as important, students learning English, like Sofía, may not have access to bilingual books at school, at home, and public libraries.
Independent	Many students of color come from collective/communal cultures where individualism, competition, independence, and not helping others are devalued. Thus, this is in opposition to independence. How do teachers understand and respond to this item on a checklist and/or nomination form?
Creative	Culturally different students are often considered "resourceful," but this may not be viewed as creative. When problem solving and problem finding are tied to academic and formal programs rather than real-world experiences, how are students rated? Are teachers making decisions with checklists, which are subjective, or objective measures?
Keen sense of justice	Students of color may ask questions tied to social injustices, particularly racial prejudice. Is this considered when educators complete referral or nomination forms?
Inquisitive	Students of color may reject simplistic and one-sided answers regarding social ills. They may press/challenge teachers to go deeper. How is this considered when educators complete referral or nomination forms?
Leader	Gang leaders share the generic characteristics of being a leader (e.g., popular, persuasive). How do teachers rate gifted students based on socially unacceptable leadership activities?

Figure 8.2. Sample characteristics of gifted with cultural considerations. *Note.* The * designates information on lack of diversity in children's literature retrieved from Ehrlich (2015).

The above propositions are consistent with those set forth by the U.S. Department of Education (1993) in *National Excellence: A Case for Developing America's Talent*, which presented a proactive and bold definition of gifted and talented, a definition that leaves no doubt that the nation must meet the needs of its gifted students, regardless of their race, culture, and income:

> Children and youth with outstanding talent perform or show the potential for performing at remarkably high levels of accomplishment when compared with others of their age, experience, or environment. These children and youth exhibit high performance capacity in intellectual, creative, and/or artistic areas, and unusual leadership capacity, or excel in specific academic fields. They require services or activities not ordinarily provided by the schools. Outstanding talents are present in children and youth from all cultural groups, across all economic strata, and in all areas of human endeavor. (p. 26)

Reflecting on Ford's Venn diagram (Figure 8.1), for the first time, the federal definition was culturally responsive rather than colorblind, considered socioeconomic status, focused on potential, addressed context, and noted that no group is more gifted than another. Embedded in the 1993 definition is the notion of equity, which will be discussed and quantified later. Sofía and DeMarkus have potential, but it may not be realized as gifted students of color whose interests and needs are neglected, and when resources and curricular materials are not responsive (e.g., few if any authentic multicultural books, lack of bilingual gifted education teachers, no gifted services). The urgency is now—they are young and eager to learn and underachievement could begin (Plucker, Giancola, Healey, Arndt, & Wang, 2015). Accordingly, we support and promote gifted and talented theories that recognize the critical role of opportunity, such as those of Tannenbaum (1983) and Gagné (1999). Both acknowledge that *chance* plays a role in whether giftedness comes to fruition and in who is identified as gifted and talented. They include and go beyond nature and nurture to contend that both matter, as do so many other factors (e.g., intrapersonal factors). In different schools, perhaps high-potential students of color would be identified as gifted; chance is at work.

Testing and Assessment

Debates abound regarding which instruments to adopt with gifted students. The debates increase relative to students of color where issues of test bias and fairness are evoked. We are not optimistic that arguments pertaining to test bias and unfairness will be resolved. Children like DeMarkus and Sofía should be kept in mind. If they are or become disinterested in school, this is counterproductive, despite what they *can* do. Children who find joy in reading, who can read, and who want to read do better than others in school and on tests. This must not be discounted on intelligence and achievement tests, nor on checklists and referral forms.

Those who adopt and administer tests, as well as interpret test score results, must do so in culturally responsive ways. The American Psychological Association (APA), American Educational Research Association (AERA), and others have clear principles and guidelines about evaluating people of color in ethical ways (e.g., see http://www.apa.org/science/programs/testing/fair-testing.pdf and http://www.apa.org/pubs/info/brochures/testing.aspx). This entails doing a critical and comprehensive evaluation of why Sofía and DeMarkus may be gifted, but their grades and test scores may show otherwise. They have limited opportunities to show their promise, potential, and possibility, and they may be on the road to underachievement (Ford, 2010). Test performance must not be interpreted void of individual and contextual considerations. Likewise, the adopted test and instrument needs to be selected with advocacy at the forefront—with the best interest of students in mind. This is culturally responsive. Figure 8.3 poses a few considerations regarding evaluating students of color. An important recommendation, particularly to address teacher underreferral of students of color, which is subjective, and to increase access overall for students of color in an objective way, is to adopt universal screening (at various grade levels) and to adopt local and building norms. Not much has been written about building norms. We argue that districts must identify gifted students in all buildings, not some. Recall the 1993 federal definition of gifted, which asserts that students should be compared to others of their experience and environment. Local norms may be insufficient. Building norms are more contextual and, thus, responsive to gifted students of color and their settings. See Ford (2015), which juxtaposes two types of school districts—one that is equitable; the other that is not.

Underrepresentation: Setting Equity Goals

Earlier, data on underrepresentation were presented. This section revisits underrepresentation, with a focus on equity. Valid questions are: "When is underrepresentation significant?", "How severe must underrepresentation be in order to require changes?", and "How severe must underrepresentation be to be considered discriminatory?" When the percentage of underrepresentation *exceeds* the designated threshold in the Equity Allowance Formula, it is beyond statistical chance; therefore, human error is operating—attitudes, expectations, measures, and policies and procedures may be biased in favor of Whites and, thus, discriminatory against students of color.

Evaluation	Cultural Considerations
Language	What accommodations are made to support culturally and linguistically different students in their preferred or primary language?
	What instruments have been adopted in the students' preferred or primary language?
Culture	To what extent will items on tests confuse students of color because of unfamiliarity, lack of experience, or lack of exposure?
	What other instrument(s) can be adopted to gather a more accurate measure of culturally different students' skills and abilities?
Income	Are data disaggregated to support students of color who are low income?
	How do low-income students of color perform on measures compared to high-income students from the same background?
Measures	Has the district adopted a variety of tests and checklists as options to use when data and patterns indicate that students of color are not performing well on certain ones (e.g., have nonverbal measures been adopted?)
	Are gifted education services/curriculum and measures aligned?
Criteria	Has the district adopted multiple criteria?
	Has the district adopted local and building norms?
Policies	Has the districted implemented universal screening? If so, at what grade level?
	Is screening ongoing?
	Are gifted underachievers removed from services, or are they supported?

Figure 8.3. Evaluating gifted students: Sample cultural considerations.

Intent matters when examining underrepresentation, depending on the legislation applied. For example, the doctrine of disparate impact holds that practices may be considered discriminatory and illegal if they have an "adverse impact" on students regarding a protected trait. Protected traits vary by statute, but most federal civil rights laws (e.g., Title VI) include race, color, religion, national origin, and gender as protected traits (Ford, 2015; Ford & Russo, 2015). Under the disparate impact doctrine, a violation of Title VI of the 1964 Civil Rights Act may be proven by demonstrating that an instrument, practice, and/or policy has a disproportionately adverse effect on students of color. Therefore, the disparate impact doctrine prohibits school personnel from using a facially neutral practice that has an unjustified adverse impact on members of a protected class. A mantra of some or many districts is that of valuing and promoting equity. We wholeheartedly support equity in both philosophy and deed. Per the Equal Employment

Representation in U.S. Schools vs. Gifted Education	U.S. Gifted Equity Goals Using EEOC 80% Rule
Black students = 19% Gifted Black students = 10%	19% x 80% = 15.2% Must increase from 10% in gifted education to minimum of 15.2%
Hispanic students = 25% Gifted Hispanic students = 16%	25% x 80% = 20% Must increase from 16% in gifted education to minimum of 20%

Figure 8.4. National equity goals applying the EEOC 80% rule.

Opportunity Commission (EEOC), equity can be quantified in the context of disparate impact. EEOC uses the 80% formula, which is described and applied below (see http://www.hr-software.net/EmploymentStatistics/DisparateImpact.htm). This is where philosophy, law, and practice sync.

Calculating the Equity Index (EI) is simple. It is not a racial quota, which is illegal at the time of this writing. Start with the percentage of each underrepresented group of students of color in the nation, state, district, and/or building; then multiply that percentage by 80% (see Figure 8.4). As previously stated, Black students are 19% of U.S. students. Thus, to be equitable, Black students should represent a *minimum* of 15.2% of students in gifted education in the U.S. (19% x 80% =15.2%). This is an increase from 10% to 15.2%. The equity goal for Hispanic/Latino students also needs to be calculated. They are 25% of students in U.S. schools, but only 16% of gifted education students. Using the EEOC 80% formula, their *minimum* representation must be 20%, which means an increase from 16% to 20% of Hispanic students in gifted education. These data highlight and reinforce the reality that our nation's gifted programs are racially segregated. The underrepresentation of Black students is not only substantial, but also beyond statistical chance, suggesting that racial discrimination is operating. As a nation and educational system, we are far from fulfilling the mandates of *Brown v. Board of Education* (1954) regarding desegregation in schools as it pertains to gifted education (Ford, 2015; McFadden v. Board of Education for Illinois School District U-46, 2013; Wright et al., 2017). Using the 80% rule, some 400,000 more Black and Hispanic students must be identified as gifted.

Where has the formula been adopted? In two court cases and by the Missouri state department of education. For details, see Ford (2013, 2015) and for specifics, see Krishnamurthy (2014; http://www.dailyherald.com/article/20140323/news/140329388), *Fisher v. Lohr* (https://www.justice.gov/sites/default/files/crt/legacy/2013/10/25/tucsonusdusp.pdf); *McFadden v. Board of Education for Illinois School District U-46* (2013); and Missouri Department of Elementary and Secondary Education (2016; https://dese.mo.gov/sites/default/files/qs-Gifted-

Underrepresented-Gifted-Students-2016.pdf). Several school districts, working with this chapter's first author, have adopted the equity formula in the overall plan to decrease underrepresentation and set measurable goals.

Culturally Responsive Gifted Education: Revised Bloom-Banks Matrix

Once students of color have been identified as gifted, then what? This begs the question for students like DeMarkus and Sofía. This section hones in on multicultural curriculum for gifted students. Ford and Harris (1999) developed a two-fold model that they called the Bloom-Banks Matrix to address the need to make learning rigorous *and* relevant for students. The Matrix, which merges the best of critical thinking (Bloom, 1956; Anderson et al., 2001) and multicultural curriculum (Banks, 2009), serves as a tool for teachers to develop lessons that offer rigor with substantive multicultural content for their students. The original Bloom-Banks Matrix was based on the original Bloom's taxonomy and later revised to accommodate the changes by Anderson et al.

In several books, James Banks has presented a concrete model containing four levels of how to infuse multicultural content into the curriculum. The four levels are contributions, additive, transformation, and social action.

1. The *contributions* level is the lowest level and most commonly adopted in schools. It focuses on elements and artifacts—food, fun, fashion, and folklore—with no regard for their meaning, significance, and history. Frequently, these artifacts are so superficial that they create and/or reinforce stereotypes, such as readings and lessons asking students to make teepees, to create totem poles, to dress as the racially different group or individual, to bring foods from their culture or the culture of other groups. The most problematic result is the creation or reinforcement of stereotypes and the dehumanizing of groups of color.

2. The *additive* level is slightly higher than contributions in Banks' model. It focuses on ideas and issues that are safe with little chance of being controversial. Students talk and read books about sexism and classism, for example, yet they do not read or learn about racism. Students learn about heroes of color who are less controversial (e.g., Martin Luther King Jr. vs. Malcolm X). Lessons and readings are an add-on that are not integral to the curriculum, such as Black History Month and Hispanic Heritage Month. Consequently, students acquire a superficial, polemic, tangential understanding of groups of color being studied.

3. The third level is *transformation,* whereby teachers endeavor to transform the curriculum with regard to ideas, concepts, themes, issues, and topics in all subject areas. Controversy is not shied away from; social ills and

inequities are addressed. This level is rigorous. Students are exposed to many points of view and to opposing perspectives, making it not polemic as in level 2. In promoting more than one viewpoint, students become critical thinkers. Also important is that students are encouraged and given opportunities to become empathic, by being asked to put themselves in the position of those facing challenges (e.g., How would you feel if you were . . .?). Mr. José was at this level with the book assignment.

4. The *social action* level is the highest in Banks's model. Students, based in particular on their learnings and experiences with transformation lessons and activities, are encouraged and enabled to make recommendations for change to improve issues and problems; if opportunity permits, they act upon those recommendations. The goal is empowering students to envision and seek change for the bettering of their own lives, the lives of others, the community, and larger society.

In 1999, Ford and Harris created the Bloom-Banks Matrix, which weds Bloom's taxonomy (1956) with Banks's multicultural model. The matrix is conceptualized as a Venn diagram but applied as a 6 x 4 model—six levels of Bloom by four levels of Banks. Figure 8.5 presents the 24-cell matrix that is grouped into four quadrants, which are depicted in four shades of gray. Quadrant 1 is low level on both models (low rigor-low relevance). Quadrant 2 is low on Bloom but high on Banks (low rigor-high relevance). Quadrant 3 is high on Banks but low on Bloom (high rigor-low relevance). Quadrant 4 is high on both (high rigor-high relevance). With Sofía's class reading in mind, we present a matrix in Figure 8.6. More sample matrices based on books, poems, events, biographies, and more can be found in Ford and Harris (1999), Ford (2011), and Wright, Ford, and Trotman Scott (in press), to name a few.

	Knowledge	Comprehension	Application	Analysis	Synthesis	Evaluation
Contributions	Students are taught and know facts about cultural artifacts, events, groups, and other cultural elements.	Students show an understanding of information about cultural artifacts, groups, and so forth.	Students are asked to and can apply information learned on cultural artifacts, events, and so forth.	Students are taught to and can analyze (e.g., compare and contrast) information about cultural artifacts, groups, and so forth.	Students are required to and can create a new product from the information on cultural artifacts, groups, and so forth.	Students are taught to and can evaluate facts and information based on cultural artifacts, groups, and so forth.
Additive	Students are taught and know concepts and themes about cultural groups.	Students are taught and can understand cultural concepts and themes.	Students are required to and can apply information learned about cultural concepts and themes.	Students are taught to and can analyze important cultural concepts and themes.	Students are asked to and can synthesize important information on cultural concepts and themes.	Students are taught to and can critique cultural concepts and themes.
Transformation	Students are given information on important cultural elements, groups, and so forth, and can understand this information from different perspectives.	Students are taught to understand and can demonstrate an understanding of important cultural concepts and themes from different perspectives.	Students are asked to and can apply their understanding of important concepts and themes from different perspectives.	Students are taught to and can examine important cultural concepts and themes from more than one perspective.	Students are required to and can create a product based on their new perspective or the perspective of another group.	Students are taught to and can evaluate or judge important cultural concepts and themes from different viewpoints (e.g., racially and culturally different groups).
Social Action	Based on information on cultural arti-facts, students make recommendations for social action.	Based on their understanding of important con-cepts and themes, students make recommendations for social action.	Students are asked to and can apply their understanding of important social and cultural issues; they make recommen-dations for and take action on these issues.	Students are required to and can analyze social and cultural issues from differ-ent perspectives; they take action on these issues.	Students create a plan of action to address a social and cultural issue(s); they seek important social change.	Students critique important social and cultural issues and seek to make national and/or international change.

Note. Based on the models of Banks (culturally responsive) and Bloom (thinking skills). Actions taken on the social action level can range from immediate and small scale (classroom and school level) to moderate (community and regional level) to large scale (state, national, and international levels). Likewise, students can make recommendations for action or actually take social action.

Figure 8.5. Ford's Bloom-Banks Matrix: Cell definitions. *Note.* From *Multicultural gifted education: Rationale, models, strategies, and resources* (2nd ed., p. 116), by D. Y. Ford, 2011, Waco, TX: Prufrock Press. Copyright 2011 by Prufrock Press. Reprinted with permission.

	Knowledge	Comprehension	Application	Analysis	Evaluation	Synthesis
Contributions	What name did the teacher give to María? Why did the teacher change María's name to Mary? Who was María named after? What country did María come from?	How are home and school alike, according to María's father (Papi)? Are you named after anyone? Does your name translate to another name? Do you have a nickname? What is the purpose of a nickname? Could Mary be a nickname for María?	Make a list of 3–5 names given to children who are Puerto Rican/Latino/Hispanic.	Do you believe it was okay for the teacher to change María's name to Mary? Explain. Do you think the teacher was unkind or uncaring by changing María's name?	Using the Internet, study Puerto Rico and write a paper summarizing your findings. Make a list of 3–5 reasons the teacher should not have changed María's name. In small groups, explain and critique viewpoints.	María's family has rice, beans, and salad for dinner one night. Make a collage of different foods, clothes, and holidays from Puerto Rico.
Additive	Why did María's family move to the mainland (United States)? How did María injure her knee?	What was causing María to not answer her teacher's questions? Why do you think the author, Alma Flor Ada, wrote this book? Define the word *disrespectful* in relation to *unkind* and *uncaring*. Think of other words (synonyms) to describe the teacher's relationship with María. What does the word *immigrant* mean?	Draw a picture of how you would feel if your teacher changed your name. Check off the list of emojis and/or GIFs that best describe María's emotions throughout the book.	What other way could the teacher have distinguished between the two Marías without changing names? If you were a teacher, would you have changed the names of students? Explain what you would have done.	Interview your teacher to see if he or she would have changed María's name. Also ask if the teacher has ever had students with the same name. How did your teacher handle this?	How would you have felt if the teacher changed your name? Write a short story, or create a song, poem, or short video expressing your feelings.

Figure 8.6. Revised Bloom-Banks Matrix applied to *My Name Is María Isabel. Note.* In the interest of space, the authors rely primarily on the first 5 out of 10 chapters in creating this matrix. We encourage teachers to create two or more separate matrices or a unit in order to engage students in a thorough discussion of the entire book.

	Knowledge	Comprehension	Application	Analysis	Evaluation	Synthesis
Transformation	Have ever moved to another country, state, city, or changed to another school? If so, did you feel like María?	How did María feel when the teacher changed her name to Mary? How did María feel moving from Puerto Rico to the mainland/U.S.?	Make a list of all of the emotions María felt in the book.	How did María feel moving from Puerto Rico to the mainland/U.S.? Use a Venn diagram to compare her feelings to other family members'.	Survey students regarding their views on changing María's name to Mary. Tally the responses and display them in a chart on a classroom wall.	María's poem "My Greatest Wish" explains her feelings about many school experiences when she felt like an outsider and unwelcomed. Write a poem or song about how you felt reading it.
Social Action	Read the book to your best friend, sister, brother, or your caregiver, mother, or father.	María felt uncomfortable as a new student. Discuss how you would have welcomed her (or any new student) to the classroom.	Work in groups to create at least three classroom activities to welcome new students to your class. Work with a teacher or family member to connect with a pen pal from another country.	Write a letter to the author, Alma Flor Ada, sharing what you like and dislike about the book.	Survey students regarding how and why names are an important part of self-identity. Critique their views on how and why names are an important part of one's self-identity to create and display in a chart titled "What's In A Name" and share the results with the teacher.	Create a song, poem, or video to share when you have new classmates. Also, ask the principal and/or guidance counselor to share it with new families.

Figure 8.6., continued

Major Takeaways

The purpose of this chapter is to apply a cultural lens to gifted education, with the goal of avoiding colorblindness and in any way discounting the role of culture in educational settings. The culture of students of color must not be discounted or ignored; doing so contributes to their underrepresentation in gifted education. We recommend that educators:

1.   receive formal training in gifted education *and* multicultural education;

2.   view all aspects of gifted education (e.g., referrals, measures, criteria, policies, definitions, theories, philosophy) through a cultural lens and aim for being culturally and linguistically responsive;

3.   create curriculum that is rigorous enough to challenge and relevant enough to engage gifted and potentially gifted students of color;

4.   establish learning opportunities that tap into and nurture the potential of students of color so that they have increased opportunities to demonstrate their gifts and talents;

5.   improve access to programs in the early years for all children, particularly culturally different, and low-income students; and

6.   adopt equity in philosophy and practice, with specific attention to the EEOC 80% formula to set minimal representation goals for students of color.

RECOMMENDED READINGS AND RESOURCES

Ford, D. Y. (2005). Welcoming all students to room 202: Creating culturally responsive classrooms. *Gifted Child Today, 28,* 28–30, 65.

Ford, D. Y. (2011). *Multicultural gifted education* (2nd ed.). Waco, TX: Prufrock Press.

York, S. (2016). *Roots and wings: Affirming culture and preventing bias in early childhood* (3rd ed.). St. Paul, MN: Redleaf Press.

CultureGrams—http://www.culturegrams.com

Sample Bloom-Banks' Matrices—https://www.drdonnayford.com/sample-ford-harris-matrices

Teaching for Tolerance, Perspectives for a Diverse America—http://perspectives.tolerance.org

REFERENCES

Ada, A. F. (1995). *My name is María Isabel.* New York, NY: Aladdin.

Anderson, L. W. (Ed.), Krathwohl, D. R. (Ed.), Airasian, P. W., Cruikshank, K. A., Mayer, R. E., Pintrich, P. R., . . . Wittrock, M. C. (2001). *A taxonomy for learning, teaching, and assessing: A revision of Bloom's Taxonomy of Educational Objectives* (Complete edition). New York, NY: Longman.

Banks, J. M. (2009). *Teaching strategies for ethnic studies* (8th ed.). New York, NY: Allyn & Bacon.

Bloom, B. (Ed.). (1956). *Taxonomy of educational objectives. Handbook I: Cognitive domain.* New York, NY: Wiley.

Brown v. Board of Education of Topeka 347 U.S. 483 (1954).

Ehrlich, H. (2015). *The diversity gap in children's literature.* Retrieved from http://blog.leeandlow.com/2015/03/05/the-diversity-gap-in-childrens-publishing-2015

Fisher v. Lohr, 821 F. Supp. 1342 (D. Ariz. 1993).

Ford, D. Y. (2010). *Reversing underachievement among gifted Black students: Theory, research and practice* (2nd ed.). Waco, TX: Prufrock Press.

Ford, D. Y. (2011). *Multicultural gifted education* (2nd ed.). Waco, TX: Prufrock Press.

Ford, D. Y. (2013). *Recruiting and retaining culturally different students in gifted education.* Waco, TX: Prufrock Press.

Ford, D. Y. (2014). Under-representation of African American and Hispanic students in gifted education: Impact of social inequality, elitism, and colorblindness. In J. P. Bakken, F. E. Obiakor, & A. F. Rotatori (Eds.), *Gifted education: Current perspectives and issues* (pp. 101–126). Bingley, England: Emerald Group.

Ford, D. Y. (2015). Recruiting and retaining Black and Hispanic students in gifted education: Equality vs. equity schools. *Gifted Child Today, 38,* 187–191.

Ford, D. Y., & Grantham, T. C. (2003). Providing access for gifted culturally diverse students: From deficit thinking to dynamic thinking. *Theory into Practice, 42,* 217–225.

Ford, D. Y., Grantham, T. C., & Whiting, G. W. (2008). Culturally and linguistically diverse students in gifted education: Recruitment and retention issues. *Exceptional Children, 74,* 289–308.

Ford, D. Y., & Harris, J. J., III (1999). *Multicultural gifted education.* New York, NY: Teachers College Press.

Ford, D. Y., & Russo, C. J. (2015). No child left behind . . . unless a student is gifted and of color: Reflections on the need to meet the educational needs of the gifted. *Journal of Law in Society, 15,* 213–239.

Gagné, F. (1999). My convictions about the nature of abilities, gifts, and talents. *Journal for the Education of the Gifted, 22,* 109–136.

Gardner, H. (1983). *Frames of mind: The theory of multiple intelligences.* New York, NY: Basic Books.

Grissom, J. A., & Redding, C. (2016). Discretion and disproportionality. *AERA Open, 2*(1), 1–25. doi:10.1177/2332858415622175

Krishnamurthy, M. (2014). U-46 gifted program gets overhaul nearly decade after lawsuit. *Chicago Daily Herald*. Retrieved from http://www.dailyherald.com/article/20140323/news/140329388

McFadden v. Board of Education for Illinois School District U-46, F. Supp. 2d., 2013, WL 3506010 (N.D. III. July 9, 2013).

McFarland, J., Hussar, B., de Brey, C., Snyder, T., Wang, X., Wilkinson-Flicker, S., . . . & Hinz, S. (2017). *Condition of education 2017*. Washington, DC: U.S. Department of Education.

Missouri Department of Elementary and Secondary Education. (2016). *Identifying and serving traditionally underrepresented gifted students: Guidance for Missouri school districts*. Retrieved from https://dese.mo.gov/sites/default/files/qs-Gifted-Underrepresented-Gifted-Students-2016.pdf.

National Association for Gifted Children. (2013). *Mandated services for gifted and talented students*. Retrieved from http://www.nagc.org/sites/default/files/Position%20Statement/Mandated%20Services%20for%20Gifted%20and%20Talented%20Students.pdf

Plucker, J. A., Giancola, J., Healey, G., Arndt, D., & Wang, C. (2015). *Equal talents, unequal opportunities: A report card on state support for academically talented low-income students*. Lansdowne, VA: Jack Kent Cooke Foundation.

Sternberg, R. J., Jarvin, L., & Grigorenko, E. L. (2010). *Explorations in giftedness*. New York, NY: Cambridge University Press.

Tannenbaum, A. J. (1983). *Gifted children*. New York, NY: Macmillan.

U.S. Department of Education. (1993). *A national excellence: A case for developing America's talent*. Retrieved from http://eric.ed.gov/?id=ED359743

U.S. Department of Education, Office of Civil Rights. (2013). *Civil rights data collection*. Retrieved from http://ocrdata.ed.gov

VanTassel-Baska, J. (1992). *Effective curriculum planning for gifted learners*. Denver, CO: Love.

Wright, B. L., Ford, D. Y., & Trotman Scott, M. (in press). Pathways to STEM: Engaging young gifted Black boys using the Color-Coded Bloom-Banks Matrix. *Gifted Child Today*.

Wright, B. L., Ford, D. Y., & Young, J. L. (2017). Ignorance or indifference? Seeking equity and excellent for under-represented students of color in gifted education. *Global Education Review, 4*(1), 45–61.

CHAPTER 9

Using the Actiotope Model of Giftedness to Bridge the Gap Between Experiences and Practice

Albert Ziegler and Wilma Vialle

Paula has been teaching for more than 30 years at a school specializing in gifted education. She loves working with her students, who are quick and dedicated learners. Her school is coeducational and comprises approximately 300 students from grades 5 to 10, 220 of whom are boarders. Admission criteria are a record of excellent academic performance and an IQ of at least 130. The final decision on admission is made by a committee after personal interviews with each student and also considers their extracurricular activities and how their interest profile aligns with the school's profile. The school has several resource rooms, excellent sports, music, and Information Technology facilities, and a counseling center staffed with five school psychologists and guidance counselors, all of whom have expertise in gifted education. The maximum class size is 20 students, and the student-to-teacher ratio is 5:4. Instruction periods, in which the official state curriculum is taught, are from Monday to Friday between 8 a.m. and 1 p.m., including breaks. However, the official state curriculum is completed in approximately 70% of the allotted time. The remaining 30% of school time is dedicated to enrichment in the respective school subjects. After their lunch break, students work individually for 2 hours on homework assignments and for 2 hours on a special interest project in small groups ranging from three to seven people. For the boarders, special projects are offered on weekends.

In 2016, the school was taken over by a new consortium, which decided to adopt a more contemporary school approach to replace the existing one that had been in force for more than 30 years. The consortium appointed Paula to put together an Innovation Team to oversee the transition to the new structure. Paula happily accepted.

In this chapter, we will report Paula's initial thought processes. She was fully cognizant that the efficiency and success of the Innovation Team would depend on the quality of her preparatory work. Along with carefully monitoring and analyzing her school and conducting a thorough examination of the relevant literature, she also consulted several experts from various backgrounds. These included experts in gifted education (representatives from other gifted schools and researchers), experts in administration and governance, parents of gifted students, and organizational psychologists and sociologists. She also consulted specialists, such as the program director of a mentoring program and the head of a school specializing in self-regulated learning. After months of preparatory work, she had accumulated answers to five crucial issues:

1. On what model of giftedness and gifted education should the new school approach be based?
2. What are the main goals of gifted education?
3. In what way can models of giftedness and gifted education assist the Innovation Team in planning the new school approach?
4. What are the key principles for the development of the new school approach?
5. What are the major action areas for the Innovation Team?

GIFTEDNESS AND GIFTED EDUCATION

Paula is an enthusiastic teacher. However, her recent examination of the literature on gifted education ended in a revelation that challenged her thoughts about optimal gifted education. She encountered an almost 25-year-old meta-analysis published by Lipsey and Wilson (1993). The authors had analyzed the average effect sizes of various educational methods, many of which were routinely used in gifted education: ability grouping, enrichment, acceleration, and pull-out programs. As the first three of the four methods were used at Paula's school, she was naturally excited to learn something about their effectiveness. To her utter dismay—even before adjusting the results for placebo effects and publication bias—the effects were, according to conventional criteria, weak or moderate, with the largest effects reported for acceleration. Later meta-analyses confirmed these low to moderate effect sizes for gifted education provisions (Kim, 2016; Steenbergen-Hu, Makel, & Olszewski-Kubilius, 2016; Steenbergen-Hu & Moon, 2011). Paula found the results sobering. For example, Steenbergen-Hu et al. (2016) found that accelerated students outperformed nonaccelerated same-age peers, however, they did not differ significantly from nonaccelerated older peers. Although this may be viewed positively in some respects (i.e., the accelerated students are able to cope with the educational demands of the work completed by older peers), Paula started to wonder what the point of acceleration (or the other gifted education methods) might be if the gifted were indistinguishable among their older peers.

Paula concluded that the effect sizes of traditional gifted provisions were not satisfactory. She searched the literature for more contemporary approaches to gifted education and concluded that a systemic approach offered the most promising prospects (Ziegler & Phillipson, 2012). She selected the Actiotope Model of Giftedness (AMG; Ziegler, 2005; Ziegler & Stoeger, 2017; Ziegler, Stoeger, & Balestrini, in press; Ziegler, Vialle, & Wimmer, 2013).

Giftedness Is a Construct

In the past, Paula noticed her colleagues occasionally committing the fallacy of reification, whereby they treated giftedness as if it were a real thing. By contrast, Paula concurred with the view of the AMG that giftedness is a construct, that is, a complex idea or theory that a particular society has created to synthesize a number of simpler elements. This is important because it means that giftedness, as a social construct rather than a concrete thing, cannot cause anything by itself (Gould, 1981).

Learning-Oriented Definition of Giftedness

Given that the literature contains more than 200 different definitions of the terms *gifted* and *giftedness* (McAlpine, 2004), it seemed naïve to Paula that anybody would expect there to be one agreed upon, correct definition of giftedness. Any definition of giftedness is a proposal for a means to understand the concept. The definition, therefore, can be more or less fruitful for educational and scientific purposes, but it can never be right or wrong.

Paula appreciated the down-to-earth conception of giftedness in the AMG, because it is learning related. According to Ziegler (2005), an individual is considered gifted when a learning pathway can be identified that will enable this individual to attain excellence in at least one domain.

The AMG definition is dynamic, interactive, and constructive. It is dynamic in that it does not describe the current state of an individual, but rather the learning prospects over time of an individual under ideal, but realistic, conditions.

It is interactive because the gifted educators play a vital part in the individual's successful pursuit of this learning pathway. It is constructive because this learning pathway does not immediately exist, but rather needs to be constructed by gifted educators or qualified personnel. Thus, a distinctive feature of the AMG's definition of giftedness is that it is completely focused on future learning rather than supposedly stable, current attributes, such as intelligence.

Resisting a dichotomous view. Paula resisted the temptation of a dichotomous view that divides students into two categories of the gifted and the nongifted, largely because research has failed to identify any meaningful and clear-cut attribute that would accurately distinguish the two groups. Cut-off points, such as the IQ-threshold of 130 used at her own school, were clearly not natural psychological categories but artificial conventions.

It came as no surprise to Paula that the sense of awe that marked the beginning of the scientific study of giftedness, characterized by the frequent use of words such as *genius* (Galton, 1869; Terman, 1922), has since been replaced by a much more realistic assessment. Even cognitive psychologists, for example, failed to identify any special thinking processes of the gifted. Rather, a witticism coined by Weisberg (2003) seems to apply: "Ordinary thinking, extraordinary outcomes" (p. 204). Viewing gifted students from a practical perspective made Paula realize that regardless of which area she targets—be it intellectual, physiological, emotional, motivational, or social development—gifted students might be outstanding in the outcomes of their learning, but not in their psychological attributes. The empirical journals focusing on giftedness research, such as *Gifted Child Quarterly*, *Journal of the Education of the Gifted*, *High Ability Studies*, *Roeper Review*, and *Talent Development & Excellence*, demonstrate that most direct comparisons of any potential distinguishing personal attributes between gifted and nongifted samples are—regardless of the respective definitions of giftedness used in the study at hand—not significant. And when differences do occur, the overlaps in the distributions are in most cases greater than 80%.

Gifted education as part of general education. Paula realized that the demythologization of the gifted with respect to their thinking abilities is not disturbing news for gifted education. Rather, it is a valuable advantage that gifted educators can make use of the experiences and research findings obtained with nongifted samples. For example, textbooks and handbooks on learning strategies or motivation that are based on research with nongifted samples are as valuable for the educator of gifted children as for the educator of nongifted children. Or, to use a more specific example, when a teacher teaches a specific subject such as the Pythagorean theorem, the didactic principles she has to consider are the same for gifted and nongifted students. Therefore, it was obvious to Paula that skills in general education and, in particular, skills related to optimizing learning should be mandatory for the school staff.

What is specific about gifted education? Paula understood that there are two characteristics that distinguish gifted education from general education. The first, paradoxically, derives from the very existence of gifted education because it grants a special status as "gifted" to some students and keeps this status back from others (Borland, 2003; Margolin, 1994). Thus, gifted education invents a reality that has consequences. One potential negative consequence, for example, was described by scholars such as Freeman (2006a, 2006b) and Heller (2004), who proposed that the labeling of the gifted might be a risk factor for their development. Other negative effects and various positive effects of labeling have been discussed by Oh et al. (2015, 2016). Further examples of the consequences of these invented realities brought about by gifted education include the effects of gifted provisions, such as all of the consequences of learning in more homogeneous high-ability groups (such as Paula's school) or the consequences of acceleration when the gifted find themselves members of learning groups with average ages sometimes markedly above their own age.

The other distinguishing characteristic of gifted education is a consequence that derives from the decision that a gifted student pursues the learning pathway to attain excellence. By definition, the gifted are the only ones who are able to take this learning pathway, and so, for example, educators need to provide them with special learning opportunities or resources. But, again, that means that experiences with nongifted samples are not irrelevant, and, in many cases, only the advanced content may differ.

The Two Overarching Aims of Gifted Education

Paula held firmly to the view that gifted education is only part of education. In particular, this means that there is no automatic assumption that a child labeled as gifted must pursue extraordinary learning outcomes. This decision is up to the gifted individual and her parents or legal guardians. Indeed, educators can have many educational goals for their students, such as the four general values emphasized at Paula's school: mutual respect, tolerance, esteem, and self-determination. However, it is evident that a school for the gifted would pursue giftedness-related educational goals alongside its general educational goals, as that is its purpose. Paula believed there are two overarching aims specific to gifted education, namely the remedial aim and the talent-development aim.

The Remedial Aim in Gifted Education

The remedial aim in gifted education has two aspects. The first is directed at possible negative outcomes resulting from the giftedness itself or from gifted education. An oft-quoted example, which is relevant to Paula's school, is the labeling of a student as gifted. Some scholars consider labeling a substantial risk factor for gifted individuals (Heller, 2004). Although some problems might be mitigated at Paula's school for the gifted, such as rejection by less gifted peers (Persson, 2010), other problems such as higher levels of competition among peers of similar ability might occur instead (Feldhusen, Dai, & Clinkenbeard, 2000).

The second remedial aim is concerned with keeping the actiotopes of the gifted students operative for talent development. In the AMG, an actiotope is defined as the entirety of the individual and the material, social, and informational environment with which this individual interacts (Ziegler et al., 2013). This aim is much more complex and requires a much higher level of expertise from a gifted educator. In particular, remedial gifted education can be subdivided into three areas that can be expressed in the questions of how the actiotope of a gifted student can:

1. maintain balance (e.g., a student sets goals that are too ambitious);
2. break out of an undesired balance (e.g., one of the teachers imposes her own ambitions on the gifted students); or
3. regain a lost balance (e.g., supporting a student who has developed self-doubts).

If an imbalance in the actiotope is detected, efforts to remediate should be immediately made and steps taken at reintegrating the actiotope's components in the direction of desired homeostatic or homeorhetic states.[1] Usually, undesired balances take on the form of self-reinforcing cycles, which might lead to various defensive reactions. For example, in order to protect her self-esteem, a student might dismiss feedback or might disengage from competitive learning environments (Crocker & Luhtanen, 2003). However, it is important to note that, from a systemic perspective, any state of an actiotope (including undesired balances) should always be viewed as reflecting an individual's best attempts at solving a problem, as dysfunctional as such an attempt might seem to an observer. To clarify, in the last example, the antipathy of a drop in self-esteem may well compel a student to prioritize maintaining self-esteem over learning and lead to the dismissal of feedback or the avoidance of learning (Baumeister, 1997).

---

1   By definition the process in which a dynamic system returns to a desired state is called *homeostasis* (e.g., regaining energy by eating). The process in which a dynamic system returns to a trajectory is called *homeorhesis* (e.g., self-motivation in order to keep learning).

The Talent Development Aim

Although the remedial aim was directed at desired homeostatic or homeorhetic states, the talent development aim is ultimately directed at acquiring highly effective action repertoires and learning. The challenge for Paula's school was to systematically arrange the students' learning environment in a way that yields learning experiences of increasing complexity that natural environments can no longer offer. In this process, new learning environments are constantly created by teachers, mentors, and counselors. It is important to align the components of the actiotope so they become increasingly coordinated and harmonious as skill levels rise.

THEORIES AS MEDIATORS BETWEEN EXPERIENCES AND PRACTICE

Before Paula could start thinking about how best to apply the AMG to practice, she reflected thoroughly on the relationship between theory and practice. The common assumption is that the relationship between theory and practice is unidirectional, whereby the theory is applied to practice. However, in the AMG a very different position is taken, which is depicted in Figure 9.1. In this model, the theory acts as a mediator between experiences denoted with $E_1, E_2, \ldots E_n$ and an intended area of application.

The experiences range from objective (e.g., findings in research studies) to subjective (e.g., practitioners' experiences), from highly controlled (e.g., experimental settings) to informal (e.g., anecdotal) experiences, and from experiences made in neutral settings (e.g., research laboratories) to experiences made in the target settings (e.g., the classrooms of Paula's school). From the outset, there is no preference in the AMG for any of these experiences as each type of experience has its own advantages and disadvantages. For example, although observations in laboratory settings might have high internal validity, they might also have low ecological validity[2], and their transfer in a practical field of application might not be easy. On the other hand, experiences collected in the classroom might have high ecological validity, but low internal validity.

Finding Relevant Experiences

There is no universal algorithm to determine the relevant experiences for a gifted educator. For example, in order to improve interests in the classroom, Paula may have:

---

2   Internal validity is the degree to which other variables can be ruled out in a study. Ecological validity refers to how closely the study resembles the natural setting.

> ➢ relied on insights from goal-setting theories and attributional retraining collected primarily in laboratory settings;
> ➢ asked experienced colleagues; and/or
> ➢ made use of her own experiences as a teacher for many years and a mother of three grown children.

The gifted educator has to decide on a case-by-case basis which are the most relevant experiences she can transfer to the intended area of application. Thus, the role of a model of giftedness is not to inform the gifted educator what to do, but rather to give her hints as to which experiences are relevant.

Although each gifted student occupies a unique position in life and no two situations are ever completely identical, the basic idea is that structural equivalence (i.e., the degree of resemblance) helps us to decide on the most relevant experiences for a particular situation. Indeed, experiences and the intended areas of application of these experiences might be correlated in patterned textures of relationships within and between actiotopes. An experience thereby gains its relevance for a potential area of application by (1) its validity and (2) the structural equivalence of the experience and the intended area of application. For example, if several teachers at Paula's school had successfully applied a particular didactic approach, this might be more informative for their context than research findings about similar didactic approaches collected with different samples in different settings with different teachers.

The Principle of Structural Equivalence

The AMG was introduced with various levels of abstraction. A convenient version for practical purposes is to view the AMG from the perspective of a learning resource approach (Ziegler & Baker, 2013; Ziegler, Chandler, Vialle, & Stoeger, in press). In general, resources are any means to an end. However, as giftedness refers to extraordinary learning prospects, the resources addressed in the AMG are exclusively those that are input to the internal processes of the actiotope that are directly or indirectly concerned with learning. If these resources are impacting the person from the environment, they are termed *exogenous resources* or *educational capital*. If they reside within the person herself, they are termed endogenous resources or learning capital.[3]

Figure 9.2 illustrates the basic process of gifted education from a learning resource perspective. The actiotope consists of the personal and the environmental components of the actiotope. The gifted educator is interested in the transforma-

---

3   Various authors use the term *capital* for resources. For example, Pierre Bordieu addresses resources used for attaining social and economic goals. In contrast, the AMG refers to resources that can be used for attaining learning goals.

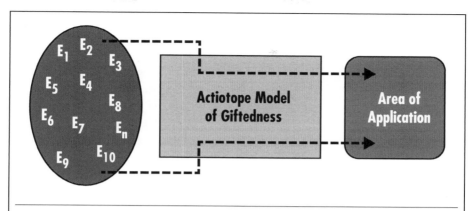

Figure 9.1. The AMG as mediator between past experiences and intended areas of application.

tion of exogenous into endogenous learning resources, which ultimately enable the gifted individuals to perform effective actions.

First aspect of structural equivalence: Desired actions in gifted education. It is a distinguishing characteristic of the AMG that it aims to support gifted students in developing effective actions of various kinds. Thus, the gifted educator should start with a list of desired actions she wants the gifted student to exhibit and then work toward these specific actions. Four kinds of actions are of special interest in the AMG:

➢ *Target actions* are the actions at which a gifted educator is directly aiming. Their number is infinite and might include prosocial behavior, assertive action, and all of those actions that constitute direct progress toward higher skill levels or excellence in a talent domain.

➢ *Auxiliary actions* are actions that support target actions. They are typically located in the environmental component of the actiotope and comprise, for example, parents who read to their children or teachers in resource rooms who set up experiments.

➢ *Anticipatory actions* aim at resource building. Examples include the learning of a foreign language at school that might only become truly useful to an individual in their later career or a learning strategy that will be used in future learning.

➢ *Regulatory actions* refer to all kinds of actions that aim at maintaining homeostasis or homeorhesis within the actiotope. Examples are phrases used for self-motivation ("don't give up!"), management of self-esteem, and increasing effort after failure.

One extremely important point of being so specific in naming the educational goals in terms of actions is that the four types of actions serve as an orientation to identify the relevant experiences that can be transferred to the desired area of application. However, in order to pick the most relevant experiences, the aspired actions give only an approximate first indication and cover only one aspect of structural equivalence. The second aspect is to find experiences that are similar with regard to the specific constellation of learning resources in the intended area of application.

Second aspect of structural equivalence: Learning resources. Ziegler and Baker (2013) outlined 10 relevant types of learning resources to which a gifted student needs access in order to develop her effective action repertoire. Definitions are given in Figure 9.3.

Paula compiled a long list to identify how much of which capitals her school and its students had at their disposal and what capitals she would desire. Examples included various ways of getting funding (economic educational capital); committed teachers, caring parents, and mentors (social educational capital); ways to foster a learning-goal oriented climate at school (cultural educational capital); learning software, books, and study desks (infrastructural educational capital); curricula, training programs, vocational training for the teacher and the school psychologists (didactic educational capital); sports programs, functional dormitories, health care center (organismic learning capital); packages of measures to enhance learning goals such as the establishment of interest groups (telic learning capital); enrichment courses for the development of various skills (actional learning capital); ample opportunities to practice skills and to build up conditional knowledge, that is, competency to use declarative or procedural knowledge in the right situation (episodic learning capital); and ample time for individual reflection and a quiet learning place (attentional learning capital).

KEY PRINCIPLES OF THE NEW SCHOOL APPROACH

Paula took some time to become familiar with the basic tenets of systemic gifted education. She was convinced that they should be condensed into principles that would guide each practical decision. After some consideration, she settled on three key principles.

Actiotopes as the Units of Analysis

According to Ragin (1987, 1992), the primary point of dispute between qualitative and quantitative approaches in social sciences is the issue of what counts as a case. Qualitative approaches focus on cases, which are usually con-

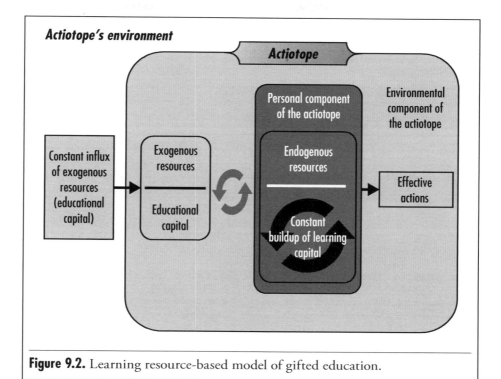

Figure 9.2. Learning resource-based model of gifted education.

stituted by individuals. In contrast, quantitative approaches focus on aggregated units, usually variables. Although the AMG prefers a qualitative approach to gifted education, a case is not constituted by a person but rather by an actiotope. Figure 9.4 illustrates this paradigm shift with regard to the unit of analysis. Gifted education is concerned with the development of actiotopes (A) as opposed to persons (P) or single attributes (denoted in Figure 9.4 with I, L, G, and S, which represent intelligence, learning strategies, gifts, and self-concept, by way of example). Each actiotope is unique, and therefore, each educational step has to be specifically tailored to the uniqueness of this actiotope.

Note that the preference for a qualitative approach by no means implies that in the AMG quantitative data, especially those from research studies, are underestimated. Indeed, they might offer relevant experiences on an aggregated level as to how to improve gifted education, which nevertheless has to be always directed at actiotopes, not on the optimization of single variables.

Systemic Thinking

Systemic gifted education aims at the development of actiotopes, which thereby enable gifted students to execute effective actions. In systemic gifted education, actiotopes acquire skills and resources, reflecting the unique action reper-

Type of Exogenous Learning Resource	Type of Endogenous Learning Resource
ECONOMIC EDUCATIONAL CAPITAL refers to any possession, money or valuables that can be invested in the initiation and maintenance of learning processes.	ORGANISMIC LEARNING CAPITAL refers to the physiological and constitutional resources of a person which are important for successful learning.
CULTURAL EDUCATIONAL CAPITAL refers to the value placed on learning and learning goals.	TELIC LEARNING CAPITAL refers to the goals a person pursues which directly or indirectly foster successful learning.
SOCIAL EDUCATIONAL CAPITAL refers to all individuals and social institutions that can directly or indirectly contribute to successful learning.	ACTIONAL LEARNING CAPITAL refers to the action repertoire of a person, that is, the totality of actions an individual is—in principle—capable of performing.
INFRASTRUCTURAL EDUCATIONAL CAPITAL refers to the material components of the environment that provide possibilities for learning.	EPISODIC LEARNING CAPITAL refers to the effective action repertoire (i.e., the stored simultaneous goal- and situation-relevant action patterns) that is accessible to an individual.
DIDACTIC EDUCATIONAL CAPITAL refers to the know-how of designing and implementing successful learning processes.	ATTENTIONAL LEARNING CAPITAL refers to the quantitative and qualitative attentional resources that an individual can apply to learning.

Figure 9.3. Definitions of the educational and learning capitals.

toires, goals, experiences, and relationships that exist only in a specific actiotope. However, an educational step is not concluded when an effective action has been executed. Each single learning step extends the previous action repertoire and thus demands coadaptations of the other components and learning resources of an actiotope. New challenges must be readjusted after each learning step. The actiotope will be exposed to new structured activities, which usually involve other people, such as teachers, school psychologists, or peers in cooperative learning communities. Sufficient learning resources must be made available for each learning step so that a gifted student can meet this new learning challenge. Learning is highly individualized, which refers not only to the individual, but also to the actiotope and the necessary coadaptations.

Learning Resources Orientation Along a Learning Pathway

One of Paula's main objectives was to provide each student with access to as many learning resources as possible. The continuity principle (Ziegler & Stoeger,

2017) states that learning resources need to be available at each point on the learning pathway, otherwise further talent development ceases. The scarcity of a single learning resource might be sufficient to collapse a whole learning pathway, as the high dropout rates among the gifted suggest (e.g., Matthews, 2009). Indeed, the development of an actiotope is not governed by the total amount of available resources, but rather by the scarcest resource among these.

SIX ACTION FIELDS FOR THE INNOVATION TEAM

Paula's teacher training at the university occurred in a conventional climate that considered education essentially as top-down in character. In this characterization, scholars conduct research and deduce powerful theories from their data, which in turn are used by practitioners to guide their educational practice. Paula has gained an important insight from her occupation with systemic thinking, however. The development of a school for the gifted is an open process. A good school is not characterized by having solutions but by the identification of crucial action fields and by constantly working toward solutions and self-optimization. Paula planned to discuss and find solutions in six action fields with the Innovation Team.

Action Field 1: Reevaluation of the General Education at the School

The simultaneous education of many actiotopes in a school for the gifted is a Herculean task. And it occurs against the backdrop of the nongiftedness-related educational goals, such as fostering social competencies, motivation, learning strategies, and skills in self-regulation. Paula is aware that these take the lion's share of the daily processes at school. Thus, the first Action Field she formulates is based on the rule of thumb that everything that optimizes normal education will also benefit gifted education. The first assignment for the Innovation Team is therefore to reevaluate thoroughly and with an open mind all nongiftedness-related educational practices and make suggestions for their improvement.

Action Field 2: Setting the Structure for a Learning Community

Systemic thinking recognizes that reality happens on many systemic levels and that systemic processes are nested within each other. Their interactions might lead to self-organizations resulting in new states with sometimes radically

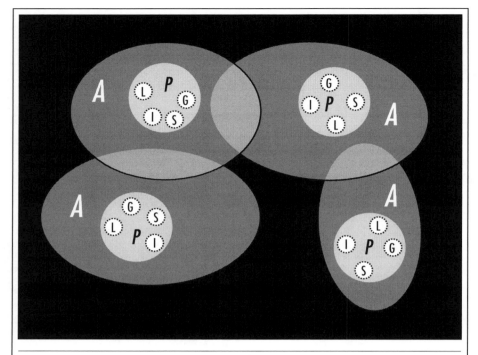

Figure 9.4. Unit of analysis in the AMG is actiotopes (A) as opposed to persons (P) or single attributes (denoted with I, G, S, and L).

different properties that propagate through the whole system (e.g., Luenberger, 1979; Michel, Wang, & Hu, 2001; Ziegler & Stoeger, 2017). Finding a magic educational formula to optimize all of these processes is an illusion. Reality is too complex for any Innovation Team to easily plan and implement an ideal school for the gifted. It is a process of trying, failing, learning, trying harder, and so on. Gifted education, therefore, is never the spelling out of a grand plan, but rather the constant optimization of current states. Paula wanted to work with the Innovation Team on a sustainable structure for her school that allowed all levels to be capable of learning and to be adaptable. The phrase "all levels" included, but was not limited to, the level of networks of her school with other institutions and social bodies, the level of school administration, the entities of the school such as the counseling center, the curriculum, the teaching practices, and individual learning of the gifted. Paula concluded she had to tackle three concrete tasks with the Innovation Team:

1. Identification of the structures, entities, practices, and processes at her school that should be kept adaptable.
2. Generation of a feedback system for each of these structures, entities, and processes.

3. Establishment of a sound method for how these structures, entities, and processes would be adapted in response to the feedback and would be responsible for its execution.

In order to make it easier for the Innovation team, Paula compiled a long list of structures, entities, and processes she would like to keep adaptable. What helped her to clarify the last two steps was to think about how to improve the current practise at her school that comprised gaining extra time by accelerating the regular curriculum and then using the extra time for enrichment. In light of the meta-analyses, she would suggest to the Innovation Team that they substitute most of the time dedicated to enrichment in groups with individual learning guided by an individual mentor. However, she must be prepared for the possibility that the Innovation Team would want to retain this practice. In this case, a sound method must be established that ensures the current practice is open to change. She would need a feedback structure that could generate information when a practice has become outdated and should be replaced by a more effective one. Solutions she could suggest to the Innovation Team range from internal measures, such as establishing a small research unit at their school directed by the counseling center, to external measures, such as establishing an expert advisory board to the school whose members could be regularly consulted. But who would decide on adaptations and changes? A committee consisting of members of the school administration, the counseling center, and the teacher body?

Paula was aware that practical questions like these have no optimal solution and no conception of giftedness can answer them. The final decision on the new conception for the school will be up to the Innovation Team and the school consortium. Fortunately, the principle of structural equivalence can guide them to find the most relevant experiences to set up a suitable structure for the whole school as a learning community that is constantly open to optimizing its own practice based on feedback. There are best-practice examples and scientific disciplines, such as organizational psychology, that have collected a multitude of relevant findings. And, more than ever, Paula is aware that the innovation concept the Innovation Team will finally settle on will be a good one, but still subject to ongoing improvement. So, as important as it is to give the school a good start and furnish it with good structures, it is much more important to keep it open to further feedback-based development.

Action Field 3: Continuing Education: Increasing the Stock of Relevant Experiences and Improving Systemic Thinking

The best direction a model of giftedness can provide is to focus the attention of gifted educators on relevant experiences and their complex systemic interactions. In its own professional development, the staff of the school will need to sharpen its systemic thinking and constantly extend the stock of relevant experiences that it can use when it sets and pursues educational goals. Paula was aware that this would put high demands on the whole school staff. However, as systemic effects are unavoidable, neglecting these would simply mean settling for suboptimal results. Mutual supervisions, team sessions, discussion groups, and workshops with external experts were some of the measures Paula suggested to the Innovation Team to this end.

Action Field 4: Implementation of a Mentoring System

Research has shown that individually guided learning by an expert or a group of experts is the most efficient means of learning (Bloom, 1984; Grassinger, Porath, & Ziegler, 2012). Therefore, Paula is convinced that a mentoring program could greatly benefit her school. Meta-analyses and reviews clearly demonstrate that mentoring is highly effective when it is professionally designed (Grassinger et al., 2012; Stoeger, Hopp, & Ziegler, 2017; Stöger & Ziegler, 2012). However, Paula appreciated the danger that negative outcomes may occur when essential characteristics of successful mentoring are not met (Allen & Eby, 2007; Schwarz, Rhodes, Chan, & Herrera, 2011). For example, common weaknesses of many mentoring programs are when mentors and mentees are not well matched, the mentors are not trained, the mentoring is not specifically tailored to the specific circumstances and resources, and the mentoring is not constantly adapted as it progresses.

There are many types of mentoring (Stöger & Ziegler, 2012), including peer-to-peer-mentoring, mentoring by external experts, parental mentoring, one-to-one or many-to-one mentoring, and so on. Paula favored a flexible, many-to-one mentoring that comprised the mentee, a teacher, a school psychologist and whenever possible, on a needs basis, an external mentor. However, Paula was open to suggestions and invited an expert on mentoring who helped the school develop a suitable mentoring program.

Action Field 5: Optimization of Individual Learning

Individual learning sessions with a mentor, a teacher or, more generally, a learning expert are highly effective. However, a learning expert will not be available 24/7, and this means that periods of solitary individual learning will be necessary. Paula decided that in order to improve individual learning, the students of her school should develop self-regulated learning (SRL) skills. These are defined as "an active, constructive process whereby learners set goals for their learning and then do monitor, regulate, and control their cognition, motivation, and behavior, guided and constrained by their goals and contextual features in the environment" (Pintrich, 2000, p. 453). In group learning settings such as classrooms, SRL is the ideal road to differentiation. For gifted students working toward excellence over an extended period of time in a specialized talent domain, SRL is even more important—and the further they progress toward excellence, the more important it becomes.

Action Field 6: Identification

An important issue for the Innovation Team was determining which students would be be admitted to the school. Paula is anticipated much discussion among the members of the Innovation Team. In some respects, the theoretical answer is obvious and simple: that is, those students with the best learning prospects. However, in reality, this is an impossible task. For example, nobody can validly compare whether a musically talented student can advance further in music than a mathematically talented student can advance in mathematics. The two domains are not directly comparable. Another problem is the time factor. A thorough identification, according to the AMG, takes days of initial testing and interviews and then follow-up contacts (Ziegler, Grassinger, Stöger, & Harder, 2012). However, this would not be feasible for her school. So what would be a practical solution?

Paula decided to suggest to the Innovation Team a form of identification that entailed five columns:

1. Achievements indicate whether an effective action repertoire has been accrued.

2. However, there are many underachievers at school who have special strengths and extraordinary learning prospects in a domain. Thus, possible high achievements in a domain like mathematics, sports, or arts should also qualify for admission into the school.

3. Of special importance are available learning resources. Assessment of learning resources can be completed with two measurement instruments that have specifically been designed to measure educational and learning capital. The applicant's former teachers from their previous schools would be asked to complete a teacher checklist. This checklist has satisfactory psychometric properties and was able to predict achievements very well (Harder, Trottler, Vialle, & Ziegler, 2015; Harder, Trottler, & Ziegler, 2013). The other instrument that should be administered to the applicants is the Questionnaire for Educational and Learning Capital (QELC; Vladut, Liu, Leana-Taşcilar, Vialle, & Ziegler, 2013; Vladut, Vialle, & Ziegler, 2015), which also has excellent psychometric properties. For example, more educational and learning capital, as measured with the QELC, is associated with higher achievements and various indicators of failure coping (Leana-Taşcilar, 2015; Vladut et al., 2015).

4. Paula was not opposed to IQ testing in principle. Indeed, the IQ can be regarded as an indication of the effectiveness of an action repertoire in the

academic domain at a given point in time. The reason for this was not because she believed that IQ tests are valid measures of human intelligence, but they are validated by academic achievements. However, it has to be kept in mind that IQ tests also have many disadvantages and their results have to be handled with great care. For example, some ethnic minorities or people from developing countries might be assigned IQ scores that substantially underrate their abilities (Flynn, 2012; Steele, 2010).

5. In personal interviews, a personal learning pathway should be jointly constructed with the applicant in order to get a clearer picture of the learning prospects of the student.

Paula's preliminary thoughts on identification have thus far referred to the selection of students for the school. However, the AMG emphasizes that identification is not primarily about the person, but about identification and constant optimization of a learning pathway. Thus, identification should not stop with admission to school; rather, the real work of identification starts at this point. It will require constantly figuring out the best learning and it needs to be done in a coordinated way. Paula suggested that the Counseling Center in cooperation with the personal mentors take the lead on this.

Conclusion

In this chapter, we followed Paula in her initial thoughts on how to develop a new approach for her school for the gifted. She was disappointed because the traditional provisions of gifted education fell short of her expectations in terms of effectiveness. Their effect sizes were markedly insufficient to help gifted students to live up to their full potential (Kim, 2016; Lipsey & Wilson, 1993; Steenbergen-Hu et al., 2016; Steenbergen-Hu & Moon, 2011). In accordance with the AMG (Ziegler et al., 2013), she realized that more effective gifted education needs the unit-of-analysis to be not only the person, but also the system of the person and her environment (Csikszentmihalyi & Wolfe, 2000).

Traditional gifted education typically had the goal of optimizing the components of a system (e.g., motivation, learning behavior) instead of seeking to optimize the ensemble of components at the level of their interactions. However, the latter goal is the hallmark of systemic gifted education (Ziegler & Phillipson, 2012). For any possible educational action, all manner of resulting positive and negative feedback loops have to be considered, thus making it necessary to take a qualitative approach to gifted education.

Gifted educators have to be aware that embracing a systemic learning approach implies also a demythologization of the gifted. Textbooks on human reasoning, memory, motivation, social competencies, and so on, do not come in duplicate with one version for the nongifted and one version for the gifted. However, this means that most of the experiences collected with nongifted samples can be transferred to the gifted.

Unique to the gifted are two broad characteristics. First, by inventing the construct of giftedness—whatever its definition might be—a new social reality is also invented. For example, every student at Paula's school is not simply a student, but a student who attends a school for the gifted. In a similar vein, every student who does not attend a school for the gifted is a student who has not attended a school for the gifted while others have. Secondly, gifted students are, by definition, those students who have extraordinary learning prospects and may attain excellence in a domain.

The AMG is especially interested in patterns and interactive processes within the actiotope and between actiotopes. Of utmost importance is the constant availability of learning resources and their interplay. However, having stated this it should be made clear again that the AMG points only to relevant experiences and uses these experiences, in turn, to find the best answers to attain the educational goals for the gifted.

The ideas introduced so far can be transferred to any field of gifted education, be it gifted counseling, summer camps, enrichment, gifted education at home, and so on. How can a model of giftedness be helpful when we deal with all of the imponderables along a learning pathway in all of these different educational settings? We have emphasized throughout this chapter that a model of giftedness does not provide answers directly, but guides us to find relevant experiences. As such, it serves as a mediator between our intended area of application and relevant experiences. It is worth mentioning that relevant experiences are by no way to be found only in the results of research studies, but also in the intelligent experiences of practitioners. Besides the validity of these observations, structural equivalence is a good orientation to identify the relevant experiences.

Paula planned six action fields for her Innovation Team. The choice of these action fields was, in part, due to the special assignment to find a new approach for her school. Indeed, this assignment ended before implementation. Nevertheless, each concrete implementation of an approach to gifted education will need to find solutions to highly similar issues. However, it will never be the execution of a grand plan; rather, it will entail the constant and arduous feedback-based effort to find the best solutions for the next learning steps of the gifted learner within a learning-resources-rich environment. It takes action in open loops in which gifted educators learn what works and what does not work for the learning of the gifted students entrusted to their care.

Major Takeaways

- A model of giftedness cannot be translated directly into practice. Instead, the model serves as a mediator between an intended area of application and relevant experiences that can guide a gifted educator to design and implement effective educational actions.

- In the AMG, relevant experiences encompass research findings as well as experiences from practice.

- The AMG is less interested in optimizing the components of a system (e.g., motivation, learning behaviour) than in optimizing the ensemble of components at the level of their interactions and in the provision of sufficient learning resources.

- Gifted education is not the execution of a grand plan, but rather the constant and arduous feedback-based effort within a learning-resources-rich environment to identify the optimal next learning steps for the gifted learner.

RECOMMENDED READINGS

Ziegler, A. (2005). The actiotope model of giftedness. In R. Sternberg & J. Davidson (Eds.), *Conceptions of giftedness* (pp. 411–434). Cambridge, England: Cambridge University Press.

Ziegler, A., & Stoeger, H. (2017). Systemic gifted education. A theoretical introduction. *Gifted Child Quarterly, 61,* 183–193. doi:10.1177/0016986217705 713

Ziegler, A., Stoeger, H., & Balestrini, D. (in press). Systemic gifted education. In C. O'Reilly, T. Cross, & J. R. Cross (Eds.), *Provisions for gifted students.* Dublin, Ireland: CTYI Press.

Ziegler, A., Chandler, K., Vialle, W., & Stoeger, H. (in press). Exogenous and endogenous learning resources in the Actiotope Model of Giftedness and its significance for gifted education. *Journal for the Education of the Gifted, 40.*

REFERENCES

Allen, T. D., & Eby, L. T. (2007). *Blackwell handbook of mentoring: A multiple perspectives approach.* London, England: Blackwell.

Baumeister, R. F. (1997). Esteem threat, self-regulatory breakdown, and emotional distress as factors in self-defeating behaviour. *Review of General Psychology, 1,* 145–174. doi:10.1037/1089-2680.1.2.145

Bloom, B. S. (1984). The 2 sigma problem. The search for methods of group instruction as effective as one-to-one tutoring. *Educational Researcher, 13,* 3–16.

Borland, J. H. (2003). *Rethinking gifted education.* New York, NY: Teachers College Press.

Crocker, J., & Luhtanen, R. K. (2003). Level of self-esteem and contingencies of self-worth: Unique effects on academic, social, and financial problems in college students. *Personality and Social Psychology Bulletin, 29,* 701–712. doi:10.1177/0146167203029006003

Csikszentmihalyi, M., & Wolfe, R. (2000). New conceptions and research approaches to creativity: Implications of a systems perspective for creativity in education. In K. A. Heller, F. J. Mönks, R. J. Sternberg, & R. F. Subotnik (Eds.), *International handbook of giftedness and talent* (pp. 81–93). Oxford, England: Pergamon Press.

Feldhusen, J. F., Dai, D. Y., & Clinkenbeard, P. R. (2000). Dimensions of competitive and cooperative learning among gifted learners. *Journal for the Education of the Gifted, 23,* 328–342.

Flynn, J. R. (2012). *Are we getting smarter? Rising IQ in the twenty-first century.* New York, NY: Cambridge University Press.

Freeman, J. (2006a). Emotional problems of the gifted child. *Journal of Child Psychology and Psychiatry, 24,* 481–485. doi:10.1111/j.1469-7610.1983.tb00123.x

Freeman, J. (2006b). Giftedness in the long term. *Journal for the Education of the Gifted, 29,* 384–403. doi:10.4219/jeg-2006-246

Galton, F. (1869). *Hereditary genius.* London, England: Macmillan.

Gould, S. J. (1981). *Mismeasure of man.* New York, NY: Norton.

Grassinger, R., Porath, M., & Ziegler, A. (2012). Mentoring: Conceptual foundations and effectivity analysis. *High Ability Studies, 21,* 27–46.

Harder, B., Trottler, S., Vialle, W., & Ziegler, A. (2015). Diagnosing resources for effective learning via teacher and parent checklists. *Psychological Test and Assessment Modeling, 57,* 201–221.

Harder, B., Trottler, S., & Ziegler, A. (2013). Die entwicklung der Nürnberger Bildungs- und Lernkapital Checkliste (NBLC) [Development of the Nuremberg educational and learning capital check list]. *Journal für Begabtenförderung, 13*(2), 37–47.

Heller, K. A. (2004). Identification of gifted and talented students. *Psychology Science, 46,* 302–323.

Kim, M. (2016). A meta-analysis of the effects of enrichment programs on gifted students. *Gifted Child Quarterly, 60,* 102–116.

Leana-Taşcılar, M. Z. (2015). The actiotope model of giftedness: Its relationship with motivation, and the prediction of academic achievement among Turkish students. *The Australian Educational and Developmental Psychologist, 32,* 41–55. doi:10.1017/edp.2015.6

Lipsey, M. W., & Wilson, D. B. (1993). The efficacy of psychological, educational, and behavioural treatment: Conformation from meta-analysis. *American Psychologist, 48,* 1181–1209.

Luenberger, D. G. (1979). *Introduction to dynamic systems; theory, models, and applications.* New York, NY: Wiley.

Margolin, L. (1994). *Goodness personified: The emergence of gifted children*. New York, NY: Aldine de Gruyter.

Matthews, M. S. (2009). Gifted learners who drop out: Prevalence and prevention. In L. V. Shavinina (Ed.), *International handbook on giftedness* (pp. 527–536). Berlin, Germany: Springer.

McAlpine, D. (2004). What do we mean by gifted and talented? In D. McAlpine &. R. Moltzen (Eds.), *Gifted and talented: New Zealand perspectives* (2nd ed., pp. 33–66). Palmerston North, New Zealand: Kanuka Grove Press.

Michel, A. N., Wang, K., & Hu, B. (2001). *Qualitative theory of dynamical systems* (2nd ed.). New York, NY: Marcel Dekker.

Oh, H., del Mar Badia Martín, M., Blumen, S., Maakrun, J., Quoc, A.-T. N., Stack, N., . . . Ziegler, A. (2016). Motivational orientations of high-achieving students as mediators of a positive perception of a high-achieving classmate: Results from a cross-national study. *Annals of Psychology, 32,* 695–701. doi:10.6018/analesps.32.3.259451

Oh, H., Sutherland, M., Stack, N., del Mar Badia Martín, M., Blumen, S., Quoc, A.-T. N., . . . Ziegler, A. (2015). A cross-cultural study of possible iatrogenic effects of gifted education programs: Tenth graders' perceptions of academically high performing classmates. *High Ability Studies, 26,* 152–166. doi:10.1080/13598139.2015.1044080

Persson, R. S. (2010). Experiences of intellectually gifted students in an egalitarian and inclusive educational system: A survey study. *Journal for the Education of the Gifted, 33,* 536–569.

Pintrich, P. R. (2000). The role of goal orientation in self-regulated learning. In M. Boekaerts, P. R. Pintrich, & M. Zeidner (Eds.), *Handbook of self-regulation* (pp. 451–502). San Diego, CA: Academic Press.

Ragin, C. C. (1987). *The comparative method: Moving beyond qualitative and quantitative strategies.* Berkeley, CA: University of California Press.

Ragin, C. C. (1992). Introduction: Cases of "What is a case?" In C. C. Ragin & H. S. Becker (Eds.), *What is a case? Exploring the foundations of social inquiry* (pp. 1–18). Cambridge, England: Cambridge University Press.

Schwarz, E. O., Rhodes, J. E., Chan, C. S., & Herrera, C. (2011): The impact of school-based mentoring on youths with different relational profiles. *Developmental Psychology, 47,* 450–462.

Steele, C. M. (2010). *Whistling Vivaldi: And other clues to how stereotypes affect us*. New York, NY: Norton.

Steenbergen-Hu, S., Makel, M. C., & Olszewski-Kubilius, P. (2016). What one hundred years of research says about the effects of ability grouping and acceleration on K–12 students' academic achievement: Findings of two second-order meta-analyses. *Review of Educational Research, 86,* 849–899. doi:10.3102/0034654316675417

Steenbergen-Hu, S., & Moon, S. M. (2011). The effects of acceleration on high-ability learners: A meta-analysis. *Gifted Child Quarterly, 55,* 39–53.

Stoeger, H., Hopp, M., & Ziegler, A. (2017). Online mentoring as an extracurricular measure to encourage talented girls in STEM (science, technology, engineering, and mathematics): An empirical study of one-on-one versus group mentoring. *Gifted Child Quarterly, 61,* 239–249. doi:10.1177/00169862177 02215

Stöger, H., & Ziegler, A. (2012). Wie effektiv ist mentoring? Ergebnisse von einzelfall- und meta-analysen [How effective are mentorings: Results from case studies and meta-analyses]. *Diskurs Kindheits- und Jugendforschung, 7,* 131–146.

Terman, L. M. (1922). A new approach to the study of genius. *Psychological Review, 29,* 310–318.

Vladut, A., Liu, Q., Leana-Taşcılar, M., Vialle, W., & Ziegler, A. (2013). A cross-cultural validation study of the Questionnaire of Educational and Learning Capital (QELC) in China, Germany and Turkey. *Psychological Test and Assessment Modeling, 55,* 462–478.

Vladut, A., Vialle, W., & Ziegler, A. (2015). Learning resources within the actiotope: A validation study of the QELC (Questionnaire of Educational and Learning Capital). *Psychological Testing and Assessment Modeling, 57,* 40–56.

Weisberg, R. W. (2003). Case studies of innovation. In L. Shavinina (Ed.), *International handbook of innovation* (pp. 204–247). Oxford, England: Elsevier Science.

Ziegler, A. (2005). The actiotope model of giftedness. In R. Sternberg & J. Davidson (Eds.), *Conceptions of giftedness* (pp. 411–434). Cambridge, England: Cambridge University Press.

Ziegler, A., & Baker, J. (2013). Talent development as adaption: The role of educational and learning capital. In S. Phillipson, H. Stoeger, & A. Ziegler (Eds.), *Exceptionality in East Asia: Explorations in the Actiotope model of giftedness* (pp. 18–39). London, England: Routledge.

Ziegler, A., Chandler, K., Vialle, W., & Stoeger, H. (in press). Exogenous and endogenous learning resources in the Actiotope Model of Giftedness and its significance for gifted education. *Journal for the Education of the Gifted, 40.*

Ziegler, A., Grassinger, R., Stöger, H., & Harder, B. (2012). Das beratungskonzept der landesweiten beratungs-und forschungsstelle für hochbegabung (LBFH). In A. Ziegler, R. Grassinger, & B. Harder (Eds.), *Konzepte der hochbegabtenberatung in der praxis* (pp. 247–269). Berlin, Germany: Verlag.

Ziegler, A. & Phillipson, S. (2012). Towards a systemic theory of giftedness. *High Ability Studies, 23,* 3–30.

Ziegler, A., & Stoeger, H. (2017). Systemic gifted education. A theoretical introduction. *Gifted Child Quarterly, 61,* 183–193. doi:10.1177/0016986217705 713

Ziegler, A., Stoeger, H., & Balestrini, D. (in press). Systemic gifted education. In C. O'Reilly, T. Cross, & J. R. Cross (Eds.), *Provisions for gifted students.* Dublin, Ireland: CTYI Press.

Ziegler, A., Vialle, W., & Wimmer, B. (2013). The Actiotope Model of Giftedness: A short introduction to some central theoretical assumptions. In S. Phillipson, H. Stoeger, & A. Ziegler (Eds.), *Exceptionality in East Asia: Explorations in the Actiotope model of giftedness* (pp. 1–17). London, England: Routledge.

CHAPTER 10

Smart Contexts for 21st-Century Talent Development

Sociocultural Approaches to Gifted Education

Jonathan A. Plucker, Jacob McWilliams, and Jiajun Guo

dvances in technology and social networking have led to unprecedented rates of change in almost every aspect of our daily lives. For example, the music industry remained relatively stable throughout most of the 20th century, broadcasting music over radio waves and selling albums in the form of first vinyl records, then cassette tapes and compact discs. The 21st century saw a shift, however, toward digital recordings and online streaming of music, radio broadcasts, and podcasts. Today, the "record store" is nearly obsolete, as a majority of consumers now choose to stream audio materials. Add in changes to how music is broadcast, from terrestrial radio stations to satellite radio to Internet stations, and the music industry today would be unrecognizable to someone from the 1990s, let alone earlier. Each of these changes has had large, unsettling impacts on music companies, the musical artists, and consumers. Aspiring musicians can subvert industry gatekeepers by performing, recording, and distributing their work independently and inexpensively, but the changing contexts also bring challenges, such as lower royalty rates and a dispersed base of potential consumers.

The rapid changes described above have occurred in almost all aspects of our lives. More people have more access to simple-to-use software and communities that can support them in generating and distributing creative, critical, and collaborative work to audiences; these audiences can in turn add to, refine, and redistribute this work to additional communities and audiences. The access and ease of use that are hallmarks of today's digitally networked technologies have led to deep changes in how education, work, and creative activity are nourished and supported. As a result, the skills and achievements that enable individuals to stand out as "gifted" or "talented" in any given field have shifted, as well. Yet our approach to gifted education and talent development has not changed at the same pace as other societal and cultural developments.

Our goal in this chapter is to share a sociocultural perspective on gifted education and talent development that addresses the importance of context in children's development. Indeed, we believe context should be the primary concern of educators working with advanced students. We begin by defining our terms, followed by a summary of sociocultural perspectives on talent development. The chapter closes with an examination of the implications of this perspective for educators.

DEFINING TERMS: WHY *CONTEXTS*?

A central premise of this chapter is that *context* is a crucial unit of analysis for understanding how talent emerges, becomes valued, and garners resources and support. We would even go so far as to say *giftedness, talent, intelligence, creativity*, and related terms need to be defined solely within context. For example, Plucker, Beghetto, and Dow (2004) centered context in their definition of creativity, describing it as, "the interaction among aptitude, process, and environment by which an individual or group produces a perceptible product that is both novel and useful as defined within a *social context*" (p. 90, emphasis in original).

Plucker et al. (2004) argued that creativity is best determined in the presence of unambiguous evidence of extraordinary achievement (i.e., both novelty and usefulness) within *a specific social context*. From this perspective, looking for universal examples of creative potential in K–12 students does not make a lot of sense. Consider an example from the first author's experiences as an elementary school teacher: He mentioned to a colleague that one of her students had done very creative work on a recent project. The teacher responded dismissively, saying, "Surely someone somewhere has done that before," implying that universal norms are what matter for creativity and talent. But a student's creativity will be highly intertwined with their personal context, that of a student in fourth grade with their particular interests and social relationships, and holding a student to a universal, context-independent standard is both silly and unhelpful regarding efforts to develop that student's creative talents.

In a similar vein, what counts as talent is defined at the cultural level, and achievements are only marked as such insofar as they align with culturally valued forms of behavior and knowledge production. Often, as Barab and Plucker (2002) noted, talent and aptitude are either revealed or concealed by social norms and expectations—and these norms and expectations can reflect societal inequities. Gardner's work on human intelligence often emphasized the important role of cultural context, noting that, "intelligence is best conceived of as the product of dynamic process involving individual competencies and the values and opportunities afforded by society" (Kornhaber, Krechevsky, & Gardner, 1990, p. 177).

As an example of this, Barab and Plucker (2002) described a student selected for an intensive academic summer program for talented students. The student struggled during the program, which emphasized collaborative projects, self-regulation, and creativity. Her initial poor performance, combined with difficult interactions with peers, led instructors to question why the student had been admitted to the program in the first place. Eventually, however, it became clear that the instructional approach emphasized in this student's home school in an urban district focused on lectures and did not foster self-regulation in students; the student, furthermore, expressed discomfort with being surrounded by middle-class, suburban peers. The context of this summer program, then, was not designed to illuminate the student's talent or aptitude, but rather provided a context that concealed her skills and invited failure. From a sociocultural perspective, the question is not "Why did this student fail?" but rather "How could the context of the summer program be modified to allow the student to succeed?"

SOCIOCULTURAL THEORY: MOVING FROM "SMART PEOPLE" TO "SMART CONTEXTS"

Our effort to emphasize the importance of context reflects a growing body of scholarship in the social sciences that advances sociocultural perspectives on learning and social production (e.g., Barab & Plucker, 2002; Chaiklin, 2003; Cole, 1996; Goos, 2014; Lave & Wenger, 1991; McDermott, 1996; Roth & Lee, 2007; Tobin, 2015; Wertsch, Tulviste, & Hagstrom, 1993). Based on the assumption that separating a person's thinking from their social and cultural environment is difficult, if not impossible, this approach considers how people interact with, and in the process reflect or resist, culturally valued ways of thinking and acting.

Sociocultural theories of learning and human development are not particularly new—at least, not much newer than other theories that are more widely embraced in the United States. Lev Vygotsky (1896–1934), widely accepted as the foundational theorist of the sociocultural approach, was a contemporary of the Swiss psychologist Jean Piaget (1896–1980)—a name that is far more well known among teachers, as Piaget's constructivist theories of learning and child development have dominated teacher education programs in the U.S. (Jones & Brader-Araje, 2002; Richardson, 1997). Vygotsky's work, on the other hand, is far less commonly taught in teacher education programs. This is due in large part to the particulars of Vygotsky's life: He lived and worked in the Soviet Union (strike one), died from tuberculosis at age 37 (strike two), and had his work largely hidden behind the Iron Curtain for decades (strike three). His most influential work, *Mind in Society*, was only published in English in 1978, more than 40 years after his death; this text has been increasingly taken up by scholars and practitioners working in the social sciences—particularly in education, psychology, and anthropology (Brown, Metz, & Campione, 1996; Davydov, 1995; Jacob, 1997).

Vygotsky's philosophical framework treats individuals as deeply situated within a social-cultural milieu. He found little value in considering individual cognition if that consideration does not account for context. Vygotsky's emphasis on the culturally situated nature of cognition and learning runs counter to the individualistic principles undergirding American educational systems. Traditional forms of teaching and assessment are designed to separate learners from their contexts, and to treat learning as ultimately an individual accomplishment that resides in individual minds (e.g., DeLay, 1996; Lorsbach & Tobin, 1992). When knowledge is decontextualized in this manner, it can be evaluated efficiently and effectively through traditional assessments, such as tests, quizzes, and projects in which individuals' discrete contributions can be identified and graded.

However, sociocultural theories position knowledge as located not only in individual heads, but across people, tools, and contexts (Lave & Wenger, 1991; Stetsenko & Arievitch, 2004; Wertsch, 1985). What counts as knowledge is activity that stretches across people, cultural artifacts, and social structures. Consider, for example, what is required for a person to drive a car from their home to the supermarket. Certainly, the driver has at some point acquired (and, ideally, retained) the expertise necessary to operate an automobile safely. This knowledge includes mastery of the ignition, transmission, steering, gas pedal, and brake. The mechanisms that comprise an automobile, however, are themselves the products of the knowledge of a multitude of people who came before our hypothetical driver. Braking systems are designed to enable safe, consistent, and effective deceleration—and in order to create such a system, car designers must themselves draw on their knowledge of driving, an awareness of how various weather conditions impact deceleration, and an acceptance of a general consensus about what constitutes sufficient braking. Each aspect of a car, then, carries with it the accumulated societal knowledge about driving.

Additionally, "safe driving" is not accomplished by a single individual. Instead, it is the collective accomplishment of all drivers on a given road or within a given system of roads. This accomplishment requires coordination across drivers, which is achieved through the use of signs (including stop signs, school zone signs, and speed limit signs) and signals (use of headlights, brake lights, and turn signals in ways that other drivers can understand and respond to). Safe driving is a category that is regulated by law enforcement and legal systems. Although any driver could theoretically identify unsafe driving practices, only police officers are imbued with the right to enforce driving laws.[1]

It follows, then, that safe driving could be defined as a collective accomplishment. The knowledge contained inside of individuals' heads is meaningless unless and until those individuals can participate effectively within the larger system of driving. Sociocultural theorists concern themselves with how individuals come to participate increasingly effectively within such systems. They might consider what values and norms are reflected within a given system and how those values and norms shape what counts as knowledgeable participation. They might also investigate the values and beliefs that are designed into individual cars, with one possible goal of identifying how these designs favor some people and limit the effective participation of others. And they certainly would examine how the design of roads, signage, and related physical conditions interact with individual drivers and cars to produce safe driving.

Talent development is likewise a complex system, with individual students and their unique abilities and potentials interacting with other students, teachers, family members, and other important people within their social circles. In addition, these interactions take place within important cultural and physical contexts (e.g., even if the classrooms were identical, the cultural context of a German and a Chinese classroom is clearly different). All of these factors impact how talent emerges and develops, and successful talent development efforts should consider all of these interactions.

Embracing sociocultural theories, then, requires reconsideration not only of how we conceptualize and position knowledge, but also of how we teach and assess students. This makes it radical in several senses at once, as will unfold in the later sections of this chapter.

---

1   A tangential, but relevant, point: Any given category of knowledge can also be reviewed for its relationship to other categories of knowledge. For example, although police officers regulate obedience to traffic laws, they also enforce a range of other norms and values in the process. In America, drivers are not regulated uniformly; people of color, and particularly Black men, are ticketed at a higher rate than are White drivers.

APPLYING SOCIOCULTURAL PRINCIPLES TO TALENT DEVELOPMENT

It is our hope, of course, that readers of this chapter emerge convinced of the utility of sociocultural theories of learning, especially in accounting for giftedness and talent development in an increasingly participatory culture. In this section, we offer a brief overview of some key tenets of sociocultural theory and offer educational applications derived from these tenets.

Tenet 1: Knowledge = "Socially Valued Forms of Thinking, Valuing, and Acting" (Or, It's Context All the Way Down)

From a sociocultural perspective, *knowledge* and *truth* are not universal concepts but are shaped by the values and norms held by communities and cultures. Literacy—a core element of knowledge—is itself defined and shaped by the valued forms of reading and writing that carry capital in a given culture. To understand this, we might trace what Brandt (2014) described as "the rise of writing" (p. 1). For most people and most of human history, Brandt wrote, writing literacy played a small role in workplace and private life. The rise of digitally networked technologies, however, has led to an increased emphasis on writing—as well as a shift in how the effectiveness of text-based communication is assessed.

We see this, for example, in the ways in which digital technologies are implicated in shifting literacy practices. Traditional forms of publication (i.e., publishing houses, print newspapers, and television shows) were for many centuries designed to filter information for audiences. Publishing was relatively expensive, so creative and critical work was published if it met criteria for quality and profit as determined by specific gatekeepers (Csikszentmihalyi, 1988).

Increasingly, digital technologies have led to what Shirky (2008) has referred to as a "publish, then filter" (p. 81) mindset (i.e., vs. the traditional "filter, then publish" approach). Creative production and publication tools are relatively inexpensive, and anybody with an Internet connection can quickly and inexpensively create and circulate creative or critical work to a wide audience. This trend offers increased opportunities for people to create, collaborate, and share their own content.

On the other hand, this *publish, then filter* model calls for different approaches to reading and analyzing texts, and for a heightened sensitivity to false, misleading, or inaccurate information. That is why critical media literacy (CML) has become an increasingly valued set of reading and writing practices (Alvermann & Hagood, 2000; Kellner & Share, 2005, 2007). CML refers to the ability to critically analyze the relationship between media, audience, information, and power. No matter how impressive gifted children's abilities are, they still need guidance in identifying relevant and important information and resisting sociocultural manipulation. In that sense, as Kellner (2011) explained, the gaining of critical media literacy is an empowering resource for individuals and citizens, gifted or not, "in learning how to cope with a seductive cultural environment" (p. 7). In other words, learning facts is helpful, but an inability to use that knowledge to evaluate information in a digitally saturated, real-world environment makes the facts useless.

It is not just literacy that is contextually bound. Computation and deduction skills are determined by the kinds of problems people encounter in the course of their everyday lives (Lave, Smith, & Butler, 1988). Talent, creativity, intelligence— and what "counts" as exceptional behavior—rely on a culture to accept them as such. The colloquialism that some inventor or composer or scientist was ahead of their time is not precisely true; it may be more accurate to say that a given person's abilities preceded a context in which their expertise or creative work was valued. For example, the American statistician and management expert W. Edwards Deming did much of his pioneering work during World War II in support of the American war effort. After the war, his approach to quality control and management fell out of favor in the U.S. as international demand for American products skyrocketed (i.e., quality control is less of a concern if everything you make is immediately sold). But General MacArthur, then leading the effort to rebuild Japan, recruited Deming to teach his methods to the Japanese, and Deming is given a great deal of credit for the postwar economic resurgence of Japan (Aguayo, 1991; The W. Edwards Deming Institute, 2016). Deming's work in the contexts of the war and postwar Japan allowed his talent to become visible and flourish; his work in the postwar U.S. was not as supportive of a context for his talent.

This type of example is also readily seen within the lives of young people. A student may not appear talented, intelligent, or creative in one setting—such as a fifth-grade math class—but they may appear highly skilled when observed keeping track of the books for their family's business afterschool and on weekends. Or consider the student who performs slightly above average on math tests but thrives in the competitive environment of the math team. Different contexts provide a range of opportunities for students' abilities to interact with diverse settings to produce talented behavior.

School systems are contexts in which certain kinds of knowledge and creativity are not only valued but also identifiable, whereas other kinds are devalued or not visible. Numerous examples of this abound in educational scholarship. For example, in *Street Mathematics and School Mathematics*, Nunes, Schliemann, and Carraher (1993) provided multiple illustrations of people who can use complex math to solve everyday problems but are unable to solve the formal math problems contained on many school-based tests. Many forms of social competency—for example, a flair for coordinating collaborative projects or an ability to curate, organize, and represent the ideas and work of peers—are crucial skills in many careers but are often devalued within formal school systems.

A sociocultural approach invites us to consider not only *what* constitutes exceptional behavior, but *why* a given context labels some kinds of behavior as exceptional while overlooking or devaluing other kinds of behavior. It also invites educators to investigate how this serves to marginalize or undervalue certain learners or certain kinds of behavior. For example, formal school settings tend to be implicitly or even explicitly hostile to student creativity, and hypothesized reasons include negative teacher attitudes toward divergent ideas and behaviors, ineffective interventions, poor quality curriculum and assessments for creative development, and lack of teacher training, among many other possible factors (see Beghetto & Plucker, in press; McLellan & Nicholl, 2013; Sternberg, 2015). Interventions could be designed to address these and other potential barriers, or we could examine how creativity emerges in real-world contexts and attempt to model those conditions within our schools. This approach is essentially what the Schoolwide Enrichment Model and higher education model of Plucker and Dow (2017) are designed to do, attempting to replicate contexts that tend to produce human creativity and innovation in out-of-school settings. A sociocultural approach examines all of the factors suggested above, but also how contextual variables, such as incentives for helping students become more creative, can be infused into school settings, providing enhanced opportunities for all students (and teachers) within the school to develop their creative talents.

Educational application. Reframe exceptional behavior. If a given learner looks *smart*, what is it about the context that enables that learner to succeed? Who else benefits from specific aspects of the context, and why? Conversely, which learners are at a disadvantage, and what might be shifted to enhance those students' learning experiences? There may be value in taking a holistic approach to education that considers other (nonacademic) contexts in which learners may be considered "high achieving." Examples include club or team sports, podcasting or other creative communication forms, participation in an online forum for fans of the Broadway musical *Hamilton*, or something else entirely. What all of these examples have in common is the assumption of a community, with community-generated values that guide effective participation. A teacher might draw on learners' mastery of locally valued forms of knowledge and participation for two purposes: First, to reflect on how school-based norms might reveal or conceal important forms of giftedness that are emphasized in other areas of importance in students' lives, and second, to guide learners in investigating and articulating the norms that shape their classrooms or school. If contexts can make a learner look more or less talented, then it follows that the ability to identify and negotiate community norms is a crucial skill.

Tenet 2: Learning and Knowledge Are Distributed Across People, Tools, and Contexts

A key principle of sociocultural theories is that knowledge does not reside in individuals' minds. Rather, learning can be defined as culturally meaningful forms of action using the tools, people, and contexts that make up human life, as seen in the safe-driving example discussed earlier.

From a sociocultural perspective, knowledge is produced collaboratively. Collaborative knowledge production has become particularly visible and powerful given the technologies that enable us to connect with thinkers and creators around the world. McWilliams and Plucker (2014) recently offered the example of digital artist and hacker Salvatore Iaconesi. He was diagnosed with brain cancer in 2012 and reached out through his virtual networks to "open source a cure." He invited medical professionals, software designers, artists, and others who have experienced illness and disability to review his medical records and participate in developing a treatment plan. The results? Not only does Iaconesi continue to live and work 5 years later, but he has extended his personal experiment into an organization he called "La Cura" (The Cure). La Cura is described as

> a global art performance about the opportunity to transform our societies to become more active, aware, caring human beings by reclaiming information and knowledge, and by feeling the desire to be part of a society whose well-being truly depends on the well-being of all of its members. (Iaconesi, n.d., para. 2)

A recent workshop he offered as part of this project "hailed the emergence of a new type of superhero: the interconnected superhero." The website (http://la-cura.it/2016/04/29/la-cura-un-supereroe-interconnettivo) described a "contrast in feelings" about Iaconesi's project:

> On the one hand, the courage and exceptional work of Salvatore who, like a superhero, sought to save humankind from the perils of non-collaboration; on the other hand, a clear emergence of the conditions that enabled a capacity and desire for interconnectedness, in support of collaboration and collective action.

The above description might easily also apply to sociocultural perspectives on giftedness and talent development. Certainly there are people who meet an agreed-upon definition of giftedness—Iaconesi, an accomplished digital artist, engineer, and technology designer, likely fits most people's definition of a highly talented person. However, giftedness is also reliant on a combination of tools, people, and communities that make exceptional behavior possible. Talent is a collaborative endeavor, accomplished through effective coordination of resources and people. This is increasingly visible and prevalent because of the emergence of digitally networked technologies, and as a result new dispositions and skills have become important factors in shaping giftedness and talent. For this reason, the emphasis in the Plucker et al. (2004) creativity definition on tangible products is important: Having a tangible product means that the combination of individual potential and talent-supporting context has interacted to produce talented outcomes.

Educational application. Talent identification and development would do well to move beyond an emphasis on individuals' knowledge and capacity for learning, and to account for the social skills that enable effective coordination of collaborative knowledge production. This is particularly important as we move toward a culture that increasingly values and enables collaborative projects and collective problem solving (Buckingham, 2003; Dede, Korte, Nelson, Valdez, & Ward, 2005; Jenkins et al., 2013; Jenkins, Purushotma, Weigel, Clinton, & Robison, 2009). Consider developing activities and assessments that evaluate students' skills at and capacity for collaborative work. As a thought experiment, explore what might happen if giftedness was a label given to groups of students instead of individual learners. Then consider what structures might enable groups to complete exceptional projects and explore powerful problems.

As an extension, it may be valuable to develop assessments to support learners' development of the social skills and cultural competencies that enable collaborative problem solving. Although these have traditionally been labeled *soft skills*, they are the crucial *knowing-how* skills that make complex, coordinated work possible (e.g., see Dilley, Fishlock, & Plucker, 2015; Plucker, Kennedy, & Dilley, 2015; Robles, 2012).

Tenet 3: Learning and Development Occur in the Zone of Proximal Development

The notion of the Zone of Proximal Development, or ZPD, is one of the most widely discussed concepts from Vygotsky's work (Chaiklin, 2003). A common definition of ZPD is that it is the distance between what a learner can independently achieve and what he or she can achieve only with support.

Interaction is the essence of learning and development in the ZPD. Without interactions, we cannot know how much support is needed for certain progress or how much growth can be achieved through certain support. For example, determining the true potential of students who breeze through their schoolwork is difficult, and the lack of challenge (i.e., never being in the ZPD) does a disservice to students who may excel at unchallenging school work but then enter the workforce without any experience succeeding in intellectually challenging contexts and, more to the point, learning how to work with others to overcome those challenges and further develop their talent in real-world contexts.

The notion of the ZPD has direct implications on how we assess and develop talent. Traditional approaches to talent identification tend to rely on individual assessments that measure learners' skills in a range of domains relative to their peers. Even in cases where multidimensional approaches to assessment are used, the assessment data may be used in inappropriate ways. For example, Renzulli (2004) noted that this approach can be a "multi-criteria smoke screen" (p. 87) because it gives the impression of examining a broader range of indicators of potential, but in most cases high grades in regular schoolwork, teacher ratings, or other criteria only serve the purpose of earning the student a "ticket" to take an individual intelligence test.

Individual intelligence tests, and the factors that commonly lead a student to be identified for testing, rely primarily on what a learner has *achieved* and not what a learner *might achieve*. This leads to talent identification situations in which the tests may produce few false positives but many false negatives, especially among disadvantaged students who have not lived and learned in contexts that allow them to develop their talents. The sociocultural perspective invites us to consider this in terms of the ZPD. Research suggests that giftedness might be described as more rapid progress in response to adult assistance (Kanevsky, 1992) or demonstrated learning in advanced-for-age ZPDs (Morelock, Brown, & Morrissey, 2003).

Educational application. Talent identification must move beyond assessing knowledge acquisition and toward a consideration of what learners may accomplish when working in their zone of proximal development. At the very least, educators should consider whether students have had the necessary opportunities to develop the skills and behaviors that are the focus of chosen identification strategies.

SMART CONTEXTS FOR THE 21ST CENTURY

In this section, we offer a more extended discussion of the kinds of shifts that might be considered in order to enact these principles in 21st-century classrooms. We attempt to show what an applied perspective for developing talent and achieving giftedness could look like, with attention to compromises that are necessary for this approach to succeed in our schools.

Identifying Talents

As noted above, standardized ability and achievement tests tend to assess abstract and usually decontextualized skills, without providing much insight into a learner's capacity for the kinds of collaborative, multidisciplinary, and complex concerns and challenges that gifted and creative learners will need to take on in order to successfully navigate the social and workplace dynamics of the coming decades. Multidimensional assessments have received a good deal of attention and interest (e.g., McBee, Shaunessy, & Matthews, 2012), but they are commonly implemented as nominate-then-test approaches that are not truly multidimensional and tend to be biased against students who have not learned in talent-friendly contexts (McBee, 2006; McBee, Peters, & Miller, 2016). Further, talent and giftedness are frequently viewed as abstract, universal categories and fail to take into account how context may reveal or obscure a learner's capacity for exceptional achievement. Asian American and White middle class students are overrepresented in talent identification and development programs, and this is not because talent disproportionately lands in the brains of these learners—rather, they are more likely to be placed in contexts that help them exhibit talented behaviors; conversely, many other minority and poor students do not have access to these contexts and therefore do not have sufficient opportunities to develop their gifts and talents (Callahan, 2005; Ford, Grantham, & Whiting, 2008; Milner & Ford, 2007; Morris, 2001; National Research Council, 2002; Plucker, Hardesty, & Burroughs, 2013).

Some approaches to talent identification aim at countering these equity concerns. One such approach is to incorporate nonstandardized tests when appropriate, such as nonverbal achievement tests and creativity assessments. Examples include the Revolving Door Identification Model (Renzulli & Reis, 1994) and WICS model (Wisdom, Intelligence, and Creativity Synthesized; Sternberg, 2003). Empirical support for these approaches is mixed (Plucker & Peters, 2016), but researchers suggest creativity assessment may counter ethnic biases and increase diversity (Kaufman, 2010; Kaufman, Plucker, & Russell, 2012). Creativity assessments may work in favor of students from historically marginalized racial or ethnic communities, whose achievement in traditional academic domains may be undervalued by systems that privilege White, middle class dispositions and students (Luria, O'Brien, & Kaufman, 2016).

Another approach that aligns with sociocultural perspectives on learning is the dynamic assessment approach. This approach is based on Vygotsky's work framing learning as rich and dynamic (Kanevsky & Geake, 2004), as well as Feuerstein's learning potential assessment (Feuerstein, Rand, Jensen, Kaniel, & Tzuriel, 1987). In this approach, students are provided with opportunities to interact with teachers or other adults. Only through this interaction can we assess how much teaching/support is needed for certain progress, or in the context of giftedness, how much progress students can make in response to certain support. For gifted students, this progress/zone is much larger than other average students so that they can reach higher levels of competency in their areas of strength.

The idea of dynamic assessment has been implemented by some educators, and it appears to work well in identifying gifted children. For example, Lidz and Macrine (2001) used a nonverbal test and followed the typical test-intervene-post-test procedure in their dynamic assessment strategy. Although the entire procedure of identification involved several sources of information, including standardized tests and teacher/parent nominations, dynamic assessment was most effective in helping identify students across ethnicity, gender, and districts (Lidz, 2002). The mechanism behind the success is clear: Although some gifted students may live in underresourced conditions that prevent them from maximizing full competence, their learning potentials as measured by the learning gains in dynamic assessments are equal to those in better environments.

Instruction for Giftedness

Embracing an alternative approach to talent identification requires talent development and gifted education, too, to shift their focus. If we adopt a socio-cultural perspective and aim to identify learners whose talent is undervalued or underestimated in current educational contexts, then our educational supports must change to accommodate those learners and help them achieve academic and workplace success. This means acknowledging that traditional views of talent and creativity still rule the day in many ways, while also enacting teaching models that center context in learning and assessment.

Indeed, a shift in pedagogy is demanded by the global concerns that our young learners will be called upon to address. The problems faced by contemporary society are complex and multidisciplinary. Concerns such as mitigating the impact of climate change on economic, ecological, and social systems; providing effective and affordable health care to vulnerable populations; and addressing the global impact of cultural intolerance require collaborative, systems-based problem-solving strategies. Contemporary education systems were not designed to prepare learners for this kind of work (Apple, 2006; Dede et al., 2005).

Gifted and talented programs are in a position to enact this change. Many classrooms and schools already embrace problem-based learning (PBL), because of its emphasis on engagement with real-world, ill-defined problems. What if PBL were extended to engage students in the kinds of contexts they may encounter outside of formal school structures? For example, rather than have students design a pretend online business in response to a PBL scenario, why not have them design a real online business (see Barab & Duffy, 2012)? Classroom instruction might then move beyond helping students *learn what* the correct answer is and place increased focus on helping students *learn how* to leverage knowledge networks and to apply expertise to complex problems. *Learning how* requires social skills, including an ability to navigate communities, discern norms for interaction, build social capital among community members, and participate in the (spoken or tacit) goals of community members. Historically, these kinds of skills have been referred to as *soft skills*, which minimizes the enormous role they play in supporting success (Sharma & Sharma, 2010; Symonds, Schwartz, & Ferguson, 2011).

Another, often de-emphasized area of importance is creating conditions in which students can present and defend their work and provide thoughtful critique of others' work. We might alternatively label this "dialogue across difference/dialogue across ideas." In order to engage effectively in this kind of dialogue, learners must be able to adopt alternative perspectives, understand differing worldviews, and justify the value of their work to those who view it from a different standpoint than they do. As the first author has previously argued (Plucker & Barab, 2005), few areas of human activity have been as consistently neglected in education as has constructive criticism (see Plucker, 2016).

Although dialogue across difference/dialogue across ideas has a clear value for those working in creative endeavors, it is also increasingly important in the "publish, then filter" culture learners will encounter any time they navigate the Internet's vast range of virtually and geographically distributed communities (Shirky, 2008). Whereas in previous generations, critical and creative work was filtered and publicized by marketing directors, editors, publicists, and other gatekeepers, today's learners often serve as their own editors and publicists. The sheer volume of user-generated content available online makes effective communication about the impact and value of a given project essential for its take-up by others in a given community.

Take the recent example of one of our colleagues, who after several recommendations decided to start listening to podcasts. As podcasting has proliferated, identifying the most interesting shows to download or stream has become increasingly difficult. She did not find online lists of the most downloaded podcasts to be helpful, so she did what many of us do in similar situations—she used social media to ask her friends for recommendations. The advice was remarkably similar across her social media "friends," which is not surprising—we tend to be friends on social media with people who share our interests. But the recommendations were unique enough that even the most experienced podcast listeners commented that they picked up new ideas from the online discussion; some people also offered suggestions for how to listen to podcasts most effectively and efficiently. In this way, our colleague's social media context became her gatekeeper. Our talented students, living and learning in highly interconnected online contexts, have the same experiences on a daily basis.

Interactions Between Instruction and Assessment

Throughout this chapter, we have asserted or implied that traditional approaches to assessment often fail to identify and validate the kinds of exceptional behavior that might enable exceptional achievement in the 21st century. Given the emphasis placed on context in the sociocultural perspective, the use of standardized tests—designed to eliminate contextual factors such as locally valued knowledge—may be particularly fraught.

Fortunately for educators, a combination of dynamic assessment models and agency over formative and summative assessments in classroom contexts offer opportunities to develop and value alternative measures. One particularly promising form of assessment has been labeled *participatory assessment* (Hickey, Honeyford, Clinton, & McWilliams, 2010; Hickey, Ingram-Goble, & Jameson, 2009; Hickey & Rehak, 2013). A participatory assessment model positions *knowledge acquisition* as secondary in relevance, when compared to *knowledgeable participation* in culturally valued practices. For example, it is a truism that today's learners are generally abysmal at geography and are unable to locate non-American countries on a world map (Carr, 2008). Ask most students to pull out their phone or tablet, however, and ask them, "Can you find Ukraine on a map?" The majority of today's young learners will nod, quickly searching for and locating Ukraine using an app.

We are not saying that procedural knowledge should be the sole goal of learning, and that semantic knowledge does not matter. Rather, sociocultural approaches to talent development emphasize that the talent is the result of the individual working successfully within their social and cultural context. From a sociocultural perspective, the question is not "Is semantic or procedural knowledge more important for talent development?" but rather "How can educational contexts be designed to allow students to exhibit talented behaviors as they work together to develop a range of new semantic and procedural knowledge?"

Participatory assessment approaches would certainly care about whether students have accurately located Ukraine, but only because a correct answer is further evidence that they have participated effectively in the valued practice of locating information via the Internet. Participatory assessment is particularly useful in appraising successful participation in the transdisciplinary, collaborative endeavors that learners might join, in the classroom and outside of it, in order to accomplish extraordinary feats of creativity and brilliance. In these endeavors, who knows the Pythagorean theorem matters less than how the group decides how much wood it will need to roof the neighborhood of tiny houses it has built to shelter a local homeless population.

Participatory assessment models, and similar assessment approaches that take into account collaboration, resist the learner-as-unit-of-interest emphasis that characterizes the vast majority of educational assessment approaches (VanTassel-Baska, 1998). They assume that knowledgeable participation involves coordination of people, artifacts, and cultural expectations, and they extend the boundaries of assessment to consider the interaction of these factors.

CONCLUSION

In this chapter, we have attempted to illustrate the potential for sociocultural theories of learning to shift how we think about talent identification and development. We emphasized a framework that considers the individual in interaction with context, collaborating with tools, other people, and cultural expectations to create generative and socially valued products. The major advantage to this approach, in our view, is the acknowledgement that context is critically important both to understanding giftedness and to developing giftedness in young people.

We acknowledge that context can be largely ignored when working with gifted students, and that focusing on individual gifted students is a time-tested approach about which many advocates and educators feel passionate. We grant that this approach may lead to high test scores and impressive educational accomplishments. But we question whether this approach is the optimal path for life success for most talented people. First, many minority and poor students are not broadly successful within this approach, nor are women in certain STEM disciplines; that constitutes probably more than half of our students, calling into question how well the traditional approach truly works. Second, perhaps individuals who are successful within the traditional approach also benefit from unnoticed contextual factors that lead to the development of their giftedness and talents (e.g., the internship example); expanding a more contextualized approach to talent development to most of our students may be a better path forward for the field. Third, we now have case studies of countries which have traditionally focused on the individualistic learning approach, such as China; that approach clearly produces amazingly high test-scorers who have a great deal of semantic knowledge . . . but many of those students are then sent to Western universities to learn how to apply that knowledge in useful and creative ways. From a sociocultural perspective, the success of the individual-as-gifted approach is limited and illusory, and a greater use of contextual approaches may produce many more instances of talent and giftedness.

This approach invites educators to consider how they prepare learners to *participate* in culturally valued projects and to work on the transdisciplinary, ill-defined problems that increasingly characterize 21st-century life. This approach makes it possible to unlock the kinds of extraordinary achievements that can enrich the world, address contemporary concerns, and advance creative and innovative mindsets in ways that may benefit all students and lead to astonishing cultural shifts.

Major Takeaways

- Traditional approaches to gifted education and talent development, much like other aspects of K–12 education, focus on the learning and talents of individual students. During identification, instruction, and assessment, the emphasis is on the student as an individual learner.

- Sociocultural theorists look at knowledge as socially valued forms of thinking and acting, emphasizing that all learning happens within important social and cultural contexts. Ignoring these contexts when working with gifted students limits our ability to prepare students for using their abilities in real-world contexts.

- Learning and knowledge are distributed across people, tools, and contexts.

- Learning and development occur in the Zone of Proximal Development (ZPD), yet most potentially talented students do not have opportunities to work within the ZPD.

- Dynamic and participatory assessment strategies are context-friendly approaches to identification and assessment within talent development efforts.

- Gifted education and talent development programs that emphasize problem-based learning with real problems, require social interaction among talented students, are aware of the cultural context in which student work is situated, and emphasize the importance of noncognitive skills in achievement have the potential to better prepare students for successful use of their talents in real-world settings.

RECOMMENDED READINGS

Hickey, D. T., & Rehak, A. (2013). Wikifolios and participatory assessment for engagement, understanding, and achievement in online courses. *Journal of Educational Multimedia and Hypermedia, 22,* 407–441.

Jacob, E. (1997). Context and cognition: Implications for educational innovators and anthropologists. *Anthropology & Education Quarterly, 28,* 3–21.

McWilliams, J., & Plucker, J. A. (2014). Brain cancer, meat glue, and shifting models of outstanding human behavior: Smart contexts for the 21st century. *Talent Development and Excellence, 6*(1), 47–55.

Plucker, J. A., & Barab, S. A. (2005). The importance of contexts in theories of giftedness. In R. J. Sternberg & J. E. Davidson (Eds.), *Conceptions of giftedness* (pp. 201–216). New York, NY: Cambridge University Press.

Wertsch, J. V. (1985). *Vygotsky and the social formation of mind.* Cambridge, MA: Harvard University Press.

REFERENCES

Aguayo, R. (1991). *Dr. Deming: The American who taught the Japanese about quality.* New York, NY: Fireside.

Alvermann, D. E., & Hagood, M. C. (2000). Critical media literacy: Research, theory, and practice in "New Times." *The Journal of Educational Research, 93,* 193–205.

Apple, M. W. (2006). Understanding and interrupting neoliberalism and neoconservatism in education. *Pedagogies, 1*(1), 21–26.

Barab, S. A., & Duffy, T. (2012). From practice fields to communities of practice. In D. Jonassen & S. Land (Eds.), *Theoretical foundations of learning environments* (2nd ed.; pp. 29–65). New York, NY: Routledge.

Barab, S. A., & Plucker, J. A. (2002). Smart people or smart contexts? Cognition, ability, and talent development in an age of situated approaches to knowing and learning. *Educational Psychologist, 37,* 165–182.

Beghetto, R. A., & Plucker, J. A. (in press). The relationship among schooling, learning, and creativity: "All roads lead to creativity" or "You can't get there from here"? In J. C. Kaufman & J. Baer (Eds.), *Creativity and reason in cognitive development* (2nd ed.). New York, NY: Cambridge University Press.

Brandt, D. (2014). *The rise of writing.* New York, NY: Cambridge University Press.

Brown, A. L., Metz, K. E., & Campione, J. C. (1996). Social interaction and individual understanding in a community of learners: The influence of Piaget and Vygotsky. In A. Tryphon & J. Vonèche (Eds.), *Piaget-Vygotsky: The social genesis of thought* (pp. 145–170). East Sussex, England: Psychology Press.

Buckingham, D. (2003). Media education and the end of the critical consumer. *Harvard Educational Review, 73,* 309–327.

Callahan, C. M. (2005). Identifying gifted students from underrepresented populations. *Theory Into Practice, 44,* 98–104.

Carr, N. (2008, July-August). Is Google making us stupid? *The Atlantic.* Retrieved from http://www.theatlantic.com/doc/200807/google

Chaiklin, S. (2003). The zone of proximal development in Vygotsky's analysis of learning and instruction. In A. Kozulin, B. Gindis, V. S. Ageyev, & S. M. Miller (Eds.), *Vygotsky's educational theory and practice in cultural context* (pp. 39–64). Cambridge, England: Cambridge University Press.

Cole, M. (1996). *Cultural psychology: A once and future discipline.* Cambridge, MA: Harvard University Press.

Csikszentmihalyi, M. (1988). Society, culture, and person: A systems view of creativity. In R. J. Sternberg (Ed.), *The nature of creativity: Contemporary psychological perspectives* (pp. 325–339). New York, NY: Cambridge University Press.

Davydov, V. V. (1995). The influence of LS Vygotsky on education theory, research, and practice. *Educational Researcher, 24*(3), 12–21.

Dede, C., Korte, S., Nelson, R., Valdez, G., & Ward, D. (2005). *Transforming learning for the 21st century: An economic imperative.* Naperville, IL: Learning Point Associates.

DeLay, R. (1996). Forming knowledge: Constructivist learning and experiential education. *Journal of Experiential Education, 19,* 76–81.

Dilley, A., Fishlock, J., & Plucker, J. A. (2015). *What we know about communication* [P21 Research Series]. Washington, DC: Partnership for 21st Century Skills. Retrieved from http://www.p21.org/our-work/4cs-research-series/communication

Feuerstein, R., Rand, Y., Jensen, M. R., Kaniel, S., & Tzuriel, D. (1987). Prerequisites for assessment of learning potential: The LPAD model. In C. S. Lidz (Ed.), *Dynamic testing* (pp. 35–51). New York, NY: Guilford Press.

Ford, D. Y., Grantham, T. C., & Whiting, G. W. (2008). Culturally and linguistically diverse students in gifted education: Recruitment and retention issues. *Exceptional Children, 74,* 289–306.

Goos, M. (2014). Creating opportunities to learn in mathematics education: a sociocultural perspective. *Mathematics Education Research Journal, 26,* 439–457.

Hickey, D. T., Honeyford, M. A., Clinton, K. A., & McWilliams, J. (2010). Participatory assessment of 21st century proficiencies. In V. J. Shute & B. J. Becker (Eds.), *Innovative assessment for the 21st century* (pp. 107–138). New York, NY: Springer.

Hickey, D. T., Ingram-Goble, A. A., & Jameson, E. M. (2009). Designing assessments and assessing designs in virtual educational environments. *Journal of Science Education and Technology, 18,* 187–208.

Hickey, D. T., & Rehak, A. (2013). Wikifolios and participatory assessment for engagement, understanding, and achievement in online courses. *Journal of Educational Multimedia and Hypermedia, 22,* 407–441.

Iaconesi, S. (n.d.). *Art is Open Source: La Cura.* Retrieved from http://www.artisopensource.net/projects/la-cura

Jacob, E. (1997). Context and cognition: Implications for educational innovators and anthropologists. *Anthropology & Education Quarterly, 28*(1), 3–21.

Jenkins, H., Kelley, W., Clinton, K., McWilliams, J., Pitts-Wiley, R., & Reilly, E. (2013). *Reading in a participatory culture: Remixing Moby-Dick in the English classroom.* New York, NY: Teachers College Press.

Jenkins, H., Purushotma, R., Weigel, M., Clinton, K., & Robison, A. J. (2009). *Confronting the challenges of participatory culture: Media education for the 21st century.* Cambridge, MA: MIT Press.

Jones, M. G., & Brader-Araje, L. (2002). The impact of constructivism on education: Language, discourse, and meaning. *American Communication Journal, 5*(3), 1–10.

Kanevsky, L. (1992). The learning game. In P. S. Klein & A. J. Tannenbaum (Eds.), *To be young and gifted* (pp. 204–243). Norwood, NJ: Ablex.

Kanevsky, L., & Geake, J. (2004). Inside the zone of proximal development: Validating a multifactor model of learning potential with gifted students and their peers. *Journal for the Education of the Gifted, 28,* 182–217.

Kaufman, J. C. (2010). Using creativity to reduce ethnic bias in college admissions. *Review of General Psychology, 14,* 189–203.

Kaufman, J. C., Plucker, J. A., & Russell, C. M. (2012). Identifying and assessing creativity as a component of giftedness. *Journal of Psychoeducational Assessment, 30,* 60–73.

Kellner, D. (2011). Cultural studies, multiculturalism, and media culture. In G. Dines & J. M. Humez (Eds.), *Gender, race, and class in media: A critical reader* (pp. 7–18). Los Angeles, CA: SAGE.

Kellner, D., & Share, J. (2005). Toward critical media literacy: Core concepts, debates, organizations, and policy. *Discourse: Studies in the Cultural Politics of Education, 26,* 369–386.

Kellner, D., & Share, J. (2007). Critical media literacy, democracy, and the reconstruction of education. In D. Macedo & S. R. Steinberg (Eds.), *Media literacy: A reader* (pp. 3–23). New York, NY: Lang.

Kornhaber, M., Krechevsky, M., & Gardner, H. (1990). Engaging intelligence. *Educational Psychologist, 25,* 177–199.

Lave, J., Smith, S., & Butler, M. (1988). Problem solving as an everyday practice. In R. I. Charles & E. A. Silver (Eds.), *The teaching and assessing of mathematical problem solving* (Vol. 3, pp. 61–81). Reston, VA: National Council of Teachers of Mathematics.

Lave, J., & Wenger, E. (1991). *Situated learning: Legitimate peripheral participation.* New York, NY: Cambridge University Press.

Lidz, C. S. (2002). Mediated learning experience (MLE) as a basis for an alternative approach to assessment. *School Psychology International, 23,* 68–84.

Lidz, C. S., & Macrine, S. L. (2001). An alternative approach to the identification of gifted culturally and linguistically diverse learners: The contribution of dynamic assessment. *School Psychology International, 22,* 74–96.

Lorsbach, A., & Tobin, K. (1992). Constructivism as a referent for science teaching. *NARST Newsletter, 30,* 5–7.

Luria, S. R., O'Brien, R. L., & Kaufman, J. C. (2016). Creativity in gifted identification: increasing accuracy and diversity. *Annals of the New York Academy of Sciences, 1377,* 44–52.

McBee, M. T. (2006). A descriptive analysis of referral sources for gifted identification screening by race and socioeconomic status. *Journal of Secondary Gifted Education, 17,* 103–111.

McBee, M. T., Peters, S. J., & Miller, E. M. (2016). The impact of the nomination stage on gifted program identification: A comprehensive psychometric analysis. *Gifted Child Quarterly, 60,* 258–278.

McBee, M. T., Shaunessy, E., & Matthews, M. S. (2012). Policy matters: An analysis of district-level efforts to increase the identification of underrepresented learners. *Journal of Advanced Academics, 23,* 326–344.

McDermott, R. (1996). The acquisition of a child by a learning disability. In S. Chaiklin & J. Lave (Eds.), *Understanding practice: Perspectives on activity and context* (pp. 269–305). Cambridge, England: Cambridge University Press.

McLellan, R., & Nicholl, B. (2013). Creativity in crisis in design & technology: Are classroom climates conducive for creativity in English secondary schools? *Thinking Skills and Creativity, 9,* 165–185.

McWilliams, J., & Plucker, J. A. (2014). Brain cancer, meat glue, and shifting models of outstanding human behavior: Smart contexts for the 21st century. *Talent Development and Excellence, 6,* 47–55.

Milner, H. R., & Ford, D. Y. (2007). Cultural considerations in the underrepresentation of culturally diverse elementary students in gifted education. *Roeper Review, 29,* 166–173.

Morelock, M. J., Brown, P. M., & Morrissey, A. M. (2003). Pretend play and maternal scaffolding: Comparisons of toddlers with advanced development, typical development, and hearing impairment. *Roeper Review, 26,* 41–51.

Morris, J. E. (2001). African American students and gifted education: The politics of race and culture. *Roeper Review, 24*(2), 59–62.

National Research Council. (2002). *Minority students in special and gifted education.* Washington, DC: National Academies Press.

Nunes, T., Schliemann, A. D., & Carraher, D. W. (1993). *Street mathematics and school mathematics.* New York, NY: Cambridge University Press.

Plucker, J. A. (2016). Creative articulation. In J. A. Plucker (Ed.), *Creativity and innovation: Theory, research, and practice* (pp. 151–163). Waco, TX: Prufrock Press.

Plucker, J. A., & Barab, S. A. (2005). The importance of contexts in theories of giftedness. In R. J. Sternberg & J. E. Davidson (Eds.), *Conceptions of giftedness* (pp. 201–216). New York, NY: Cambridge University Press.

Plucker, J. A., Beghetto, R. A., & Dow, G. T. (2004). Why isn't creativity more important to educational psychologists? Potentials, pitfalls, and future directions in creativity research. *Educational Psychologist, 39,* 83–96.

Plucker, J. A., & Dow, G. T. (2017). Attitude change as the precursor to creativity enhancement. In R. A. Beghetto & J. C. Kaufman (Eds.), *Nurturing creativity in the classroom* (2nd ed., pp. 190–211). New York, NY: Cambridge.

Plucker, J. A., Hardesty, J., & Burroughs, N. (2013). *Talent on the sidelines: Excellence gaps and America's persistent talent underclass.* Storrs: University of Connecticut, Center for Education Policy Analysis. Retrieved from http://cepa.uconn.edu/mindthegap

Plucker, J. A., Kennedy, C., & Dilley, A. (2015). *What we know about collaboration* [P21 Research Series]. Washington, DC: Partnership for 21st Century Skills. Retrieved from http://www.p21.org/our-work/4cs-research-series/collaboration

Plucker, J. A., & Peters, S. J. (2016). *Excellence gaps in education: Expanding opportunities for talented youth.* Cambridge, MA: Harvard Education Press.

Renzulli, J. S. (2004). Introduction to identification of students for gifted and talented programs. In J. S. Renzulli & S. M. Reis (Eds.), *Identification of students for gifted and talented programs.* Thousand Oaks, CA: Corwin Press.

Renzulli, J. S., & Reis, S. M. (1994). Research related to the Schoolwide Enrichment Triad Model. *Gifted Child Quarterly, 38,* 7–20.

Richardson, V. (1997). *Constructivist teacher education: Building a world of new understandings.* London, England: Falmer.

Robles, M. M. (2012). Executive perceptions of the top 10 soft skills needed in today's workplace. *Business Communication Quarterly, 75,* 453–465.

Roth, W.-M., & Lee, Y.-J. (2007). "Vygotsky's neglected legacy": Cultural-historical activity theory. *Review of Educational Research, 77,* 186–232.

Sharma, G., & Sharma, P. (2010). Importance of soft skills development in 21st century curriculum. *International Journal of Education & Allied Sciences, 2*(2), 39–44.

Shirky, C. (2008). *Here comes everybody: The power of organizing without organizations.* New York, NY: Penguin.

Sternberg, R. J. (2003). WICS as a model of giftedness. *High Ability Studies, 14,* 109–137.

Sternberg, R. J. (2015). Teaching for creativity: The sounds of silence. *Psychology of Aesthetics, Creativity, and the Arts, 9,* 115–117.

Stetsenko, A., & Arievitch, I. M. (2004). The self in cultural-historical activity theory: Reclaiming the unity of social and individual dimensions of human development. *Theory & Psychology, 14,* 475–503.

Symonds, W. C., Schwartz, R., & Ferguson, R. F. (2011). *Pathways to prosperity: Meeting the challenge of preparing young Americans for the 21st century.* Cambridge, MA: Harvard Graduate School of Education.

Tobin, K. (2015). The sociocultural turn in science education and its transformative potential. In C. Milne, K. Tobin, & D. DeGennaro (Eds.), *Sociocultural studies and implications for science education* (Cultural Studies of Science Education, Vol. 12). Dordrecht, The Netherlands: Springer.

VanTassel-Baska, J. (1998). *Excellence in educating gifted & talented learners.* Denver, CO: Love.

The W. Edwards Deming Insitute. (2016). *Timeline.* Retrieved from https://deming.org/deming/timeline

Wertsch, J. V. (1985). *Vygotsky and the social formation of mind.* Cambridge, MA: Harvard University Press.

Wertsch, J. V., Tulviste, P., & Hagstrom, F. (1993). A sociocultural approach to agency. In E. Forman, N. Minnick, & C. A. Stone (Eds.), *Contexts for learning: Sociocultural dynamics in children's development* (pp. 336–356). New York, NY: Oxford University Press.

CHAPTER 11

Transforming Gifted Education Into Talent Development

PRACTICAL CONSIDERATIONS AND ADVOCACY ADVANTAGES

Rena F. Subotnik, Paula Olszewski-Kubilius, and Frank C. Worrell

*I*magine a scenario where you wake up as principal of an elementary school. You are standing in front of parents explaining the implementation of a new gifted program. In this dream, you are describing to the audience how you will be serving high IQ children with a daily program designed to enhance and support the participating children's gifts. The next night you are once again in the limelight at a parent meeting rationalizing a new program for mathematically talented students, selected by virtue of demonstrated interest, achievement, and creativity in mathematics. What arguments would you use in each case? Which program would be easier for you to explain to the parents and to other audiences in your professional world?

We contend that just as schools support their athletes and musicians because their gifts are explicit to their audiences and identified by virtue of performance, programs that focus on domain-specific giftedness in the academic realm are more likely to be welcomed by the school community. Clearly, these arguments are not airtight. We hope in this chapter to acknowledge drawbacks while leaving readers as supporters of the domain-specific talent development approach to gifted education.

What Does It Mean to Be Gifted?

In 2011, Subotnik, Olszewski-Kubilius, and Worrell synthesized the psychological literature on giftedness. This review of the literature led to the development of the following definition:

> Giftedness is the manifestation of performance or production that is clearly at the upper end of the distribution in a talent domain even relative to other high functioning individuals in that domain. Further, giftedness can be viewed as developmental in that in the beginning stages, potential is the key variable, in later stages, achievement is the measure of giftedness, and in fully developed talents, eminence is the basis on which this label is granted. Psychosocial variables play an essential role in the manifestation of giftedness at every developmental stage. Both cognitive and psychosocial variables are malleable and need to be deliberately cultivated. (Subotnik et al., 2011, p.7)

How Did We Come to This Definition?

Several key drivers led to the crystallization of this definition. Foremost, gifted education is critical to fulfilling society's need for future innovators, those who will create products and services that enrich and improve our lives. The goal of gifted education should therefore be to enable more individuals to make eminent contributions through explicit education and training. Another motivator for us was dispelling prevailing false negative (e.g., nerdy, aloof) and false positive (e.g., will make it on their own) stereotypes about gifted children. A review of the literature also resulted in insights about differences in talent development trajectories across domains. This knowledge allows for different perspectives on persistent, perplexing educational issues, such as achievement gaps and inequalities in educational opportunities, and has the potential to result in more children having their talents identified and nurtured. A fourth driver was to benefit the study of exceptional *academic* talent based on extensive research on talent development in sport and the performing arts, which has long emphasized the role of domain-specific abilities and psychosocial skills. A final stimulus for our work was to enable other researchers in psychology to value studying exceptional ability and giftedness and how these topics inform variables associated with achievement, such as self-concept and motivation.

Components of the Model

Domain-specific abilities. At the base of our position/definition of what it means to be gifted is the lack of empirical evidence that high *general* cognitive ability, or IQ, is the *sole* predictor of *exceptional* adult achievement (Subotnik, Karp, & Morgan, 1989; Terman & Oden, 1959). Although IQ is one of the most consistent predictors of academic and occupational outcomes (Brody, 1997; Nisbett et al., 2012), it accounts, on average, for about 25% of the variance in academic achievement (Neisser et al., 1996). Additionally, there is evidence from longitudinal studies that individuals with high IQs in childhood do not necessarily aspire to or achieve eminence in adulthood (Subotnik, Kassan, Summers, & Wasser, 1993), and that the relationship between IQ and educational opportunity or schooling is bidirectional (Ceci & Williams, 1997). Yet, the use of general cognitive ability measures such as IQ has dominated practice in gifted education in schools (National Association for Gifted Children, 2014–2015).

In contrast, substantial evidence supports domain-specific abilities as having strong predictive validity in terms of adult accomplishment, and this is true for domains as varied as sports, the performing arts, and the STEM fields. The combination of high mathematical and spatial reasoning abilities is related to STEM career choice and success (Lubinski, 2016; Park, Lubinski, & Benbow, 2007); spatial ability is useful for predicting success in fields, such as chemistry, dentistry, and engineering, and areas of the visual arts (Hegarty, 2004; Hegarty, Keehner, Khooshabeh, & Montello, 2009; Hsi, Linn, & Bell, 1997; Sorby, Casey, Veurink, & Dulaney, 2013; Stieff, 2013; Winner & Casey, 1992); musicality and pitch perception have been identified as important to singing talent (Watts, Barnes-Burroughs, Andrianopoulos, & Carr, 2003); and technical and tactical skills distinguished elite players in field hockey (Elferink-Gemser, Visscher, Lemmink, & Mulder, 2010). Moreover, there is evidence that domain-specific skills, notably spatial skills, are malleable and can be developed through intervention (Uttal et al., 2013).

Considerable debate among scholars who study giftedness pits the role of ability against practice, specifically deliberate practice (Drake & Winner, in press; Ericsson, 1996b; Macnamara et al., in press). It is our contention that practice and study are critical to the development of talent, but ability matters as well, and higher ability may enable individuals to set goals for deliberate practice, benefit from it at faster rates, and reach higher levels of performance. Deliberate practice may largely account for intra-individual differences in skill levels, that is, significant improvement, but may be less predictive of interindividual performance differences (Macnamara et al., in press).

Domain trajectories. Different domains have different trajectories, with different starting points, peaks, and endpoints (see Figure 11.1). In some domains, such as violin performance or mathematics, talent can emerge in early childhood,

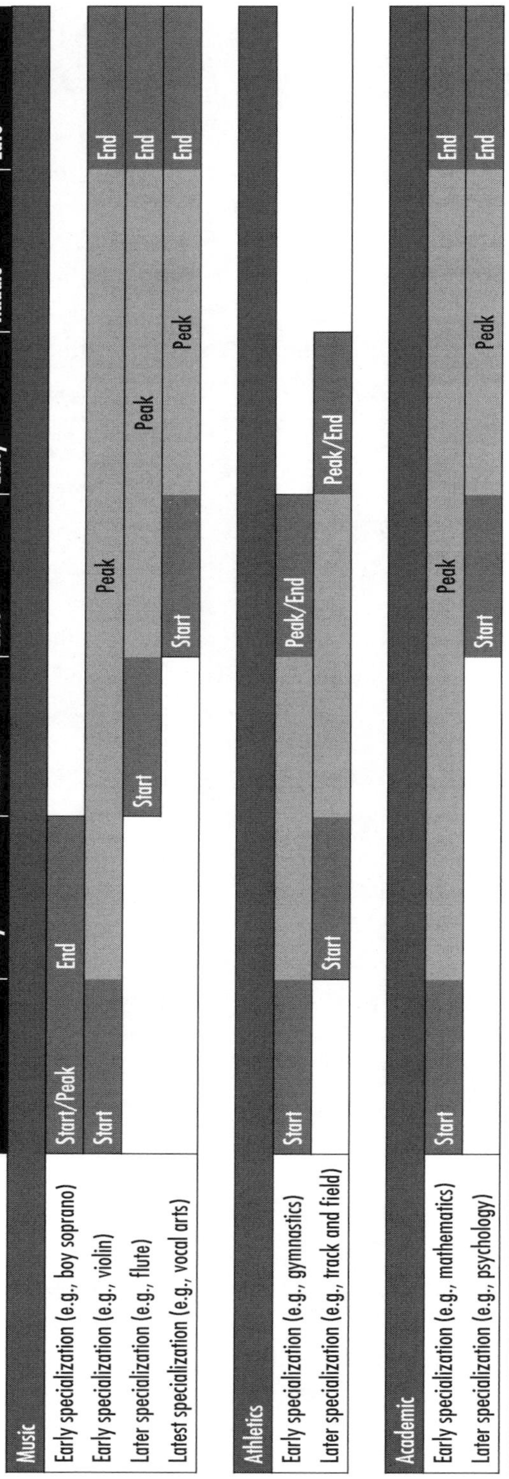

Figure 11.1. Starts, peaks, and end points for various domains of talent.

especially if early opportunities and enrichment are provided. The emergence of talent in other domains is dependent upon acquisition of basic skills (e.g., writing) or physical development (e.g. sports, wind instruments). In a few domains, talent may not be evident until adulthood (e.g., diplomacy), as a constellation of skills and wealth of experiences are required to develop needed abilities. Variation in the trajectories among talent domains is informative as to when identification or talent mining could or should start. It should also be noted that individuals can vary in their entry due to lack of opportunity, but in domains that have shorter career trajectories, such as gymnastics or figure skating, lack of appropriate early opportunity can severely limit or even truncate progress.

Opportunities offered and taken. Also, common across domains is the importance of opportunities to develop talent in the domain; however, the nature and purpose of these opportunities varies depending upon the stage of talent development. In the early stages, opportunities provide exposure to domains and enable early indications of talent to emerge and be noticed. Playful engagement elicits enthusiasm, joy, and motivation. As interest begins to coalesce, opportunities help individuals acquire crucial basic skills and technical competencies. Deliberate practice at this stage is needed to solidify and automatize skills so that individuals can devote more energy to creativity in the domain.

As individuals progress in their domain of talent, experiences that provide exposure to authentic work and contact with adult professionals enhance the likelihood of successful progress. That is, enculturation into the domain—including learning about the values and mores of the talent field, the paths and varied roles for professionals, the various gatekeepers, benchmarks for progress, and standards of excellence—and developing social networks can be motivating and intensify commitment that sustains individuals through difficult times and setbacks. Content knowledge is almost always the focus of school and formal courses, but these other aspects of talent development can be acquired through special mentoring programs, opportunities to do research in laboratories, and other supplemental or outside-of-school activities.

As opportunities are typically linked to resources, they are usually much more available to individuals from families in the middle and upper classes. Consequently, one role of public schools is to identify and provide opportunities to children from lower socioeconomic status backgrounds. Equally important, however, is that students and families from all backgrounds take advantage of opportunities (e.g., participating in competitions, summer programs, and in-school programs), if they wish to maximize the development of the children's talent. As children move from playful engagement in a domain to the acquisition of skills, they must exert increased commitment of time to domain-specific activities, and a concomitant decrease in time spent engaging in other activities. The amount of time an individual spends in deliberate practice is correlated highly with how skilled the individual becomes (Ericsson, 1996a; Ericsson, Krampe, & Tesch-Römer, 1993). In sum, appropriate opportunities at an early stage can both build motivation and help children acquire the self-confidence, persistence, and resiliency to partake of increasingly challenging talent development opportunities.

Psychosocial skills. Throughout their journey, students need assistance with psychosocial skills that support high achievement, and the role played by these skills varies by stage of talent development. For example, being teachable and open to instruction and feedback from teachers or mentors is critical when a student is acquiring the foundational techniques of the domain. At later points, a good teacher will encourage his or her students to "bite back" when they have strong evidence for a different approach (Jarvin & Subotnik, 2015). A positive response to challenging work and competition is important as one traverses to higher stages in the talent domain. Resiliency and a thick skin are especially needed when individuals start putting forth their unique and creative ideas and work for review and critique. Students learn resilience from failure when messages by significant others communicate that failure provides opportunities for growth. Students acquire mindsets that emphasize effort and improvement if reinforced by teachers, coaches, and mentors.

Availability of opportunities outside of school. Talented students ought to have access to appropriate challenging programs within school *and* outside of school (see Subotnik et al., 2011), especially children who are socioeconomically disadvantaged and students living in rural areas. Lack of resources and geographical proximity to community or university-based programs may hinder the development of students from these groups, and we argue that schools must take on the additional responsibility, typically assumed by parents of more advantaged children, of accessing or providing outside-of-school opportunities for these children.

In some highly specialized areas, such as video production and anime, students participate in online communities of practice where they develop products and submit them to peers for critique, feedback, and assistance. Some talent domains, such as sports and music, are developed largely outside of school, although school may provide initial exposure and opportunity for exceptional ability to be noticed. For these domains, identifying excellent and expert instructors, coaches, or training programs is especially important, as well as facilities and organizational structure. For example, specialized schools exist in the performing arts and, in sports, online schools are used to help athletes complete academic work around intense practice schedules.

But, even for academic areas, talent development requires both in-school and outside-of-school opportunities. Typically, students and families seek summer programs offered by universities and community organizations. Some students arrange to work with professors or mentors on independent research projects. In fact, high-level adult creative accomplishments in the STEM fields is associated with a rich and varied dose of STEM educational experiences during high school and college (Wai, Lubinski, Benbow, & Steiger, 2010).

HOW ARE GIFTS AND TALENTS DEVELOPED?

Typically, gifted education specialists have tended to view talent development as a process that begins with entrance into formal schooling and ends at the end of high school, with little coordination between services and programming from one level of schooling to the next. Thoughtfully sequenced continuous programming is rare and talent development paths are interspersed with gaps. However, if one views talent development as the deliberate transformation of domain-specific abilities to competencies, expertise, and beyond, a systematic approach is necessary. Talent development that results in expertise or creative production requires long-term commitment to an articulated sequence of programs within and outside of school, and the gaps that occur in the course of typical school transitions can derail the talent development process. Advantaged families can often fill in these gaps with supplemental, tuition-based programming, but youth without the resources are left behind. This view of talent development requires teachers to enhance their role by providing experiences that prepare students to successfully transition to the next stage of talent development.

Based on evidence that domain-specific skills are malleable and need to be developed with instruction, practice, interaction with peers, and coaching in psychosocial skills, we offer a model of growth based on the expertise literature as well as the work of Benjamin Bloom (1985) and his colleagues. In this conception, abilities transform into competencies, competencies into expertise, and on some occasions, expertise will generate notably outstanding performances or great ideas (Olszewski-Kubilius, Subotnik, & Worrell, 2016; see also Jarvin & Subotnik, 2015).

Each domain has a set of skills, content knowledge, and behavioral expectations that are associated with success and growth. Those domains that have explicit benchmarks, usually in performance areas such as sports, music, and dance, make it easier for children and their supporters to know how well they are progressing and what needs to be remediated or improved. In the case of most academic domains, however, progress may be associated solely with academic achievement in school contexts. Although important, academic success may not parallel the path to creative productivity. For example, many gifted adolescents wishing to explore research experiences in university laboratories during the summer or after school find themselves unprepared for conducting science that is not based on prescribed answers or given problems. Even winners of high prestige Olympiad competitions have trained themselves to take on difficult problems with a set of correct solutions, ones that can be solved in hours rather than days or years.

Bloom and his colleagues (1985) identified characteristics of teachers associated with beginning or "falling in love" with a domain, those who supported youngsters in developing an identity as a participant in a domain, and finally those teachers who coached their mentees to find their individual creative voice. The first stage involves joyful interaction and recognition that initial motivation may come from wanting to please parents or teachers on the part of children. Over time, many children who fall in love with an area, field, or topic want to learn the skills and knowledge that provide entry into being a novice scientist or historian. As children move on to achieving competence and expertise in a field, they need teachers who are knowledgeable and connected to the domain. Learning new skills may be tedious, yet good teachers are prepared to imbue their students with the values and special beauty of the domain. With practice, more skills become automatic, and new and exciting challenges take up more of the time devoted to acquiring expertise.

Depending on the domain, school age youth may achieve a significant level of expertise and even reach national level recognition for creative performance or ideas. Access to outstanding coaches and programs is especially important during this stage of development. Psychosocial skills play an outsize role in helping individuals deal with competition or stage fright, and pushback from supporters of the status quo. The performance domains incorporate psychosocial skills deeply in their training, and it is time for the academic domains to consider ways in which these skills can be incorporated as well.

Applying the Model

Based on the literature, we highlighted two categories of individuals who pursue creative domains and careers. One is the *performer* who uses his or her body, voice, or expression to interpret a piece of music, written word, or physical challenge. A second category we call the *producer*, or one who choreographs, composes, invents, or researches a problem. Both sets of talented people have some similarities in how their talents are developed, and some clear differences (see Figure 11.2). As we have noted, talent development of *both* performers and producers involves mastering domain content and skill, which is accomplished through practice and study driven by commitment and drive. In addition to motivation and commitment, other psychosocial variables play an important role in enhancing or inhibiting talent development, including self-confidence and strategic risk-taking. Finally, it is likely that these two categories of gifted individuals are socialized into the values of the domain by skilled mentors, teachers, or coaches.

	Performers	Producers
Similarities	Must master the content within the domain	
	Need guided and deliberate practice and/or study	
	Must have commitment and motivation	
	Domain values are inculcated by mentors	
	Psychosocial variables limit or enhance success	
Differences	What you need to practice is more clearly defined—results of practice seen more easily	Tasks are more diffuse, long term, and multi-component
	Judgments of experts are trusted throughout the process	Judgments for selection in academic disciplines, at least at the pre collegiate level, are not trusted, and objective basis serve as a stand-in
		Judgments of experts are trusted in fields such as composition, playwriting, and visual arts
	Physical abilities are important—you do not have them forever, which constrains the arc of talent development	Physical abilities do not serve as central constraints to the arc of talent development
	Greater winnowing and fewer opportunities over time	Room for a greater number of producers, particularly in domains designated to target societal need
	More current focus on psychosocial-skills training	Little current focus on psychosocial-skills training
	The outcome of excellence and creativity is clearer—better sense of knowing the path and where you are going	Outcome of excellence is clear only in some areas—e.g., academic publications, grants, awards
	Domain is appreciated more widely by the public	Domain is mainly appreciated by insiders

Figure 11.2. Comparison of performers versus producers. From "Rethinking giftedness and gifted education: A proposed direction forward based on psychological science" (p. 31), by R. F. Subotnik, P. Olszewski-Kubilius, & F. Worrell, 2011, *Psychological Science in the Public Interest, 12,* 3–54. Copyright 2011 by R. F. Subotnik, P. Olszewski-Kubilius, and F. Worrell. Reprinted with permission of the authors.

On the other hand, time plays a major role in *differentiating* between performers and producers. Performers often have a limited range of years when they are operating at their peak. In some early specialization domains, such as gymnastics or violin, the childhood years need to be devoted to skill development. Additionally, benchmarks for progress are more explicit in the performance domains than in academic domains, particularly during the school years. This discrepancy is also reflected in the degree of trust that experts in the performance domains elicit from the field. That is, the judgments of talent scouts, no matter how subjective their methods for identifying talent, are greatly valued. Concurrently, school-based evaluators are typically not allowed to be the sole arbiters of selection, and their judgments must be accompanied by an abstract test of achievement or intelligence. Additionally, psychosocial skills are taught more explicitly to elite performers as an inherent part of their training. Finally, the performance domains are more appreciated by the public than are production domains, most especially those considered academic. For all of these reasons, we argue that some lessons learned from the performance domains can be applied to talent development in academic domains during childhood and adolescence.

Identification in music. What are some lessons that can be learned from the preparation of musicians that can be applied to teaching and learning academic subjects in and out of school? First, talent is identified in a content valid way from the earliest years. That is, talent in music is identified by watching someone play or sing. In young children, attention is paid to pitch and general musicality. As children move from potential to the achievement stage, the audition is not random. The repertoire of an audition is made public and those with the wherewithal to apply know what they need to prepare. Clearly, many potentially talented children and their families are left out of the process because they do not know where to look to find a teacher and instrument, or they may not have the resources to participate.

The benchmarks for success are determined each year in a traditional music program by way of a "jury," or performance in front of the entire faculty for their musical area (e.g., strings). Success in the jury allows one to continue in the program. Each student has lessons to focus on individual strengths and weaknesses, and teachers prepare each student to face challenges of performance like stage fright or loss in a concerto competition. Good music programs also tailor their programs for different outcomes, whether soloist, orchestra player, or music teacher.

Identification in mathematics. Mathematics is one of the few academic domains in which talent can emerge early. This early potential is often demonstrated in a young child's effort to "mathematize" the world. A rage to count objects and observe patterns can be indicative of a capacity for exceptional mathematical reasoning. If fueled by parents, a child may enter formal schooling with very advanced mathematical computational and reasoning skills. Often, these children come to the attention of teachers and they become candidates for early acceleration in math. In these cases, early opportunity plays a significant role in not only developing mathematical talent but also in enabling it to be observed and noticed. This outcome is not the case for all children with potential talent in math, particularly children who come from socioeconomically disadvantaged backgrounds. For children in these circumstances, it is important that their preschools and elementary schools provide early enrichment opportunities for playful exploration of mathematical concepts. Through these opportunities, children with talent who demonstrate a mathematical cast of mind (Krutetskii, 1976), exceptional interest, and a faster learning rate can be identified.

The domain of mathematics has reliable and valid instruments to assess children's academic development. Most typically used achievement tests by schools have subtests that assess computation, concepts, and reasoning. These can be used to initially identify children who may need a broader curriculum or a faster pace of instruction. Additionally, mathematics lends itself readily to subject area acceleration, and children who are advanced can be placed with older students for their mathematics instruction. Another path forward is through afterschool clubs that serve as avenues for identifying potential among individual students in different arenas of mathematics that are not part of the school curriculum. Because interest and motivation develop with exposure to interesting mathematics, afterschool or in-school enrichment is essential at all grades during elementary school and serves as a means to identify "late bloomers." Families with resources often begin to supplement their child's school-based learning in math with summer and weekend programs or even online courses. These opportunities give students access to similarly interested and talented peers, as well as advanced instruction.

By middle school, above-grade level testing should be used to assess mathematical reasoning ability. There is a long history of using the math subtests of the ACT or SAT with seventh and eighth graders, and more recently, the PSAT 8/9 with fourth through sixth graders to discern levels of advanced mathematical reasoning ability. Scores on above-grade-level tests have immediate utility for placement in mathematics in middle school and also predictive validity for future accomplishments in math-related careers. Ample research shows that middle school students with high scores on the SAT-M are more likely to pursue STEM careers as adults (Lubinski, 2016). Scores on these tests can distinguish between students who need one year of acceleration in math from those that need to be accelerated several years. Interest and motivation to work and expend effort on advanced math should be a consideration in placement in accelerated mathematics opportunities and programs.

Many schools group students in middle school for math and enable high-achieving students to complete Algebra I before grade 9, but this is likely insufficient acceleration for many gifted students. Students with access to summer programs often use these programs to accelerate their mathematics learning, by completing a year of mathematics in the summer, and thereby qualifying for the mathematics course 2 years ahead when they return to school at the end of the summer. Additionally, schools with high percentages of low-income and minority students are less likely to offer advanced classes in mathematics in middle school, despite the fact that 25% of these students score above the 90th percentile on NAEP tests (Loveless, 2016), and it is essential that opportunities to engage in advanced mathematics with similarly able peers are offered to these students as well.

A robust school-based talent development program would include other opportunities, such as afterschool math clubs and participation in math competitions such as Math Olympiads. These outside-of-school and extracurricular programs are an important part of a talent development program in mathematics, as they give students peer support for their interests, cultivate motivation and commitment, enable students to benchmark their progress against peers, and help develop essential psychosocial skills, such as positive attitudes toward challenge and competition.

Students with mathematical talent and interest should be advised by school counselors to take a variety of classes beyond advanced math classes, as well as mentorships with professional mathematicians. Many students with exceptional math interest and ability may eventually pursue careers in mathematics or in mathematically based STEM fields, such as engineering and physics. Counselors can assist in identifying good matches to math-related careers, some with a more direct, applied focus such as biomedical engineering. Summer programs often have courses that provide initial exposure to fields such as engineering and robotics. Students who are especially interested in pure math should be directed to special summer programs for the most mathematically talented students that focus, for example, on number theory, and online or dual credit courses that allow them to take math courses typically reserved for college students. A robust talent development program includes outside-of-school opportunities, and while schools cannot be expected to offer all of these, they can be expected to help students identify opportunities. For their part, summer programs and organizations that offer supplemental programs must ensure that students from low-income families also have access.

Students with interests in mathematics and related careers need to be actively counseled about the importance of seeking research mentorships and internships, not only for their own development but also because of the advantages that accrue from networking and mentoring by adult professionals. Engagement at a deeper and more authentic level offers enculturation into the values and mores of the field and can help students decide if they are a good fit. It is often from these experiences that students get the best advice about matters such as deciding on academic versus industry career paths, criteria for choosing a graduate program, and the importance of identifying a major professor or mentor. Some high schools dedicate faculty to facilitate independent research on the part of students, sometimes to prepare students for participation in science competitions such as the Regeneron Science Talent Search, and many colleges offer opportunities for funded undergraduate research. Counseling and advising is especially important for students who do not have family members who can guide them. Undergraduates who wish to pursue graduate training should connect with research faculty to get laboratory-based experiences, or work with graduate students and professors on authentic projects; these opportunities can also result in advice regarding graduate schools, internships, and further training.

Identification in technology. Many young children show interest in technology, and it is not unusual to see preschoolers engaging in games on iPhones and iPads. Some may go on to develop a fascination with programming languages. Attraction to linguistic or numerical codes, code breaking, or in "making" things may provide clues to a burgeoning interest in programming beyond working with technology tools such as computers. Some schools offer an articulated technology sequence, but more often, offerings are minimal, designed to help students acquire basic skills in the service of academic learning (e.g., Word or Excel), or courses are offered as electives or via clubs or afterschool programs. Many parents supplement with outside-of-school courses and programs.

A trajectory for talent programming and web or application design might be to start with learning languages such as Scratch, Alice, or Logo. Students can then progress to more advanced languages such as Greenfoot, Ruby on Rails, and Python, and introductory web design. More advanced learners study Java, C++, SQL, and Objective C and take AP Computer Science in high school. For children with a desire to learn software development and gaming, Minecraft and courses in animation, digital or graphic design, audio and video production, or cyber security would provide an articulated sequence of skill development culminating in courses that preview adult work in technology. Those pursuing robotics and electronics can start by studying WeDo, LEGO Mindstorms, and NXT, moving on to Arduino and courses in electrical engineering.

In this domain, given our current school system, much will need to be learned outside of school through clubs, additional courses taken in out-of-school settings, and online communities. Another source for courses would be MOOCs and dual-enrollment courses offered via community colleges and universities. Although schools many not offer the wide range of options needed by students with interests in these areas of technology, they can advise students on what courses they should take depending upon their skill levels, and potentially where to find them.

Identification in writing. Talent in writing may manifest early in word play, verbal analogies, word games, or early reading. It may proceed to a passion for writing short stories, plays, or poetry, or creating books, newspapers, or magazines. A language arts program in school that enables students to acquire a strong foundation in expressing ideas in writing using appropriate vocabulary and grammar will largely be the focus of instruction in elementary and middle school. But most schools do not systematically look for nor develop creative writing abilities, which involve developing both creativity and technique. Students with writing talent will need ample opportunities to engage in various forms such as persuasive writing and creative writing (e.g., short stories and poetry), and to share and receive critical feedback on their work. They also need to become comfortable with editing and revising as they refine their work.

Middle and high school courses that provide a strong curriculum on literary analysis will enable students to study and learn from the techniques of various writers. During high school, programs that preview writing for careers such as journalistic writing, fantasy fiction writing, graphic novels, or writing for marketing and public relations, travel, or scientific publications, facilitate exploration and identity development within the talent field. There are many creative writing competitions and students should be encouraged to participate in them, as they will provide opportunities for them to benchmark their skill development, receive guidance from professional writers, and meet other budding writers.

Extracurricular activities and clubs such as a speech club or debate can hone thinking skills and developing confidence in putting oneself forward. Drama clubs are often attractive to creative students as well as high school activities such as yearbook and literary magazines. In addition, students should be helped to identify publication outlets for their work. Similar to other domains, a school cannot offer all of the courses and opportunities needed by talented writers, and writing courses offered via distance education or dual enrollment will be important. However, schools can provide guidance on the trajectory for writers, help students find appropriate programs and courses and encourage their participation in them, and connect them with mentors or professional writers who can also assist in guiding them on a career path.

Evaluation of Success in a Talent Development Program

Overall, the measure of a "good" talent development program is that children and youth who want to pursue their talent in a domain have the necessary experiences and courses available to them to continue on a path of developing skills and competencies in their talent domain, starting from early exposure through expertise. Schools may not be able to offer all of these courses in all domains, but they should be responsible for giving the best possible advice and guidance to enable students to achieve their goals over the long term. These outcomes will only occur if teachers and other school personnel, parents, and coaches are aware of the opportunities available in their districts, communities, states, and even nationally that can enhance the development of talent. For participants, success would mean that they maintained and enhanced their interest in the domain and that they acquired and mastered benchmarks sufficient to moving toward developing expertise in the domain. If queried about their satisfaction with the program and the support they received, they would be able to report that they were well prepared to move forward.

As for evaluating the success of programs, we endorse record keeping and data collection that would promote continuous improvement toward maintaining and enhancing participant interest in the domain and evidence that students are reaching benchmarks for that domain. These data will allow programs to evaluate if they have provided appropriate instruction and supports to their talented students by using national standards in science, mathematics, music, or sports as a point of reference; reflected in their students moving on to the next level successfully and maybe at an earlier age. Schools and programs will also need to develop connections with programs at the next level to see who continued and who did not and why. Certainly, no program should expect that every participant will pursue a career in a domain he or she explored in school, but all program participants should be prepared to apply what they have learned to whatever pathway they choose. Keeping track of these outcomes can help programs to educate children about different futures inside and outside of the domain.

Major Takeaways

Let us get back to the principal's two dreams that served as the introduction to this chapter. Upon reflection, in which situation would you want to find yourself—defending traditional gifted education or promoting talent development? We hope that we have provided readers with sufficient evidence and argument for choosing talent development.

- By focusing on domain-specific rather than global talent, more children can be served, and devoting resources to talent development in specific academic domains, such as mathematics or writing, is easier to explain than supporting a program for students with high IQs, especially if these students are not producing strong academic work.

- From the performance domains, we have learned that most of the psychosocial skills needed to facilitate growth can be strengthened or taught. The idea of coaching for high performance is a unique contribution of the talent development model.

- Talent development done properly involves integration of in-school and out-of-school community-based programs and beyond. Involving the community in the vicinity of a school cannot but be helpful in promoting support for the students and the program. Helping young people discover and engender their talents is a win-win for everyone.

RECOMMENDED READINGS

Olszewski-Kubilius, P., Subotnik, R. F., & Worrell, F. C. (2015). Conceptions of giftedness and the development of talent: Implications for counselors. *Journal of Counseling and Development, 93,* 143–152. doi:10.1002/j.1556-6676.2015.00190.x

Olszewski-Kubilius, P., Subotnik, R. F., & Worrell, F. C. (2017). The role of domains in the conceptualization of talent. *Roeper Review, 39,* 59–69. doi:10.1080/0278319 3.2017.1247310

Subotnik, R. F., Olszewski-Kubilius, P., & Worrell, F. (2011). Rethinking giftedness and gifted education: A proposed direction forward based on psychological science. *Psychological Science in the Public Interest, 12,* 3–54. doi:10.1177/1529100611418056

Subotnik, R. F., Olszewski-Kubilius, P., & Worrell, F. C. (2015). Nurturing the young genius. *Scientific American Mind, 23*(4), 60–67.

Worrell, F. C., Olszewski-Kubilius, P., & Subotnik, R. F. (2012). Important issues, some rhetoric, and a few straw men: A response to comments on "Rethinking Giftedness and Gifted Education." *Gifted Child Quarterly, 56,* 224–231. doi:10.1177/0016986212456080

REFERENCES

Bloom, B. J. (Ed.). (1985). *Developing talent in young people.* New York, NY: Ballantine Books.

Brody, N. (1997). Intelligence, schooling, and society. *American Psychologist, 52,* 1046–1050. doi:10.1037/0003-066X.52.10.1046

Ceci, S. J., & Williams, W. M. (1997). Schooling, intelligence, and income. *American Psychologist, 52,* 1051–1058. doi:10.1037/0003-066X.52.10.1051

Drake, J. E., & Winner, E. (in press). Why deliberate practice is not enough: Evidence of talent in drawing. In D. Z. Hambrick, G. Campitelli, & B. N. Macnamara (Eds.), *The science of expertise. Behavioral, neural, and genetic approaches to complex skill.* New York, NY: Psychology Press.

Elferink-Gemser, M. T., Visscher, C., Lemmink, K. A. P. M., & Mulder, T. (2010). Multidimensional performance characteristics and standard of performance in talented youth field hockey players: A longitudinal study. *Journal of Sports Sciences, 25,* 481–489. doi:10.1080/02640410600719945

Ericsson, K. A. (1996a). The acquisition of expert performance: An introduction to some of the issues. In K. A. Ericsson (Ed.), *The road to excellence: The acquisition of expert performance in the arts and sciences, sports, and games* (pp. 1–50). Mahwah, NJ: Erlbaum.

Ericsson, K. A. (Ed.). (1996b). *The road to excellence: The acquisition of expert performance in the arts and sciences, sports, and games.* Mahwah, NJ: Erlbaum.

Ericsson, K A., Krampe, R. T., & Tesch-Römer, C. (1993). The role of deliberate practice in the acquisition of expert performance. *Psychological Review, 100,* 363–406. doi:10.1037/0033-295X.100.3.363

Hegarty, M. (2004). Mechanical reasoning by mental simulation. *Trends in Cognitive Sciences, 8,* 280–285. doi:10.1016/j.tics.2004.04.001

Hegarty, M., Keehner, M., Khooshabeh, P., & Montello, D. R. (2009). How spatial abilities enhance, and are enhanced by, dental education. *Learning and Individual Differences, 19,* 61–70. doi:10.1016/j.lindif.2008.04.006

Hsi, S., Linn, M. C., & Bell, J. E. (1997). The role of spatial reasoning in engineering and the design of spatial instruction. *Journal of Engineering Education, 86,* 151–158. Retrieved from http://jee.org/1997/april/505.pdf

Jarvin, L., & Subotnik, R. F. (2015). Academic talent development in North America and Europe. *Asia Pacific Education Review, 16,* 297–306. doi:10.1007/s12564-015-9370-0

Krutetskii, V. A. (1976). *The psychology of mathematical abilities in school children.* Chicago, IL: University of Chicago Press.

Loveless, T. (2016). *How well are American students learning?* The 2016 Brown Center Report on American Education (Vol. 3, No. 5). Washington, DC: The Brookings Institution.

Lubinski, D. (2016). From Terman to today: A century of findings on intellectual precocity. *Review of Educational Research, 86,* 900–944. doi:10.3102/0034654316674576

Macnamara, B. N., Hambrick, D. A., Frank, D. J., King, M. J., Burgoyne, A. P., & Meinz, E. J. (in press). Deliberate practice and the deliberate practice view. In D. Z. Hambrick, G. Campitelli, & B. N. Macnamara (Eds.), *The science of expertise. Behavioral, neural, and genetic approaches to complex skill.* New York, NY: Psychology Press.

National Association for Gifted Children. (2014–2015). *State of the states in gifted education.* Washington, DC: Author.

Neisser, U., Boodoo, G., Bouchard, T. J., Jr., Boykin, A. W., Brody, N., Ceci, S. J., Halpern, D. F., . . . Urbina, S. (1996). Intelligence: Knowns and unknowns. *American Psychologist, 51,* 77–101. doi:10.1037/0003-066X.51.2.77

Nisbett, R., Aronson, J., Blair, C., Dickens, W., Flynn, J., Halpern, D., & Turkheimer, E. (2012) Intelligence: New findings and theoretical developments. *American Psychologist, 67,* 130–159. doi:10.1037/a0026699

Olszewski-Kubilius, P., Subotnik, R. F., & Worrell, F. C. (2016). Aiming talent development toward creative eminence in the 21st century. *Roeper Review, 38,* 140–152. doi:10.1080/02783193.2016.1184497

Park, G., Lubinski, D., & Benbow, C. P. (2007). Contrasting intellectual patterns predict creativity in the arts and sciences: tracking intellectually precocious youth over 25 years. *Psychological Science, 18,* 948–952. doi:10.1111/j.1467-9280.2007.02007.x

Sorby, S., Casey, B., Veurink, N., & Dulaney, A. (2013). The role of spatial training in improving spatial and calculus performance in engineering students. *Learning and Individual Differences, 26,* 20–29. doi:10.1016/j.lindif.2013.03.010

Stieff, M. (2013). Sex differences in the mental rotation of chemistry representations. *Journal of Chemical Education, 90,* 165–170. doi:10.1021/ed300499t

Subotnik, R. F., Karp, D., & Morgan, E. (1989). High IQ children at midlife: An investigation into the generalizability of Terman's genetic studies of genius. *Roeper Review, 11,* 139–144. doi:10.1080/02783198909553190

Subotnik, R. F., Kassan, L., Summers, E., & Wasser, A. (1993). *Genius revisited: High IQ children grown up.* Norwood, NJ: Ablex.

Subotnik, R. F., Olszewski-Kubilius, P., & Worrell, F. (2011). Rethinking giftedness and gifted education: A proposed direction forward based on psychological science. *Psychological Science in the Public Interest, 12,* 3–54. doi:10.1177/1529100611418056

Terman, L. M., & Oden, M. H. (1959). *The gifted group at mid-life: 35 years' follow-up of the superior child.* Stanford, CA; Stanford University Press.

Uttal, D. H., Meadow, N. G., Tipton, E., Hand, L. L., Alden, A. R., Warren, C., & Newcombe, N. S. (2013). The malleability of spatial skills: A meta-analysis of training studies. *Psychological Bulletin, 139,* 352–402. doi:10.1037/a0028446

Wai, J., Lubinski, D., Benbow, C. P., & Steiger, J. H. (2010). Accomplishment in science, technology, engineering, and mathematics (STEM) and its relation to STEM educational dose: A 25-year longitudinal study. *Journal of Educational Psychology, 102,* 860–871. doi:10.1037/a0019454

Watts, C., Barnes-Burroughs, K., Andrianopoulos, M., & Carr, M. (2003). Potential factors related to untrained singing talent: A survey of singing pedagogues. *Journal of Voice, 17,* 298–307. doi:10.1067/S0892-1997(03)00068-7

Winner, E., & Casey, M. B. (1992). Cognitive profiles of artists. In G. Cupchik & J. Laszlo (Eds.), *Emerging visions of the aesthetic process* (pp. 154–170). New York, NY: Cambridge University Press.

CHAPTER 12

Advanced Academics

A RESPONSE TO INTERVENTION PERSPECTIVE ON GIFTED EDUCATION

Scott J. Peters, Heidi Erstad, and Michael S. Matthews

WHAT DOES IT MEAN TO BE GIFTED/TALENTED?

To address what it means to be "gifted" under the Advanced Academic perspective (Peters, Matthews, McBee, & McCoach, 2014), it's important that we first clarify the basis for this definition and address the question of why educational systems choose to identify students as *gifted* in the first place. Our premise is that gifted education should have the same goal as any other educational intervention or curriculum in schools—that is, to assure that all students are challenged in their learning to the degree necessary to develop to their full potential. To meet this goal, we argue that *gifted* education programs and services are needed only when and if students are not otherwise having their instructional needs met. An example might help illustrate this point because it's the main *raisons d'être* for gifted education.

Andrew is 16 years old and attends Emerson High School. He just finished taking AP Calculus BC as a sophomore. Luckily for him, the school has a scope and sequence in place such that any student—no matter when he or she takes this particular class—always has a class to take the next year. In this case, his school has an advanced math option available in which students who have completed AP Calculus BC are able to take college-level Calculus 3 as part of their high school schedule. Andrew subsequently enrolls in this class, and there is every reason to believe he will be appropriately challenged by this curriculum. This course is not considered to be a part of gifted education, but rather is available to anyone who needs it—that is, anyone who has demonstrated her or his readiness for Calculus 3 content by successfully completing AP Calculus BC—in order to continue to develop her or his mathematics skills. By enrolling in this class, Andrew's learning needs are met and no further intervention is necessary.

Lucy is 16 years old and attends Thoreau High School. She just finished a combined course on geometry and trigonometry, which typically is a junior-level class, as a sophomore. The school offers no additional math coursework beyond Algebra II, which she completed during her freshman year. Because taking any other available math class at her school (or no math class at all) would fail to develop her math abilities, she is flagged as in need of a supplementary (gifted) intervention. This designation alerts the building team that an individualized plan needs to be developed to allow Lucy to access additional math courses through dual enrollment, either at another high school or online. In this case, gifted education services are necessary in order to make sure Lucy continues to grow and develop her math abilities. Without the options provided by gifted services, she would remain underchallenged in the area of mathematics.

These two cases go a long way to defining what "giftedness" is according to the Advanced Academics perspective. The Advanced Academics (AA) perspective sees "giftedness" as an educational designation unique to the K–12 school setting. In other words, although it is possible to be gifted, talented, or eminent in adulthood or in areas of study not covered in school, the AA perspective is school-contingent. In this usage, there is no such thing as giftedness outside of the K–12 educational context. Put simply, gifted is an educational label that denotes an unmet need beyond the reach of universal services provided to students in a school.

It's a well-established principle in education that students have individual levels of readiness, or needs, that should inform instruction targeted at their current level of prior knowledge. If a student is not in his or her Zone of Proximal Development[1] with regard to a particular domain or content area and the student's

---

1   The theoretical basis for this perspective is Vygotsky's concept of the Zone of Proximal Development (ZPD; Vygotsky, 1978). Stated briefly, the ZPD is the area of learning that lies between what a child can do on her or his own and what he or she can accomplish with the assistance of another more knowledgeable person, such as a teacher. Vygotsky suggested that new content can only be learned effectively when it is presented within the child's ZPD; instruction at a lower level is boring or represents material already mastered, while instruction at too high a level will be above the learner's comprehension. Notably, the ZPD is conceptualized as differing across individuals.

advanced current level of need cannot be met through the standard universal curriculum and instructional practices, then that student has an unmet need that should be addressed under the larger umbrella of gifted education. The actual level of student ability is irrelevant, except to the extent that it aligns with the level of content available. Where gifted education kicks in is when those needs are on the advanced end of the spectrum and are not met by existing services in the learner's current educational placement.

In the examples above, Andrew had a higher level of math achievement (calculus), but in fact, had no unmet need. Andrew's need for above-level math was already being addressed through existing pathways—part of universal programming for students. Therefore, no special intervention, gifted service, or any accompanying label was warranted (see, for example, Matthews, Ritchotte, & Jolly, 2014). Alternatively, Lucy, even with her relatively lower level of math achievement compared to Andrew, would require a gifted intervention to remain challenged because no other options are available in her school setting. From an Advanced Academics perspective, this discrepancy or mismatch between a school's available level of instruction and a given student's learning needs is the essential element of giftedness and gifted education.

In other words, from an Advanced Academics perspective, schools do not identify students as *gifted* simply because of a high level of measured ability or achievement. Instead, the only appropriate reason for a "gifted" label is because the label comes with an educationally necessary intervention or service. This is the same as with any other educational designation (e.g., learning disabled, visually impaired). Labels have no value in their own right, but rather, they are useful when they secure a means through which to provide students with an appropriately matched educational service.

The alternative to what we propose is not hard to imagine, given that it is actually happening in most schools. In most states and school districts, simply having high ability or achievement, compared to others the same age and regardless of prior opportunity, is sufficient to assign students the label of giftedness (National Association for Gifted Children [NAGC] & Council of State Directors of Programs for the Gifted [CSDPG], 2015). For several important reasons, we suggest that this tradition of finding and designating "gifted" as a within-child characteristic is, in fact, a hindrance to the goal of ideal challenge.

First, a label of "gifted" has acquired the connotation of a desirable status that some are fortunate enough to possess, as some kind of incentive or reward, even as such status remains unattainable to others. What's more, designating a child as "gifted" suggests that this construct is permanent, applies to all domains, and that the label was endowed in some way rather than being developed through access and opportunity.

Additionally, schools' preoccupation with a binary identification of students as "gifted" or "not" suggests two homogenous levels of need for each group. The gifted label is a blunt tool for addressing the far more finely nuanced challenge of meeting students' individual instructional needs. For instance, despite a label of gifted, some students could be vastly underchallenged yet remain so because gifted programming in their school is not aligned to address the areas in which students have demonstrated advanced need. It is also possible to remain underchallenged if the learner's measured ability is not considered high enough to be designated as gifted. In the state of New Mexico, for example, a measured IQ score of 130 or higher is required to be labeled as gifted and served under those programs. Isaac (pseudonym), an 8-year-old student one of us (Peters) met there, was scoring at the high school level for math, topping out the Measures of Academic Progress in mathematics. However, he wasn't eligible for gifted services because his IQ score didn't meet the 130 threshold. This is what happens when the label of giftedness is assigned without consideration for the level of unmet need: Some students will be labeled even though they have no unmet need (Andrew), while others will not be identified even though they are drastically underchallenged (Isaac). To provide for those students who require more challenge, the degree of current educational mismatch must be a consideration in deciding who is and is not labeled as gifted, if that term is to remain the gateway to appropriate educational services.

Our point being: What we *call* students who are underchallenged to the point of needing something else to continue learning matters far less than the services and supports we *actually provide* to them. This is why we prefer the concept of Advanced Academics (AA). From the AA perspective, any student who has a learning need that is beyond the reach of whole-class or even partially differenti-ated classroom instruction should be considered gifted and provided a service that corresponds with her or his particular level of need. In one school, a 16-year-old might be gifted if she needs calculus; in another—because of a strong focus on remediation in the grade-level classroom—even a child who is only slightly above "grade-level proficiency" might need a gifted intervention. As another example, a kindergartner who enters school reading may or may not need a gifted service, depending on the focus of instruction and level of differentiation found within her or his classroom.

With an Advanced Academics perspective, simply knowing a child's current level of achievement is insufficient to make the decision regarding gifted ser-vices. Instead, the school also must consider how that student's current level of achievement compares to what he or she is being taught. If the student cannot be challenged in the existing classroom or through the universal level of instruc-tion—whatever that may be in this specific setting—then a gifted intervention is necessary to further support him or her. In this manner, a student with an IQ of

145 could, but does not automatically, require gifted services simply because of this high level of ability.

As we have demonstrated, if the label of "gifted" is to remain the gateway to appropriate educational services for students who require more challenge, the degree of current educational mismatch must be the primary consideration. Giftedness and its associated historical connotations simply are not helpful when planning actual support and services for students.

In the world of perfectly differentiated and individualized instruction where there are no barriers to accessing appropriately challenging curriculum, no specialized "other" interventions are necessary. Taken to an extreme, if a school offers such a flexible schedule of such a wide range of curricular offerings that every student can access appropriately challenging curriculum and instruction, then gifted education and Advanced Academics do not need to exist.

For the real world, we advocate that schools operationalize Advanced Academics within a Response to Intervention (RtI) framework (see, for example, Johnsen, Parker, & Farah, 2015). Within an RtI framework, systems and interventions are in place to allow for all students to be challenged, regardless of how far above typical performance they are. Figure 12.1 depicts how schools provide multiple levels of services and supports to match the needs of students:

As illustrated in Figure 12.1, the school (or grade level or course) begins by identifying significant College and Career Readiness outcomes (A). They then apply a screening process (B) with multiple data sources to identify students' current level of performance on this outcome. For students moderately- or well-above benchmark, the school has in place some methods for digging deeper (C) to verify and/or learn more about their level of need. This digging deeper process helps teams match supports to needs (D), identifying the intensity and type of support students will need to continue to grow, more closely assuring that each student is learning within his or her ZPD.

In healthy and sustainable systems, Tier 1, or the universal level of support (i.e., differentiated instruction around core curriculum, ongoing collaboration, and strategic assessment) meets the learning needs of the vast majority of students. Tier 2, or selected level, of Advanced Academic services are added for students whose moderate learning needs extend beyond the universal (E); Tier 3, or intensive level of Advanced Academic services are provided for those few students whose current performance is multiple grade levels above peers/benchmark, to the degree that they really require an individualized learning plan (F).

Thus, the essential question when deciding whether a student is in need of an Advanced Academic intervention is whether or not his or her needs are being met through the universal/Tier 1 level of support. If a school offers an honors U.S. history course as well as a general-level U.S. history course, for example, then the combined range of needs that could be met by those courses would be part of the

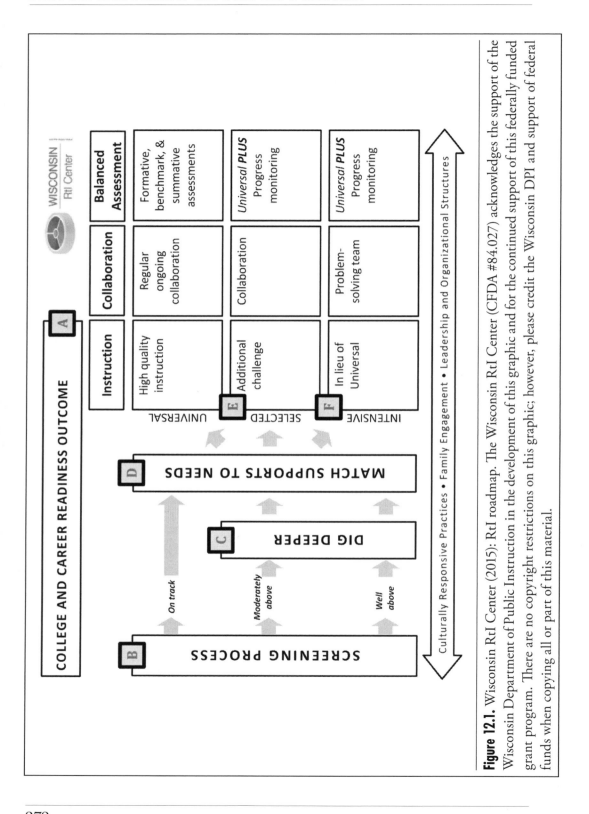

Figure 12.1. Wisconsin RtI Center (2015): RtI roadmap. The Wisconsin RtI Center (CFDA #84.027) acknowledges the support of the Wisconsin Department of Public Instruction in the development of this graphic and for the continued support of this federally funded grant program. There are no copyright restrictions on this graphic; however, please credit the Wisconsin DPI and support of federal funds when copying all or part of this material.

Tier I/universal level of services. Students whose needs are outside of the reach of these services would require and receive a different form or level of support.

How Do People Develop Their Gifts and Talents?

As discussed above, the goal of Advanced Academics is the same as for any other educational service—to assure students are challenged and grow and develop in their learning. Similarly, Advanced Academics seeks to develop student skills the same way a person learns any new skill—by interacting with content that is just above that which they can perform on their own and have already mastered. This is the very definition of the Zone of Proximal Development. Regardless of whether an eighth grader is working on letter recognition or is in the process of writing her own novels, she will only be able to develop and further refine her skills if what she is being taught is just beyond what she can accomplish independently. In this view, there is nothing particularly unique about developing the skills of "gifted" learners.

What might stand out as somewhat different about the Advanced Academics perspective is that it acknowledges that all levels of talent or even measured ability are influenced by the individual's past opportunity to learn (see, for example, Flores, 2007). Although this might seem intuitive or even obvious, the implications of this point are considerable. First, such a perspective means that a one-time identification process is out of the question. Just because a student is not demonstrating high ability or achievement right now, does not mean that he or she doesn't have the potential to do so at a future point in time. Rather, it could signify that, in this area, the learner has not yet had the opportunity to develop this talent because of a lack of or limited prior exposure.

For this reason, schools need to be sure they are giving students opportunities to develop and demonstrate talents on an ongoing basis. In contrast, in conventional gifted education approaches, identification and program placement decisions are traditionally made on the basis of *already developed* talent, advantaging students whose familial resources have afforded them greater prior exposure to opportunities to learn. Additionally, higher family income also tends to be associated with higher levels of cultural capital, which can be thought of as knowledge and attitudes that accompany learning and make it possible within a specific cultural context. For example, awareness of college admissions requirements and their procedures and timeline is one form of cultural capital that is associated with high family income, likely in large part because higher income families are more likely to have members who themselves have attended college. Analogous examples could be drawn from many areas of K–12 education, including gifted education.

Of course, exposure alone is not enough. For some domains or skills, once a student's interest in and talent for a domain is piqued, she might be able to develop that talent further on her own. Reading is a classic example. There are few barriers to independent development of a person's reading ability, assuming ongoing access to a library or the Internet. However, with most other skills and content areas this isn't true. A student who has a talent for math isn't as likely to be able to develop algebra skills using a book from the local library. Some will, but this is far less universal than is the case with reading. This is why we say that exposure alone is not enough.

Once a given level of readiness is observed, an educational system that is adaptable and that includes services for varying levels of readiness needs to be available for most learners to fully develop their abilities in mathematics or other content domains. Because it clearly is responsive to these varied learning needs, we are very supportive of the Response to Intervention approach.

Nothing we have said so far suggests that classroom differentiation or existing gifted curricular models are necessarily bad or ineffective. In the Advanced Academics perspective, however, learning happens for identified gifted kids just as it happens for anyone—through scaffolded interaction with novel, appropriately challenging content. In this view, there is no such thing as "gifted" curriculum. What advanced learners require to continue to grow and develop depends on their starting level of need. For some this might require content that is "lower" in level of rigor than others. This is something that is particularly unique to the Advanced Academic model.

How Can Educators Develop Their Students' Talents?

Early in 2017, two of us (Peters and Matthews) were involved in a project that sought to understand just how many students in the United States were working a year or more above the grade level in which they were enrolled (Peters, Rambo-Hernandez, Makel, Matthews, & Plucker, 2017). We did this to produce a very rough yet readily generalizable estimate of how many students might be capable of working beyond the level of their classroom instruction, given the strong focus on grade-level standards that dominates the United States education system. To examine this question, we looked at state datasets for California, Texas, and Wisconsin. What we found was that anywhere from 20%–49% of students were already scoring a year or more above grade-level proficiency in English language arts, and 16%–35% were a year or more advanced in math. When we looked at national data from the Northwest Evaluation Association's Measure of Academic Progress (MAP), we found that almost 25% of students were 2 or more years advanced in reading. Note that while these were multistate data, the MAP data were not representative of the entire nation because individual districts choose whether or not to administer MAP.

This study's implications are simple: There are large numbers of "grade-level" students whose learning needs actually fall well above their age-based grade level. The next question becomes, are these learners too far from being on grade level for a single teacher to reach? That's a harder question. Still, it brings us to our advice to educators on how to develop their students' talents.

The most important thing schools can do to develop the skills and talents of "gifted" students (as we define them) is to blur the fixed lines surrounding age-based grade levels and to put policies and procedures in place that allow students to access content outside of their traditionally rigid, age-based grade level. Right now, most K–12 schools are set up with strict age-based grade-level placements where the main factor that determines what a student is taught is how old they are (within rather random-seeming 12-month age bands that most commonly span September through August). This completely age-based system is one extreme on a continuum. The other extreme—which is rarely, if ever, implemented—is age-irrelevant instruction in which learning opportunities are based entirely on readiness and need.

Neither of these extremes is ideal. At the age-based end of the continuum, many students will be taught content that is too easy or too difficult to benefit them. The needs-based end of the continuum has a slightly different set of problems; setting up classrooms based solely on need would involve mixing a wide range of ages, and also would require offering remedial courses that likely would be dominated by low-income students because of the strong association between family income and academic achievement (see Peters & Engerrand, 2016 and discussion of opportunity to learn earlier in this chapter). Luckily, the two extremes of the continuum are not the only options available. Instead, there are ways to blur the lines separating age-based classrooms and curricula that can balance the need for diverse learning experiences and the wide ranges of academic needs that students have. What we propose is using a schoolwide RtI approach.

Instead of relying on the heroic efforts of individual teachers to meet the full range of their students' needs, a schoolwide RtI approach draws on the assets and resources within a school and its surrounding local community to plan and provide differentiation and talent development at the universal level of support; problem solve for groups and individual students whose academic needs extend beyond the universal level; and review the effectiveness of the school/district's system of support for advanced learning.

To accomplish these tasks, schools need to establish and hold sacred intentional collaboration times and purposeful teaming structures to accomplish essential functions that support advanced learning. Let's look at each collaborative team function in greater detail.

1. Plan and Provide Differentiation and Advanced Learning Strategies at the Universal Level of Support

Meeting this first function often occurs as a part of existing grade-level or content area collaborative teams. These teams use unit preassessment, available benchmark and screening assessments, student portfolios, and observational data to address the question: *How will we respond when students have exceeded grade-level standards and benchmarks?*

Building and district-level Advanced Academics specialists support teachers within these general education contexts by providing resources and strategies to help teachers extend the reach of the universal level of support. At this level, specialist teaching staff and coaches make arrangements with general education teachers to co-plan, model, co-teach, and/or provide instructional coaching to support implementation of differentiation and talent development strategies within the regular classroom.

2. Problem Solve for Advanced Academic Groups and Individuals (i.e., Students Whose Academic Needs Extend Beyond the Universal Level)

Establishing a robust, differentiated universal level of support is necessary, yet insufficient to fully address the needs of students whose academic learning needs extend beyond the level of the school's typical instruction. Many schools already have existing teams in place to problem solve possible new approaches for those students whose achievement is moderately or significantly below grade level. The purpose of these teams—that is, to problem solve how to more effectively meet specific student learning needs—can, and should, be extended to include meeting the needs of advanced learners. Membership on such teams is necessarily fluid, depending upon expertise needed, the amount of prior direct contact between team members and the student in instructional settings, and these individuals' projected involvement in implementing plans of support. Team membership may include the Advanced Academics specialist, one or more classroom teachers, specialists who bring expertise in other specific fields (e.g., special education, ESL), the school counselor, and a principal or other representative of the school's administrative team.

These Advanced Academic teams are responsible for digging deeper into specific student needs, setting goals for growth, matching supports to needs, and monitoring the progress of students to gauge whether the plans of support are working for small instructional groups and for individual students alike. Specifically, this team oversees the following tasks by addressing the accompanying questions:

➤ *Dig deeper and set goals*: What is the student's precise level of current performance, and what are its associated learning needs? How do we know? What learning goals would provide the appropriate level of challenge for this student?

➤ *Create a plan of support*: Which evidence-based practices or programs would best meet students' needs? At what level of intensity? Who will implement the practices or programs? How often? When? What type and amount of training and support will those delivering these practices or programs need to implement them successfully?

➤ *Consider the development of social-emotional skills (e.g., managing perfectionism), of college and career readiness habits and skills (e.g., persistence, time management), and of a healthy academic identity (e.g., sense of agency and authority) that students will need to be successful in Advanced Academic settings*: What type of supports do groups of students/each individual student need to enable their success in Advanced Academics settings? How will these be addressed in the plan? How will the student/family be given a stake in developing the plan?

➤ *Monitor progress and adjust accordingly*: How will progress be monitored? How often? By whom? How will the student be involved in this process? In what way(s) and how often will parents be informed of their child's progress? How often and when will the team meet to assess student progress? Is the student making expected/sufficient progress toward his or her goal? What needs to happen in response if sufficient progress is not evident? Should the evidence-based practices or programs be continued, be changed, or be implemented with greater intensity? Do we need to set a more ambitious goal for this individual student's learning?

Collaborative teams are guided by discussion and documentation protocols to assure equitable consideration across the school and district. We've included a sample Advanced Learning Plan (see Figure 12.2) and Progress Monitoring Documentation Form (see Figure 12.3) from the Wauwatosa School District in Wisconsin to illustrate this point.

WAUWATOSA SCHOOL DISTRICT
‹ Your Educational Community ›

Selected & Intensive Gifted & Talented Services
Options for Advanced Learning Plan

For Internal Use Only
Directions: Use this form to help determine GT services for each student. Chosen services should be listed on the student's Advanced Learning Plan.

Modified Learning Environment:		
___ Cluster Grouping ___ In-Class Flexible Grouping ___ Cross-Grade Level Grouping ___ Subject Advancement	___ Early Entrance ___ Grade Level Advancement ___ Distance or Online Learning Options	___ Individualized Academic Program ___ Other:
Options for Curriculum/Instruction Modification:		
___ Preassessment ___ Change of Pace ___ Curriculum Compacting ___ Advanced Levels of Thinking (Depth & Complexity) ___ Creative/Critical Problem Solving Strategies ___ Tiered Assignments ___ Independent Study ___ Inquiry Circles ___ Early instruction in advanced research skills ___ Learning Contracts ___ Interest Centers or Groups	___ R.A.F.T. s ___ Enrichment/Extension Projects ___ Extension Menus (Tic-tac-toe) ___ Most Difficult First ___ Khan Academy ___ NWEA Skills Navigator ___ Access to Leveled Texts/Resources ___ Emphasis on Choice of Content, Process, or Product ___ Orbital Studies ___ Advanced Use of Technology	___ Flexible counseling group ___ Competition (specify) ___ Content Extensions (e.g. Math Extension Units) (specify) ___ Specialized curricula (e.g. M2 or M3 Math Units) (specify) ___ Advanced online content (specify) ___ School or community talent opportunity (specify) ___ Other:
Behavioral/Affective Areas of Focus:		
___ Self-efficacy ___ Confidence ___ Motivation ___ Resilience ___ Self-awareness ___ Social skills ___ Peer relations	___ Perfectionism ___ Independence ___ Organization ___ Curiosity ___ Openness to risk-taking ___ Self-advocacy ___ Work rate (too fast or slow)	___ Communication skills ___ Collaborative skills ___ Stress management ___ Connection of effort to success ___ Reversing underachievement ___ Cultural identity ___ Other:

Figure 12.2. Wauwatosa advanced learning plan options. From "Wauwatosa Advanced Student Learning Plan," developed by Jeanne Paulus, Wauwatosa School District, Wauwatosa, WI. Reprinted with permission of Wauwatosa School District.

Area of Identification & Tier:

SMART Goal(s) (Include acceptable evidence and tool used to monitor progress):

Provider: Classroom Teacher

Setting:

Month	Acceptable Evidence of Student Progress Toward Goal (Teacher Updates)	Frequency of Teacher/ Student Sessions (Teacher updates)	Progress (See key below) (Teachers & Coaches/Reading Specialists update)	Action(s) taken (See key and include rationale for next steps) (Teachers & Coaches/Reading Specialists update)	Date & Notes of Classroom Observations and/or Teacher Meetings (Instructional Coach and/or Reading Specialist updates)
October	Baseline Data:				**Teacher Meeting Required** to Create ALPs
November/ December					
January					

Progress Key: If data indicate...	Mark as...	Action Key: Consider these actions	Mark action taken as...
No progress toward goal	-	Improve fidelity, Intensify instruction, or Change intervention	FIDELITY *or* INTENSITY *or* CHANGE
Sufficient progress	+	Continue with no changes	CONTINUE
Goal is met	++	Intensify instruction, or Change intervention Raise goal	INTENSITY *or* CHANGE

Figure 12.3. Progress monitoring form. From "Wauwatosa Advanced Student Learning Plan," developed by Jeanne Paulus, Wauwatosa School District, Wauwatosa, WI. Reprinted with permission of Wauwatosa School District.

3. Reviewing the Effectiveness of the School's System of Support for Advanced Learners

This final team function is frequently the responsibility of the school or district's G/T Committee or Curriculum and Instruction team. To serve this function, this team reviews student outcome data and systems-level implementation data, determining the extent to which the school is meeting the needs of the students whose needs extend beyond the universal, and evaluating whether this is sufficient. For example, the team may disaggregate screening data for its advanced learners to gauge whether they are achieving expected growth across the school. This team may also look at progress monitoring data as a whole to gauge the effectiveness of the school's existing programs and practices for meeting the needs of students that fall beyond the reach of the universal level of instruction.

Critically, this team also considers whether the school is disproportionately underidentifying or underserving specific subpopulations of its students (e.g., by gender, by economic status, by race/ethnicity, by English proficiency level). This team can then create hypotheses, gather additional data as needed, and develop plans of action based on a thorough analysis of the data, rather than on conjecture or emotion alone. Even in the absence of the gifted label, efforts to meet the needs of all learners will be ineffective if some groups of learners are disproportionately present within the most advanced learning settings (see *cultural competence* sidebar).

Schools with effective and sustainable RtI systems leverage all of the strengths, strategies, and resources they have available into a coordinated response system to support learners. Establishing this coordinated continuum

Cultural competence in teaming and collaborative decision making. Responsive schools recognize that perceptions of student ability based on student demographic characteristics and past opportunities to learn play a significant role in decision making about advanced academics, especially where the race and culture of the students served differ from those who have historically achieved school success. Collaborative team members demonstrate cultural competence by first understanding their own identity and the myriad ways that culture operates in schools. They examine their own biases and maintain high beliefs for all learners from all backgrounds. Teams actively consider whether cultural mismatches in systems and structures, and historical policies and practices, may inhibit student success, no matter how well intentioned. They then willingly place the locus of responsibility for change on professionals and the school, not on the students and families they serve.

of supports is the first critical step in creating a system that as a whole responds quickly and effectively to student needs beyond the reach of the universal level of support. When schools have developed an articulated continuum of supports, collaborative teams are able to match students to instructional and affective supports quickly, with the confidence that their decisions are sound because of their sound underlying foundation in a thoughtful and responsive professional culture. The creation of student and staff schedules and other routine operational tasks become easier because of the underlying supporting structure and program goals. With a defined continuum of supports, schools are better positioned to provide targeted professional development and support to staff delivering interventions and additional challenges.

CONCLUSION

By addressing the needs of all learners within their Zone of Proximal Development, the Advanced Academics perspective within a schoolwide RtI system builds upon the strengths of traditional gifted education approaches, while minimizing the drawbacks we have observed in current educational practice. Readers who wish to learn more about this approach are encouraged to pursue the recommended readings listed below, particularly the 2014 book by Peters et al. in which we have developed the Advanced Academics perspective in greater detail.

Major Takeaways

- What the educational program is called is less important than how it is structured, for the purposes of meeting the educational needs of the school's advanced learners.

- The key factor in the Advanced Academics approach is matching instruction closely with students' current readiness to learn.

- A schoolwide Response to Intervention (RtI) framework offers an appropriate and widely used structure within which the Advanced Academics approach can be implemented.

- Intentional collaboration is key to successful implementation and sustainability of Advanced Academics within an RtI system.

RECOMMENDED READING

Matthews, M. S., Ritchotte, J. A., & Jolly, J. L. (2014). What's wrong with giftedness? Parents' perceptions of the gifted label. *International Studies in Sociology of Education, 24,* 372–393. doi:10.1080/09620214.2014.990225

McBee, M. T., Peters, S. J., & Miller, E. M. (2016). The impact of the nomination stage on gifted program identification. *Gifted Child Quarterly, 60,* 258–278. doi:10.1177/0016986216656256

McBee, M. T., Peters, S. J., & Waterman, C. (2014). Combining scores in multiple-criteria assessment systems: The impact of combination rule. *Gifted Child Quarterly, 58*, 69–89. doi:10.1177/0016986213513794

Peters, S. J., & Engerrand, K. G. (2016). Equity and excellence: Proactive efforts in the identification of underrepresented students for gifted and talented services. *Gifted Child Quarterly, 60*, 159–171. doi:10.1177/0016986216643165

Peters, S. J., Matthews, M. S., McBee, M. T., & McCoach, D. B. (2014). *Beyond gifted education: Designing and implementing advanced academic programs*. Waco, TX: Prufrock Press.

Vygotsky, L. S. (1978). *Mind in society: The development of higher psychological processes* (M. Cole, V. John-Steiner, S. Scribner. & E. Souberman, Trans.). Cambridge, MA: Harvard University Press.

Wisconsin RtI Center. (2015). *Continuum of supports implementation tools*. Retrieved from http://www.wisconsinrticenter.org/administrators/rti-in-action/implementation-tools-in-a-continuum-of-supports.html

REFERENCES

Flores, A. (2007). Examining disparities in mathematics education: Achievement gap or opportunity gap? *High School Journal, 91*(1), 29–42.

Johnsen, S. K., Parker, S. L., & Farah, Y. N. (2015). Providing services for students with gifts and talents within a Response-to-Intervention framework. *Teaching Exceptional Children, 47*, 226–233. doi:10.1177/0040059915569358

Matthews, M. S., Ritchotte, J. A., & Jolly, J. L. (2014). What's wrong with giftedness? Parents' perceptions of the gifted label. *International Studies in Sociology of Education, 24*, 372–393. doi:10.1080/09620214.2014.990225

National Association for Gifted Children, & The Council of State Directors of Programs for the Gifted. (2015). *2014–15 state of the states in gifted education: Policy and practice data*. Washington, DC: Authors.

Peters, S. J., & Engerrand, K. G. (2016). Equity and excellence: Proactive efforts in the identification of underrepresented students for gifted and talented services. *Gifted Child Quarterly, 60*, 159–171. doi:10.1177/0016986216643165

Peters, S. J., Matthews, M. S., McBee, M. T., & McCoach, D. B. (2014). *Beyond gifted education: Designing and implementing advanced academic programs*. Waco, TX: Prufrock Press.

Peters, S. J., Rambo-Hernandez, K., Makel, M., Matthews, M. S., & Plucker, J. A. (2017). Should millions of students take a gap year? Large numbers of students start the school year above grade level. *Gifted Child Quarterly, 61*, 229-238. doi:10.1177/0016986217701834

Vygotsky, L. S. (1978). *Mind in society: The development of higher psychological processes* (M. Cole, V. John-Steiner, S. Scribner, & E. Souberman, Trans.). Cambridge, MA: Harvard University Press.

Wisconsin RtI Center. (2015). *Continuum of supports implementation tools.* Retrieved from http://www.wisconsinrticenter.org/administrators/rti-in-action/implementation-tools-in-a-continuum-of-supports.html

CHAPTER 13

Creative Deep Thinking

TALENT SUPPORT NETWORKS FOSTERING THE DISCOVERY OF UNEXPECTED SIMPLICITY AND THE DEVELOPMENT OF AUTONOMY, INTEGRITY, AND WISDOM[1]

Peter Csermely

T he 21st century regularly produces situations and challenges that have never been experienced during the written history of humankind. The increasing global impact on Earth's ecosystems, the 24-hours-a-day global social presence, artificial intelligence surpassing several aspects of human thinking, and the incoming medical revolution and robot-world are just a few of those entirely new situations that need novel solutions at both the level of the individuals and the society. This pressing need makes gifted people the "life insurance" of our planet in the coming decades.

Daniel Kahneman (2011) introduced the concept of "fast and slow thinking" a few years ago. Fast thinking is mobilized if we encounter a situation that was experienced prior. However, a slower, contemplative thinking is required if we would like to discover a new solution for a novel situation. This contemplative, deep thinking is related to creativity, because it allows the mind to free itself from

1   The author thanks the large number of enthusiastic persons for their volunteer work in the talent support networks listed in this paper. The Hungarian Talent Support Network is supported by the Hungarian Talent Program and by the EU Structural Funds grant "Hungary of Talents" (EFOP-3.2.1-15). The Hungarian Templeton Program was supported by the Templeton World Charity Foundation (TWCF0117). Network-science related research in the author's group is supported by the Hungarian National Science Foundation (OTKA K115378).

social pressure and conventional solutions. Creative, deep thinking is generally considered to be important for a successful life (Byers, 2014). It is a warning sign that contemplation has become increasingly difficult in the rush of our century.

Wisdom—as an orienting knowledge about what is good and right—may be considered as a major help to solve the most important problems of mankind (Fischer, 2015). Practicing deep thinking helps the gradual development of wisdom.

Importantly, deep thinking is not only useful to induce creative ideas at the level of the individual, but also mobilizes the wisdom of crowds at the societal level (Surowieczki, 2004) in the process of deliberative democracy (Bessette, 1980; Dewey, 1927; Guttmann & Thompson, 2004; Habermas, 1984, 1987; Neblo, Esterling, Kennedy & Lazer, 2010). Deep thinking combines our starting idea with a high number of potential contexts. This process helps to rephrase the starting idea and leads to its creative, novel versions (Byers, 2014; Fischer & Hommel, 2012).

Deep thinking is—by far—not only complicating the original idea, but often embarks to its much simpler, much more elegant form. As the 1932 Nobel Physics Laureate Werner Heisenberg noted in a conversation with Albert Einstein:

> If nature leads us to mathematical forms of great simplicity and beauty . . . we cannot help thinking that they are "true," that they reveal a genuine feature of nature. . . . You must have felt this too: The almost frightening simplicity and wholeness of relationships which nature suddenly spreads out before us and for which none of us was in the least prepared. (as cited in Thiessen, 2012, p. 156)

This unexpected simplicity may lead to especially powerful forms of novel solutions that are able to mobilize people and may soon become a generally accepted and established response as a part of human culture.

Gifted people have a special responsibility to use their talent to participate in finding out novel solutions to the challenges of our century. This chapter focuses on the practices of talent support actions that may foster contemplation, creative; deep thinking; and deliberative discussions of gifted people. Importantly, the chapter links these practices to the development of wisdom, as an emergent property of mind that can be obtained by the successful integration of life experiences, where success means a balanced, impartial, and independent life and is guided by universal love—as explained in the next section. Summarizing three case studies of talent support programs, this chapter shows that developing deep thinking and wisdom is an important, but heretofore not well-developed, aspect of gifted education.

CREATIVE, DEEP THINKING AS A PART OF GIFTEDNESS HELPING THE DEVELOPMENT OF WISDOM

Creativity is often considered as a centerpiece of the multiple ingredients of giftedness (Gardner, 1993; Kaufman, Plucker, & Russell, 2012; Renzulli, 1986; Sternberg & Davidson, 2005). Deep thinking requires repeated cycles of the creative process allowing both divergent and convergent thinking periods (Campbell, 1960; Csermely, 2015; Osborn, 1953; Simonton, 1999; Sowden, Pringle, & Gabora, 2015). Many types of talented young people make, select, and reselect thousands of combinations of ideas in each hour (if not in each minute). How could this intensive thinking process contribute to the development of wisdom? This section will try to find some initial segments of a possible answer to this question.

Characterization of the Concept of Wisdom

The content of wisdom is often specified as a list of propositions that were endorsed by wise people of many cultures (Fischer, 2015). Table 13.1 lists a few key quotations on the nature of wisdom. Table 13.2 summarizes nine common propositions of Buddha, Confucius, Jesus Christ, and Socrates (Carter, 1998; Confucius, 1190/2010; The Holy Bible, 1837; Plato, 399 BC/2014; Xenophon, 371 BC/2001) about wisdom adapted from the excellent summary of Fischer (2015). Wisdom can be understood as an orienting knowledge about what is virtuous, good, and right, leading to inner peace and lasting happiness (Fischer, 2015).

From the content of Tables 13.1 and 13.2, wisdom emerges not as a thinking process, but as an emergent property of the mind that can be obtained by the successful integration of life experiences, where "successful" means balanced, impartial, and independent. Wisdom, as an emergent property of mind, when emerged, directs the thinking process. The concept of "emergent property" is used here as a property of a complex system that its building blocks do not have. Life and consciousness are typical emergent properties of complex systems (Novikoff, 1945). As detailed later in this section, integration of life experiences is not an even process: crisis events, major decisions of life, extreme joy, and suffering, if their lessons became internalized in a balanced way, all play crucial role in the development of wisdom. Importantly, wise people always understood the limits of their knowledge and their bounded rationality (Fischer, 2015). This agrees well with the conceptualization of wisdom as an emergent property, which implies an endless possibility to develop wisdom as the maturing mind becomes more and more aware of the universe.

TABLE 13.1

Quotations on the Nature of Wisdom

Quotation	Reference
the beginning of her [*wisdom*] is the most true desire of discipline	Book of Wisdom 6:18, The Holy Bible 1837, page 605
The heart that is well prepared for any fate hopes in adversity, fears prosperity	Horace, The Golden Mean, Odes 2.10, 13 BC/2003
Information, the knowledge of facts, though ever increasing, is by its very nature limited. Wisdom is infinite, it includes knowledge and the way of action	Krishnamurti, 2008, page 66
when feelings arise, wisdom is blocked	Lin-Chi, 1993, page 25
wisdom, that is from above first indeed is chaste, then peaceable, modest, easy to be persuaded, consenting to the good, full of mercy and good fruits, without judging, without dissimulation.	St. James' Epistle 3:17, The Holy Bible 1837, page 1174
the application of tacit knowledge as mediated by values toward the achievement of a common good (a) through a balance among multiple intrapersonal, interpersonal, and extrapersonal interests and (b) in order to achieve a balance among responses to environmental contexts: adaptation to existing environmental contexts, shaping of existing environmental contexts, and selection of new environmental contexts.	Sternberg, 1998, page 353
I must make myself indifferent to all created things in regard to everything which is left to my freedom of will and is not forbidden. Consequently, on my own part, I ought not to seek health rather than sickness, wealth rather than poverty, honor rather than dishonor, long life rather than a short one, and so on in all other matters. I ought to desire and elect only the thing which is more conducive to the end for which I am created.	St. Ignatius of Loyola, 1548/1991, page 130
And if I should have prophecy, and should know all mysteries, and all knowledge; and if I should have all faith, so that I could remove mountains, and have not charity, I am nothing.	St. Paul's First Epistle to the Corinthians 13:2, The Holy Bible 1837, page 1117

TABLE 13.2

*Nine Common Propositions of the Buddha, Confucius,
Jesus Christ, and Socrates About Wisdom*

The greatest commandment to love each other: hatred ceases by love and good deeds.
Treat others as you would like others to treat yourself.
Respect your father and mother.
Good people and children make good company.
Not material things but virtuous thoughts and actions bring lasting happiness.
Fate does not always reward virtue by material things but it is irrational not to accept fate.
Observe your own errors and learn from others'.
Knowledge about social beings is more important than knowledge about the physical universe.
Death is nothing to fear, for either it will be simply the end of consciousness or it will be a new experience. Not knowing about it for sure motivates virtuous behavior here and now. Confronting the thought of death and thinking it through, can relief from the fear of death.

Adapted from Table 1 of Fischer (2015) summarizing statements from the Dhammapada (Carter, 1998) the Analects (Confucius, 1190/2010) the New Testament (The Holy Bible, 1837), the Apology of Plato (Plato, 399 BC/2014) and the Memorabilia of Xenophon (Xenophon, 371 BC/2001).

Wisdom emerges as a balanced state of mind. Identification of the "golden mean" as a source of moral virtue was a key idea of many ancient religions and philosophies, like in Buddhism (Kalupahana, 1986) and in the works of Confucius (1190/2004) and Aristotle (349 BC/1926), in close relation with beauty, symmetry, harmony, and truth. Horace's (13 BC/2003) famous ode on The Golden Mean was interpreted as the expression of wisdom in the form of internal freedom that is not following the extremities of the environment, but inversely acts against them (Ritoók, 2009). Internal freedom of the balanced mind gives independence and develops personal integrity. Independence of mind is a major element of Krishnamurti's (2008) works and the balanced state of mind is a central concept of Sternberg's (1998) balance concept of wisdom. Internal freedom and independence are related to autonomy (the best developed Stage 6 of Kohlberg; Kohlberg, Levine, & Hewer, 1983) and integrity.

In agreement with the concept of wisdom as a balanced state of mind, attaining wisdom implies: (1) a continuous and intensive attention to others (where "others" means the whole world); (2) recognition of others' interests; (3) ability to induce abstract rules from repeated situations; (4) ability of long-term thinking; (5) prioritization, resetting of priorities and explanation of the reasons, why the priorities were reset; (6) ability to decide whether the current situation is "usual" or "extraordinary," requiring one to apply former rules or just inversely to break them; (7) ability to decide whether the environment requires adaptation, can be changed or has to be exchanged for a different environment (adapt, fight, or flight); and—last but not least—(8) an intensive and long practice of creative, deep thinking. Because the emergence of wisdom may need a lifetime experience, motivation (a "most true desire"; see Table 13.1) to develop wisdom becomes a crucial factor in its achievement.

The statements in Tables 13.1 and 13.2 emphasize that wisdom requires impartial judgment. Mastering of impartial judgment implies a state of noble indifference. Feelings may overemphasize some past experiences over others, and may either push the mind toward a certain, restricted path, or may forbid the mind to try others. Stoics suggested to transform passions to clear judgment, self-discipline, and a peace of mind (Graver, 2009). Importantly, nonextreme emotions by emphasizing certain solutions and disqualifying others guide the mind by restricting its search to a much smaller domain of possible solutions and allowing reasonably fast decisions, as demonstrated by Damasio (1994).

Importantly, universal love is crucial to attain wisdom. Universal love acts like a compass and drives the mind continuously toward the feeling of the flow of life. This "life-flow" is conceptually the same as living in harmony with the Tao of the world, thus with the source, pattern, and substance of everything that exists taken together. Similarly, universal love-induced "life-flow" is close to the moral virtues and meditation of the Noble Eightfold Path of Buddhism extending and guiding the two paths related to insight and wisdom (Carter, 1998). "Life-flow" is also close to the concept of a lifetime effort to achieve common good. However, it is important to note here that "common good" became a widely abused political category recently used in the sense of the optimal solution for a numerical majority of a certain smaller group of people (like the citizens of a country or the inhabitants of a town). Universal love and consequently attained "life-flow" extend the meaning of the "common good" much beyond the benefits of the members of the society, and include a large number of other extrapersonal factors in the sense of Sternberg (1998), including the protection of the environment and, ultimately, God (Tables 13.1 and 13.2).

Crucial decision points requiring a high level of wisdom are usually not equally occurring in different segments of life. Their distribution seems to follow a scale-free distribution (Barabasi, 2010; Csermely, 2009). In a usual day of ours we most probably do not have any such crucial decision points. As a rough approximation, 10 times more important decisions often come 10 times less frequently. Hundred times more important decisions often come a hundred times less frequently. Crucially important decisions that may come only in a few cases in a whole lifetime may need fast action. This is when wisdom becomes especially important. Fortunately, time is rather relative in the sense that the restricted moment of a crucially important decision can be subjectively extended. Still, the mind has to be exercised to preserve its impartial judgment, noble indifference, and—most of all—universal love and life-flow in these exceptional moments of crucial decisions. Purposeful slow-down at a moment that urges an exceptionally speedy decision is an especially useful exercise of the impartial, autonomous, noble indifference of wise minds.

Slowing down in critical moments is especially useful in the sense that it allows the exercise of the joy and playfulness of creative, deep thinking just at the moment when they are needed the most. Critical slow-down is a well-known phenomenon of complex systems, when they arrive close to a crucial decision point (Scheffer et al., 2009). This decision point can be imagined as a saddle between two valleys. The complex system (e.g., the mind) stays in a saddle of the "decision-landscape," and has the choice to go to the valley either to its right or left. In reality, the number of choices are often multiple. Thus, the complex system has a high number of possibilities for where to go, which—at that very moment—do not seem to be far from each other, because they all start at the same decision point of the crucially important saddle. Creative, deep thinking explores many of these possibilities, and the wise mind may imagine the whole situation with the multitude of possible decisions and their consequences by raising above itself and looking to the whole situation from a bird's-eye view. Freezing the moment can greatly help to obtain this impartial, autonomous distance and grand-view, which are both needed to make a wise decision at this exceptionally important point of life.

In summary, practice of contemplative, deep thinking not only increases the chances to reach highly creative, originally novel solutions, but also allows the gradual development of wisdom. Mastering of contemplation develops a feeling of "life-flow," which finds joy in the changing situations of life, because they allow the exercise of the real depth of thinking, rebalance the mind, and develop wisdom. Wisdom enables the individual to reach freedom from social pressure leading to independence, internal freedom, autonomy, and integrity.

Talent support programs help gifted young individuals, if they are exposing them to occasions when they may exercise deep thinking, rewarding them with creative thoughts, giving them motivation, and showing them the path to develop wisdom. The closing part of the chapter will list several ways this goal may be achieved and will show—by the example of three case studies of talent support programs—what initial steps may be taken to expose talented young people to previously unexpected situations and social environment to give them a chance for deep thinking and development of their wisdom.

HOW DOES UNEXPECTED SIMPLICITY
RELATE TO CREATIVE, DEEP THINKING?

The divergent mode of creative thinking often produces ideas that are unexpected. The convergent mode of creative thinking often selects those ideas that are relatively simple. Ideas that have an elegant short form have a much higher chance to get memorized, to be remembered, and to be spread in the society. Unexpectedly simple ideas are much more complex to generate than to describe (Chater, 1999). Repeated cycles of divergent and convergent thinking constitute the deep thinking process and often result in the finding of unexpectedly simple descriptions of the situation or of the solutions to the challenges it caused. Guiding the mind toward unexpected simplicity is a part of the lifetime experience, which is called *wisdom*. Moreover, wisdom, when developed, selects the most important meaning of surrounding events and facts and highlights their surprisingly simple essence.

HOW MAY TALENT SUPPORT NETWORKS
FOSTER CREATIVE, DEEP THINKING?

Henri Poincaré (1908/2014) highlighted that the most useful ideas may emerge from those combinations, which are connecting distant regions of human knowledge. He wrote,

> Among chosen combinations the most fertile will often be those formed of elements drawn from domains which are far apart. Not that I mean as sufficing for invention the bringing together of objects as disparate as possible; most combinations so formed would be entirely sterile. But certain among them, very rare, are the most fruitful of all. (p. 386)

This notion was supported by recent studies showing that (a) significantly greater attention was triggered by Facebook messages that combined topics seldom discussed together (Bail, 2016); (b) the emergence of creative, high-complexity, innovative solutions required both the separation and occasional reconnection of distant social groups (Derex & Boyd, 2016; Michelucci & Dickinson, 2016; Reia, Herrmann & Fontanari, 2017); (c) the overlap between cognitively distant groups led to larger creative success of video game developers (de Vaan, Vedres, & Stark, 2015); and (d) the inclusion of unusual combinations of prior work often occurred in highest-impact science (Uzzi, Mukherjee, Stringer, & Jones, 2013). These studies showed that key ingredients of creativity can be rationalized as network phenomena of human concepts and social acquaintances.

In a similar, but much earlier study, Granovetter (1973) emphasized the importance of nonredundant information in finding novel solutions to social problems. Granovetter's analysis demonstrated that nonredundant information often comes by cross-cutting dense social circles. Importantly, intercommunity contacts were also shown to increase social cohesion and social stability (Csermely, 2009; Granovetter, 1973).

Social networks may also induce and foster deep thinking. Distinguished thinkers and/or people whose mindsets developed in different social and cultural contexts help to rephrase the starting idea and to attain a bird's-eye view, where the context of the starting idea suddenly emerges (Byers, 2014; Csermely, 2008). This process often leads to an idea that is more original and/or shows the signs of unexpected simplicity.

Talent support networks may design programs that purposefully expose talented people to situations and acquaintances, which crosscut social circles and cultural boundaries. Such experiences provide an access to novel information and build a novel context of the original information. This becomes a particularly efficient and motivating process, if the novel acquaintances are talented, creative people themselves.

Repeated exposures of talented people to groups with different social and cultural backgrounds will increase their networking ability. Networking is a key success factor in a modern society (Christakis & Fowler, 2011; Csermely, 2009). It is important that talent support networks should take extreme care, when organizing the exposure of talented people to various novel situations, to their acceptance by the novel environment. This "acceptance factor" gives an additional benefit to expose talented people to other, different types of talented people. The reason is that talented people themselves already realized the pain of being not accepted, and many times are willing to give acceptance of the other talented young individual. They know that this will increase the acceptance of themselves, and they also enjoy the amusing novelty of different mindsets and behaviors. Getting the repeated experience of "being accepted" increases the "I am safe" feeling of talented people and encourages them to make even larger excursions out of the "comfort zone" of their original social network.

Importantly, talent support networks need to organize discussions on major questions of mankind, allowing the practice of deep, contemplative, deliberative thinking, as well as the development and defense of moral judgments and wisdom. Importantly, joint projects, especially in the form of good purpose actions increasing social responsibility may build motivation to commit talented people to find greater joy in developing their deep thinking and wisdom.

The three intermingled activities of (1) experiencing cross-cutting social circles and cultural boundaries, (2) increased networking skills, and (3) initiation of deep thinking through good purpose joint projects will also enable talented people to a larger influence of social opinion and lead to community actions. Importantly, creative, deep thinking is a key leadership skill, related to strategic and visionary thinking (Puccio, Mance, & Murdock, 2011). If creative deep thinking is paired with unexpected simplicity and a wisely focused, strong emotional background, it may inflict a new trend, and may strongly engage the followers' self-concepts in the interest of the mission. In this way, creative, deep thinking may significantly contribute to charismatic leadership (Shamir, House, & Arthur, 1993).

APPLYING THE CONCEPT: EXPERIENCES OF THREE TALENT SUPPORT PROGRAMS

In this section, I summarize my experiences on the exposure to novel situations, development of networking skills, and encouragement of deep thinking obtained in three talent support networks.

Talent support network 1: Hungarian Network of Research Students (http://www.kutdiak.hu/en). I established this network in 1996 to give top-level scientific research to high school students (see Csermely, 2003, for a detailed overview). We have had 300–500 scientific projects completed in each of the past 20 years. As a crucial contribution to the project, mentor-student pairs often bridged different social circles. As one of the examples, József Horváth, a child of underprivileged, Roma origin in the countryside of Hungary was exposed to state-of-art molecular biology methods developing a better classification of mouth tumors. This became his research project during his bachelor's and master's degree studies, and led to his (currently final stage) doctoral project. He became a role model on how to span social circles and fulfill one's dreams. Brigitta Sipőcz summarized her experiences at age 17 as follows:

> I met a new world here. I learned perseverance and endurance during my years of research. The friendly atmosphere helped me to overcome my shyness, and the wide variety of topics in the mentor database made me realize what am I really interested in life and pursue it with full devotion.

In the last 15 years she pursued the same goal in scientific research, became a successful astronomer, and discovered 35 minor planets—among many others.

A key ingredient for the network's success was rather unexpected. The movement—now in its 21st year of providing research opportunities to more than 10,000 young students—flourishes because of the social network it makes between the students themselves. Scientific conferences, and, as a key event, an annual one-week research camp for the 80 best students of Hungary and neighboring countries provided the opportunity for students to develop a strong social cohesion. Importantly, the contemplative, creative, deep thinking of the students was mobilized by the fact that the network is directed by the students themselves. As an example of this ownership feeling, student members of the research camp each year extensively discuss the future aims, means, and finances of the group (Csermely, 2003; Csermely, 2013).

Talent support network 2: The Hungarian Templeton Program (http://templetonprogram.hu/en). This program was established by the Hungarian Talent Support Network (Csermely, 2013) and selected 314 Hungarian Junior Templeton Fellows between ages 10–29 with exceptional cognitive talent from more than 20,000 applicants. Fellows received a one-year intensive, personalized development program offering 500 different programs lasting altogether for 2,000 hours.

Fellows could choose from the 500 types of programs according to their individual needs (where the initial in-depth interview and further consultations with Fellows, their parents, and teachers established a "personal development program," giving advice in the choice) and could "purchase" the programs for "Talents," the virtual currency of the program. Fellows received 200 Talents to be spent on programs during the year. Fellows altogether spent 31,200 Talents to participate in different programs and gained 8,500 Talents for giving public lectures, writing articles for the website or for publication, and for attending group meetings (for a lecture, publication, or group meeting, 5 Talents could be earned). Fellows altogether attended 5,400 programs. An average program cost 6 Talents. Fellows individually attended 16 programs as an average.

Fellows felt that these programs provided lifelong experiences for them (only 5 of the 314 could not mention any in the fourth quarterly report). For 126 Fellows the summer camps, for 70 Fellows the mentoring cooperations (including 17 Fellows mentioning the "Personal consultation with an Excellence" option), for 66 Fellows the group meetings, and for 33 Fellows the site visit at CERN, Switzerland, were these special experiences. Fewer Fellows were involved in the following programs, but all of them named them as their most significant experience: LEAF Summer Camp, Speak Academy, to give a lecture at Templeton Talks and Networking Days, Milestone, and visiting the European Union Parliament at Brussels. All other programs of the 500 were mentioned at least once.

Fellows considered the exposure to novel situations and social contacts as the most important benefits of the program. The self-organization of the Fellows' network and now, after finishing the year of the program, their alumni network led to several joint good purpose actions. A cohort of the Fellows defined a key element of wisdom as the ability to "fly over the ground," which it meant as the freedom of the wise person, who is (1) able to overcome the strong emotions of past experiences, which either bind the decision to certain modes or prohibit others; (2) free from social pressure; and (3) free from the burdens of life (Fuszek, 2017). Discussions of the meaning of wisdom with gifted individuals pointed out the scarcity of occasions when talented young people may think about the way to attain wisdom in our rushing century. At the same time, participants of these discussions realized the importance of contemplative thinking and planned to set aside much more time for contemplative, deep thinking in the future (Fuszek, 2017).

Talent support network 3: The Youth Platform of the European Talent Support Network. The European Talent Support Network was established by the European Council for High Ability (http://echa.info) in 2014 to increase cooperation between organizations in gifted education and talent support, to share best practices, and to organize exchanges of talented young people and their teachers. By 2017, the Network had close to 300 cooperating organizations from 50 countries of Europe and other continents (http://etsn.eu/map-of-etsn/).

After the successful first European Youth Summit in March 2016, the Network established a Youth Platform, which became a fast-growing group of talented young people. Youth Platform members enjoyed and greatly appreciated the opportunity to learn the approaches and opinions of talented young people from several continents. Members organized the 2nd Youth Summit in March 2017 in Budapest, having twice as many participants from 17 countries than the first summit. They initiated several joint actions.

1. **Talented Youth Survey (TYS).** This project is focused on surveying the experiences of gifted students in terms of education, social integration, satisfaction with projects created for them, and other issues. The Youth Platform team will create an online survey for this project.

2. **Talents for Talented (TfT).** The long-term aim of this project is to help underprivileged children to join the Youth Platform and take part in its activities. Platform members discuss and create different projects, such as charity evenings, volunteer or exchange programs, and ways to help people living in bad circumstances in a concrete way.

3. **Youth Expedition of Science (YES).** Youth Platform members create a regular face-to-face event for talented people interested in natural sciences, humanities, and engineering. Interested members create their own research proposals and implement them with the help of their peers and the support of experts.

During the Innovation Day of the Summit, an additional seven project ideas were created. The most popular ones (determined by vote) were: an International Mentoring

Program, a Cultural Exchange Program for talented people from Talent Centres/Points, a Youth Platform YouTube channel, and a Social Network for talented people (UTalent). The Youth Platform is creating teams for these projects.

All of the three talent support programs showed the potential for how deep thinking and social responsibility could be induced in networks of young talented people. At this stage, the results of these occasions have not been tested systematically. However, the initial personal experiences showed that the approaches shown in this chapter are useful for further systematic exploration.

CONCLUSION

Gifted people have a special responsibility to mobilize their talent to find out solutions to the challenges of our century never experienced before. This chapter focused on the possibilities of talent support actions to promote creative, deep thinking, contemplation, and deliberative discussions of gifted people. Experiences of gifted young people cross-cutting social circles and cultural boundaries, their increased networking skills, as well as the initiation of their deep thinking by discussions and good purpose joint projects all emerged as important tools to achieve the above goals. Importantly, the chapter showed that creative, deep thinking, contemplation, and deliberative discussions contribute to the development of wisdom, as an emergent property of mind, which can be obtained by the successful integration of life experiences, where "successful" means balanced, impartial, and independent and is guided by universal love. Agreeing with Andreas Fischer (2015), regretfully "neither teachers nor ministers of education seem to sufficiently understand what wisdom is and why or how wisdom should be taught" (p. 80). An important future task of talent support programs will be to use the methods described in this chapter to increase creative, deep thinking, and guide talented young people toward discoveries of unexpected simplicity and wisdom, helping them to attain charismatic leadership skills.

Major Takeaways

- It is an important goal of talent support actions to promote deep thinking, contemplation, and deliberative discussions of gifted people. These experiences are related, can be built up systematically, and lead to the development of autonomy, integrity, and wisdom in the long term.

- Experiences of gifted young people cross-cutting social circles and cultural boundaries, their increased networking skills, as well as the initiation of their deep thinking by discussions and good purpose joint projects emerged as important tools to increase their potential and awareness to develop wisdom.

- The initial personal experiences of the three case studies listed showed that the above approaches are useful for further systematic exploration. Talent support programs should measure the efficiency of these methods to initiate deep thinking, autonomy, integrity, and wisdom.

RECOMMENDED READING

Christakis, N. A., & Fowler, J. H. (2011). *Connected: The surprising power of our social networks and how they shape our lives—How your friends' friends' friends affect everything you feel, think, and do.* Boston, MA: Back Bay Books.

Csermely, P. (2009). *Weak links: Stabilizers of complex systems from proteins to social networks.* Heidelberg, Germany: Springer Verlag. doi:10.1007/978-3-540-31157-7

Kahneman, D. (2011). *Thinking, fast and slow.* London, England: Allen Lane.

REFERENCES

Aristotle. (349 BC/1926). *Nicomachean ethics* (H. Rackham, Trans.) Cambridge, MA: Harvard University Press.

Bail, C. A. (2016). Combining natural language processing and network analysis to examine how advocacy organizations stimulate conversation on social media. *Proceedings of the National Academy of Sciences, 113,* 11823–11828. doi:10.1073/pnas.1607151113

Barabasi, A. L. (2010). *Bursts: The hidden patterns behind everything we do, from your e-mail to bloody crusades.* New York, NY: Plume.

Bessette, J. M. (1980). Deliberative democracy: The majority principle in republican government. In R. A. Goldwin & W. A. Schambra (Eds.), *How democratic is the Constitution?* (pp. 102–116). Washington, DC: American Enterprise Institute for Public Policy Research.

Byers, W. (2014). *Deep thinking: What mathematics can teach us about the mind.* Singapore: World Scientific Publishing. doi:10.1142/9789814618045

Campbell, D. (1960). Blind variation and selective retention in creative thought as in other knowledge processes. *Psychological Review, 67,* 380–400. doi:10.1037/h0040373

Carter, J. N. (1998). *The Dhammapada.* Oxford, England: Oxford University Press.

Chater, N. (1999). The search for simplicity: A fundamental cognitive principle? *The Quarterly Journal of Experimental Psychology: Section A, 52,* 273–302.

Christakis, N. A., & Fowler, J. H. (2011). *Connected: The surprising power of our social networks and how they shape our lives.* Boston, MA: Back Bay Books.

Confucius. (1190/2004). *The doctrine of the mean.* Kila, MT: Kessinger.

Confucius. (1190/2010). *The Analects of Confucius.* Auckland, New Zealand: The Floating Press.

Csermely, P. (2003). Recruitment of the youngest generation to science. A network of youth excellence and communication strategies for high school student researchers. *EMBO Reports, 4,* 825–828. doi:10.1038/sj.embor.embor927

Csermely, P. (2008). Creative elements: Network-based predictions of active centres in proteins, cellular and social networks. *Trends in Biochemical Sciences, 33,* 569–576. doi:10.1016/j.tibs.2008.09.006

Csermely, P. (2009). *Weak links: Stabilizers of complex systems from proteins to social networks.* Heidelberg, Germany: Springer Verlag. doi:10.1007/978-3-540-31157-7

Csermely, P. (2013). The appearance and promotion of creativity at various levels of interdependent networks. *Talent Development & Excellence, 5,* 115–123.

Csermely, P. (2015). *Plasticity-rigidity cycles: A general adaptation mechanism.* Retrieved from http://arxiv.org/abs/1511.01239

de Vaan, M., Vedres, B., & Stark, D. (2015). Game changer: The topology of creativity. *American Journal of Sociology, 120,* 1144–1194. doi:10.1086/681213

Damasio, A. (1994). *Descartes' error: Emotion, reason, and the human brain.* New York, NY: Putnam.

Derex, M., & Boyd, R. (2016). Partial connectivity increases cultural accumulation within groups. *Proceedings of the National Academy of Sciences, 113,* 2982–2987. doi:10.1073/pnas.1518798113

Dewey, J. (1927). *The public and its problems.* Athens, OH: Swallow Press.

Fischer, A. (2015). Wisdom—The answer to all the questions really worth asking. *International Journal of Humanities and Social Science, 5,* 73–83. Retrieved from http://www.ub.uni-heidelberg.de/archiv/19786

Fischer, R., & Hommel, B. (2012). Deep thinking increases task-set shielding and reduces shifting flexibility in dual-task performance. *Cognition, 123,* 303–307. doi:10.1016/j.cognition.2011.11.015

Fuszek, C. (Ed.). (2017). *The nature of wisdom. Thoughts of Hungarian Templeton Fellows about wisdom.* Budapest: Association of Hungarian Talent Support Organizations.

Gardner, H. (1993). *Creating minds.* New York, NY: Basic Books.

Granovetter, M. (1973). The strength of weak ties. *American Journal of Sociology, 78,* 1360–1380. doi:10.1086/225469

Graver, M. (2009). *Stoicism and emotion.* Chicago IL: University of Chicago Press.

Gutmann, A., & Thompson, D. (2004). *Why deliberative democracy?* Princeton, NJ: Princeton University Press.

Habermas, J. (1984). *Theory of communicative action* (Vol. 1). Boston, MA: Beacon Press.

Habermas, J. (1987). *Theory of communicative action* (Vol. 2). Boston, MA: Beacon Press.

The Holy Bible. (1837). Dublin, Ireland: Richard Coyne.

Horace. (13 BC/2003). *Odes, 2.10* (A. S. Kline, Trans.). Retrieved from http://www.poetryintranslation.com/PITBR/Latin/HoraceOdesBkII.htm#anchor_Toc39742784

Kahneman, D. (2011). *Thinking, fast and slow.* London, England: Allen Lane.

Kalupahana, D. J. (1986). *Nāgārjuna: The philosophy of the middle way.* Albany: State University of New York Press.

Kaufman, J. C., Plucker, J. A., & Russell, C. A. (2012). Identifying and assessing creativity as a component of giftedness. *Journal of Psychoeducational Assessment, 30,* 60–73. doi:10.1177/0734282911428196

Kohlberg, L., Levine, C., & Hewer, A. (1983). *Moral stages: A current formulation and a response to critics.* Basel, NY: Karger.

Krishnamurti, J. (2008). *Education and the significance of life.* New York, NY: HarperOne.

Lin-Chi. (1993). *Zen teachings.* Boston, MA: Shambala Publications.

Michelucci, P., & Dickinson, J. L. (2016). Human computation. The power of crowds. *Science, 351,* 32–33. doi:10.1126/science.aad6499

Neblo, M., Esterling, K. M., Kennedy, R. P., & Lazer, D. (2010). Who wants to deliberate—and why? *American Political Science Review, 104,* 566–583. doi:10.1017/S0003055410000298

Novikoff, A. B. (1945). The concept of integrative levels and biology. *Science, 101,* 209–215. doi:10.1126/science.101.2618.209

Osborn, A. F. (1953). Applied imagination: Principles and procedures of creative problem solving. New York, NY: Charles Scribner's Sons.

Plato. (399 BC/2014). *Apology.* Seattle, WA: CreateSpace Independent Publishing Platform.

Poincaré, H. (2014). *Foundations of science.* Cambridge, UK: Cambridge University Press.

Puccio, G. J., Mance, M., & Murdock, M. C. (2011). *Creative leadership: Skills that drive change.* Los Angeles, CA: SAGE. (Original work published 1908.)

Reia, S. M., Herrmann, S., & Fontanari, J. F. (2017). The impact of centrality on cooperative processes. *Physical Review E, 95,* 022305. doi:10.1103/PhysRevE.95.022305

Renzulli, J. S. (1986). The Three-Ring Conception of Giftedness: A developmental model for creative productivity. In R. J. Sternberg & J. E. Davidson (Eds.), *Conceptions of giftedness* (pp. 53–92). New York, NY: Cambridge University Press.

Ritoók, Z. (2009). Horace and the golden mean. In *Desire, poetry and cognition. Selected essays* (pp. 359–366). Budapest, Hungary: Osiris.

Shamir, B., House, R. J., & Arthur, M. B. (1993). The motivational effects of charismatic leadership: A self-concept based theory. *Organization Science, 4,* 577–594. doi:10.1287/orsc.4.4.577

Scheffer, M., Bascompte, J., Brock, W. A., Brovkin, V., Carpenter, S. R., Dakos, V., . . . Sugihara, G. (2009). Early-warning signals for critical transitions. *Nature, 461,* 53–59. doi:10.1038/nature08227

Simonton, D. K. (1999). *Origins of genius: Darwinian perspectives on creativity.* New York, NY: Oxford University Press.

Sowden, P., Pringle, A., & Gabora, L. (2015). The shifting sands of creative thinking: Connections to dual process theory and implications for creativity training. *Thinking Reasoning, 21,* 40–60. doi:10.1080/13546783.2014.885464

St. Ignatius of Loyola. (1548/1991). *The spiritual exercises and selected works.* Mahwah NJ: Paulist Press.

Sternberg, R. J. (1998). Balance theory of wisdom. *Review of General Psychology, 2,* 347–365.

Sternberg, R. J., & Davidson, J. E. (Eds.). (2005). *Conceptions of giftedness* (2nd ed.). New York, NY: Cambridge University Press.

Surowiecki, J. (2004). *The wisdom of crowds.* New York, NY: Anchor, Doubleday.

Thiessen, D. (2011). *Bittersweet destiny: The stormy evolution of human behavior.* Piscataway, NJ: Transaction.

Uzzi, B., Mukherjee, S., Stringer, M., & Jones, B. (2013). Atypical combinations and scientific impact. *Science, 342,* 468–472. doi:10.1126/*science*.1240474

Xenophon. (371 BC/2011). *Memorabilia.* Ithaca, NY: Cornell University Press.

CHAPTER 14

Achievement Orientation Model

UNDERSTANDING HOW WHAT WE BELIEVE DETERMINES WHETHER WE ACHIEVE[1]

Del Siegle, D. Betsy McCoach, and Emma Bloomfield

Most teachers recall certain students who left lasting impressions on them for a multitude of reasons. For some, memories of excellence and outstanding achievement abound, while for others, anguish over potential never realized lingers. Educators often wonder why certain talented students never achieve to their maximum potential, agonizing over this question long after the students are no longer in their class. Our encounters with students similar to the one we are about to describe prompted us to develop the Achievement Orientation Model to better understand giftedness and the self-perceptions that regulate individuals' ability to manifest their gifts.

Anne was a high school freshman in Algebra I. She struggled greatly throughout her first year of high school. Chronic tardiness, using inappropriate language with teachers, skipping classes, and picking fights (both verbal and physical) with other students were just a few commonplace activities in her day. At the same time, it was abundantly clear she was a highly capable student. She demonstrated that she knew the content by answering questions in class and completing practice problems both in class and after school, yet her grades were consistently low, given

---

1   Some of this information was adapted from Siegle, D., McCoach, D. B., & Roberts, A. (2017). Why I achieve determines whether I achieve. *High Ability Studies, 28,* 59–72. doi:10.108 0/13598139.2017.1302873

her strong ability. She seldom completed homework assignments and classroom assessments. She did not value the academic goals of high school. Anne's home life was tumultuous, and she prioritized survival over academics. She did not see the prospect of attending college as a reality given her circumstances, she did not enjoy mathematics for mathematics sake, she was not a self-proclaimed "good student," and she did not see any relevance in the algebra content. As will be made clear in this chapter, the Achievement Orientation Model demonstrates how this concept of valuing a task, along with other beliefs, is essential to academic success. Working with Anne over the course of the school year was a struggle, and she barely passed Algebra 1. Fortunately, over the course of the next 3 years, she realized that college was in her future and achieving success in high school became important to her. If we knew then what we know now based on our work developing the Achievement Orientation Model, we would have been better equipped to address the needs of Anne and other students like her, whose paths we have crossed over our combined two decades of teaching. We hope this chapter renews educators' confidence in their ability to make a difference in the lives of the students they work with in schools.

WHAT DOES IT MEAN TO BE GIFTED?

In the Achievement Orientation Model, giftedness involves performance, rather than some measure of potential. Although we agree that individuals vary greatly on their potential to achieve, ultimately their accomplishments determine their giftedness rather than their latent potential. Therefore, our model supports a developmental perspective of giftedness that fits well with the work of those who support a talent development approach to giftedness (Subotnik, Olszewski-Kubilius, & Worrell, 2011; see also Chapter 11, this volume). Although we do not attempt to address who is or is not gifted with our model, we do address what attitudes and beliefs gifted individuals possess when they pursue achievement. Renzulli (2005) preferred to label individuals' behaviors as gifted rather than the individuals themselves, and we agree with that perspective. Rather than labeling a particular student as gifted, Renzulli has recommended that the behaviors students are displaying be labeled. For him, gifted is used as an adjective or adverb, and he suggests that giftedness is brought to bear upon some performance area. In his Three-Ring Conception of Giftedness, giftedness is a behavior that comes to fruition in certain (but not all) people, at certain times (but not all of the time), and under certain circumstances. The Achievement Orientation Model addresses the beliefs individuals have about themselves and their environment when those conditions exist. According to Renzulli, giftedness is something students do, not something they are, and it occurs when students are task committed and use their above-average ability in creative ways (see also Renzulli & Reis, this volume).

Gagné (2005, this volume) distinguished between the terms *gifted* and *talented*; gifts are the raw material, and talents are the byproduct of developing that material. In his Differentiated Model of Giftedness and Talent, individuals turn their gifts into talents. This transformation occurs through the interaction of a developmental process, catalysts (such as the environment and intrapersonal characteristics), and chance. The Achievement Orientation Model addresses the attitudes individuals possess during that transformational process.

The National Association for Gifted Children (2010) also recognized the developmental nature of giftedness in their definition:

> Gifted individuals are those who demonstrate outstanding levels of aptitude (defined as an exceptional ability to reason and learn) or competence (documented performance or achievement in top 10% or rarer) in one or more domains. Domains include any structured area of activity with its own symbol system (e.g., mathematics, music, language) and/or set of sensorimotor skills (e.g., painting, dance, sports).
>
> The development of ability or talent is a lifelong process. It can be evident in young children as exceptional performance on tests and/or other measures of ability or as a rapid rate of learning, compared to other students of the same age, or in actual achievement in a domain. As individuals mature through childhood to adolescence, however, achievement and high levels of motivation in the domain become the primary characteristics of their giftedness. Various factors can either enhance or inhibit the development and expression of abilities. (para. 1–2)

We believe individuals' attitudes are key in the development and expression of ability, and we suggest that individuals have control over developing their giftedness through positive attitudes. We are not suggesting that everyone has the potential to be gifted. Certainly some students are able to learn material or develop skills more easily, quickly, or earlier than other students, and some students are also better able to grasp complex and complicated ideas than others. However, these advantages are not sufficient to predict long-term differences in success later in life. As Geoff Colvin (2008) wrote in *Talent Is Overrated*, "talents are much less important than we think" (p. 35). What determines a difference in the long term is what students do with their gifts.

For most high-achieving individuals, the process of becoming gifted involves hours of deliberate practice that focuses on tasks beyond the individuals' current level of comfort and competence (Ericsson, 2002). It requires feedback from a knowledgeable coach who can guide them through the process and also help them learn how to coach themselves (Ericsson, Prietula, & Cokely, 2007). In order to sustain this practice, individuals generally require a growth mindset (Dweck, 2006) where they recognize that abilities are malleable and can be improved with concentrated effort. It also involves time to develop giftedness to reach a high level of expertise. Although domains of talent have unique developmental trajectories across the life span, it generally takes a minimum of 10,000 hours of deliberate practice over 10 years to achieve expertise (Ericsson et al., 2007; Subotnik et al., 2011). Obviously, giftedness is not something that just happens to individuals. Therefore, the attitudes individuals have about themselves and their tasks influence whether they are willing to expend the effort necessary to develop their giftedness. From our perspective, individuals who possess a set of three attitudes (self-efficacy, goal valuation, and environmental perceptions) and a resultant behavior (self-regulation) are more likely to develop and utilize their abilities for high levels of achievement. We discuss these in more detail throughout the remainder of this chapter.

HOW ARE GIFTS/TALENTS DEVELOPED?

The constructs featured in most achievement models tend to be organized around beliefs about the perceived capacity to do different tasks and the reasons for doing different tasks (Pintrich, Marx, & Boyle, 1993; Wigfield & Cambria, 2010). The Achievement Orientation Model combines these. According to the Achievement Orientation Model, developing one's talent is a choice individuals make based on a set of self-perceptions in three areas—self-efficacy, goal valuation, and environmental perceptions—which collectively influence individuals' motivation, and subsequently interact with self-regulation to promote engagement and ultimately achievement. Accordingly, individuals must possess positive affect in the areas of self-efficacy, goal valuation, and environmental perceptions. The intensity of their positivity in the three areas need not be equally strong, but it must be positive. The interaction of self-efficacy, goal valuations, and environmental perceptions is multiplicative and their relationship with self-efficacy is additive. The three attitudes of self-efficacy, goal valuation, and environmental perceptions operate in a multiplicative manner similar to Simonton's (2005) Emergenic-Epigenetic model in which all elements need to be present before giftedness is revealed. If any of the three do not meet a threshold value, students may fail to be motivated. Intense positivity in one of the three areas does not compensate for negativity in another area. However, beliefs and values are not

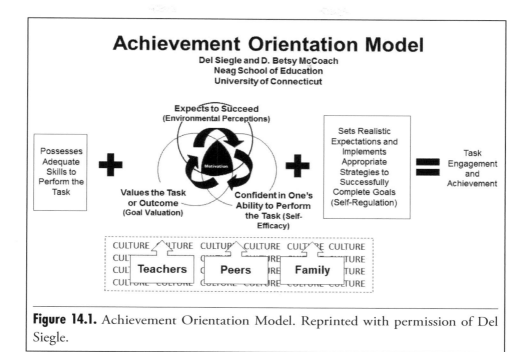

Figure 14.1. Achievement Orientation Model. Reprinted with permission of Del Siegle.

sufficient: The addition of the self-regulation metacognitive process ultimately results in achievement (Brigandi, 2015). Therefore, the model is a combination of multiplicative and additive features. If any one of the three attitude components is missing, regardless of the strength of the others, individuals lack the motivation to self-regulate and achievement may falter. Although lacking the product of the three attitudes hinders motivation, possessing it does not guarantee achievement, because self-regulation is still necessary. Societal and cultural values also influence students' beliefs and values in the three areas of self-efficacy, goal valuation, and environmental perceptions, as well as their self-regulation, through students' interactions with peers, parents, and teachers. Figure 14.1 depicts this process.

Self-Efficacy

Bandura introduced the concept of self-efficacy in 1977, when he defined it as "the conviction that one can successfully execute the behavior required to produce the outcome" (p. 79). Decades of research support the positive relationship between believing one has the capacity to perform an academic task and actual academic achievement (Artino, 2012; Multon, Brown, & Lent, 1991; Robbins et al., 2004). Individuals with low self-efficacy toward a task are more likely to avoid it, while those with high self-efficacy are more likely to attempt it. These individuals will work harder at the task and will persist longer in the face of difficulties (Ames & Archer, 1988; Bandura, 1977, 1986; Schunk, 1981; Schunk & Pajares, 2013).

Goal Valuation/Meaningfulness

In addition to believing they have the skills to be successful, students must also value tasks and find them meaningful before they engage. This appears to be a critical issue for some gifted underachievers (McCoach & Siegle, 2003). Many gifted underachievers have high self-efficacy, but fail to achieve in school because they do not value their schoolwork (McCoach & Siegle, 2003). Such was the case with the student we described at the start of this chapter.

Individuals find tasks meaningful for different reasons. These reasons will vary from one person to another, but they often fall into four categories: attainment value or importance, intrinsic or interest value, utility value or usefulness of the task, and cost (Eccles & Wigfield, 1995). Children's achievement values affect their self-regulation and motivation because goals influence how children approach, engage in, and respond to academic tasks (Hidi & Harackiewicz, 2000). Additionally, Wigfield and Eccles (1992) suggested that individuals weigh the cost and benefits in determining whether they wish to pursue certain activities.

Environmental Perceptions

Not only can individuals' perceptions of self and the value of tasks lead to differences in achievement, individuals' perceptions of the supportive nature of their environment can also lead to differences in achievement (Pekrun, 2006). People must not only believe they have the skills to do well and value the related task, they must also believe their efforts are supported and will not be thwarted; therefore, putting forth effort is not a waste of time and energy.

Some environmental factors are within individuals' control, others are not. The environmental perceptions construct in the Achievement Orientation Model is similar to, but not synonymous with, Rotter's (1966) locus of control. Students with external locus of control views believe others are in control and may question the support they receive in their environment. Therefore, external locus of control can negatively influence achievement with gifted students (Moore, 2006). However, students with internal locus of control beliefs may feel in control, but not necessarily supported by their environment. Achievement for students with internal locus of control can be thwarted when they perceive their environment blocking their efforts. Ogbu (1978) suggested that people put effort into areas where they believe they can be successful, and in environments where they believe they are supported. The environmental perceptions factor captures the importance of the interaction between the person and the environment, as well as the perception of that environment on achievement motivation (French, Rodgers, & Cobb, 1974; Lewin, 1935; Ritchotte, Matthews, & Flowers, 2014; Zeigler & Phillipson, 2012).

Students who believe they can learn the material, find it meaningful, and trust their environment engage in the learning process, set realistic expectations, and self-regulate their learning. Although self-regulation may serve as the engine, propelling students toward achievement, the path to self-regulation and eventual achievement begins with positive views about one's ability to succeed, the friendliness of the environment, and the importance of the task at hand.

Self-Regulation

Self-regulation is the ability to monitor and control behavior according to the demands of the situation (Cook & Cook, 2009). The importance of self-regulation for learning is well documented in the literature (Zimmerman, 2011). In some sense, the three attitudes we just described could be considered components of self-regulated learning. For example, goals are a central construct in most self-regulation theories (Locke & Latham, 2002; Pintrich, 2000; Zimmerman, 2000). Findings from meta-analyses support self-efficacy as an important contributor to self-regulation (Colquitt, LePine, & Noe, 2000). Students need to be motivated to use self-regulation strategies; they need the will to engage in self-regulated learning as well as the skills to self-regulate (McCombs & Marzano, 1990). Certainly, self-regulation is essential for high levels of performance. In the Achievement Orientation Model, self-efficacy, goal valuation, and environmental perceptions provide prerequisite motivation; however, the ability to self-regulate at high levels is essential for obtaining eminence in a given domain (Ericsson, Krampe, & Tesch-Römer, 1993). Therefore, we cannot overstate the importance of self-regulation in attaining the highest levels of achievement.

HOW IS GIFTEDNESS MANIFESTED?

We do not propose a system for identifying and evaluating gifted students. However, we can provide recommendations for enhancing the beliefs and values we propose in the Achievement Orientation Model and suggestions on how to address them under different educational conditions. In order to develop gifts and talents, students must first develop self-efficacy, goal valuation, and positive environmental perceptions. Improved student attitudes in these three areas will allow for maximum growth in areas of strength because these three beliefs together create the self-regulation and motivation required for academic achievement. We choose to organize this information around the components of the model.

Self-Efficacy: "Am I Smart Enough?"

Ultimately, students need to be able to affirmatively answer, "Yes" to the above question. Before attempting any task, individuals must believe they have the necessary skills or ability to perform it. This is true whether individuals are auditioning for a play or tackling a difficult mathematics problem. Although a number of factors influence students' confidence to tackle challenging situations, their past performance (Usher & Pajares, 2006) and the performances of others around them (Britner & Pajares, 2006) have dramatic effects.

In an educational setting, self-efficacy influences: (1) the activities students select, (2) how much effort they put forth, (3) how persistent they are in the face of difficulties, and (4) the difficulty of the goals they set. Students with low self-efficacy do not expect to do well. They do not believe they have the skills to do well and tend to avoid tasks for which they are not efficacious. Gifted students with low self-efficacy often do not achieve at a level that is commensurate with their abilities. The connection between self-efficacy and achievement grows stronger as students advance through school and is highly predictive of achievement at the college level (Wood & Locke, 1987).

Bandura (1986) established that self-efficacy emerges from four sources: past experiences, observations of others, verbal persuasion, and physiological clues. The common saying, "Success breeds success" hits the mark with self-efficacy. Students who have been successful in the past will tend to believe that they can be successful in the future. Unfortunately, students who have previously performed below their own or others' expectations probably lack confidence in their skills and may believe they are not good enough to succeed at challenging tasks.

Educators can increase students' confidence by helping them recognize their past successes and the role that effort played in their achievements. By helping students acknowledge their past growth, educators help promote future growth. For example, parents and teachers can keep samples of students' work throughout the year and periodically review this previous work with students. This helps students recognize their growth and improvement. At the end of the school year, when students review their work from the beginning of the year, they are amazed by how easy that earlier work now appears. Student portfolios can effectively be used for this purpose.

Along these same lines, teachers and parents can video record their students as the students are engaged in different activities. Once again, students should periodically review these recordings to recognize their improvement. For example, a young person who has been taking violin lessons for a number of years may not believe she has been making any progress. However, the student will notice striking differences in her performance when comparing a recently recorded performance with one that was recorded 6 months or a year ago.

Parents and teachers can also help students chart the progress of various activities. This might include the number of words spelled correctly on weekly spelling assignments or the student's progress mastering multiplication or addition facts. Students enjoy updating their charts to record new accomplishments; with each update, they become aware of the progress they are making.

Parents and teachers can also verbally recognize students' progress. Successful students are those who understand they have the skills to do well while simultaneously recognizing the important role effort plays in high levels of achievement. Therefore, feedback provided to students must contain (1) recognition of their skill and (2) attribution of its development to the student. Feedback and compliments should also be specific. Praise such as "Good work!" provides students with very little information about what they did well and does little to help them recognize their ability or to help build their confidence that they have ability. Compliments should include what students specifically did well, such as, "You've learned to include appropriate topic sentences in each paragraph you write." In addition to specifically recognizing the skill students have mastered, this compliment also recognizes that the students have developed the skills. By using such phrases as "you have learned," "you are becoming," and "your practice paid off," parents and teachers are sending students messages that the students themselves are responsible for their skill development and the skills they currently possess. With additional effort, students can also be responsible for acquisition of future skills.

Over the last decade, educators and researchers have become concerned not only about whether students are efficacious about their abilities, but how they believe they obtained their abilities and the skills they need to be successful (Makel, Snyder, Thomas, Malone, & Putallaz, 2015; Siegle, 2012; Siegle & Langley, 2016; Siegle, Rubenstein, Pollard, & Romey, 2010; Snyder, Barger, Wormington, Schwartz-Bloom, & Linnenbrink-Garcia, 2013). Dweck's (2006, 2012) work on growth mindsets propelled this issue to the forefront for practitioners and researchers. Dweck (2012) stressed the importance of students seeing talents and abilities as dynamic and malleable qualities. Students who see their abilities as something they can develop, rather than simply a fixed trait, are more motivated to learn and persevere in the face of obstacles, are more resilient after setbacks, and ultimately achieve more. It is this growth mindset that leads to positive achievement behaviors (Dweck, 2006).

Goal Valuation: "Is This Important to Me?"

For many gifted students, the curriculum and instructional strategies they encounter in school are not meeting the intellectual stimulation and need for cognition they seek. Failure of the school environment to meet students' needs can lead to declines in academic motivation and interest (Wang & Eccles, 2013).

Therefore, valuing the goals of school and finding them meaningful are essential attitudes for achievement. This also includes valuing other activities where individuals demonstrate talent. Liddell and Davidson (2004) stressed the important role valuing tasks plays in achievement: "Students perform better on those skills that they value and this may be influenced by underlying motivation to master the skill" (p. 52).

The Achievement Orientation Model was designed on the assumption that the necessary prerequisite skills for achievement have already been established. Because knowledge and skill development have traditionally been a focus of the educational system, we will not dwell on this aspect here. Efforts made to ensure that rigorous curricula are available at all ages, and vertically aligned across grades for continuity, provide the necessary foundation of skills and knowledge. Effective curriculum for gifted students is appropriately challenging, is taught at an accelerated pace, has complexity in the organization of the content, and has greater depth (Little, 2012). Many gifted students already know much of the material they encounter in their regular classrooms (Reis, Westberg, Kulikowich, & Purcell, 1998). Gifted students generally enjoy learning and do not want to be bored in school. They often equate lack of challenge with boredom (Gallagher, Harradine, & Coleman, 1997). It is important that students encounter curriculum that is within their zone of proximal development (Little, 2012; Vygotsky, 1978). Students are more likely to value activities they find intellectually stimulating.

Students whose interests and goals are incorporated into the curriculum show greater motivation and use self-regulatory strategies more often. They also have higher academic self-concept and subjective task values (Wang & Eccles, 2013).

Generally, gifted students naturally enjoy higher order thinking tasks (Rimm, Siegle, & Davis, 2018) and have a *need for cognition*. Need for cognition is "the tendency for an individual to engage in and enjoy thinking" (Cacioppo & Petty, 1982, p. 116). This overall stable motivational intrinsic trait is not necessarily domain-specific and is malleable (Cacioppo & Petty, 1986; Preckel, Holling, & Vock, 2006). Students high in need for cognition are more likely to engage in learning processes and complex thinking activities (Meier, Vogl, & Preckel, 2014), and earn higher school grades (Ackerman & Heggestad, 1997; Preckel et al., 2006). Preckel et al. (2006) found that lower values in need for cognition correlated with underachievement, even more strongly than achievement motivation. Students with need for cognition want to understand and find meaning in their experiences. Higher levels are associated with an increased appreciation of debate, evaluation of ideas, and problem solving (Dole & Sinatra, 1998).

Students find their school tasks meaningful for a variety of reasons, and these reasons can vary from one student to another. Some students see themselves as good students. They identify as someone who does well in school, and this identity motivates them to work hard on whatever school-related task they encounter.

Other students have a clear vision of their future and see the important role education plays in achieving their future aspirations. These students see school as a vehicle to future success. Another group of students does well in school when the topic interests them. Student interest can be a powerful motivator for academic achievement. Each of these examples represents different ways that students make learning experiences meaningful. For example, one student in a language arts class may work for top grades because she wants to attend a prestigious college or earn an important college scholarship. A second student may hope to become a writer and wants to sharpen his writing skills. A third student may simply enjoy writing. Although each of these students is motivated to achieve in language arts, each is motivated to do well for a different reason.

Educators can make school more meaningful for students and increase student motivation by capitalizing on these motivating factors. For example, teachers can begin every lesson with an explanation of how the information students are learning is useful and why students are learning it. Teachers can also help students see beyond an immediate task to its long-term benefits. This strategy is more effective if teachers and adults work with students to understand students' short and long-term goals. Over a century ago, Friedrich Nietzsche noted that "the future influences the present as much as the past" (BrainyQuote, n.d). What students wish to achieve in the future certainly influences the effort they place on current tasks. Helping students set short- and long-term goals is an effective strategy in making school more meaningful. Short-term goals are generally more effective with young people who sometimes have trouble relating to longer term goals. The purpose is to help students who do not particularly enjoy an academic task recognize a positive outcome it produces.

Topics are also more meaningful when students understand what occurred before and after them. For example, someone who grew up with film cameras is more likely to be impressed with the digital camera of today than someone who has only known digital cameras. By understanding what came before digital photography, what was happening at the time digital photography was developed, and the effects of digital photography, individuals will have a greater appreciation for digital photography. This principle can be applied to any new content students are asked to embrace (Kaplan, 2006).

Additionally, educators should pay attention to student interests. Interest is one of the strongest self-reported predictors of achievement across a wide variety of domains (Siegle et. al, 2010). When students are interested in topics, they tend to excel at them. Adults can encourage their children to incorporate their interests into their school projects. Educators can learn students' interests and tie those interests to the topics students are learning. Offering students a choice of tasks to complete can also be an effective strategy for engaging students. Students appreciate being given options even when the options reflect equally challenging tasks.

Finally, there are times when rewarding students for doing well is the best motivator (Jovanovic & Matejevic, 2014). However, some researchers (Deci, Koestner, & Ryan, 1999) warn that educators and parents should avoid providing rewards when students are already motivated to perform tasks. Developing a reward system for an intrinsically motivated student might actually be detrimental for that student's long-term intrinsic motivation. However, when students are not motivated and other strategies such as setting goals or exploring student interests are ineffective, a reward system for completing work and performing well can be useful. Rewards should be used sparingly, however, and students should be weaned off of them as they gain confidence and appreciation for performing the task.

Because gifted students often master their school content earlier than other students, educators can also make learning more meaningful by providing engaging material that is optimally challenging. Classroom activities should be appropriate to students' current knowledge and skill levels and, like all learning, be designed to be intellectually stimulating.

Environmental Perceptions: "Can I Be Successful Here?"

As previously noted, students must believe they have the prerequisite skills to perform a task and also believe it is important to attempt the task. However, these two attitudes are not sufficient motivators by themselves. Students must also view their learning environment as supportive. In other words, they must see their learning environment as friendly and likely to support a positive outcome if they put forth effort. Successful students believe that environmental factors such as parents, teachers, peers, and the curriculum support their effort and do not prevent them from being successful. Phrases such as "You don't understand," "I can't learn the way he teaches," or "It doesn't matter what I do, I won't be successful," are indicators that students do not view their learning environment as friendly. In other words, they do not believe they can succeed even if they try.

Students' perceptions of the support they are receiving in their environment may or may not be accurate. These perceptions of the supportive nature of the environment are as important as the actual academic environment in promoting motivation and engagement in school (Wang & Eccles, 2013). For example, the learning environment is not always supportive of gifted students. Some teachers are threatened by gifted students. Cross (1997) suggested that, in some situations, low motivation may represent a coping strategy whereby students strive to adapt to an anti-intellectual school environment. As we previously discussed, the curriculum may not be appropriate. When students inhabit an unfriendly environment, they have three options: change their behavior to be successful in the environment, change the environment to meet their needs, or find a more appropriate environment where they can be successful. Sternberg (2001) suggested that wisdom involves determining which of these three options will most likely lead to success for the individual. Most of these changes require the support and assistance of teachers and parents. Educators and parents can discuss with gifted students what is within their control, what is not within their control, and the best option for being successful.

Students should also understand that their perceptions of the situation might be distorted. One successful strategy for addressing this is a technique called *active listening*. Active listening involves paraphrasing back to the student what he or she says (Robertson, 2005). The purpose is threefold. First, it lets the student know that the listener is interested in what the student is saying. Second, it is meant to clarify for the listener what the student is saying to ensure that the listener actually does understand. Third, it allows the student to reflect on and clarify what he or she is saying. Through this reflective process, the student and listener often come to understand hidden issues that may be bothering the student.

No single strategy works with every student. However, a combination of the strategies presented here can help to increase the motivation of gifted and talented students. Developing motivation patterns takes time. Ultimately, the decision to achieve and pursue giftedness lies with the student. With the support of caring teachers, parents, and friends, talented individuals can develop their talents and lead fulfilling lives.

CONCLUSION

Ultimately, for students to achieve academic success, a variety of factors need to be enacted, or prevented from occurring. Student environmental perceptions and self-perceptions affect academic achievement. Curriculum needs to be chosen carefully to include the interests and goals that are of high value to the student; it also needs to be accelerated when needed, taught in-depth, and taught with greater complexity in organization (Little, 2012; Wang & Eccles, 2013). Students who have high self-efficacy are more likely to develop approach goal orientations, showing a growth mindset that is more likely to affect positively their achievement process (Schunk & Pajares, 2013). All of these attitudes and beliefs about achievement influence whether students achieve, to what extent students achieve, and in which context they achieve. Self-regulation helps propel students toward action. However, without the prerequisite attitudes we have described, students find it difficult to engage and develop self-regulation behaviors.

Major Takeaways

- We vary greatly in our potential to achieve; however, ultimately our accomplishments determine our giftedness rather than latent potential.

- The beliefs and values we hold toward ourselves, given tasks, and achievement itself influence what tasks we seek, and whether we accomplish them.

- Our self-perceptions in the three areas of self-efficacy, goal valuation, and environmental perceptions interact to motivate us to self-regulate our behaviors and subsequently engage and achieve.

- Societal and cultural values influence our attitudes in the three areas of self-efficacy, goal valuation, and environmental perceptions, as well as our ability to self-regulate.

RECOMMENDED READINGS

Dweck, C. S. (2006). *Mindset: The new psychology of success.* New York, NY: Random House.

Siegle, D. (2013). *The underachieving gifted child: Recognizing, understanding, and reversing underachievement.* Waco, TX: Prufrock Press.

Subotnik, R. F., Olszewski-Kubilius, P., & Worrell, F. C. (2011). Rethinking giftedness and gifted education: A proposed direction forward based on psychological science. *Psychological Science in the Public Interest, 12,* 3–54.

REFERENCES

Ackerman, P. L., & Heggestad, E. D. (1997). Intelligence, personality, and interests: Evidence for overlapping traits. *Psychological Bulletin, 121,* 219–245.

Ames, C., & Archer, J. (1988). Achievement goals in the classroom: Students' learning strategies and motivation processes. *Journal of Educational Psychology, 80,* 260–267.

Artino, A. R. (2012). Academic self-efficacy: From educational theory to instructional practice. *Perspectives on Medical Education, 1,* 76–85. doi:10.1007/s40037-012-0012-5

Bandura, A. (1977). Self-efficacy: Toward a unifying theory of behavioral change. *Psychological Review, 84,* 191–215.

Bandura, A. (1986). *Social foundations of thought and action: A social cognition theory.* Englewood Cliffs, NJ: Prentice-Hall.

BrainyQuote. (n.d.). *Friedrich Nietzsche quotes.* Retrieved from https://www.brainyquote.com/quotes/quotes/f/friedrichn107170.html

Brigandi, C. B. (2015). *Gifted secondary school students and enrichment: The perceived effect on achievement orientation* (Unpublished doctoral dissertation). University of Connecticut, Storrs.

Britner, S. L., & Pajares, F. (2006). Sources of science self-efficacy beliefs of middle school students. *Journal of Research in Science Teaching, 43,* 485–499. doi:10.1002/tea.20131

Cacioppo, J., & Petty, R. (1986). Central and peripheral routes to persuasion: An individual difference perspective. *Journal of Personality and Social Psychology, 51,* 1032–1043.

Colquitt, J. A., LePine, J. A., & Noe, R. A. (2000). Toward an integrative theory of training motivation: A meta-analytic path analysis of 20 years of research. *Journal of Applied Psychology, 85,* 678–707. doi:10.1037/0021-9010.85.5.678

Colvin, G. (2008). *Talent is overrated: What really separates world-class performers from everybody else.* New York, NY: Penguin Books.

Cook, J. L., & Cook, G. (2009). *Child development: Principles and perspectives* (2nd ed.). New York, NY: Pearson.

Cross, T. L. (1997). Psychological and social aspects of educating gifted students. *Peabody Journal of Education, 72,* 180–200.

Deci, E., Koestner, R., & Ryan, R. M. (1999). A meta-analytic review of experiments examining the effects of extrinsic rewards on intrinsic motivation. *Psychological Bulletin, 125,* 627–668.

Dole, J. A., & Sinatra, G. M. (1998). Reconceptualizing change in the cognitive construction of knowledge. *Educational Psychologist, 33,* 109–128. doi:10.1080/004 61520.1998.9653294

Dweck, C. S. (2006). *Mindset: The new psychology of success.* New York, NY: Random House.

Dweck, C. S. (2012). Mindsets and malleable minds: Implications for giftedness and talent. In R. F. Subotnik, A. Robinson, C. M. Callahan, & E. J. Gubbins (Eds.), *Malleable minds: Translating insights from psychology and neuroscience to gifted education* (pp. 7–18). Storrs: University of Connecticut, The National Research Center on the Gifted and Talented.

Eccles, J. S., & Wigfield, A. (1995). In the mind of the actor: The structure of adolescents' achievement task values and expectancy-related beliefs. *Personality and Social Psychology Bulletin, 21,* 215–225.

Ericsson, K. A. (2002). Attaining excellence through deliberate practice: Insights from the study of expert performance. In C. Desforges & R. Fox (Eds.), *Teaching and learning: The essential readings* (pp. 4–37). Oxford, England: Blackwell. doi:10.1002/9780470690048.ch1

Ericsson, K. A., Krampe, R. T., & Tesch-Römer, C. (1993). The role of deliberate practice in the acquisition of expert performance. *Psychological Review, 100,* 363–406.

Ericsson, K. A., Prietula, M. J., & Cokely, E. T. (2007). The making of an expert. *Harvard Business Review.* Retrieved from https://hbr.org/2007/07/the-making-of-an-expert

French, J. R. P., Jr., Rodgers, W., & Cobb, S. (1974). Adjustment as person-environment fit. In G. V. Coelho, D. A. Hamburg, & J. E. Adams (Eds.), *Coping and adaptation* (pp. 316–333). New York, NY: Basic Books.

Gagné, F. (2005). From gifts to talents: The DMGT as a developmental model. In R. J. Sternberg & J. E. Davidson (Eds.), *Conceptions of giftedness* (2nd ed., pp. 98–119). New York, NY: Cambridge University Press.

Gallagher, J., Harradine, C. C., & Coleman, M. R. (1997). Challenge or boredom? Gifted students' views on their schooling, *Roeper Review, 19,* 132–136.

Hidi, S., & Harackiewicz, J. M. (2000). Motivating the academically unmotivated: A critical issue for the 21st century. *Review of Educational Research, 70,* 151–179.

Jovanovic, D., & Matejevic, M. (2014). Relationship between rewards and intrinsic motivation for learning—Researches review. *Procedia–Social and Behavioral Sciences, 149,* 456–460. doi:10.1016/j.sbspro.2014.08.287

Kaplan, S. (2006, July). *Gifted students in a contemporary society: Implications for curriculum.* Keynote at the 29th Annual Confratute, Storrs, CT.

Lewin, K. (1935). *A dynamic theory of personality: Selected papers.* New York, NY: McGraw-Hill.

Liddell, M. J., & Davidson, S. K. (2004). Student attitudes and their academic performance: Is there any relationship? *Medical Teacher, 26,* 52–56.

Little, C. A. (2012). Curriculum as motivation for gifted students. *Psychology in the Schools, 49,* 695–705. doi:10.1002/pits.21621

Locke, E. A., & Latham, G. P. (2002). Building a practically useful theory of goal setting and task motivation: A 35-year odyssey. *American Psychologist, 57,* 705–717

Makel, M. C., Snyder, K. E., Thomas, C., Malone, P. S., & Putallaz, M. (2015). Gifted students' implicit beliefs about intelligence and giftedness. *Gifted Child Quarterly, 59,* 203–212. doi:10.1177/0016986215599057

McCoach, D. B., & Siegle, D. (2003). Factors that differentiate underachieving gifted students from high-achieving gifted students. *Gifted Child Quarterly, 47,* 144–154.

McCombs, B. L., & Marzano, R. J. (1990). Putting the self into self-regulated learning: The self as agent in integrating will and skill. *Educational Psychologist, 25,* 51–69.

Meier, E., Vogl, K., & Preckel, F. (2014). Motivational characteristics of students in gifted classes: The pivotal role of need for cognition. *Learning and Individual Differences, 33,* 39–46.

Moore, M. M. (2006). *Variations in test anxiety and locus of control orientation in achieving and underachieving gifted and nongifted middle school students* (Unpublished doctoral dissertation). University of Connecticut, Storrs.

Multon, K. D., Brown, S. D., & Lent, R. W. (1991). Relation of self-efficacy beliefs to academic outcomes: A meta-analytic investigation. *Journal of Counseling Psychology, 38,* 30–38.

National Association for Gifted Children. (2010). *Redefining giftedness for a new century: Shifting the paradigm* [Position statement]. Retrieved from https://www.nagc.org/sites/default/files/Position%20Statement/Redefining%20Giftedness%20for%20a%20New%20Century.pdf

Ogbu, J. U. (1978). *Minority education and caste.* New York, NY: Academic Press.

Pekrun, R. (2006). The control-value theory of achievement emotions: Assumptions, corollaries, and implications for education and practice. *Educational Psychology Review, 18,* 315–341.

Pintrich, P. R. (2000). The role of goal orientation in self-regulated learning. In M. Boehaerts, P. R. Pintrich, & M. Zeidner (Eds.), *Handbook of self-regulation* (pp. 451–501). San Diego, CA: Academic Press.

Pintrich, P. R., Marx, R. W., & Boyle, R. A. (1993). Beyond cold conceptual change: The role of motivational beliefs and classroom contextual factors in the process of conceptual change. *Review of Educational Research, 63,* 167–199.

Preckel, F., Holling, H., & Vock, M. (2006). Academic underachievement: Relationship with cognitive motivation, achievement motivation, and conscientiousness. *Psychology in the Schools, 43,* 401–411.

Reis, S. M., Westberg, K. L., Kulikowich, J. M., & Purcell, J. H. (1998). Curriculum compacting and achievement test scores: What does the research say? *Gifted Child Quarterly, 42,* 123–129.

Renzulli, J. S. (2005). The Three-Ring Conception of Giftedness: A developmental model for promoting creative productivity. In R. J. Sternberg & J. E. Davidson (Eds.), *Conceptions of giftedness* (2nd ed., pp. 246–279). New York, NY: Cambridge University Press.

Rimm, S. B., Siegle, D., & Davis, G. A. (2018). *Education of the gifted and talented* (7th ed.). Boston, MA: Pearson.

Ritchotte, J. A., Matthews, M. S., & Flowers, C. P. (2014). The validity of the Achievement-Orientation Model for gifted middle school students: An exploratory study. *Gifted Child Quarterly, 58,* 183–198. doi:10.1177/0016986214534890

Robbins, S. B., Lauver, K., Le, H., Davis, D., Langley, R., & Carlstrom, A. (2004). Do psychosocial and study skill factors predict college outcomes? A meta-analysis. *Psychological Bulletin, 130,* 261–288.

Robertson, K. (2005). Active listening: More than just paying attention. *Australian Family Physician, 34,* 1053–1055.

Rotter, J. (1966). Generalized expectancies for internal vs. external control of reinforcement. *Psychological Monographs, 80,* 1–28.

Schunk, D. H. (1981). Modeling and attributional effects on children's achievement: A self-efficacy analysis. *Journal of Educational Psychology, 73,* 93–105.

Schunk, D. H., & Pajares, F. (2013). Competence perceptions and academic functioning. In A. J. Elliot & C. S. Dweck (Eds.)., *Handbook of Competence and Motivation* (pp. 85–104). New York, NY: Guilford Press.

Siegle, D. (2012). Recognizing both effort and talent: How do we keep from throwing the baby out with the bathwater? In R. F. Subotnik, A. Robinson, C. M. Callahan, & E. J. Gubbins (Eds.), *Malleable minds: Translating insights from psychology and neuroscience to gifted education* (pp. 233–243). Storrs: University of Connecticut, The National Research Center on the Gifted and Talented.

Siegle, D., & Langley, S. D. (2016). Promoting optional mindsets among gifted children. In M. Neihart, S. Pfeiffer, & T. L. Cross (Eds.), *The social and emotional development of gifted children: What do we know?* (2nd ed., pp. 269–280). Waco, TX: Prufrock Press.

Siegle, D., McCoach, D. B., & Roberts, A. (2017). Why I achieve determines whether I achieve. *High Ability Studies, 28,* 59–72. doi:10.1080/13598139.2017.1302873

Siegle, D., Rubenstein, L. D., Pollard, E., & Romey, E. (2010). Exploring the relationship of college freshman honors students' effort and ability attribution, interest, and implicit theory of intelligence with perceived ability. *Gifted Child Quarterly, 54,* 92–101.

Simonton, D. K. (2005). Genetics of giftedness: The implications of an emergenic-epigenetic model. In R. J. Sternberg & J. E. Davidson (Eds.), *Conceptions of giftedness* (2nd ed., pp. 312–326). Cambridge, England: Cambridge University Press.

Snyder, K. E., Barger, M. M., Wormington, S. V., Schwartz-Bloom, R., & Linnenbrink-Garcia, L. (2013). Identification as gifted and implicit beliefs about intelligence: An examination of potential moderators. *Journal of Advanced Academics, 24,* 242–258.

Sternberg, R. J. (2001, July). *Successful intelligence.* Presentation at Annual Edufest Institute, Boise, ID.

Subotnik, R. F., Olszewski-Kubilius, P., & Worrell, F. C. (2011). Rethinking giftedness and gifted education: A proposed direction forward based on psychological science. *Psychological Science in the Public Interest, 12,* 3–54.

Usher, E. L., & Pajares, F. (2006). Sources of academic and self-regulatory efficacy beliefs of entering middle school students. *Contemporary Educational Psychology, 31,* 125–141.

Vygotsky, L. S. (1978). *Mind in society: The development of higher psychological processes.* Cambridge, MA: Harvard University Press.

Wang, M. T., & Eccles, J. S. (2013). School context, achievement motivation, and academic engagement: A longitudinal study of school engagement using a multidimensional perspective. *Learning and Instruction, 28,* 12–23.

Wigfield, A., & Cambria, J. (2010). Students' achievement values, goal orientations, and interest: Definitions, development, and relations to achievement outcomes. *Developmental Review, 30,* 1–35. doi:10.1016/j.dr.2009.12.001

Wigfield, A., & Eccles, J. S. (1992). The development of achievement task values: A theoretical analysis. *Developmental Review, 12,* 1–46.

Wood, R. E., & Locke, E. A. (1987). The relationship of self-efficacy and grade goals to academic performance. *Educational and Psychological Measurement, 47,* 1013–1024.

Ziegler, A., & Phillipson, S. N. (2012). Towards a systemic theory of gifted education. *High Ability Studies, 23,* 3–30. doi:10.1080/13598139.2012.679085

Zimmerman, B. J. (2000). Attaining self-regulation: A social cognitive perspective. In M. Boekaerts, P. R., Pintrich, & M. Zeidner (Eds.), *Handbook of self-regulation* (pp. 13–39). San Diego, CA: Academic Press.

Zimmerman, B. J. (2011). Motivational sources and outcomes of self-regulated learning and performance. In B. J. Zimmerman & D. H. Schunk (Eds.), *Handbook of self-regulation of learning and performance* (pp. 49–64). New York, NY: Taylor and Francis.

CHAPTER 15

A Model for Eliminating Excellence Gaps

Jonathan A. Plucker, Scott J. Peters, and Stephanie Schmalensee

The lack of diversity in gifted education has been a concern within the field for decades. No matter how you define giftedness and gifted education, the data tell the same story: Identified gifted and talented students tend not to be racially or socioeconomically diverse, and outcomes for advanced students across racial and economic subgroups are highly unequal (Plucker, Hardesty, & Burroughs, 2013; Wright, Ford, & Young, 2017). But given these data and long-standing concerns about them, why has American progress toward achieving equity in advanced educational achievement been so halting? More to the point, why do American students appear to be *losing* ground according to some measures? The American educational system is past the point of knowing about the concept and scope of excellence gaps—the differential rates with which students of various subgroups achieve at advanced levels. The collective knowledge has now begun to focus on how to address them.

This lack of progress is due in large part to the emphasis of the American K–12 educational system on minimum competency and the rates with which various subgroups achieve minimum competency. This emphasis has been long in coming with growing attention to such equity in the original Elementary and Secondary and Education Act, the No Child Left Behind Act, and the Every Student Succeeds Act. American education is only now starting to see a focus beyond minimum competency in federal and state policy (but only just starting). The traditional focus on basic competency in K–12 schools poses several problems for schools and society at large. First, achievement gaps exist at many levels. Minimum competency gaps are prioritized because of the national and state policy focus described above, but there is no reason why inequality in achievement at higher levels of performance should be ignored. The emphasis placed on minimum competency is manifested in state accountability systems, how test results are interpreted and used at the school and classroom level, and how teachers are evaluated. As noted by Neal and Schanzenbach (2010), when advanced achievement and closing excellence gaps are not considered educational priorities, it should not be surprising that high-ability students and their education receive relatively little attention. This lack of attention affects low-income and racial/ethnic minority students disproportionately, as these students are less likely to receive advanced educational services at their local, public schools.

How Excellence Gaps Develop

To further our analysis of excellence gaps, we would like to sketch some examples of how a range of factors combine to create very large gaps between what otherwise similar children can achieve and actually are achieving. Even if students attend well-resourced public schools in suburban areas, with considerable family and educator support, excellence gaps still emerge as students move through the school system. As of the 2013–2014 school year, African American and Latino/a students were significantly underrepresented in identified K–12 gifted populations. At the advanced achievement level, the numbers are even worse. On the 2015 National Assessment of Educational Progress for science, 5% of Asian and 2% of White students scored advanced compared to less than .5% of African American, Native American, or Hispanic students. Even when attending otherwise high-quality schools, years of distinctly different opportunities, levels of support, and levels of resources—all against the backdrop of racial, socioeconomic, and perhaps gender bias (some unintentional, some not)—contribute to unequal educational opportunity to learn. Those experiences are additive over time and can result in students of similar initial ability achieving at very different levels. When students attend poorly resourced schools, lack family support, or do not have access to high-quality educators, the differences between these levels of achievement can become enormous. The wide variability in school quality in the United States, based largely on family income, is all too common. These disparate levels of achievement get wider over time as some students continue to benefit from in- and out-of-school resources while others do not. We refer to these differences as *excellence gaps*.

Excellence gaps are obvious across all levels of education, across all content areas, and on all academic assessments. For example, recent performance on the

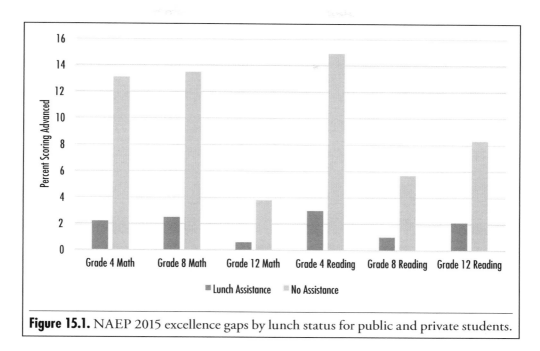

Figure 15.1. NAEP 2015 excellence gaps by lunch status for public and private students.

National Assessment of Educational Progress (NAEP) is summarized in Figure 15.1. Across several grade levels and content areas, stark differences can be found between students who qualify for lunch assistance and those who do not regarding the percentage who score at the advanced level. Many of these gaps are growing as economically vulnerable students' performance stagnates, yet that of their less vulnerable peers increases.

When educational opportunities at any level are not offered as part of the public educational system, then some families will seek them at their own cost and some will not or cannot. This is one of the reasons that educational achievement and family income are so highly correlated—money is often directly linked to access educational opportunity. Families who are aware of supplementary options, can afford them, have the time to seek them out and enroll their children in them, and are willing to do so even when such content is not part of the local school's curriculum, will take advantage of such opportunities in order to further their child's learning. Some of this is due to financial capital and some due to cultural capital—the culture of knowing and being willing to challenge the system. All parents would want to provide advanced opportunities to their children, but only some have that option due to financial, cultural, logistical, or political barriers. This strong association between socioeconomic status and opportunity is not written in stone. In fact, as Finn and Wright (2015) discussed in their recent book on the topic, this association is not present in many other developed nations.

Although excellence gaps are caused by many factors as highlighted in the examples above, a major factor is that talent development and educational excellence come with opportunity, psychological, and financial price tags. Because advanced education has generally been either an afterthought or very low priority in K–12 education, families that seek to challenge their academically talented students have to pursue options outside of the public system—private schools, after-school and weekend programs, summer experiences, and more recently, Internet-based options. If the family is aware of the other opportunities (opportunity), believes their child is qualified for and deserving of them (psychological), and can afford them (financial), then the student is in pretty good shape.

A discussion of academic excellence gaps would be left wanting if it did not mention the hidden costs that aid in the creation of excellence gaps. But they are "hidden" only in the sense that the affordability of these aspects of talent development are taken for granted by some families, but the accessibility of these options are either very limited for many students, or the options simply are not known to them. For example, if the single parent of a talented student does not own a car, taking the student on public transportation to a distant afterschool or weekend enrichment program may mean working fewer hours or simply missing an entire shift of work. Or consider the role of unpaid internships for high school and college students—students in economically secure families can afford to take an unpaid (or poorly paid) internship, and they often have the professional connections to make such internships happen. But a poor, loan-strapped college student may not be able to learn about internship opportunities, and even if she does, the lost income from not having a summer job may be too high a cost to bear. And if we layer geographical concerns on top of all of these other factors (How many good unpaid internships are located in low-income urban and rural communities?), something that seems attractive to many families becomes a wedge that drives either end of the excellence gap further apart.

Excellence gaps are similar to minimal competency gaps in that they are complex and have come to be after years of unequal educational opportunities. Most of these opportunities (or lack thereof) take place before students begin formal education, which is part of the reason why it is so hard for schools to do anything about them. In the following section, we outline some areas of potential when it comes to addressing excellence gaps.

REDUCING EXCELLENCE GAPS

We believe there is a path forward for increasing the number of talented students in the United States and, perhaps more importantly, shrinking excellence gaps and eliminating, once and for all, the country's talent underclass. Plucker and Peters (2016) recently reviewed existing empirical studies to identify the most

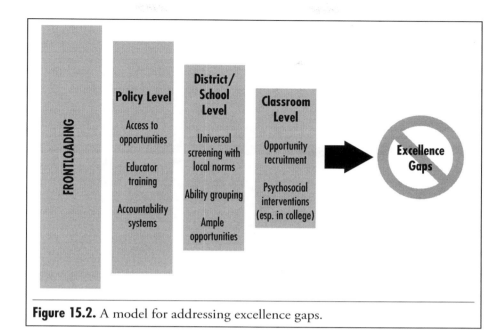

Figure 15.2. A model for addressing excellence gaps.

promising practices for reducing excellence gaps. They generally found promising avenues but few empirically supported interventions. In the next section, we highlight areas where they found advanced education (and the racial, ethnic, and income inequality that often comes with it) has seen greater attention or appear to be on the verge of some positive change. We also offer several recommendations that should have a positive effect on the number of advanced achievers who come from low-income or racial/ethnic minority families. If educators, families, and communities want to take a big swing at excellence gaps, the following suggestions represent the research community's best evidence for a path forward.

After reviewing the available research and model programs around the country, Plucker and Peters (2016) recommended the following approach that reflects the current state of the art for addressing and eventually eliminating excellence gaps (see Figure 15.2). The model includes six sets of interventions: closing opportunity gaps, universal screening with local norms, flexible ability grouping, K–12 accountability systems with relevant indicators, educator training and support, and psychosocial interventions (primarily at the college level). The model is not meant to be exhaustive, instead focusing on the most promising avenues for shrinking excellence gaps while educators wait for comprehensive childhood poverty measures to be put in place—something we believe would go a long way to mitigating all achievement gaps. We do not mean to imply that we need either childhood poverty reduction *or* the following educational and policy interventions, but rather that we need *both* (see Plucker & Peters, 2016). Most educators and advocates cannot address poverty reduction on their own, but they can affect the following issues directly in their own school districts or indirectly by working with state-level policymakers.

Realistic Opportunities

The three keys to opportunity for advanced learning are: (1) successful communication, (2) belief and acceptance, and (3) low barriers to access. If an opportunity for developing the talents of students exists, the students and their caregivers need to know the opportunity exists, they need to believe they should be taking advantage of the opportunity, and they need a realistic chance of accessing the opportunity. Each of these three criteria is necessary but not sufficient for an opportunity to move from being a nice idea to a real benefit for a talented student. Educators have done a good job in recent years of raising awareness about opportunity gaps (e.g., Carter & Welner, 2013; Nores & Barnett, 2014), but recent research suggests that beliefs in the desirability of accessing opportunities may not be as widespread as commonly assumed.

In the intervention model, responsibility for providing, ensuring access to, and encouraging participation in opportunities for talent development is spread among policymakers, administrators, and teachers, but these responsibilities are of equal concern to all stakeholders in K–12 education. Consider the hypothetical case of a poor, high-ability student attending an urban school with few, if any, opportunities for advanced learning. If the district addresses this problem by creating an afterschool program for advanced students in math, the student may still not be able to attend if the program is held 2 miles away from the student's school, or if there is a participation fee to help cover the cost of the program. And if the program is moved to the student's school and all fees are waived, the student's family/caregivers may not understand the value of the opportunity or believe that the student should participate (in rural areas, we often hear stories of families declining participation over a fear that students will leave the community if their talents are developed). Merely creating an opportunity does not address excellence gaps, as access to and communication about the importance of the opportunity are key pieces in seeing an opportunity become realized.

A cautionary note on technology: Much of the rhetoric around technology in our schools focuses on the many advantages and opportunities that are enabled by increasing presence and sophistication of educational technology. Indeed, these advantages are tremendous in theory—with distance education alone, there should no longer be an issue of a student not being able to take an advanced course due to a lack of resources or insufficient numbers of talented students in their home school. But as Hardesty, McWilliams, and Plucker (2014) noted, the presence of technology does not necessarily guarantee its effective use or that students have the technological knowledge and experience that allows them to use the technologies. And, of course, many students do not have advanced technology or Internet access outside of the school day. Opportunities are best conceptualized as theoretical constructs that do not become real until they became positive student outcomes.

Universal Screening and Local Norms

Nonuniversal screening for advanced learning needs will miss many qualified students, and those students will be disproportionately from underrepresented populations (e.g., Card & Giuliano, 2016b; Grissom & Redding, 2016; Hamilton et al., in press; McBee, Peters, & Miller, 2016). For example, the National Research Center on Gifted Education found that low-income students were much less likely to be identified for participation in gifted education programs than their similarly talented peers who were not low-income (Hamilton et al., in press). Part of this is due to low referral rates—certain student populations are never tested for advanced learning needs, which makes it hard to know they exist. Assessments or systems used to identify talent should be administered universally to all eligible students. This could take the form of testing or observing all second-grade students instead of only those who received a teacher recommendation. This will involve some increased time and money, but it will also mean the fewest students from low-income or minority families are missed. There is also some middle ground between testing all students and testing only the top 5% or 10%. If screening thresholds are set lower (e.g., the top 30%), then a happy balance can be found. This is one of the clearest action steps that gifted or advanced programs should take. If addressing underrepresentation and excellence gaps is truly a goal, then moving toward universal assessment is a must. A small but growing number of states, including Colorado, Alabama, Ohio, and South Carolina, are mandating and—in some cases—providing the financial resources for universal screening (Plucker, Glynn, Healey, & Dettmer, in press).

Advanced or gifted learners are often identified by comparing their performance on some measure to the performance of other students from across the nation. In this fashion, a national norm comparison is used as the criterion. Unfortunately, because of school segregation and the unequal opportunity factors discussed above, this results in broad student underrepresentation. A benefit to universal screening is that it would make the application of local norms very easy, because data would be available on all students. Local norms as an identification method moves the comparison group from the rest of the nation (as in national norms) to the rest of a particular student's school or district—hence local. Plucker and Peters (2016) discussed that implementing local norms would increase the number of identified advanced learners in the schools with the largest numbers of low-income and minority students. Of course, simply identifying and labeling students is not likely to have much of an effect on their learning, but if they are identified and then provided with additional support, local norms could have an effect on excellence gaps.

Of course, educators also need to proactively seek out students of potential who also come from low-income or minority families. Universal screening and local norms can help these efforts, but additional efforts are necessary, such as using group-specific comparisons and allowing teachers to recommend students into certain programs even if the student's test scores would not otherwise qualify them for the program (Peters & Engerrand, 2016). That said, such proactive identification cannot be implemented in isolation. Students who are identified via alternative criteria need to be provided additional support in order to be successful. Mentoring, tutoring by older peers from similar communities, or additional support from school staff need to all be considered (see our discussion of frontloading below). As a simple rule, with any differentiated identification process comes the need for differentiated services.

Ability Grouping

There is little question that grouping by prior achievement can be an effective strategy for promoting educational excellence (Gentry & Tay, this volume; Steenbergen-Hu, Makel, & Olszewski-Kubilius, 2016). In addition to benefitting high achievers over a wide range of settings, content areas, and studies, ability grouping research provides evidence of helping close excellence gaps (e.g., Card & Giuliano, 2016a; Robinson, 2008). We see great promise in trying to narrow the range of achievement that any single teacher is expected to instruct in a general classroom setting. We also believe there are ways to do this that are flexible and do not set up students for low expectations. Any district looking to implement grouping should do so with care and with an eye toward what effects such a practice will have on excellence gaps. Additional information on effective grouping practices is available in Gentry and Tay's chapter in this volume.

K–12 Accountability Systems

Some interventions that may reduce excellence gaps are focused at the state policy level. These are important for educators to understand, as they can exert pressure on their local representatives to create and implement proexcellence and antigap policies that set the context in which educators can help more students reach high levels of achievement. One such state policy is each state's K–12 school accountability system. Due to the new federal guidelines provided as a result of the Every Student Succeeds Act (ESSA), states are reconceptualizing their accountability systems. As we write this chapter, many states are submitting their state plans for ESSA to the U.S. Department of Education. States generally tinker with their systems routinely, but ESSA has important implications for those systems that will encourage and allow for major retooling. Accountability systems have a demonstrable effect on education policy and student outcomes, yet few states have much in the way of excellence indicators in their systems' data points (Plucker, Giancola, Healey, Arndt, & Wang, 2015). Adding such indicators would send an important message that advanced learning and growth for all students is important and obtainable for all K–12 public school students (Neal & Schanzenbach, 2010).

Unfortunately, in very few states can schools earn credit on their district report cards for closing excellence gaps (Petrilli, Griffith, Wright, & Kim, 2016; Plucker et al., in press). Changing state policies to allow for excellence gap closure to be included on school report cards would allow schools to devote resources (such as the Title I funds now allowed to be used for advanced learners thanks to ESSA) to receive credit for their work toward greater equity in this area. It is not clear to us why any single "gap" closure would be preferred over another. If a local school community is seeing talents in its low-income, African American, Native American, or Hispanic students going underdeveloped, it should not be penalized for devoting money and effort to this goal.

Of course, districts could create district-level or school-level goals for closing excellence gaps on their own. Many teachers now craft Student Learning Outcomes/Objectives (SLOs) as a form of goal setting and personal evaluation. District or building leadership could encourage or mandate that these goals include the closing of excellence gaps, the identification of larger numbers of advanced learners from underrepresented populations, or the growth of advanced learners beyond grade-level proficiency. In addition to crafting a plan for how a building will close minimal proficiency gaps, schools could be required to also include a plan for how they will close excellence gaps related to target populations. Schools could also just be allowed to create any equity goals they like rather than states mandating a focus on minimal competency.

Educator Preparation and Support

Another state-level policy issue that helps set the context for successful school- and classroom-level interventions is preservice training. Future administrators, teachers, and school counselors are usually not required to receive any content in their preparation programs regarding the education of talented students or the need to shrink excellence gaps. Plucker et al. (in press), in a review of state-level policies, found that only six states require preservice training of any of these groups of future educators, with no state requiring it of all three groups. Given that these policies are required but not necessarily monitored, it is fair to conclude that the percentage of K–12 educators who enter the classroom with even cursory knowledge of just an awareness of excellence gaps is negligible.

The federal Higher Education Opportunity Act (HEOA), reauthorized in 2008, made three substantive changes regarding teacher training. It required teacher-training programs to instruct their students in the identification of student learning needs that included the needs of advanced learners; it required that teacher-training programs instruct their students in how to differentiate instruction for advanced learners and otherwise meet their learning needs; and it required that state report cards on the quality of teacher training programs include criteria on how the earlier two requirements are being addressed and evaluated. If all states and teacher training programs had indeed done all of this, every teacher who completed his or her program over the last 5–8 years would have received some training regarding how to challenge advanced learners. Unfortunately, we have little reason to think that states followed the intent of HEOA with regard to advanced learners.

All of this points to a relatively easy recommendation for states to implement: Enforce the HEOA requirements related to advanced learners. Teacher training regarding students who are already at proficiency is embarrassingly weak. If states want to address the low overall rates of advanced achievement or specifically excellence gaps, they should require teacher preparation programs to include content on how to identify when students are being underchallenged, how to differentiate curriculum in order to better meet their needs, how to implement student acceleration processes, and how to support underrepresented learners in their work toward advanced achievement. In our experience in teacher education, advanced learners tend to receive one or two lessons of attention, *at most*, within a larger class about special education. With this as the state of affairs, it should be no surprise that teachers focus more on remediation than on developing excellence.

Plucker and Peters (2016) noted that ESSA requires that any state and district that accepts Title II money must report on how those funds were used to increase the capacity of teachers to reach all students. Importantly, the definition of "all students" specifically includes gifted and talented students. If states want to address excellence gaps, they could proactively enforce this requirement or even focus a state priority on the closure of excellence gaps through staff professional development. Unlike with HEOA where the mandates were weakly enforced (at best), states could implement extensive oversight to Title II funds to make sure that they are being used to develop educator ability to reach *all* students. Title II-supported interventions could include, for example, a district training its teachers in the use of the Mentoring Mathematical Minds curriculum for high-potential English language learners (Cho, Yang, & Mandracchia, 2015; Gavin et al., 2007). Similarly, a district could seek to expand the pre-AP programs for low-income students in order to close excellence gaps and increase overall rates of achievement. A range of options is possible if a state takes on this issue as a priority with its Title II funds. Because most states are just beginning to determine how the ESSA rules and requirements will be implemented, this seems like the perfect time.

Proactive professional development. K–12 educators learn almost nothing about advanced learners in teacher training programs. Because of this, schools need to take on this task on their own. Now that Title II funds can be used for this purpose, even fewer barriers remain. We do not mean to suggest that schools begin putting their teaching staffs through license or master's degree programs in gifted education. Instead, they should seek out support or teacher training that will help general educators increase their capacity to challenge an even wider range of students. How do I differentiate for an elementary student who is reading at the high school level? What materials are best for a middle school student who is ready for trigonometry? How can we decide how and whether or not to accelerate a child to the next grade level without missing important content? What does supporting African American students look like in advanced education? These questions and many more can be addressed via proactive attention to advanced learners within a single district. Districts tend to have extensive control over what in-services they put on and what conferences their staff attend and topics related to advanced learning should be in the rotation just like any other topic of need.

Psychosocial Interventions in College

One of the most popular recent interventions in all of education involves the use of psychosocial interventions to increase student soft skills that may lead to improved learning and overall achievement. Psychologists have long known that motivation, attitude, and the social context of the learning environment are all strongly predictive of success. Based on this, it seems reasonable to investigate excellence gap interventions that are based not on student learning changes directly, but rather that focus on psychosocial variables. For example, can excellence gaps in science be closed not by changing science instruction but by interventions affecting student identity and personality? These interventions often focus on constructs such as grit, growth mindset, and stereotype threat reduction (see Yeager & Walton, 2011). Psychosocial interventions tend to be brief and, according to proponents, associated with long-term academic benefits.

The potential role of these constructs in mediating and shrinking excellence gaps is enticing, which is probably one reason why they continue to be discussed with such enthusiasm in the educational excellence research community. The idea that students who exhibit high levels of grit, growth mindsets, and positive self-beliefs are more likely to perform at advanced levels than students with low grit, fixed mindsets, and self-limiting beliefs is enticing; there is some evidence to suggest these constructs also differentiate between high-ability individuals and various levels of success (e.g., Blackwell, Trzesniewski, & Dweck, 2007). However, controversies exist about the distinctiveness of these constructs and whether they are causes or effects. Regardless, we think it's safe to say that noncognitive factors matter in the development of talent, but that the research base is too young to be used to plan excellence gap interventions on this basis (Abuhassàn & Bates, 2015; Rimfeld, Kovas, Dale, & Plomin, 2016).

Despite the potential of these interventions, these research areas do not yet provide very helpful information for shrinking excellence gaps. A great case in point is the research on self-affirmation interventions. These relatively brief interventions usually involve students reflecting on positive aspects of their lives and themselves, usually in writing, with the hope that these self-affirmations, by forcing students to present themselves with evidence of hardiness, resilience, and success, will help them move past stereotype threat and other psychological roadblocks to achievement. These interventions can also be expected to carry over to other students in a particular class. If targeted at particular populations, this intervention could help mitigate excellence gaps.

In one of the better, more exhaustive research programs to date, researchers studied the effects of a brief self-affirmation in several cohorts of students in a diverse school beginning in seventh grade (Cohen, Garcia, Apfel, & Master, 2006; Cook, Purdie-Vaughns, Garcia, & Cohen, 2012). They found convincing evidence that such interventions closed racial achievement gaps (as measured by student GPA), with Black students benefiting from the intervention much more than White students. The researchers also found evidence that starting the intervention earlier in the school year yielded significant benefits. But the academic benefits were largely experienced by low-performing and moderate-performing students, not high-performing students. Subsequent research found similar results (Nguyen & Ryan, 2008).

Although Plucker and Peters (2016) strike a cautionary note in a review of these psychosocial interventions due to their lack of replicability and are pessimistic about their potential impact at the K–12 level, the research on the impact of stereotype threat interventions on *college excellence gaps* is convincing (e.g., Good, Aronson, & Harder, 2008; Walton & Cohen, 2011). These interventions are also cost effective and rarely time intensive, suggesting that they can be applied widely. Any comprehensive approach to addressing excellence gaps needs to consider the role of psychosocial interventions at the college level while the field waits for more convincing evidence for K–12 students.

FRONTLOADING

The foundation of the entire excellence gap mitigation model is frontloading. Briggs, Reis, and Sullivan (2008) discussed that within gifted education, frontloading means preparing students for advanced programs before they even have the chance to be identified or to enroll. Even though the goal is to close the excellence gap for underprivileged students, just placing more underprivileged students into advanced high school courses will not solve the problem. Placing students into advanced courses without first preparing them for advanced course rigor is almost always a prescription for failure. The goal for closing the excellence gap is to address the foundational framework that goes into the creation of the gap in the first place. Once the foundation creating the excellence gap is addressed, our educational system will be best prepared to shrink the excellence gap and best serve underprivileged students. As a result, an intervention designed to increase the performance of poor students in advanced, junior-year courses should not begin when students start that course. They should instead be exposed to more rigorous curriculum leading up to those courses, helping ensure that they have the intellectual skills and academic habits that will allow them to thrive when they encounter the advanced opportunity.

As a case in point, Weiler and Walker highlighted the use of frontloading within a school with a large Latino population. In this school, AP mathematics courses were taken primarily by Caucasian students. Weiler and Walker (2009) noted that when students in remedial math courses were offered an accelerated math track in order to access upper level math classes in high school, students not only were excited to partake in such a program but also excelled in the program—the material for the later AP math program was frontloaded in order to increase the chance that underrepresented students would be identified and be successful. Students were offered a summer program to fast-track them through geometry and onto higher math courses earlier in their high school years. Being able to frontload math courses earlier in high school opened additional doors for students in AP classes as well as into the college years. With all of the potential interventions discussed earlier, it's important to highlight just how important frontloading actually is to any effort to mitigate excellence gaps. The lack of educational opportunity that causes many of these gaps needs to be backfilled by proactive interventions if such gaps are ever to narrow.

As we reflect on what is known about excellence gaps, we can't help but feel that they are becoming well understood and that the research base has moved to a point where interventions meant to address them are sorely needed. The concept of excellence gaps has existed at least since 2008, and in that time they have become more and more well understood. Much of what we described in this chapter relates to promising or potential avenues for mitigating excellence gaps.

Research supports these inferences, but as with any area of science, the next step is to evaluate the model empirically to determine the degree to which it results in smaller disparities in rates of advanced achievement.

Major Takeaways

- Excellence gaps are differences in advanced achievement among groups of students defined by race/ethnicity, gender, socioeconomic status, and English language ability.

- The interest in excellence gaps has begun to grow not only for policy makers but also among educators.

- With this interest, the need for research-based interventions and best practices to reduce these gaps has also grown.

- Research suggests a range of promising interventions for shrinking excellence gaps, including opportunities, improved educator training, universal screening using local norms, state K–12 accountability systems, ability grouping, and psychosocial interventions at the college level.

- Frontloading is the foundation of any efforts to shrink excellence gaps; interventions should be conceptualized as multiyear efforts to prepare students to succeed when they encounter rigorous curriculum and instruction.

RECOMMENDED READINGS

Plucker, J. A., & Peters, S. J. (2016). *Excellence gaps in education: Expanding opportunities for talented youth.* Cambridge, MA: Harvard Education Press.

Plucker, J. A., Giancola, J., Healey, G., Arndt, D., & Wang, C. (2015). *Equal talents, unequal opportunities: A report card on state support for academically talented low-income students.* Lansdowne, VA: Jack Kent Cooke Foundation.

Grissom, J. A., & Redding, C. (2016). Discretion and disproportionality: Explaining the underrepresentation of high-achieving students of color in gifted programs. *AERA Open, 2*(1), 1–25.

Harris, B., & Plucker, J. A. (2014). Achieving equity and excellence: The role of school mental health providers in shrinking excellence gaps. *Gifted Child Today, 37,* 110–116.

REFERENCES

Abuhassàn, A., & Bates, T. C. (2015). Grit: Distinguishing effortful persistence from conscientiousness. *Journal of Individual Differences, 36,* 205–214.

Blackwell, L. S., Trzesniewski, K. H., & Dweck, C. S. (2007). Implicit theories of intelligence predict achievement across an adolescent transition: A longitudinal study and an intervention. *Child Development, 78,* 246–263.

Briggs, C. J., Reis, S. M., & Sullivan, E. E. (2008). A national view of promising programs and practices for culturally, linguistically, and ethnically diverse gifted and talented students. *Gifted Child Quarterly, 52,* 131–145.

Card, D., & Giuliano, L. (2016a). Can tracking raise the test scores of high-ability minority students? *The American Economic Review, 106,* 2783–2816.

Card, D., & Giuliano, L. (2016b). Universal screening increases the representation of low-income and minority students in gifted education. *Proceedings of the National Academy of Sciences, 113,* 13678–13683.

Carter, P. L., & Welner, K. G. (Eds.). (2013). *Closing the opportunity gap: What America must do to give every child an even chance.* New York, NY: Oxford University Press.

Cho, S., Yang, J., & Mandracchia, M. (2015). Effects of M3 curriculum on mathematics and English proficiency achievement of mathematically promising English language learners. *Journal of Advanced Academics, 26,* 112–142.

Cohen, G. L., Garcia, J., Apfel, N., & Master, A. (2006). Reducing the racial achievement gap: A social-psychological intervention. *Science, 313,* 1307–1310.

Cook, J. E., Purdie-Vaughns, V., Garcia, J., & Cohen, G. L. (2012). Chronic threat and contingent belonging: protective benefits of values affirmation on identity development. *Journal of Personality and Social Psychology, 102,* 479–496.

Finn, C. E., & Wright, B. L. (2015). *Failing our brightest kids: The global challenge of educating high-ability students.* Cambridge, MA: Harvard Education Press.

Gavin, K. M., Casa, T. M., Adelson, J. L., Carroll, S. R., Sheffield Jensen, L., & Spinelli, A. M. (2007). Mentoring Mathematical Minds—A research-based curriculum for talented elementary students. *Journal of Advanced Academics, 18,* 566–585.

Good, C., Aronson, J., & Harder, J. A. (2008). Problems in the pipeline: Stereotype threat and women's achievement in high-level math courses. *Journal of Applied Developmental Psychology, 29,* 17–28.

Grissom, J. A., & Redding, C. (2016). Discretion and disproportionality: Explaining the underrepresentation of high-achieving students of color in gifted programs. *AERA Open, 2*(1), 1–25.

Hamilton, R., McCoach, D. B., Tutwiler, M. S., Siegle, D., Gubbins, E. J., Callahan, C. M., . . . Mun, R. U. (in press). Disentangling the roles of institutional and individual poverty in the identification of gifted students. *Gifted Child Quarterly.*

Hardesty, J., McWilliams, J., & Plucker, J. A. (2014). Excellence gaps: what they are, why they are bad, and how smart contexts can address them . . . or make them worse. *High Ability Studies, 25,* 71–80.

Higher Education Opportunity Act, 20 U.S.C. § 110-315 (2008)

McBee, M. T., Peters, S. J., & Miller, E. M. (2016). The impact of the nomination stage on gifted program identification: A comprehensive psychometric analysis. *Gifted Child Quarterly, 60,* 258–278. doi:10.1177/0016986216656256

Neal, D., & Schanzenbach, D. W. (2010). Left behind by design: Proficiency counts and test-based accountability. *The Review of Economics and Statistics, 92,* 263–283.

Nguyen, H. H. D., & Ryan, A. M. (2008). Does stereotype threat affect test performance of minorities and women? A meta-analysis of experimental evidence. *Journal of Applied Psychology, 93,* 1314–1334.

Nores, M., & Barnett, W. S. (2014). *Access to high quality early care and education: Readiness and opportunity gaps in America.* New Brunswick, NJ: Center on Enhancing Early Learning Outcomes. Retrieved from http://ceelo.org/wp-content/uploads/2014/05/ceelo_policy_report_access_quality_ece.pdf

Peters, S. J., & Engerrand, K. G. (2016). Equity and excellence: Proactive efforts in the identification of underrepresented students for gifted and talented services. *Gifted Child Quarterly, 60,* 159–171. doi:10.1177/0016986216643165

Petrilli, M. J., Griffith, D., Wright, B. L., & Kim, A. (2016). *High stakes for high achievers: State accountability in the age of ESSA: Volume I.* Washington, DC: Thomas B. Fordham Institute.

Plucker, J. A., Giancola, J., Healey, G., Arndt, D., & Wang, C. (2015). *Equal talents, unequal opportunities: A report card on state support for academically talented low-income students.* Lansdowne, VA: Jack Kent Cooke Foundation.

Plucker, J. A., Hardesty, J., & Burroughs, N. (2013). *Talent on the sidelines: Excellence gaps and America's persistent talent underclass.* Storrs: University of Connecticut, Center for Education Policy Analysis.

Plucker, J. A., & Peters, S. J. (2016). *Excellence gaps in education: Expanding opportunities for talented youth.* Cambridge, MA: Harvard Education Press.

Rimfeld, K., Kovas, Y., Dale, P. S., & Plomin, R. (2016). True grit and genetics: Predicting academic achievement from personality. *Journal of Personality and Social Psychology, 111,* 780.

Robinson, J. P. (2008). Evidence of a differential effect of ability grouping on the reading achievement growth of language-minority Hispanics. *Educational Evaluation and Policy Analysis, 30,* 141–180.

Steenbergen-Hu, S., Makel, M. C., & Olszewski-Kubilius, P. (2016). What one hundred years of research says about the effects of ability grouping and acceleration on K–12 students' academic achievement: Findings of two second-order meta-analyses. *Review of Educational Research, 86,* 849–899.

Walton, G. M., & Cohen, G. L. (2011). A brief social-belonging intervention improves academic and health outcomes of minority students. *Science, 331,* 1447–1451.

Weiler, S. C., & Walker, S. (2009). Desegregating resegregation efforts: Providing all students opportunities to excel in advanced mathematics courses. *Brigham Young University Education and Law Journal, 2009,* 341–364. Retrieved from http://digitalcommons.law.byu.edu/elj/vol2009/iss2/5

Wright, B. L., Ford, D. Y., & Young, J. L. (2017). Ignorance or indifference? Seeking excellence and equity for under-represented students of color in gifted education. *Global Education Review, 4,* 45–61.

Yeager, D. S., & Walton, G. M. (2011). Social-psychological interventions in education: They're not magic. *Review of Educational Research, 81,* 267–301.

CHAPTER 16

The Genetic Side of Giftedness

A NATURE-NURTURE DEFINITION AND A FOURFOLD TALENT TYPOLOGY

Dean Keith Simonton

The very first scientific study devoted to the genetic side of giftedness was an article that Francis Galton published in 1865, and which he expanded into a full monograph in his classic 1869 book on *Hereditary Genius*. By studying family lineages, or "pedigrees," Galton hoped to prove that talent or genius was born, not made. However, when Galton's views were attacked for ignoring important environmental influences (Candolle, 1873), he backed off a bit by introducing the nature-nurture issue in the study of talent development (Galton, 1874). For example, he was the first investigator to examine the impact of family background, such as birth order. Nevertheless, Galton was clearly more interested in nature than nurture, devoting much of his career to developing methods that became the basis of modern behavioral genetics (Galton, 1883, 1889). Behavioral genetics has since shed considerable light on the role of biological inheritance in the emergence of genius, talent, and giftedness (e.g., Johnson & Bouchard, 2014).

Even so, many investigators have strongly doubted that nature has any influence whatsoever, instead arguing that genius (giftedness or talent) is entirely made, not born (e.g., Howe, Davidson, & Sloboda, 1998). Of special significance is the developmental impact of what has been called *deliberate practice* (Ericsson, 2014). Purportedly, exceptional performance in many domains, whether sports, games, arts, or sciences, requires an individual to devote a full decade to the laborious acquisition of the requisite knowledge and skills. Hence arises the "10-year rule." If Albert Einstein, Pablo Picasso, or Michael Jordan stood head and shoulders above their contemporaries, they just must have engaged in more deliberate practice than everybody else.

An unfortunate feature of much research is the tendency to attract attention—such as increased citations—by advocating extreme positions on difficult questions, the nature-nurture issue decidedly among them (Simonton, 2000). The downside of this practice for our understanding of giftedness is that the complex interactions between genetic and environmental factors tend to get overlooked (Hambrick, Macnamara, Campitelli, Ullén, & Mosing, 2016). Worse yet, in minimizing the function of one or the other side of the debate, proponents of single-factor explanations tend to vastly oversimplify the supposed operation of the neglected factor. That oversimplification is certainly apparent in the advocates of deliberate practice as the sole factor in talent development—a point that I wish to elaborate in this chapter. As will be seen below, the genetics of genius, talent, or giftedness is far more complex and nuanced than these extremists realize. I begin by showing that any innate gift or talent for a given domain must be defined in terms of deliberate practice for the definition to feature any scientific validity. I then focus specifically on the genetics side of the foregoing demonstration, showing that nature most likely operates in a far more complex and dynamic manner than often realized. A gift or talent does not work anything like the inheritance of eye color or even height. After these two arguments are presented, I close by discussing some implications for practice.

DEFINING TALENT WITH RESPECT TO DELIBERATE PRACTICE

Most human individual differences, whether physical, cognitive, or dispositional, are not governed by a single gene. Indeed, those that are, such as Huntington's disease, tend to be abnormal rather than normal. Hence, most characteristics, even rather simple ones, such as height, are subject to polygenic inheritance—inheritance is quantitative rather than discrete. Moreover, the normal distribution so often observed for human characteristics is usually the direct consequence of there being so many genes underlying those characteristics. The classic bell curve describing individual differences in general intelligence provides a well-known example. The sum of many random variables is normally distributed.

Yet the genetics of giftedness gets yet more complicated. Except for intellectual giftedness, which is defined by high performance on a general intelligence test, talents usually operate within domains of actual achievement. For example, Galton's (1865, 1869) inquiries into hereditary talent or genius included exceptional achievers in leadership (politics, war, religion, and law), creativity (science, literature, painting, and music), and sports (rowing and wrestling). Each domain would require a distinctive profile of cognitive abilities, dispositional traits, and sometimes, in the case of sports, physical capacities (Simonton, 2017). Because almost all individual differences feature substantial heritability coefficients (Bouchard, 2004), those profiles provide the basis for the possession of a talent in the domain. For example, talent as a scientist can be defined by a set of cognitive abilities and dispositional traits that are highly predictive of scientific achievement and that possess a nontrivial degree of inheritability (Simonton, 2008). Admittedly, numerous environmental factors will also play an extremely significant role in the development of characteristics making up the domain-specific profile (e.g., Damian & Simonton, 2014). Accordingly, at the minimum, domain-specific giftedness entails two sets of factors, the genetic and the environmental. These two sets underlie the development of the requisite cognitive abilities, dispositional traits, and perhaps physical capacities leading to extraordinary achievement within a given domain.

Nonetheless, we must recognize that the environmental factors must be stratified according to when in talent development they begin to exert their effects. For example, some developmental factors begin in early childhood, such as birth order, whereas others initiate much later, such as formal training in the domain, which may not start until late adolescence or early adulthood. Most significantly, the environmental influence of deliberate practice, which has received so much attention in recent research, has a later onset than most other factors. The gifted child must first identify a specific domain of achievement before such specialized training can even begin, and that may not even occur until adolescence or even adulthood. Furthermore, because deliberate practice is obviously more domain-specific than earlier environmental factors, such as family background, it most often makes sense to separate this factor out. That end will be accomplished next.

Multivariate Recursive Model of Talent Development

Figure 16.1 proves a very basic model that is already far more complicated than most researchers' implicit or explicit assumptions about talent development. The model describes the causal relations among six *sets* of variables, where each set can contain any number of variables. The sets are defined as follows:

> EP = *exceptional performance*, as assessed by one or more criteria. For example, exceptional performance in the sciences could be judged by publications, citations, and awards (Simonton, 2016b).

> ➤ *DP = deliberate practice*, again as gauged by one or more indicators. For instance, expertise in musical composition might demand special training in keyboard, analysis, history, harmony, counterpoint, orchestration, vocal writing, and ensemble conducting.
> ➤ *CA = cognitive abilities*, which might include, in, choreography, for example, general intelligence, musical intelligence, spatial-visual intelligence, and kinesthetic intelligence (cf. Gardner, 1983).
> ➤ *PT = personality traits*, which might encompass, for a domain in the expressive arts, high openness to experience, high introversion, low conscientiousness, and high emotional instability (Feist, 1998).

Finally, at the top of the figure, where it all begins, are the two sets of variables that represent nature and nurture:
> ➤ *GF = genetic factors* underlying the variables in either *CA* (cognitive abilities) or *PT* (personality traits); and
> ➤ *EF = environmental factors* influencing variables in either *CA* or *PT*.

The obvious question that must be addressed is how to determine what variables should go into each of the six sets. The answers are implied by the arrows in Figure 16.1. These represent the direct effects from the variables in one set to the variables in another set. Unlike path diagrams, where each arrow represents only a bivariate effect (a path or partial regression coefficient), each arrow in the diagram conveniently indicates all direct effects collectively, as a kind of short hand. To see how this works, we should always start with the set *EP*, which contains all of the necessary criteria variables for judging exceptional performance in a domain. We then identify all of the variables in sets *CA*, *DP*, and *PT* that directly predict or determine those criteria variables, whether singly or collectively. Hence, $CA \rightarrow EP$ contains all of the cognitive abilities that are significantly associated with one or more performance criteria, with corresponding inferences for $DP \rightarrow EP$ and $PT \rightarrow EP$. These three sets encompass all of the direct influences on exceptional performance (albeit for sports we would most likely have to include the set *PA* containing all relevant physical abilities that impinge on either *DP* or *EP* or both; Simonton, 2017). Notice that sets *CA* and *PT* (cognitive abilities and personality traits) can each include another set of variables that may not directly influence exceptional performance but rather that only have an indirect effect owing to their impact on *DT*, the deliberate practice variables. For instance, a personality trait like conscientiousness may be far more important in enhancing vocal or instrumental exercises requisite for musical performance than in the actual performance itself, where other traits become more crucial, such as self-confidence.

But where do these cognitive abilities and personality traits come from? The response is given in the two sets that include all genetic and environmental factors.

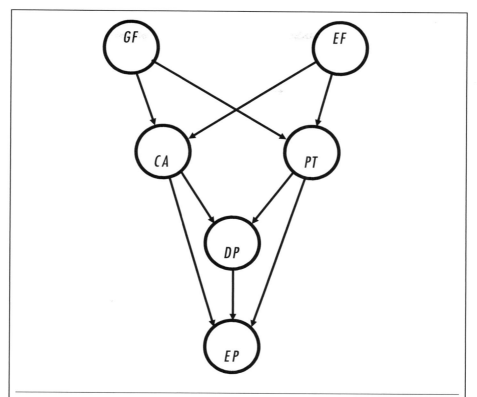

Figure 16.1. Hypothesized recursive model specifying individual differences in exceptional performance (*EP*) as a direct function of corresponding individual differences in deliberate practice (*DP*), cognitive abilities (*CA*), and personality traits (*PT*), and as an indirect function of genetic factors (*GF*, i.e., "nature") and environmental factors (*EF*, i.e., "nurture"), with *DP*, *CA*, and *PT* providing the mediating variables. Here *GF*, *EF*, *CA*, *PT*, *DP*, and *EP* each indicate entire *sets* of variables rather than single variables, where *CA* and *PT* contain phenotypic variables and *GF* genotypic variables. Accordingly, the arrows linking the sets imply multiple potential direct effects from variables in one set to variables in the other set. The variables themselves in each set may be either observed or latent (as holds for set *GF*). Figure modified from Simonton (2014, with permission of the author) to apply to exceptional performance of any kind rather than just to creativity.

Thus, *GF* contains all genetic influences on either cognitive abilities or personality traits, which is equivalent to saying that it encompasses all pertinent abilities and traits that feature substantial heritabilities. For instance, almost any intellectual domain, such as philosophy, would certainly include the inherited portion of general intelligence (Simonton & Song, 2009). Likewise, set *EF* contains all of those environmental influences on the two sets of individual differences. For example, the set would include all "diversifying experiences"—such as multicultural backgrounds or traumatic events—which can play a substantial role in talent development in many artistic domains (Damian & Simonton, 2014).

It is critical to realize that all of the relations in Figure 16.1 are presumed to be both direct and nonspurious. Any indirect effects should be accommodated by the direct effects. Hence, although genetic factors certainly exert indirect effects on exceptional performance, those effects operate only via their direct effects on either cognitive abilities or dispositional traits (and the latters' direct effects on either deliberate practice or exceptional performance). Spurious relations are those that disappear once other variables higher up (or earlier) in the causal model are statistically controlled within the model. It is for this reason, for instance, that no arrows are presumed to connect cognitive abilities and personality traits. Any correlations between variables in the two sets, such as the positive correlation between general intelligence and openness to experience, are presumed to reflect underlying shared genetic and environmental factors, such as coming from intellectually stimulating homes favored by highly intelligent parents (Scarr & McCartney, 1983).

Admittedly, the multivariate recursive model illustrated in Figure 16.1 is highly simplified. Some of these oversimplifications will be discussed later. Yet even this simple model suffices to demonstrate the complexities inherent in any definition of talent or giftedness.

Defining Innate Talent or Giftedness

So where is talent or giftedness in the model? Although all innate individual differences are found in set *GF*, talent cannot be located in the set *GF*, because none of these variables are specified to have direct effects on exceptional performance. Instead, the impact of genetic factors operates solely through cognitive abilities and personality traits, which in their turn impinge directly on exceptional performance or else operate indirectly via their effects on deliberate practice, which then affects exceptional performance. Accordingly, a talent or gift for a particular domain must be defined by the following four indirect effects: (a) *GF* → *CA* → *EP*, (b) *GF* → *PT* → *EP*, (c) *GF* → *CA* → *DP* → *EP*, and (d) *GF* → *PT* → *DP* → *EP* (Simonton, 2014; cf. Simonton, 2017). These four forms of talent can be grouped into two developmental categories.

1. *More-bang-for-the-buck effects*: (a) *GF* → *CA* → *EP* and (b) *GF* → *PT* → *EP*. These two indirect effects represent the major ways that genetic endowment can influence exceptional performance after individual variation in deliberate practice has already been accounted for (i.e., statistically controlled). Put differently, given two persons with exactly the same level

of deliberate practice on all relevant components of that expertise, one person can still perform better than the other, and that enhancement may be partly attributable to genetic factors underlying cognitive abilities and personality traits. In creative domains, an obvious example would be openness to experience, which would allow one creative individual to get more out of an identical amount of domain-specific expertise (McCrae & Greenberg, 2014).

2. *Better-faster effects*: (c) $GF \rightarrow CA \rightarrow DP \rightarrow EP$ and (d) $GF \rightarrow PT \rightarrow DP \rightarrow EP$. These two indirect effects, operating by means of deliberate practice, concern how quickly or how well a person masters the requisite domain-specific expertise. Not only may some individuals attain complete mastery at a precocious age, but at times, the acceleration may be so pronounced as to produce a child prodigy. Although not all child prodigies and precocious children grow up to become adult geniuses, some do (Winner, 2014). In fact, in domains like mathematics, music, and chess, such accelerated mastery may be the norm rather than the exception (Campitelli, Gobet, & Bilalic, 2014; Kell & Lubinski, 2014; McPherson, 2016). For instance, the most prolific and eminent classical composers are more prone to have been highly precocious if not outright prodigies (Simonton, 2016a).

Notice that the genetic influences responsible for the two effects need not overlap. Variables that enhance exceptional performance for a given amount of expertise need not be identical to those that accelerate the acquisition of that expertise. Even so, the sum total of all more-bang-for-the-buck and better-faster effects constitute a person's talent in a given domain.

It must be pointed out that the recursive causal model diagrammed in Figure 16.1 has never been fully tested on even a single domain of exceptional achievement. Instead, it was put forward as an integrative agenda for future research that would guide investigations around the current impasse of either-or, nature-versus-nurture inquiries (Simonton, 2014). That said, parts of the model have been tested, and these tests confirm that individual difference variables contained in *GF* must account for a significant proportion of variance in performance as mediated by cognitive abilities and personality traits (Ilies, Gerhardt, & Le, 2004; Simonton, 2007, 2008).[1] A reasonable ballpark estimate is that those genetic fac-

---

1   The procedures for making these estimates are too complex to describe here, so many a simple example suffice to show how genetic influence can be estimated from already published data (viz. a meta-analysis). Each arrow from *GF* to either *CA* or *PT* is associated with a particular coefficient, namely, *h*, which represents the square root of the variable's heritability coefficient. Then each arrow from *CA* or *PT* to either *DP* or *EP* would have a corresponding path coefficient β that represents the impact of the particular cognitive ability or personality trait (a.k.a. the standardized partial regression coefficient). An effect on either *DP* (better-faster effects) or *EP* (more-bang-for-the-buck effects) for a particular genetic characteristic in *GF* would then be defined by *h* × β. To

tors can account for roughly 20% of the performance variance. This percentage is not trivial. Indeed, it puts the impact of nature at about the same level as the nurture influence of deliberate practice variables contained in *DP* (see Macnamara, Hambrick, & Oswald, 2014). Furthermore, given the difficulties involved in attaining elite levels of achievement, that proportion may provide the edge that puts the talent over the top. The upshot is then a Nobel laureate, the world chess champion, Olympic gold medalist, or the victor at the Van Cliburn International Piano Competition.

TALENT DEVELOPMENT AS COMPLEX, MULTIPLICATIVE, AND DYNAMIC

As already noted, the model presented in Figure 16.1 is tremendously oversimplified—despite its rather complex implications. For example, no allowance was made for genetic-environment interactions that make it virtually impossible to separate nature and nurture (Johnson & Bouchard, 2014). Various feedback loops can occur elsewhere in the model, too, such as a two-way interaction between deliberate practice and exceptional performance (cf. Ullén, Hambrick, & Mosing, 2016). Nonetheless, rather than delve into all of these complications, I think it more useful to examine the upper left-hand corner of the figure, focusing on the genetic factors to the exclusion of all else in the model. Even the genetic factors alone, independent of what happens afterward, can overthrow commonplace misconceptions of giftedness or talent. Below let us examine three distinctions: (a) simple versus complex talents, (b) additive versus multiplicative talents, and (c) static versus dynamic talents.

SIMPLE VERSUS COMPLEX TALENTS

The specific content of *GF* in the model presented in Figure 16.1 depends on the domain. To be sure, certain cognitive abilities and personality traits will show up in many, if not most, sets of genetic factors. General intelligence is a

offer a concrete example, if h_{Op}^2 is the heritability of openness to experience (*Op* in *GF*) and $\beta_{Ct,Op}$ is the path coefficient going from openness to the number of citations a scientist receives in the professional literature (*Ct* in *EP*), then one arrow going from *GF* to *EP* would have the value $h_{Op} \times \beta_{Ct,Op}$. Hence, if $h_{Op}^2 = .57$ (from Bouchard, 2004) and $\beta_{Ct,Op} = .19$ (from Grosul & Feist, 2014), then $h_{Op} \times \beta_{Ct,Op} = .14$. Only if this product approached zero could we ever infer that openness entailed no genetic contribution whatsoever to scientific citations. The total aggregate genetic effect is then a complex function of all separate genetic effects, a function that adjusts for any shared variance among the abilities or traits (for full examples, see Ilies et al., 2004; Simonton, 2008).

prime example. Yet even when domains share abilities and traits, those variables will feature distinctive weights. For instance, openness to experience would have a higher weight in the arts than in the sciences (Simonton, 2009).

At this point it becomes essential to recognize not only that the contents of *GF* will vary across talent domains, but also the number of variables contained in a set can vary across those domains. At one extreme are simple talents that depend on a single polygenic ability or trait. If we were willing to consider fluid intelligence as a special talent domain, then it might provide an example. Indeed, if the ability to taste phenylthiocarbamide (PTC) were considered a domain, then that talent would be governed by a single gene! For sure, most talent domains include multiple genetic factors encompassing both cognitive abilities and personality traits. Yet even these can vary greatly in their complexity. For example, exceptional performance in architecture or choreography no doubt requires a larger set of abilities and traits than does chess or pure mathematics. In general, if a talent domain depends on a larger number of cognitive abilities and personality traits, then its complexity will tend to increase, given that almost all abilities and traits have at least some genetic basis (Bouchard, 2004).

Notably, as complexity increases, the number of alternative talent profiles will also tend to increase (Simonton, 2001). This tendency happens because tradeoffs can take place between the various abilities and traits. A person who is higher on a certain ability might be lower on a certain trait, but the total amount of talent remains the same, just the composition of that talent varies. The situation is analogous to psychometric tests: The more items making up the test, the larger the number of different ways of attaining the same overall test score (except, of course, when someone scores 100%). The greater variety of talent profiles has important repercussions for gifted education, as will be seen later.

Additive Versus Multiplicative Talents

So far we have been operating under the implicit assumption that the diverse genetic factors involved in talent development contribute in an additive fashion. Just like in linear multiple regression, the contribution of each variable within *GF* is first weighted by the appropriate amount and then simply added up with the other weighted contributions to produce the overall amount of estimated talent. Yet it has been argued that genius, talent, or giftedness does not operate in this simple additive fashion. Instead, inheritance is *emergenic* (Lykken, 1998; Simonton, 1999). That is, a specific configuration of abilities and traits are required in such a way that if any requisite is missing, then the talent will not exist. To give a simple example, high general intelligence is useless if a person totally lacks motivation, just as extreme motivation in the absence of sufficient general intelligence will get the person nowhere.

Emergenic inheritance can be formally expressed as multiplicative rather than additive (Simonton, 1999). Instead of adding all of the variables together, the variables are multiplied together. Because any contributing factor below a certain threshold can be set to zero, multiplicative integration involves ratio scaled variables. Given that zero times any number equals zero, then the absence of the ability or trait means that the talent will not manifest itself no matter how high a person might score on the other abilities and traits. Tradeoffs are not permitted. As will be seen shortly, emergenic talent has critical implications for practice.

Static Versus Dynamic Talents

Too often, people conceive genetic inheritance as operating in a static fashion: A person may possess a certain talent at birth, and then that latent capacity is just developed through environmental influences. Any coming and going in talent, or changes in the domain of talent, can be ascribed to the impact of the environmental factors, particularly during education and training. Yet even when the environmental factors are held constant, the genetic factors can change over the course of development. For example, the heritability of many abilities and traits can actually increase over time, so that identical twins reared apart in separate environments still can become more similar to each other as they age (Bouchard, 2004). Hence, a person's genetic constitution is not a constant, but rather unfolds in what has been called *epigenetic growth* (Simonton, 1999; not to be confused with epigenetics). Hence, a domain-specific talent might not even exist until after the individual enters adolescence or even adulthood. At the same time, a talent might vanish. An all-too-common example takes place when mental illness begins to appear in the late teens or early adulthood, and thereby undermines a person's deliberate practice or exceptional performance. After all, talent can also entail the absence of any trait that proves debilitating (i.e., mental health is the inverse of mental illness; Simonton, 2001).

Of course, the exact impact of this consideration depends on the trajectory, so inferences must often become tentative (Simonton, 1999). Nonetheless, this contrast will also have consequences for practice, even if in a most general manner.

IMPLICATIONS FOR PRACTICE

To appreciate the extreme complexity of giftedness, talent, or genius, I will draw two sets of inferences. I begin by introducing a fourfold typology based on the distinctions between simple and complex talents and between additive and multiplicative talents (Simonton, 2005). As if this typology was not intricate enough, I then introduce the complications that would be caused by dynamic (epigenetic) growth in one or more abilities or traits (cf. Simonton, 2001).

Fourfold Typology

As long as a given domain talent contains at least two variables in *GF* (see Figure 16.1), then the simplicity-complexity and additive-multiplicative dimensions are independent of each other. Obviously, the latter dimension makes no sense if there is nothing to add or multiply. This orthogonality then yields the typology in Table 16.1. As is apparent in the table, the four types of giftedness can be distinguished according to the following eight consequences:

1. *Character profiles*—As already noted earlier, the more distinct abilities and traits contained in *GF*, the more diverse the profiles can be for the corresponding talent domain. The range of potential tradeoffs increases with the number of characteristics. This impact of enhanced complexity holds for both additive and multiplicative talents (albeit in the latter case no essential component can be completely absent). To illustrate, the character profiles are likely more diverse for choreographers than for chess players.

2. *Cross-sectional distribution*—How are combined abilities and traits in *GF* distributed across individuals? In turns out that the expected distribution is normal for additive talent domains, but highly skewed for multiplicative talent domains (Simonton, 1999, 2005). Moreover, in the case of domains that are both complex and multiplicative, the skew becomes even more pronounced. This contrast is extremely provocative because domains involving exceptional performance most often exhibit extremely skewed cross-sectional distributions (O'Boyle & Aguinas, 2012; Walberg, Strykowski, Rovai, & Hung, 1984). Elite performers are found at the upper end of a very long, stretched-out tail. This elitism holds, for example, in the case of creative productivity, a small percentage of the creators in any domain accounting for most of the creative output.

3. *Proportion ungifted*—This consequence now concentrates on the lower end of the cross-sectional distribution, the bottom where talent can be considered absent altogether. For additive talent domains, the proportion who are ungifted is small, and the proportion becomes even smaller as the domain becomes more complex. In the latter case, it becomes increasingly unlikely that someone would not have anything going for them! Yet for multiplicative domains, the reverse is true. Not only is the proportion of the ungifted large, but the proportion increases with increases in complexity—remembering again that it takes only one absent ability or trait to nullify the other characteristics!

TABLE 16.1

Fourfold Typology of Giftedness: Simple Versus Complex and Additive Versus Multiplicative Giftedness

Consequences	Additive		Multiplicative	
	Simple	Complex	Simple	Complex
Character profiles	Uniform	Diverse	Uniform	Diverse
Cross-sectional distribution	Normal	Normal	Skewed	Extremely skewed
Proportion ungifted	Small	Extremely small	Large	Extremely large
Familial inheritance	Highest	High	Low	Lowest
Developmental trajectories	Few	Numerous	Few	Numerous
Developmental onset	Early	Earliest	Later	Latest
Identifiability	Highest	High	Low	Lowest
Instruction/ training strategies	Few	Numerous	Few	Numerous

Note. Simple types of giftedness are those in which the number of genetic components is small, perhaps even unidimensional, whereas complex types are those in which the number of components is large and hence highly multidimensional. Table adapted from Simonton (2005, p. 320), with permission of the author.

4. *Familial inheritance*—This repercussion provides a striking contrast with Galton's (1865, 1869) original attempt to demonstrate that talent and genius clustered into family lines. Such pedigrees can be expected if the talent domain depends on additive integration, with the pedigrees being even more conspicuous for simple domains. Yet the emergenic inheritance that provides the basis for multiplicative integration would yield rather contrasting outcomes, familial connections being far less common, and especially rare for complex talent domains (Simonton, 2005; see also Kogan & Kangas, 2006; Lykken, McGue, Tellegen, & Bouchard, 1992). Great talents in such domains can emerge seemingly out of nowhere!

5. *Developmental trajectories*—Now we turn to two consequences that deal more specifically with development, the first concerning the trajectories and the second the onset of those trajectories. The first follows closely what was observed for character profiles. The simple-complex dimension can differentiate talent domains, but the additive-multiplicative distinction proves irrelevant (Simonton, 2005). The more complex the domain, the greater the number of alternative growth patterns. The only qualification

is that the number of alternative trajectories may be less than the number of profiles to the extent that some cognitive abilities or personality traits have indistinguishable trajectories—the same developmental age curves.

6. *Developmental onset*—Unlike in the preceding, the additive versus multiplicative distinction does have important repercussions for the onset of talent development. The general expectation is that multiplicative talents tend to kick in later relative to additive talents. That delay happens because emergenic gifts require that *all* of the component abilities and traits begin to develop, whereas regular additive gifts only require just one for the process to start (Simonton, 2005). Note, too, that complex and additive talents have even earlier onsets, given the larger number of ways that development can begin, whereas complex and multiplicative talents have even later onsets, given the larger number of ways that some essential component might not have initiated development.

7. *Identifiability*—Gifted education most often cannot even begin until giftedness is first identified. Yet as seen in Table 16.1, the identifiability of talent depends on the nature of the domain. Simple domains are easier than complex domains, and additive domains are easier than multiplicative domains. This inference fits with what was said earlier about character profiles, familial inheritance, and developmental trajectories and their onset. There's just too little to go on when trying to identify the talented when their gifts reside in complex and multiplicative domains. Early telltale talent indicators will not exist (Simonton, 1999, 2001).

8. *Instruction/training strategies*—Once a talented youth is finally identified, whether early on or rather late, nurture can become matched with nature. Gifted education can then begin in earnest. Yet even at this juncture, the youth's further education becomes more complicated if the nurturing seeks to go beyond a one-size fits all strategy. After all, two talents in the same nominal domain may possess distinctive genetic profiles. One may have special gifts in a specific set of abilities whereas the other may have special gifts in a specific set of traits, each with their own contrasting set of tradeoffs. Tailoring training to innate talents would be no easy task.

Even if the implications of the fourfold typology are already daunting, we must still add a final consideration.

Epigenetic Growth

The outcomes shown in Table 16.1 do not incorporate the complications introduced by cognitive abilities or personality traits that are dynamic rather than static—that exhibit epigenetic growth. The existence of such variables in *GF* implies that: (a) character profiles may become increasingly complex over time; (b) the proportion of ungifted can also change, most likely decreasing as the "late bloomers" begin to check in; (c) both the developmental trajectories and the onset of those trajectories may display more longitudinal variability; and (d) both the identification criteria and the instruction/training strategies may become more contingent on each youth's distinctive growth pattern (Simonton, 1999, 2001). Sometimes talents will be overlooked, as "false negatives," and other times identified talents will turn out to be "false positives." Hit rates for "true" positives and negatives would decline. Moreover, the best nature-nurture match with respect to instruction and training may be temporally unstable. Gifted education would be very, very hard to do.

CONCLUSION

A talent or gift for exceptional achievement is not a simple lump of genetic assets, like a big bag of gold put in a safe deposit box at the moment of birth. Instead, it is often multidimensional, involving a profile of cognitive abilities and personality traits that are subject to both genetic and environmental factors. Furthermore, the impact of the genetic factors must be assessed in the context of deliberate practice: Nature must be evaluated in light of nurture. This definitional dependence becomes manifest in both the more-bang-for-the-buck and the better-faster effects. Complicating matters all the more is the possibility of emergenic inheritance and even epigenetic growth, which distort the cross-sectional distributions of talent, including the proportion of ungifted, as well as undermine familial inheritance and talent identification. Talent is not what people think it is.

Perhaps, in the future, means can be found to circumvent these unfortunate complications. But that will not happen until researchers take these potential complexities into full consideration in their empirical work. With a little luck, investigators may understand the genetic side of giftedness to the point that practitioners "working in the trenches" can be offered more precise advice on how to identify and nourish gifted children.

Major Takeaways

- Although innate talent and deliberate practice are often conceived as having a competitive either/or relationship in talent development, talent must necessarily be defined in terms of deliberate practice.

- One example involves *more-bang-for-the-buck effects* in which some individuals attain higher levels of performance than can be explicable in terms of practice effects alone.

- Another example entails *better-faster effects* in which individuals acquire domain-specific skill and knowledge more quickly per unit of deliberate practice.

- Besides the above effects, it is necessary to consider that the genetic contribution to talent development often operates according to emergenic inheritance and epigenetic growth.

- These complications can render development complex, multiplicative, and dynamic rather than simple, additive, and static.

RECOMMENDED READINGS

Simonton, D. K. (2005). Giftedness and genetics: The emergenic-epigenetic model and its implications. *Journal for the Education of the Gifted, 28,* 270–286.

Simonton, D. K. (2013). If innate talent doesn't exist, where do the data disappear? In S. B. Kaufman (Ed.), *The complexity of greatness: Beyond talent or practice* (pp. 17–26). New York, NY: Oxford University Press.

Simonton, D. K. (2014). Creative performance, expertise acquisition, individual-differences, and developmental antecedents: An integrative research agenda. *Intelligence, 45,* 66–73.

REFERENCES

Bouchard, T. J., Jr. (2004). Genetic influence on human psychological traits: A survey. *Current Directions in Psychological Science, 13,* 148–151.

Campitelli, G., Gobet, F., & Bilalic, M. (2014). Cognitive processes and development of chess genius: An integrative approach. In D. K. Simonton (Ed.), *The Wiley handbook of genius* (pp. 350–374). Oxford, England: Wiley.

Candolle, A. de. (1873). *Histoire des sciences et des savants depuis deux siècles.* Geneva, Switzerland: Georg.

Damian, R. I., & Simonton, D. K. (2014). Diversifying experiences in the development of genius and their impact on creative cognition. In D. K. Simonton (Ed.), *The Wiley handbook of genius* (pp. 375–393). Oxford, England: Wiley.

Ericsson, K. A. (2014). Creative genius: A view from the expert-performance approach. In D. K. Simonton (Ed.), *The Wiley handbook of genius* (pp. 321–349). Oxford, England: Wiley.

Feist, G. J. (1998). A meta-analysis of personality in scientific and artistic creativity. *Personality and Social Psychology Review, 2,* 290–309.

Galton, F. (1865). Hereditary talent and character. *Macmillan's Magazine, 12,* 157–166, 318–327.

Galton, F. (1869). *Hereditary genius: An inquiry into its laws and consequences.* London, England: Macmillan.

Galton, F. (1874). *English men of science: Their nature and nurture.* London, England: Macmillan.

Galton, F. (1883). *Inquiries into human faculty and its development.* London, England: Macmillan.

Galton, F. (1889). *Natural inheritance.* London, England: Macmillan.

Gardner, H. (1983). *Frames of mind: A theory of multiple intelligences.* New York, NY: Basic Books.

Grosul, M., & Feist, G. J. (2014). The creative person in science. *Psychology of Aesthetics, Creativity, and the Arts, 8,* 30–43.

Hambrick, D. Z., Macnamara, B. N., Campitelli, G., Ullén, F., & Mosing, M. A. (2016). Beyond born versus made: A new look at expertise. *The Psychology of Learning and Motivation, 64,* 1–55.

Howe, M. J. A., Davidson, J. W., & Sloboda, J. A. (1998). Innate talents: Reality or myth? *Behavioral and Brain Sciences, 21,* 399–442.

Ilies, R., Gerhardt, M. W., & Le, H. (2004). Individual differences in leadership emergence: Integrating meta-analytic findings and behavioral genetics estimates. *International Journal of Selection and Assessment, 12,* 207–219.

Johnson, W., & Bouchard, T. J., Jr. (2014). Genetics of intellectual and personality traits associated with creative genius: Could geniuses be Cosmobian Dragon Kings? In D. K. Simonton (Ed.), *The Wiley handbook of genius* (pp. 269–296). Oxford, England: Wiley.

Kell, H. J., & Lubinski, D. (2014). The Study of Mathematically Precocious Youth at maturity: Insights into elements of genius. In D. K. Simonton (Ed.), *The Wiley handbook of genius* (pp. 397–421). Oxford, England: Wiley.

Kogan, N., & Kangas, B. L. (2006). Careers in the dramatic arts: Comparing genetic and interactional perspectives. *Empirical Studies of the Arts, 24,* 43–54.

Lykken, D. T. (1998). The genetics of genius. In A. Steptoe (Ed.), *Genius and the mind: Studies of creativity and temperament in the historical record* (pp. 15–37). New York, NY: Oxford University Press.

Lykken, D. T., McGue, M., Tellegen, A., & Bouchard, T. J., Jr. (1992). Emergenesis: Genetic traits that may not run in families. *American Psychologist, 47,* 1565–1577.

Macnamara, B. N., Hambrick, D. Z., & Oswald, F. L. (2014). Deliberate practice and performance in music, games, sports, education, and professions: A meta-analysis. *Psychological Science, 25,* 1608–1618.

McCrae, R. R., & Greenberg, D. M. (2014). Openness to experience. In D. K. Simonton (Ed.), *The Wiley handbook of genius* (pp. 222–243). Oxford, England: Wiley.

McPherson, G. (Ed.). (2016). *Musical prodigies: Interpretations from psychology, music education, musicology and ethnomusicology.* New York, NY: Oxford University Press.

O'Boyle, Jr., E., & Aguinas, H. (2012). The best and the rest: Revisiting the norm of normality of individual performance. *Personnel Psychology, 65,* 79–119.

Scarr, S., & McCartney, K. (1983). How people make their own environments: A theory of genotype → environmental effects. *Child Development, 54,* 424–435.

Simonton, D. K. (1999). Talent and its development: An emergenic and epigenetic model. *Psychological Review, 106,* 435–457.

Simonton, D. K. (2000). Methodological and theoretical orientation and the long-term disciplinary impact of 54 eminent psychologists. *Review of General Psychology, 4,* 13–24.

Simonton, D. K. (2001). Talent development as a multidimensional, multiplicative, and dynamic process. *Current Directions in Psychological Science, 10,* 39–43.

Simonton, D. K. (2005). Giftedness and genetics: The emergenic-epigenetic model and its implications. *Journal for the Education of the Gifted, 28,* 270–286.

Simonton, D. K. (2007). Talent and expertise: The empirical evidence for genetic endowment. *High Ability Studies, 18,* 83–84.

Simonton, D. K. (2008). Scientific talent, training, and performance: Intellect, personality, and genetic endowment. *Review of General Psychology, 12,* 28–46.

Simonton, D. K. (2009). Varieties of (scientific) creativity: A hierarchical model of disposition, development, and achievement. *Perspectives on Psychological Science, 4,* 441–452.

Simonton, D. K. (2014). Creative performance, expertise acquisition, individual-differences, and developmental antecedents: An integrative research agenda. *Intelligence, 45,* 66–73.

Simonton, D. K. (2016a). Early and late bloomers among classical composers: Were the greatest geniuses also prodigies? In G. McPherson (Ed.), *Musical prodigies: Interpretations from psychology, music education, musicology and ethnomusicology* (pp. 185–197). New York, NY: Oxford University Press.

Simonton, D. K. (2016b). Giving credit where credit's due: Why it's so hard to do in psychological science. *Perspectives on Psychological Science, 11,* 888–892.

Simonton, D. K. (2017). Does talent exist? Yes! In J. Baker, S. Cobley, J. Schorer, & N. Wattie (Eds.), *Routledge handbook of talent identification and development in sport* (pp. 11–18). London, England: Routledge.

Simonton, D. K., & Song, A. V. (2009). Eminence, IQ, physical and mental health, and achievement domain: Cox's 282 geniuses revisited. *Psychological Science, 20,* 429–434.

Ullén, F., Hambrick, D. Z., & Mosing, M. A. (2016). Rethinking expertise: A multifactorial gene-environment interaction model of expert performance. *Psychological Bulletin, 142,* 427–446.

Walberg, H. J., Strykowski, B. F., Rovai, E., & Hung, S. S. (1984). Exceptional performance. *Review of Educational Research, 54,* 87–112.

Winner, E. (2014). Child prodigies and adult genius: A weak link. In D. K. Simonton (Ed.), *The Wiley handbook of genius* (pp. 297–320). Oxford, England: Wiley.

About the Editors

Jonathan Plucker, Ph.D., is the Julian C. Stanley Endowed Professor of Talent Development at Johns Hopkins University, where he works in the Center for Talented Youth and School of Education. He graduated with a B.S. in chemistry education and M.A. in educational psychology from the University of Connecticut, then after briefly teaching at an elementary school in New York, received his Ph.D. in educational psychology from the University of Virginia. His research examines educational psychology, education policy, and talent development, with more than 200 publications to his credit and more than $40 million in external funding to support his work. Recent books include *Excellence Gaps in Education* with Scott Peters (Harvard Education Press), *Intelligence 101* with Amber Esping (Springer), *Creativity and Innovation* (Prufrock), and *Toward a More Perfect Psychology* with Matt Makel (APA). He is a Fellow of the American Psychological Association, Association for Psychological Science, American Educational Research Association, and American Association for the Advancement of Science. Prof. Plucker is the recipient of the 2012 Arnheim Award for Outstanding Achievement from APA and 2013 Distinguished Scholar Award from the National Association for Gifted Children. He is president-elect of NAGC.

Anne N. Rinn, Ph.D., is an associate professor of educational psychology at the University of North Texas, where she also serves as Director of the Office for Giftedness, Talent Development, and Creativity. She has an undergraduate degree in psychology from the University of Houston and a doctorate in educational psychology from Indiana University. She has authored more than 50 publications related to the social and emotional development of gifted individuals and the psychosocial skills necessary for the development of talent. She is an active member of the National Association for Gifted Children and the American Educational

Research Association, holding leadership positions in both organizations, and is the incoming coeditor of the *Journal for Advanced Academics.*

Matthew C. Makel, Ph.D., is the Director of Research for Duke University's Talent Identification Program. His research focuses on academic talent development and research methods. Matt earned his Ph.D. in educational psychology from Indiana University, an master's degree in developmental psychology from Cornell University, and his bachelor's degree in psychology from Duke University, where he first started working with academically talented students while an undergraduate. Previously, he coedited with Jonathan Plucker the book *Toward a More Perfect Psychology: Improving Trust, Accuracy, and Transparency in Research.* His work has earned multiple awards for Excellence in Research from the MENSA Foundation, and he is the recipient of the 2017 Early Scholar Award from the National Association for Gifted Children.

About the Authors

Susan G. Assouline, Ph.D., directs the Belin-Blank Center at the University of Iowa, holds the Myron and Jacqueline N. Blank Endowed Chair in Gifted Education, and is a professor of school psychology. She is especially interested in identification of academic talent in elementary students and coauthored (with Ann Lupkowski-Shoplik) both editions of *Developing Math Talent: A Comprehensive Guide to Math Education for Gifted Students in Elementary and Middle School*. She also is codeveloper of the *Iowa Acceleration Scale*, a tool designed to guide educators and parents through decisions about grade-skipping students. In 2015, she coedited *A Nation Empowered: Evidence Trumps the Excuses Holding Back America's Brightest Students*. She is the 2016 recipient of the National Association for Gifted Children (NAGC) Distinguished Scholar Award and the 2017 University of Iowa Faculty Excellence Award.

George Betts, Ed.D., currently president of the National Association for Gifted Children, is Professor Emeritus at the University of Northern Colorado. He is the founder and former director of the Center for the Education and Study of the Gifted, Talented, and Creative and the Summer Enrichment Program (SEP). He is an internationally acclaimed speaker and consultant who specializes in supporting organizations in implementing and refining programs for gifted and talented learners. Dr. Betts served on the board of NAGC for several terms and received the 1990–1991 Distinguished Service Award. In 2003, NAGC selected Dr. Betts as one of the 50 most influential leaders in the history of gifted education (*Profiles of Influence in Gifted Education*). In 2006, he received the prestigious M. Lucile Harrison Award for Professional Excellence at the University of Northern Colorado.

Emma Bloomfield received her bachelor's degree in mathematics from Smith College in 2003. She earned her master's degree in educational leadership from

Central Connecticut State University in 2007. For the past 12 years, she has been teaching high school mathematics. She has taught in two urban public schools in Connecticut, first at New Britain High School and then at Windsor High School. Bloomfield is now working with the Renzulli Center for Creativity, Gifted Education, and Talent Development at the University of Connecticut while pursuing her Ph.D. in educational psychology.

Linda Brody, Ed.D., directs the Study of Exceptional Talent (SET) and the Diagnostic and Counseling Center (DCC) at the Johns Hopkins Center for Talented Youth (CTY). She also supervises the publication of CTY's *Imagine* magazine. SET provides academic advising and advocates for appropriately challenging opportunities for students with exceptionally advanced abilities, while the DCC offers psychoeducational assessments and other services with a special focus on twice-exceptional students. Linda, who earned her doctorate in gifted education from Johns Hopkins, has worked for more than 30 years as a counselor, researcher, and advocate for gifted children. Her research interests focus on evaluating the efficacy of intervention strategies, especially acceleration, and on special populations including the highly gifted, gifted girls, and twice-exceptional students. She received the Distinguished Service Award from the National Association for Gifted Children in 2015.

Robin Carey, Ph.D., is an educator with more than 30 years as a teacher, gifted education facilitator, programming coordinator, and instruction support services director with a passion for serving the needs of diverse learners. As the director of educational programming in the Douglas County School District in Colorado, Robin facilitated the areas of English Language Development, Gifted Education, and Literacy Interventions. She is a lifetime member of the National Association for Gifted Children, and was inducted into the Colorado Academy of Educators for the Gifted, Talented, and Creative in 2002. Robin earned her Ph.D. in Educational Administration and Policy Studies from the University of Denver, where she focused her dissertation research on the effective utilization of the Response to Intervention framework to meet the needs of all learners, with a lens for gifted learners.

Nicholas Colangelo, Ph.D., is Dean Emeritus of the College of Education, University of Iowa and Director Emeritus, Belin-Blank Center for Gifted Education, University of Iowa. His areas of research in gifted education are counseling issues, affective development, and the academic and social effects of acceleration.

Peter Csermely, Ph.D., is a professor at Semmelweis University (Budapest, Hungary). His major field of study is the adaptation of complex networks (http://www.linkgroup.hu). In 1995, Dr. Csermely launched a highly successful initiative that has provided research opportunities for more than 10,000 gifted high school students so far. In 2006, he established the Hungarian National Talent

Support Council (http://www.tehetseg.hu/en), running a talent support network involving more than 200,000 people. In 2012, he became the president of the European Council for High Ability, which started a European Talent Support Network in 2015 that now has more than 300 nodes in 35 countries of Europe and several other continents (http://etsn.eu/map-of-etsn). He has written and edited 13 books (including *Weak Links* at Springer) and published 270 research papers. Dr. Csermely was the member of the Wise Persons' Council of the president of Hungary; is a member of the Hungarian Academy of Sciences and Academia Europaea and an Ashoka Fellow; was a Fogarty, a Howard Hughes, and a Rockefeller Scholar, as well as a Templeton Awardee; and received several other national and international honors and awards, including the 2004 Descartes Award of the European Union.

Heidi Erstad, M.S., has more than 30 years of experience in the field of education as classroom teacher, staff development consultant, Gifted and Talented Coordinator, Director of Instruction, Research and Evaluation Coordinator, and adjunct instructor. She currently serves as a Regional Technical Assistance Coordinator at the Wisconsin RtI Center, helping schools implement multilevel systems of supports to ensure the success of all of the students they serve. Her areas of focus include systems of support for mathematics, gifted and talented student needs, culturally responsive practices, and eliminating race-based inequities.

Donna Y. Ford, Ph.D., is a professor of Education and Human Development in the College of Education at Vanderbilt University and Cornelius Vanderbilt Endowed Chair. Primarily conducting research in gifted education and multicultural/urban education, her work focuses on the achievement gap; recruiting and retaining culturally different students in gifted education; multicultural curriculum and instruction; culturally competent teacher training and development; African American identity; and African American family involvement. A prolific writer, she has published hundreds of articles, chapters, and books, as well as served on numerous editorial boards. Her many awards include the Research Award from the Shannon Center for Advanced Studies; American Educational Research Association (AERA)'s Early Career and Career Awards; NAGC's Early and Senior Scholars Award; the National Association of Black Psychologist's Esteemed Scholarship Award; and CEC-TAG's Outstanding Service Award. As Vanderbilt University SEC Faculty Award recipient, she is humbled by her numerous awards from student organizations.

Françoys Gagné, Ph.D., spent most of his professional career in the Department of Psychology at l'Université du Québec à Montréal (UQAM). He devoted his research and teaching activities to the field of talent development. Officially retired since 2001, Professor Gagné maintains regular publishing activities and accepts numerous international keynoting invitations. He has authored more than 150 articles and book chapters, and been invited to teach and/or keynote in more than 20 countries. Professor Gagné has gained international renown through his theory of talent development: the Differentiating Model of Giftedness and Talent (DMGT), recently updated and renamed Integrative Model of Talent Development (IMTD). He has received many professional prizes, including the prestigious Distinguished Scholar Award (1996) from the National Association for Gifted Children.

Marcia Gentry, Ph.D., Professor and Director of the Gifted Education Resource Institute, is an engaged scholar and has received grants worth several million dollars supporting her work with programming practices and underrepresented populations in gifted education. She actively participates in the field, frequently contributing to the literature, regularly serving as a speaker, and working with her doctoral students.

Tarek C. Grantham, Ph.D., is a professor at the University of Georgia whose research focuses on equity for underrepresented students in advanced programs, creativity policy, and parent engagement. Dr. Grantham coedited *Gifted and Advanced Black Students in School: An Anthology of Critical Works* (2011), and *Young, Triumphant, and Black: Overcoming the Tyranny of Segregated Minds in Desegregated School* (2013). He has provided leadership through the National Association for Gifted Children (e.g., Board of Directors, Special Populations Network, Javits/Frasier Teacher Scholar Program), the Council for Exceptional Children (e.g., The Association for the Gifted), and AERA (e.g., Research on Giftedness, Creativity and Talent SIG).

Jiajun Guo, Ph.D., received his doctorate in educational psychology at the University of Connecticut. Before that, he received his bachelor's degree and master's degree in psychology and special education at East China Normal University. His areas of interest include developing creativity measurement instruments and assessment tools, talented and gifted education, development of creative potentials, teaching creativity in the classroom, and use of technology in creativity enhancement. His work has been published in *Roeper Review*, *Thinking Skills and Creativity*, and *Creativity. Theories–Research–Applications*.

Blanche Kapushion, Ph.D., is an educator with more than 30 years as a classroom teacher, program coordinator for outdoor education, elementary principal and director of gifted and talented for Jefferson County Schools in Colorado. In her tenure as president of the Colorado Association of Gifted and Talented, Blanche led efforts of this organization to lobby for legislation to support gifted learners in Colorado. She is a lifetime member of the National Association for Gifted Children, and was inducted into the Colorado Academy of Educators for the Gifted, Talented, and Creative in 2003. Blanche was awarded a lifetime achievement recognition from the Western Academic Talent Search: Center for Bright Kids in 2016 for her support and advocacy of gifted children. Blanche earned her Ph.D. in educational administration and policy studies from the

University of Denver, focusing her dissertation research on the effect of reading reform models.

Ann Lupkowski-Shoplik, Ph.D., is the Administrator for the Acceleration Institute and Research at the Belin-Blank Center for Gifted Education and an adjunct professor in the Department of Psychological and Quantitative Foundations, both at the University of Iowa. She founded and directed the Carnegie Mellon Institute for Talented Elementary Students (C-MITES) at Carnegie Mellon University for 22 years, which provided a talent search and educational programs for gifted students as well as professional development for teachers. Together with Dr. Susan Assouline, she wrote *Developing Math Talent: A Comprehensive Guide to Math Education for Gifted Students in Elementary and Middle School* (2nd ed.). She is also a coauthor of the *Iowa Acceleration Scale* with Susan Assouline, Nicholas Colangelo, Jonathan Lipscomb, and Leslie Forstadt; and coeditor of the 2015 report on academic acceleration, *A Nation Empowered: Evidence Trumps the Excuses Holding Back America's Brightest Students*, with Susan Assouline, Nicholas Colangelo, and Joyce VanTassel-Baska.

Michael S. Matthews, Ph.D., is Professor and Director of the Academically & Intellectually Gifted graduate programs at the University of North Carolina at Charlotte. He is coeditor of *Gifted Child Quarterly*, and recently served on the Board of Directors of the National Association for Gifted Children. Dr. Matthews also currently chairs the Special Interest Group—Research on Giftedness, Creativity, and Talent of the American Educational Research Association. His research interests include assessment and identification of gifted children; research methods; education policy; science learning; motivation and underachievement; and parenting, including homeschooling, of gifted learners. His scholarship also includes a focus on gifted and academically advanced learners from diverse backgrounds, particularly English learners. Dr. Matthews is the author or editor of five books, around 40 peer-reviewed journal articles, and numerous book chapters. His work has been recognized with the Early Scholar Award from NAGC, the Michael Pyryt Collaboration Award from AERA SIG—Research on Giftedness, Creativity, and Talent, and the Legacy Book Award from the Texas Association for the Gifted and Talented.

D. Betsy McCoach, Ph.D., is a professor in the Measurement, Evaluation and Assessment program at the University of Connecticut (UCONN). Dr. McCoach has coauthored more than 100 peer-reviewed journal articles, book chapters, and books, including *Instrument Design in the Affective Domain* and *Multilevel Modeling of Educational Data*. Dr. McCoach founded the Modern Modeling Methods conference, held annually at UCONN. She is also the Director of DATIC, which hosts workshops on a variety of modeling methods. Dr. McCoach is co-Principal Investigator for the National Center for Research on Gifted Education and has served as Principal Investigator, co-Principal Investigator, and/or research methodologist for several other federally funded research projects/grants. Dr. McCoach's research interests include gifted education, instrument design, latent variable modeling, longitudinal modeling, and multilevel modeling.

Jacob McWilliams, Ph.D., earned an MFA in creative writing from Colorado State University and a Ph.D. in Educational Psychology, with a concentration in gender, sexuality, and policy studies, from Indiana University. His scholarship focuses on transgender-inclusive pedagogies, trauma-informed pedagogies, and educational policy for LGBTQ learners. He is the coordinator for the Women and Gender Center at the University of Colorado Denver.

James L. Moore III, Ph.D., is the Interim Vice Provost for Diversity and Inclusion and Chief Diversity Officer at The Ohio State University, where he is also the inaugural executive director of the Todd Anthony Bell National Resource Center on the African American Male and the EHE Distinguished Professor of Urban Education in the College of Education and Human Ecology. From 2015 to 2017, he served as a program director for Broadening Participation in Engineering at the National Science Foundation in Arlington, VA, and, from 2011 to 2015, he was an associate provost for Diversity and Inclusion at The Ohio State University. Dr. Moore is internationally recognized for his work on African American males. His research agenda focuses on school counseling, gifted education, urban education, higher education, multicultural education/counseling, and STEM education. Additionally, he is a past member of the Board of Directors of the National Association for Gifted Children.

Paula Olszewski-Kubilius, Ph.D., is the director of the Center for Talent Development at Northwestern University and a professor in the School of Education and Social Policy. Over the past 32 years, she has created programs for all kinds of gifted learners and written extensively about talent development. She has served as the editor of *Gifted Child Quarterly*, as the coeditor of the *Journal of Secondary Gifted Education*, and on the editorial boards of *Gifted and Talented International*, *Roeper Review*, and *Gifted Child Today*. She is on the board of trustees of the Illinois Mathematics and Science Academy and the Illinois Association for the Gifted. She also serves on the advisory boards for the Center for Gifted Education at William & Mary and the Robinson Center for Young Scholars at the University of Washington. She is past-president of the National Association for Gifted Children and received the Distinguished Scholar Award in 2009 from NAGC.

Scott J. Peters, Ph.D., is an associate professor of educational foundations and the Richard and Veronica Telfer Endowed Faculty Fellow at the University of Wisconsin–Whitewater, where he teaches courses related to educational measurement, research methods, and gifted and talented education. His primary research area involves gifted and talented student identification and talent development with a focus on students from underrepresented populations. His scholarly work has appeared in *Teaching for High Potential*, *Gifted Child Quarterly*, the *Journal of Advanced Academics*, *Gifted and Talented International*, the *Journal of Career and Technical Education Research*, *Ed Leadership*, *Gifted Child Today*, and *Pedagogies*. He is the first author of *Beyond Gifted Education: Designing and Implementing Advanced Academic Programs* and *Designing Gifted Education Programs and Services: From Purpose to Implementation*, both from Prufrock Press, and the coauthor (along with Jonathan Plucker) of *Excellence Gaps in Education: Expanding Opportunities for Talented Students*, published by Harvard Education Press.

Steve Portenga, Ph.D., has dedicated himself to understanding the performing brain, by integrating theories of human performance, neuroscience, technology, and behavior change. His mission with iPerformance Consultants is to help performers across a variety of domains develop their talent to its fullest potential, perform consistently in the upper range of their abilities, and manage performance pressure. He has brought his passion for the psychology of high performance to a variety of situations, including writing the American Psychological Association's definition of performance psychology; serving as founding member of APA's Coalition for the Psychology of High Performance; serving as a member of the National Association for Gifted Children's Presidential Task Force on the Whole Gifted Child; and serving as director of performance psychology for USA Track & Field at the London 2012 Olympic Games. He has worked with franchises in every major professional sport, including team captains and future Hall of Famers; has numerous academic publications; and is an invited speaker internationally for high performance groups.

Sally M. Reis, Ph.D., is the former Vice Provost for Academic Affairs, and is currently the Letitia Neag Morgan Chair in Educational Psychology, a Board of Trustees Distinguished Professor, and a University Teaching Fellow at the University of Connecticut. She was a teacher for 15 years, 11 of which were spent working with gifted students on the elementary, junior high, and high school levels. She has authored or coauthored more than 250 articles, books, book chapters, monographs, and technical reports. Her research interests are related to special populations of gifted and talented students, including students with learning disabilities, gifted females, and diverse groups of talented students. She is also interested in extensions of the Schoolwide Enrichment Model, both for gifted and talented students and as a way to expand offerings and provide general enrichment to identify talents and potentials in students who have not been previously identified as gifted. She is the codirector of Confratute, the longest-running summer institue in the development of gifts and talents.

Joseph S. Renzulli, Ed.D., is a professor of educational psychology at the University of Connecticut, where he also has served as the director of the Renzulli Center for Creativity, Gifted Education, and Talent Development. His research has focused on the identification and development of creativity and giftedness in young people, and on curricular and organizational models for differentiated learning environments that contribute to total school improvement. A focus of his work has been on applying the pedagogy of gifted education to the improvement of learning for all students. Dr. Renzulli is a UConn Distinguished Professor and holds Honorary Doctor of Laws Degrees from McGill University and the University of Camilo José Cela in Spain. The American Psychological Association named Dr. Renzulli among the 25 most influential psychologists in the world, and in 2009, Dr. Renzulli received the Harold W. McGraw, Jr. Award for innovation in education, considered by many to be the "Nobel Prize for educators."

Stephanie Schmalensee is a school psychologist who currently works as a research assistant at Johns Hopkins University. She is completing her doctorate in school psychology at Indiana University.

Dean Keith Simonton, Ph.D., is Distinguished Professor Emeritus of Psychology at the University of California, Davis. His more than 500 publications largely concern genius, creativity, talent, and leadership. Past honors include the William James Book Award, the George A. Miller Outstanding Article Award, the Theoretical Innovation Prize in Personality and Social Psychology, the Sir Francis Galton Award for Outstanding Contributions to the Study of Creativity, the Rudolf Arnheim Award for Outstanding Contributions to Psychology and the Arts, the E. Paul Torrance Award for Creativity, and three Mensa Awards for Excellence in Research. In 2014, he edited *The Wiley Handbook of Genius*.

Del Siegle, Ph.D., is Director of the National Center for Research on Gifted Education (NCRGE) and Associate Dean for Research and Faculty Affairs in the Neag School of Education at the University of Connecticut. He is a past-president of the National Association for Gifted Children (NAGC) and recently finished a term as coeditor of *Gifted Child Quarterly*. In 2016, he received the Palmarium Award, which is given yearly to the individual most exemplifying the vision of a future in which giftedness will be understood, embraced, and systematically nurtured throughout the nation and the world. Prior to becoming a professor, Siegle worked with gifted and talented students in Montana.

Rena F. Subotnik, Ph.D., is Director of the American Psychological Association Center for Psychology in Schools and Education (CPSE). One of the Center's missions is to generate public awareness, advocacy, clinical applications, and cutting-edge research ideas that enhance the achievement and performance of children and adolescents with gifts and talents in all domains. Her recent publications reflect her scholarship on applications of psychological science to gifted education, talent development in specific domains, and psychological strength training for academically gifted children and youth. She has been supported in this work by the National Science Foundation, the American Psychological Foundation, and the Association for Psychological Science.

Juliana Tay is a doctoral candidate at Purdue University, where she is pursuing a degree in gifted education. She worked in Singapore for 11 years as the subject head for art, where she supervised a team of art teachers and design programs for high-ability art students. Since coming to United States, Juliana worked as the coordinator of student programs in the Gifted Education Resource Institute at Purdue University. She is currently a research assistant on the Total School Cluster Grouping project, focusing on the evaluation and implementation of the intervention. Her research interests include gifted art learners, issues in identification for art giftedness, and evaluation of gifted programs.

Wilma Vialle, Ph.D., is a professor in educational psychology at the University of Wollongong, Australia. Her research interests are predominantly concerned with giftedness and talent development. She is the chief editor of the journal *Talent Development and Excellence* and is on the editorial board of several international journals. Wilma is also on the Executive Board of the International Research Association for Talent Development and Excellence (IRATDE). In 2006, she was awarded the Eminent Australian award by the Australian Association for the Education of the Gifted and Talented (AAEGT) for her contributions to gifted education.

Frank C. Worrell, Ph.D., is a professor of school psychology at the University of California, Berkeley. His areas of expertise include talent development/gifted education, at-risk youth, cultural identities, scale development and validation, teacher effectiveness, and the translation of psychological research findings into practice. Dr. Worrell is a Fellow of the Association for Psychological Science, the American Educational Research Association, and five divisions of the American Psychological Association, and a former Editor of Review of Educational Research.

Brian L. Wright, Ph.D., is an assistant professor of early childhood education in the Department of Instruction and Curriculum Leadership in the College of Education at the University of Memphis, where he teaches undergraduate- and graduate-level courses. His research and numerous publications (articles and book chapters) examine high-achieving African American males in urban schools pre-K–12, racial-ethnic identity development of boys and young men of color, African American males as early childhood teachers, and teacher identity development.

Albert Ziegler, Ph.D., is the Chair Professor for Educational Psychology at the University of Erlangen-Nuremberg, Germany. He has published approximately 350 books, chapters, and articles in the fields of talent development, excellence, educational psychology, and cognitive psychology. He serves as the Secretary General of the International Research Association for Talent Development and Excellence (IRATDE) and as the editor-in-chief of *Talent Development and Excellence*. His main interests in the field of talent development and excellence are the development of exceptional performances, the Actiotope Model of Giftedness, and training programs.